Praise for Elisabeth Rosenthal

"An eye-opening discussion . . . [An] impc
interviewer her goal was to 'start a very loud conversation' that will be 'difficult politically to ignore.' We need such a conversation—not just about how the market fails, but about how we can change the political realities that stand in the way of fixing it." —*The New York Times Book Review*

"Patients can save thousands of dollars by purchasing *An American Sickness* by Elisabeth Rosenthal." —*New York Journal of Books*

"An authoritative account of the distorted financial incentives that drive medical care in the United States . . . Every lawmaker and administration official should pick up a copy of *An American Sickness*. Then, at last, the serious debate could begin." —*The Washington Post*

"Elisabeth Rosenthal's meticulous history of the crisis in American healthcare should be required reading for our generation. I have not read another volume that diagnoses the 'deeply, perhaps fatally, flawed' system of health insurance and delivery with such lucidity, dissects its critical shortcomings, and provides such a clear prescription for its ills. Bold, imaginative, tautly written, and filled with fury and compassion, this book will serve as the definitive guide to the past and future of health care in America."
—Siddhartha Mukherjee, Pulitzer Prize–winning author of *The Emperor of All Maladies* and *The Gene*

"With healthcare reform becoming one of the main issues of the current administration, *An American Sickness* could not be more timely or alarming."
—*The New York Review of Books*

"Bold, insightful, well-researched analysis." —*Nature*

"Health care has a dark side, too, where greed and self-delusion allow healthcare providers and drug and device manufacturers to treat patients less like vulnerable fellow human beings and more like ATM machines. That dark side is on vivid display in *An American Sickness*, Elisabeth Rosenthal's groundbreaking book that makes it impossible not to be shocked, if not enraged, by the gulf between the good care that is possible and the profiteering our healthcare industrial complex so often engages in."
—*Washington Monthly*

"Dr. Elisabeth Rosenthal, a physician turned tenacious reporter, shows how the 'highly dysfunctional' American healthcare system turned the Gentle Art of Healing into a Greedy Arsenal of Profit, where everybody does well—except the patient. She also teaches us how to fight back against useless treatments, outrageous fees, and bewildering bills."
    —T. R. Reid, bestselling author of *A Fine Mess, The Healing of America, The United States of Europe, The Chip*, and *Confucius Lives Next Door*

"In this in-depth analysis of a malfunctioning system, Rosenthal makes a compelling case against the hospital and pharmaceutical executives behind the 'money chase,' and it's hard to imagine a more educated, credible guide. . . . The patients she interviewed share mind-boggling stories. . . . She builds her case with one damning statistic after another. . . . Rosenthal presents solutions both personal and societal in this commanding and necessary call to arms."   —*Booklist* (starred review)

"*An American Sickness* will give you many new reasons to avoid getting sick, but also the resources to help protect your finances and your life if you do. Elisabeth Rosenthal's remarkable, outrage-inducing book reveals how each attempt to check the health industry's excesses has been exploited for monetary gain. Both a fascinating history of dysfunction, and a clear manifesto for change."   —Sheri Fink, MD, PhD, Pulitzer Prize–winning author of *Five Days at Memorial* and *War Hospital*

"Provocatively analyzes . . . Rosenthal unveils with surgical precision the 'dysfunctional medical market' . . . A startling cascade."
                                     —*Publishers Weekly* (starred review)

"A blast across the bow of the entire healthcare industry . . . Throughout, the author blends extensive research with human interest . . . A scathing denouncement."   —*Kirkus Reviews*

"Through vivid, heart-wrenching stories and trenchant analysis, Libby Rosenthal unveils the irrationality, indifference, harmfulness, and downright unfairness of the American healthcare system that can often seem more driven by profit than caring and compassion. She also offers tremendously helpful advice to patients on how to navigate the system to ensure they get the best outcomes."
    —Ezekiel J. Emanuel, MD, PhD, chair of the Department of Medical Ethics and Health Policy at the University of Pennsylvania and author of *Reinventing American Health Care*

PENGUIN BOOKS

AN AMERICAN SICKNESS

Dr. Elisabeth Rosenthal was for twenty-two years a reporter, correspondent, and senior writer at *The New York Times* before becoming the editor in chief of Kaiser Heath News, an independent journalism newsroom focusing on health and health policy. She holds an MD from Harvard Medical School, trained in internal medicine, and has worked as an ER physician. She lives in New York City and Washington, D.C.

An American Sickness

HOW HEALTHCARE BECAME
BIG BUSINESS AND HOW
YOU CAN TAKE IT BACK

ELISABETH ROSENTHAL

PENGUIN BOOKS

PENGUIN BOOKS
An imprint of Penguin Random House LLC
375 Hudson Street
New York, New York 10014
penguin.com

First published in the United States of America by Penguin Press,
an imprint of Penguin Random House LLC, 2017
Published with a new afterword in Penguin Books 2018

ISBN 9780143110859 (paperback)

THE LIBRARY OF CONGRESS HAS CATALOGED THE
HARDCOVER EDITION AS FOLLOWS:
Names: Rosenthal, Elisabeth, 1956– author.
Title: An American sickness : how healthcare became big business and how
you can take it back / Elisabeth Rosenthal.
Description: New York : Penguin Press, 2017.
Identifiers: LCCN 2016042934 | ISBN 9781594206757 (hardcover) |
ISBN 9780698407183 (e-book)
Subjects: LCSH: Health care—United States. | Medical care—United States. |
Medical policy—United States. | BISAC: MEDICAL / Health Policy. |
BUSINESS & ECONOMICS / Insurance / Health. | POLITICAL
SCIENCE / Public Policy / Social Policy.
Classification: LCC RA395.A3 .R655 2017 | DDC 362.10973—dc23
LC record available at https://lccn.loc.gov/2016042934

Printed in the United States of America
12th Printing

DESIGNED BY MEIGHAN CAVANAUGH

Dedicated to all the patients, doctors, and other healthcare professionals who so generously shared their stories and experiences to bring this book to life. Waiving privacy concerns, they agreed to have their real names appear in print. In the hope of contributing to change in our healthcare system, they spent hours digging up copies of their bills, insurance statements, correspondence, and other documents to provide verification. I'm deeply grateful for their help, commitment, and courage.

They—and all Americans—deserve better, more affordable healthcare.

Contents

Part II

DIAGNOSIS AND TREATMENT: PRESCRIPTIONS
FOR TAKING BACK OUR HEALTHCARE

An American Sickness

Complaint: Unaffordable Healthcare

I n the past quarter century, the American medical system has stopped focusing on health or even science. Instead it attends more or less single-mindedly to its own profits.

Everyone knows the healthcare system is in disarray. We've grown numb to huge bills. We regard high prices as an inescapable American burden. We accept the drugmakers' argument that they have to charge twice as much for prescriptions as in any other country because lawmakers in nations like Germany and France don't pay them enough to recoup their research costs. But would anyone accept that argument if we replaced the word *prescriptions* with *cars* or *films*?

The current market for healthcare just doesn't deliver. It is deeply, perhaps fatally, flawed. Even market economists themselves don't believe in it anymore. "It's now so dysfunctional that I sometimes think the only solution is to blow the whole thing up. It's not like any market on Earth," says Glenn Melnick, a professor of health economics and finance at the University of Southern California.

Nearly every expert I've spoken with—Republican or Democrat, old or young, adherent of Milton Friedman or Karl Marx—has a theoretical explanation as to why the United States spends nearly 20 percent of its gross domestic product on healthcare—more than twice the average of developed countries. But each one also has a story of personal exasperation about the last time a family member or a loved one was hospitalized or rushed to an emergency room or received an incomprehensible, outrageous bill.

Stephen Parente, Ph.D., a health economist at the University of Minnesota and an adviser to John McCain in the 2008 presidential election, believes that studies overstate the excessive healthcare spending in the United States. But when he talks about the hospitalization of his elderly mother, his dispassionate academic tone shifts to one I've heard thousands of times, brimming with frustration:

> There were a dozen doctors all sending separate bills and I couldn't decipher any of them. They were all large numbers and the insurance paid a tiny fraction. Imagine if a home contractor worked this way? He estimates $125,000 for your kitchen and then takes $10,000 when it's done? Would anyone ever renovate?

Imagine if you paid for an airplane ticket and then got separate and inscrutable bills from the airline, the pilot, the copilot, and the flight attendants. That's how the healthcare market works. In no other industry do prices for a product vary by a factor of ten depending on where it is purchased, as is the case for bills I've seen for echocardiograms, MRI scans, and blood tests to gauge thyroid function or vitamin D levels. The price of a Prius at a dealership in Princeton, New Jersey, is not five times higher than what you would pay for a Prius in Hackensack and a Prius in New Jersey is not twice as expensive as one in New Mexico. The price of that car at the very same dealer doesn't depend on your employer, or if you're self-employed or unemployed. Why does it matter for healthcare?

We live in an age of medical wonders—transplants, gene therapy, life-saving drugs, and preventive strategies—but the healthcare system remains fantastically expensive, inefficient, bewildering, and inequitable. Faced with disease, we are all potential victims of medical extortion. The alarming statistics are incontrovertible and well known: the United States spends nearly one-fifth of its gross domestic product on healthcare, more than $3 trillion a year, about equivalent to the entire economy of France. For that, the U.S. health system generally delivers worse health outcomes than any other developed country, all of which spend on average about half what we do per person.

Who among us hasn't opened a medical bill or an explanation of benefits statement and stared in disbelief at terrifying numbers? Who hasn't puzzled over an insurance policy's rules of co-payments, deductibles, "in-network" and "out-of-network" payments—only to surrender in frustration and write a check, perhaps under threat of collection? Who hasn't wondered over, say, a $500 bill for a basic blood test, a $5,000 bill for three stitches in an emergency room, a $50,000 bill for minor outpatient foot surgery, or a $500,000 bill for three days in the hospital after a heart attack?

Where is all that money going?

BEFORE BECOMING A REPORTER for the *New York Times,* I went to Harvard Medical School and then trained and worked as a physician at what is now New York-Presbyterian Hospital, a prestigious academic center.* To

---

*After completing this book in September 2016, I left the *New York Times* to become editor in chief of Kaiser Health News, a fast-growing nonprofit independent news venture of the Kaiser Family Foundation, dedicated to expanding investigations and impactful projects in the healthcare arena. The Kaiser Family Foundation and Kaiser Health News have no relation at all to Kaiser hospitals or Kaiser Permanente. The Kaiser name is associated with many different organizations.

explore the American system and its ills, I've fallen back on the "history and physical," an organized and disciplined form of record keeping that every doctor uses. The so-called H&P is a remarkable template for understanding complex problems, such as sorting out a patient's multitude of symptoms, in order to come to the proper diagnosis and to allow for effective treatment. The H&P has predictable components:

- chief complaint: What major symptoms does the patient notice?
- history of the present illness and review of systems: How did the problem evolve? How has it affected each organ separately?
- diagnosis and treatment: What is the underlying cause? What can be done to resolve the patient's illness or symptoms?

What you are reading right now is the chief complaint: hugely expensive medical care that doesn't reliably deliver quality results. Part 1 of this book, "History of the Present Illness and Review of Systems," charts the transformation of American medicine in a little over a quarter century from a caring endeavor to the most profitable industry in the United States—what many experts refer to as a medical-industrial complex. As money became the metric of good medicine, everyone wanted more and cared less about their original mission. The descent happened sector by sector, and we will explore it that way: insurers, then hospitals, doctors, pharmaceutical manufacturers, and so on.

First as the child of an old-fashioned doctor—my father was a hematologist—then as an MD, and finally during my years as a health-care reporter for the *Times*, I've had a lifetime front-row seat to the slow-moving heist. I have spent months poring over financial statements, tax documents, patient charts, and bills trying to explain why, for example, a test that costs $1,000 at one of the nation's leading academic hospitals costs $7,000 at some small community hospitals in New Jersey—and the equivalent of only about $100 in Germany and Japan.

These days our treatment follows not scientific guidelines, but the logic of commerce in an imperfect and poorly regulated market, whose big players spend more on lobbying than defense contractors. Financial incentives to order more and do more—to default to the most expensive treatment for whatever ails you—drive much of our healthcare. The central mantra of "innovation" in the past decade has been "patient-centered, evidence-based care." But isn't that the very essence of medicine? What other kind of medical care could there be?

ALL THE HARROWING TALES in this book occurred despite the 2010 passage and 2014 enactment of the Patient Protection and Affordable Care Act (the ACA, also known as "Obamacare"). The ACA is not a failure,* as some still assert, but the "affordable" in its name was an overreach to win over votes and public opinion. (Healthcare bills all have happy names affixed for the sell, including the newest mixed bag, the 21st Century Cures Act.) After endless compromises with the medical industry to enable its passage, the ACA was mostly a bill to make sure that every American could have access to health insurance. But it didn't directly do much, if anything, to control runaway spending or unsavory business practices. Washington being what it is, I doubt we'll ever see the "Take Back America's Healthcare" bill or the "Stop Robbing Patients" bill.

Likewise, such tales will no doubt continue under the administration of Donald J. Trump, who vowed to "repeal and replace Obamacare with something better" during the 2016 campaign. As many experts pointed out, the president did not actually have the power to repeal the law, just like that, whole cloth. Within days after the election, he said he would likely keep certain provisions—such as guaranteeing access to insurance for those with preexisting conditions—and would allow for a prolonged

*For a fuller discussion, see chapter 11.

grace period so that the twenty-two million people who'd obtained insurance through Obamacare would not go without, while the "better" option could be devised. Whatever its final outlines, that Republican replacement plan (Trumpcare? PatriotCare?) is certain to expose patients to more market forces—meaning it is more imperative than ever to understand the convoluted (il)logic behind the extravagant prices we pay.

IT IS EASY TO feel helpless. Our sense of medical urgency combined with bureaucratic confusion is a debilitating cocktail. But we, the patients, can actually do a lot to wrest control of our health from the ledgers of the medical-industrial complex.

Part 2 of this book, "Diagnosis and Treatment," offers not only advice and recommendations that will make your insurers, doctors, and hospitals more affordable and responsive to you but also a range of potential, and politically viable, government fixes that would tamp down the costs and the financial crimes imposed on our bodies in the name of health.

The next steps are up to us. There are self-help strategies you can implement tomorrow to reduce your medical expenses, not to mention political solutions that could revamp American healthcare once and for all if you understand how to effectively press for their deployment. They're not mutually exclusive. We can start now.

EACH MARKET HAS certain rules that are determined by the conditions, incentives, and regulations under which it operates. Currently, we buy and sell medical encounters and accoutrements like commodities, but how do participants in the marketplace make purchasing choices? Prices are often unknowable and unpredictable; there's little robust competition for our business; we have scant information on quality to guide our decisions; and very often we lack the power ourselves to even choose.

The rules governing the delivery of healthcare in the United States have grown out of the market's design. The type of healthcare we get these days is exactly what the market's financial incentives demand. So we have to get wise to them, and be smarter, far more active participants in this ugly, rough–and–tumble world. More important, we have to change the rules of the game, with different incentives and new types of regulation. I've set out the current rules at the end of this introduction. And I'll be referring to them as you read on. In Part 1, you'll see how they play out, and their terrible effects on the health and finances of patients, as illustrated by real-life case studies.

The economist Adam Smith spoke of an "invisible hand" with respect to income distribution. But in American healthcare, there's a different type of invisible hand at work: it's on the till.

ECONOMIC RULES OF THE DYSFUNCTIONAL MEDICAL MARKET

1. More treatment is always better. Default to the most expensive option.
2. A lifetime of treatment is preferable to a cure.
3. Amenities and marketing matter more than good care.
4. As technologies age, prices can rise rather than fall.
5. There is no free choice. Patients are stuck. And they're stuck buying American.
6. More competitors vying for business doesn't mean better prices; it can drive prices up, not down.
7. Economies of scale don't translate to lower prices. With their market power, big providers can simply demand more.
8. There is no such thing as a fixed price for a procedure or test. And the uninsured pay the highest prices of all.
9. There are no standards for billing. There's money to be made in billing for anything and everything.
10. Prices will rise to whatever the market will bear.

Part I

HISTORY OF THE
PRESENT ILLNESS
AND REVIEW OF
SYSTEMS

1

THE AGE OF INSURANCE

Jeffrey Kivi, fifty-three, a chemistry teacher at New York's prestigious Stuyvesant High School, has a Ph.D. in chemistry and worked as a researcher at the pharmaceutical company Abbott Laboratories for twenty years. He has a good idea of what medical treatment should cost. Since childhood, he has suffered from a condition called psoriatic arthritis, a disease where an overly enthusiastic immune system attacks the skin, causing rashes, and the joints, causing crippling arthritis.

When he was getting his Ph.D. at Purdue University in Indiana, his disease flared up so frequently that he was on high doses of prednisone, a steroid that quells the immune system's attack on the bone. Even with that, he "had severe problems with [his] feet, ankles, knees, hips, and lower back/sacroiliac joints—often to the point of being unable to work and even walk."

About fifteen years ago, important new arthritis drugs hit the market. His rheumatologist, Dr. Paula Rackoff, said he was a good candidate. The medicine worked wonders: every six weeks, a drug called Remicade was infused into his veins in an outpatient clinic at Beth Israel Hospital, where

Dr. Rackoff practiced. The treatment cost $19,000 each visit, but Mr. Kivi, as a New York City civil servant, has excellent insurance under EmblemHealth. He paid nothing himself. On the new medicine he could stand for many hours teaching his classes and navigate Stuyvesant's labyrinthine network of hallways. The results were transformative.

Then in 2013 Dr. Rackoff moved her practice about fifteen blocks north to NYU Langone Medical Center. The support services were better and she wanted to practice in a more academic environment, she told her patients. The setup would be more convenient for Mr. Kivi too. Unlike Beth Israel, the NYU Langone infusion clinic was open nights and weekends, so he didn't have to find a substitute teacher or use sick time to get his treatment.

At first, he was impressed by the Langone Center for Musculoskeletal Care, where services were distinctly more upmarket. "I thought it might be a bit more expensive," he said, noting that at NYU he was greeted at the front desk by a patient navigator who walked him to his small private infusion cubicle, equipped with Internet, a television, bottled water, and snacks. (See **Rule 3: Amenities and marketing matter more than good care.**)

But the charges that started posting on his insurance Web site, as submitted by NYU, shocked him: the first three-hour infusion at the new hospital, in May, was billed at $98,575.98, the second in June at $110,410.82, and from July on they were billed at $132,791.04. It was the same dose as always, in the same form, prescribed by the same doctor.

Both Mr. Kivi and I, independently, spent some weeks trying to get an explanation of the charges from NYU. A pharmacist mixed up the drug. A nurse put the IV into his arm. But beyond that Mr. Kivi just sat occupying a chair for several hours. How did that merit these kinds of bills?

When Mr. Kivi complained to the NYU billing office, a patient-care representative offered a range of nonexplanations:

She tried to tell me that, although she had no idea how much profit NYU is making, she was sure that it couldn't be all that much. After all, there are shipping costs, storage costs, and other administrative costs associated with a hospital facility. Really? Enough to justify $120,000 billed to EmblemHealth for a single dosage administered? In the end, she said that I should pay no attention to how much money my insurance company was being forced to pay. After all, it's not costing me anything.

When I tried to pick up the investigation where Mr. Kivi left off, the explanations got even less convincing. The public affairs department told me Mr. Kivi was an "outlier" because he was getting aggressive treatment and he is large. Remicade is dosed according to weight and, at over six feet and nearly four hundred pounds, Mr. Kivi does get a relatively large dose. But even so, the wholesale price of Mr. Kivi's dose of Remicade should only have been about $1,200, a drug researcher at another hospital told me.

As we slid down the rabbit hole of medical pricing, things only got darker and darker. NYU Langone, it turns out, has a financial interest in Remicade and potentially stands to profit each time the drug is used. One of Remicade's inventors is Dr. Jan Vilcek, a professor at NYU and an immigrant from Slovakia who donated a share of his patent royalties to Langone Medical Center in gratitude for help reestablishing his career in the United States. NYU sold most of its rights to the royalties in 2007 for $650 million, but it still receives payment if the profits from the drug rise above an undisclosed bar. With charges like $132,000, chances are that the bar will be crossed.

But there was a bigger shocker for Mr. Kivi: instead of taking issue with the price and securing a deep discount, his insurer came through with almost all of the cash. "I was stunned when the first infusion bill finally showed up on my account," Mr. Kivi wrote to me. "Emblem-Health paid $73,931.98 for the first single infusion!! I couldn't believe my eyes!! This was for the same drug at the same dosage as I'd always gotten. Nothing had changed. And then it went up to $99,593.27 for subsequent times." The capitulation so angered Mr. Kivi that he decided to switch to a drug he could give himself at home, though it did not work as well.

(See **Rule 10: Prices will rise to whatever the market will bear.**)

Emblem was shelling out $1 million a year to NYU Langone for Mr. Kivi's treatments, and because he is a New York City teacher that means all residents were paying some share with their tax dollars. Why would an insurer pay such an exorbitant price for a drug?

The History: In the Beginning

Claims forms and explanations of benefits now seem as native to medicine as oxygen and water are to the earth, but it is important to remember that health insurance is a relatively novel invention, one whose mission has changed dramatically in recent decades.

The very idea of health insurance is in some ways the original sin that catalyzed the evolution of today's medical-industrial complex. The people who founded the Blue Cross Association in Texas nearly a century ago had no idea how their innovation would spin out of control. They intended it to help the sick. And, in the beginning, it did.

A hundred years ago medical treatments were basic, cheap, and not terribly effective. Often run by religious charities, hospitals were places where people mostly went to die. "Care," such as it was, was delivered at dispensaries by doctors or quacks for minimal fees.

Disease was very time consuming. Without antibiotics and nonsteroidal medicines, or anesthetics and minimally invasive surgery, sickness and injury took much longer to heal. The earliest health insurance policies were designed primarily to compensate for income lost while workers were ill. Long absences were a big problem for companies that depended on manual labor, so they often hired doctors to tend to workers. In the 1890s, lumber companies in Tacoma, Washington, paid two enterprising doctors 50 cents a month to care for employees. It was perhaps one of the earliest predecessors to the type of employer-based insurance found in the United States today.

As medical treatments and knowledge improved in the early twentieth century, the concept of insurance evolved. The archetype for today's insurance plans was developed at Baylor University Medical Center in Dallas, Texas (now part of Baylor Scott & White Health, since it merged with another health system in 2013, forming a giant healthcare conglomerate), which was founded in 1903 in a fourteen-room mansion by the Baptist Church. A devout cattleman provided the initial $50,000 in funding to open what was then called the Texas Baptist Memorial Sanitarium, "a great humanitarian hospital." By the 1920s, more and more Texans were coming for treatment. When Justin Ford Kimball, a lawyer who was Baylor's vice president, found out that the hospital was carrying a huge number of unpaid bills, he offered the local teachers' union a deal. For $6 a year, or 50 cents a month, teachers who subscribed were entitled to a twenty-one-day stay in the hospital, all costs included. But there was a deductible. The "insurance" took effect after a week and covered the full costs of hospitalization, $5 a day, which is about $105 in 2016 dollars.

Soon, employees for the *Dallas Morning News* and local radio stations were also signing up for what we today would call catastrophic care insurance. It was a good deal. The cost of a twenty-one-day hospitalization, $525, would have bankrupted many at the time. In that era, given the treatments available, within twenty-one days you were likely dead or cured.

Within a decade, the model spread across the country. Three million people had signed up by 1939 and the concept had been given a name: Blue Cross Plans. The goal was not to make money, but to protect patient savings and keep hospitals—and the charitable religious groups that funded them—afloat. Blue Cross Plans were then not-for-profit.

Despite this, before World War II, when most treatments were still relatively unsophisticated and cheap, few Americans had health insurance. The invention of effective ventilators, breathing machines that moved air in and out of the lungs, enabled a vast expansion of surgery suites and intensive care units. That meant more people could be saved, including soldiers injured during the war and victims of polio outbreaks.

Transformative technologies rapidly spread across the developed world. Abbott Laboratories made and patented the first intravenous anesthetic, thiopental, in the 1930s. Massachusetts General Hospital started the first anesthesia department in the United States in 1936. The first intensive care unit (ICU) armed with ventilators opened during a polio epidemic in Copenhagen in the early 1940s.

Five dollars a day and a twenty-one-day maximum stay were no longer enough. Insurance with a capital *I* was increasingly needed. A private industry selling direct to customers could have filled the need—as it has for auto and life insurance. But a quirk of history and some well-meaning policy helped etch in place employer-based health insurance in the United States. When the National War Labor Board froze salaries during and after World War II, companies facing severe labor shortages discovered that they could attract workers by offering health insurance instead. To encourage the trend, the federal government ruled that money paid for employees' health benefits would not be taxed. This strategy was a win-win in the short term, but in the long term has had some very losing implications.

The policies offered were termed *major medical,* meaning they paid for extensive care but not routine doctor visits and the like. The original purpose of health insurance was to mitigate financial disasters brought about by a serious illness, such as losing your home or your job, but it was never intended to make healthcare cheap or serve as a tool for cost control. Our expectations about what insurance should do have grown.

Blue Cross and its partner, Blue Shield, were more or less the only major insurers at the time and both stood ever ready to enroll new members. The former covered hospital care and the latter doctors' visits. Between 1940 and 1955, the number of Americans with health insurance skyrocketed from 10 percent to over 60 percent. That was before the advent of government programs like Medicare and Medicaid. The Blue Cross/Blue Shield logo became ubiquitous as a force for good across America. According to their charter, the Blues were nonprofit and accepted everyone who sought to sign up; all members were charged the same rates, no matter how old or how sick. Boy Scouts handed out brochures and preachers urged their congregants to join. By some accounts, Blue Cross Blue Shield became, like Walter Cronkite, one of the most trusted brands in postwar America.

But the new demand for health insurance presented a business opportunity and spawned an emerging market with other motivations. Suddenly, at a time when medicine had more of value to offer, tens of millions of people were interested in gaining access and expected their employers to provide insurance so they could do so. For-profit insurance companies moved in, unencumbered by the Blues' charitable mission. They accepted only younger, healthier patients on whom they could make a profit. They charged different rates, depending on factors like age, as they had long done with life insurance. And they produced different types of policies, for different amounts of money, which provided different levels of protection.

Aetna and Cigna were both offering major medical coverage by 1951. With aggressive marketing and closer ties to business than to healthcare, these for-profit plans slowly gained market share through the 1970s and 1980s. It was difficult for the Blues to compete. From a market perspective, the poor Blues still had to worry about their mission of "providing high quality, affordable health care for all."

By the 1990s, the Blues, which offered insurance in all fifty states, were hemorrhaging money, having been left to cover the sickest patients. In 1994, after state directors rebelled, the Blues' board relented and allowed member plans to become for-profit insurers. Their primary motivation was not to charge patients more, but to gain access to the stock market to raise some quick cash to erase deficits. This was the final nail in the coffin of old-fashioned noble-minded health insurance.

Many of the long-suffering Blue plans seized the business opportunity. Blue Cross and Blue Shield of California was particularly aggressive, gobbling up its fellow Blues in a dozen other states. Renamed WellPoint, it is the biggest of the for-profit companies descended from the original non-profit Blue Cross Blue Shield Association; today it is the second-largest insurer in the United States. Most of its plans still operate under the name Anthem BlueCross BlueShield, but in New York the plans operate under the Emblem brand. The insurer for New York City teachers, which reimbursed about $100,000 for each of Jeffrey Kivi's outpatient infusions, has evolved a long way from its not-for-profit mission and $5-a-day hospital payments.

WellPoint's first priority appears no longer to be its patient/members or even the companies and unions that choose it as an insurer, but instead its shareholders and investors. As in any for-profit enterprise, executives are compensated for how well they perform that financial function and are compensated well. In 2010 WellPoint had intended to hike premiums in California by 39 percent, before an attorney general effectively nixed the plan. CEO Angela Braly received total annual compensation of more than $20 million in 2012, despite the fact that she resigned under pressure that year because the company revenues were down. Joe Swedish, the new CEO appointed in 2013, is a longtime healthcare executive who served at the for-profit Hospital Corporation of America. His starting salary and bonus totaled about $5 million, not including stock options.

Then, in August 2014, WellPoint announced that it planned to change its name to Anthem Blue Cross (pending approval by shareholders), presumably to take advantage of whatever nostalgic good feelings patients had retained toward the Blues, before raising premiums on some of its California ACA policies by 25 percent in 2015. Dave Jones, California's vocal insurance commissioner, accused Anthem of "once again imposing an unjustified and unreasonable rate increase on its individual members." Using his bully pulpit to publicly voice his objections was Jones's only recourse, since he, like many state insurance commissioners, can make only non-binding determinations and has no legal authority to deny rates. To express their collective frustration, members gathered signatures for a MoveOn.org petition: "Anthem Blue Cross: Stop Playing Politics with Our Premiums." They urged their insurer "to stop spending corporate funds on political campaigns, disclose everything it has spent directly or indirectly on political campaigns, and use the money to lower rates for Anthem policyholders and California taxpayers."

In 1993, before the Blues went for-profit, insurers spent 95 cents out of every dollar of premiums on medical care, which is called their "medical loss ratio." To increase profits, all insurers, regardless of their tax status, have been spending less on care in recent years and more on activities like marketing, lobbying, administration, and the paying out of dividends. The average medical loss ratio is now closer to 80 percent. Some of the Blues were spending far less than that a decade into the new century. The medical loss ratio at the Texas Blues, where the whole concept of health insurance started, was just 64.4 percent in 2010.

The framers of the Affordable Care Act tried to curb insurers' profits and their executives' salaries, which were some of the highest in the U.S. healthcare industry, by requiring them to spend 80 to 85 percent of every premium dollar on patient care. Insurers fought bitterly against this provision. Its inclusion in the ACA was hailed as a victory for consumers. But even that apparent "demand" was actually quite a generous gift when you consider that Medicare uses 98 percent of its funding for healthcare and only 2 percent for administration.

Why did EmblemHealth agree to pay nearly $100,000 for each of Jeffrey Kivi's infusions, even though they cost only $19,000 at another hospital just down the street? First, it's less trouble for insurers to pay it than not. NYU is a big client that insurers don't want to lose, and an insurer can compensate for the high price in various ways—by raising premiums, co-payments, or deductibles. Second, now that they suddenly have to use 80 to 85 percent rather than, say, 75 percent of premiums on patient care, insurers have a new perverse motivation to tolerate such big payouts. In order to make sure their 15 percent take is still sufficient to maintain salaries and investor dividends, insurance executives have to increase the size of the pie. To cover shortfalls, premiums are increased the next year, passing costs on to the consumers. And 15 percent of a big sum is more than 15 percent of a smaller one. No wonder 2017 premiums for the most common type of ACA plan are slated to rise by double digits in many cities, despite economists' assurances that the growth of healthcare spending is slowing.

To some extent insurers do better if they negotiate better rates for your care. But that is true only under certain circumstances and in a limited way. "They are methodical money takers, who take in premiums and pay claims according to contracts—that's their job," said Barry Cohen, who owns an Ohio-based employee benefits company. "They don't care whether the claims go up or down twenty percent as long as they get their piece. They're too big to care about you."

In fact, history shows that once a procedure is covered by insurance, its sticker price generally goes up because patients are largely insulated from the cost. (For example, when patients had to pay for physical therapy on their own, the cost was likely under $100 a session, significantly less than the $500 an insurer will approve today for a forty-five-minute treatment in a major metropolitan area.) As in Mr. Kivi's case, insurers often dole out payments for services that no consumer would countenance—and, worse, they pay repeatedly. Hundreds of insured patients get infusions costing tens of thousands of dollars at NYU Langone; unlike Mr. Kivi, most do not complain about the price tag.

Instead of bargaining for decent prices, insurers refine their messaging to cultivate loyalty, whether or not it is deserved. Explanation of benefits statements tout how much an insurer "saved" you. "You saved 96%!" crowed Cigna about an overpriced one-night hospital stay at NYU Langone, a calculation explained like this: of the hospital's $99,469 bill (not including doctors' fees), Cigna paid its negotiated discounted rate of $68,240 and the patient had to contribute $3,018. Is that overwhelming cost really something to be upbeat about?

Once acceptance of health insurance was widespread, a domino effect ensued: hospitals adapted to its financial incentives, which changed how doctors practiced medicine, which revolutionized the types of drugs and devices that manufacturers made and marketed. The money chase was on: no one was protecting the patients.

2

THE AGE OF HOSPITALS

Heather Pearce Campbell, an attorney, had always relied on Swedish Medical Center in Seattle for her healthcare. She delivered her first child, a son, there in 2012, and when she became pregnant again in 2014, she returned to Swedish for prenatal treatment.

But her first sonogram, in October, revealed an ectopic pregnancy: the embryo was developing in one of the delicate, narrow fallopian tubes, a dangerous, potentially fatal complication. Within a couple of hours, Ms. Campbell was in the OR, where a surgeon removed the tube, along with the embryo and a part of her uterus.

"I was in there way less than one day, so it was pretty surprising to end up seeing a bill for $44,873.90," said Ms. Campbell of the first bill she received six weeks later, which covered only the hospital portion of the charges. But there was an even bigger surprise on the bill: her entire treatment was labeled simply "miscellaneous." The cost dwarfed the $25,000 a few years before for her two-day stay after a C-section. The bill indicated that Aetna had paid Swedish its discounted negotiated rate of $17,264.56 for her stay and she was expected to send an additional sum of $875.

For Ms. Campbell, it was a tipping point into outrage and action: "Miscellaneous? Forty-five thousand dollars?" she said. "I'm thinking 'Wow, is that how they bill?' That's a really big number!" She called the hospital and demanded a breakdown of charges. She was told "we don't normally send those," but then she pointed out that it was her right, by law. She waited. It never arrived.

When she started getting threatening calls from the hospital demanding payment in January, she protested that she'd never received the itemized bill. "The woman said, 'If you want an itemized bill you can drive over right now and get it, otherwise we're turning you over to collections.'" She filed a complaint concerning "deceptive and obstructive billing practices" with the state attorney general.

THE COST OF HOSPITAL SERVICES has grown faster than costs in other parts of our healthcare system. From 1997 to 2012, the cost of hospital services grew 149 percent, while the cost of physician services grew 55 percent. The average hospital cost per day in the United States was $4,300 in 2013, more than three times the cost in Australia and about ten times the cost in Spain.

Why?

"It's like asking Willie Sutton why he robs banks: that's where the money is," said Dr. David Gifford, a former director of the Rhode Island Department of Health. Market economists I've spoken with variously refer to hospitals as "sharks" or "spending machines." With few if any market forces to effectively curb their behavior, they raise prices as much as they can. Because most hospitals are nonprofit institutions, they have no shareholders to answer to and cannot legally show a "profit"; therefore, they spend excess income on executive compensation and building Zen gardens and marble lobbies.

A longtime finance executive with major American hospitals describes his field as an extractive industry:

> There is an army of consultants running around hospitals. A whole phalanx of firms is there to improve revenue, improve compensation, and get a piece of the pie. Ten to 15 percent of revenue goes to billing and collection companies and contractors to do things like claims and preapproval—those jobs don't even exist in Europe. And hospitals go to Wall Street for bond issues to build new wings, so the bankers are at the trough, too. We have so much surplus capacity, which should lead to falling prices. But instead we get the opposite: It's a market failure, but it follows certain logic. This is not a healthcare system, it's an industry, and at every point there's a way to make money.

A Doctor's View: One Hospital's Journey from Charity to Profit

Providence Portland Medical Center in Portland, Oregon, has undergone a transformation in the past quarter century, which is typical of hundreds of hospitals in the United States. Like many hospitals, Providence has its roots in nineteenth-century religious charity, and most have retained vestiges in their names: Baptist, Mercy, Methodist, Trinity, Presbyterian, Mount Sinai. Healthcare has become a great way for the Catholic Church, in particular, to collect money. From 2001 to 2011, the number of American hospitals affiliated with the Catholic Church grew by 16 percent, as the number of public and secular nonprofit hospitals dropped 31 percent and 12 percent, respectively. Eight of the ten largest nonprofit hospital systems in the United States have religious affiliations and names.

Providence was founded by nuns from an order in Montreal called the Sisters of Providence. In the 1850s, some of the dedicated sisters traveled for months to establish an outpost in the Pacific Northwest. (An earlier unsuccessful attempt had ended up in what is now Chile.) Once ensconced on the American frontier, in addition to taking in orphans, the sisters made home visits to the sick, and "the community came to rely on these compassionate women in times of illness and death." By 1858 they had opened St. Joseph Hospital in Fort Vancouver, the first permanent hospital in the region. By 1902 they were running thirty hospitals, orphanages, and schools in the Northwest. "Whatever concerns the poor is always our affair," said Mother Joseph, the order's leader during that period.

In 1977 Dr. Frank McCullar, a newly minted pediatrician, accepted a job in the outpatient department at Providence. Though not religious, he had trained, in part, at St. Mary's Hospital, another Catholic health provider, in Rochester, New York, which had also been staffed by nuns. He was inspired by their sense of calling. Providence also had an impressive national reputation. In 1960 Dr. Albert Starr, a Portland heart surgeon, revolutionized the treatment of heart disease by coinventing and then implanting the first successful artificial heart valve. Millions of patients who would otherwise now be dead have benefited from that discovery. Dr. Starr then opened a heart institute at Providence, where he operated for decades. (He is still, at ninety, chairman of Oregon Health & Science University's Knight Cardiovascular Institute.) He was a medical rock star, a hero, a genuine draw. Yet "I never saw him on a billboard," said Dr. McCullar. "Marketing and advertising were considered unethical and looked down on—it just wasn't done." But that and everything else about

Providence had changed by the time Dr. McCullar retired from Providence, just a few years ago.

In the 1960s Medicare arrived to cover hospital payments. Between 1968 and 1980 the number of Americans under sixty-five covered by good private insurance was at its peak (about 80 percent, compared with about 67 percent in 2007). Because patients were no longer directly forking out cash or writing checks for their care, hospitals began charging more for their services. The original Blues plan at Baylor had paid by the week for hospitalization, but now hospitals like Providence charged for each service and each encounter. In a world populated by doctors, nurses, and nuns, no one really knew how to figure out how much it cost the hospital to remove an appendix, for example. But there was no harm in aiming high, because insurers usually paid whatever was requested.

With lots of money rolling in, the hospital needed to hire businesspeople to manage it. When Dr. McCullar joined Providence, the emergency room and its associated walk-in clinics had one administrator who paid bills, hired support staff, and took care of patient complaints. Within a decade the number of administrators seemed to be doubling.

In the early 1980s, the increasingly powerful hospital administrators (many of whom sans nuns' habits held degrees in business or healthcare administration) modified Providence's "core values" to include "stewardship" of resources in addition to its long-standing guiding principles of "respect," "compassion," "justice," and "excellence." According to Dr. McCullar, "They paid more attention to the bottom line than to the tradition of medicine."

By the late 1980s, Providence had hired professional coders to translate doctors' exams into medical bills. Physicians were given stock phrases to use to describe their exams and told what procedures to perform to ensure better revenue—instruction that became commonplace at many hospitals. The doctors began receiving statements each month that showed how much money their examinations brought in, relative to those of their colleagues. Relations between the administration and the doctors became increasingly testy. The physicians in Dr. McCullar's group asked to see what the hospital had billed Medicare on their behalf. Some doctors were concerned about overcharging. Others wanted to make sure they were getting their fair share. Providence refused and threatened to fire those who insisted on disclosure.

By the late 1990s the hospital said it no longer wanted to pay a salary to doctors in the ER and clinics; instead, it would treat them as independent contractors. "That turned us into a business also," Dr. McCullar said. "We negotiated contracts that stipulated what percent of revenues we deserved." Providence's marketers also required the doctors to attend what Dr. McCullar calls "charm school." The seminars were run by a group of physician consultants who had started the Foundation for Medical Excellence in Portland. "I tried to get the administration to look harder at quality outcomes—like infection rates—but they didn't, and that's more expensive." With canny marketing, Providence grew its business, aggressively advertising cardiac care and a state-of-the-art "stroke center." A new building was adorned with marble columns and featured a fountain with jumping salmon; after more renovation, granite countertops were added and expensive art was displayed. "It became like the Providence Marriott," Dr. McCullar said. "I was embarrassed to have poor patients come here."

When Dr. McCullar arrived in Portland in 1977, Providence comprised two sister hospitals: Providence Medical Center and, across town, St. Vincent. By the time he retired, the Providence Network had absorbed many smaller hospitals and bought the practices of internists, cardiologists, and neurologists. Providence Health & Services is now the third-largest nonprofit hospital system in the United States, operating in Oregon, Washington, California, Alaska, and Montana. In 2013 it had revenues of $2.6 billion and about $2 billion in assets. Its CEO is paid about $3.5 million a year. Yet it still describes itself as "a not-for-profit

Catholic health care ministry" continuing "a tradition of caring that the Sisters of Providence began more than 158 years ago." It lists nuns from Providence Ministries as its "sponsors." The senior vice president of the health system received a papal medal from John Paul II, the Cross Pro Ecclesia et Pontifice, for his service after he retired in 2001.

In fact, Providence's "tradition" comprises a weird mix of Mother Teresa and Goldman Sachs: one day it is donating $250,000 to help build a new teaching hospital in Haiti to replace one destroyed by the 2010 earthquake, and the next its new offshoot, Providence Ventures, is announcing the launch of a $150 million venture capital fund, led by a former Amazon executive.

ONE OF THE HOSPITALS that Providence Health & Services took into its fold in 2012 was Seattle's Swedish Medical Center, where Heather Pearce Campbell had surgery for her ectopic pregnancy. The affiliation changed both its medical and its financial practices.

Swedish, a secular hospital, had long offered abortions and contraceptive services. Once under Providence's Catholic umbrella it would not. To mollify the outraged community, Swedish quickly said it would help underwrite a nearby Planned Parenthood center to perform those services. At a press conference, Lauren Simonds, executive director of NARAL Pro-Choice Washington, asked a hospital spokesman what would happen if a pregnant woman was suffering from a life-threatening emergency, such as an ectopic pregnancy, turned up at its door. The hospital's reply was boilerplate: Swedish "will provide all emergency services required by women in an emergency situation." Was it possible that Swedish could no longer itemize a bill for "termination," even if it was to save Ms. Campbell's life, and that's why the services she received were categorized as "miscellaneous"?

The merger is also likely the reason for the improbably escalating prices that Ms. Campbell has noticed on Swedish bills, since a huge conglomerate like Providence Health & Services can throw its weight around in insurance negotiations. (See **Rule 7: Economies of scale don't translate to lower prices. With their market power, big providers can simply demand more.**)

Behind the Scenes: How Hospitals Got New Business Models

After two decades with community service organizations and nurses' unions, Peg Graham went to Yale for a master of public health as well as to Pace University for an MBA to understand the mechanics of hospital finance. For much of the 1980s and 1990s, she then worked at a series of hospitals in New York City. Now semiretired, she gave me one of the textbooks she used early in her career, the fifth edition of *The Financial Management of Hospitals,* by Howard J. Berman and Lewis E. Weeks, published in 1982. A lens into a bygone era, it portends what was to come at a critical juncture in hospital history. "The financial structure of a hospital, due to legal and philosophical constraints, has not developed in the same manners as that of the commercial corporation," the authors noted. At the top of a sample hospital organization chart, they placed the "Board of Trustees," with "Administration," "Medical Staff," and "Ladies Auxiliary" beneath.

"Hospitals are big businesses," according to Berman and Weeks. "The [philanthropic] benefactor alone cannot subsidize hospital operations." They argued that an antiquated structure grounded in medicine and philanthropy had to change. And it did. Over the course of her career,

Ms. Graham watched with distress as concerns about finance rose to dominate those about patients and healthcare in hospital decision making.

In the 1980s she watched as "head nurses" morphed into "clinical nurse-managers" who were adept in fields like compliance or quality assurance and attuned to the business of medicine. To the chagrin of bedside nurses, this new breed of managers coordinated staffing levels with statistical analyses of payment and calculations of baseline nurse-patient ratios. "What disappeared was the head nurse who fiercely protected the patients on her ward and didn't give a damn about the financials," Ms. Graham told me.

Then, Ms. Graham served as a special assistant to a doctor who held an entirely new executive position in hospital infrastructure: the chief medical officer, or CMO. The top of the doctors' totem pole had traditionally been occupied by the physician in chief and surgeon in chief, older, respected practitioners who ran rounds and were called in to review difficult cases. The CMO was also a physician, but his primary allegiance was to the executive suite, and his mission was to use his professional influence to make the ad hoc practice of medicine by the army of doctors at the hospital function as a profitable business. He and his deputies in each department were in charge of "realizing efficiencies"—like trimming the length of hospital stays and convincing doctors to use one kind of stethoscope or to give their hospitalized patients generic drugs.

The good times were rolling for hospitals between 1967 and 1983, when hospitals set their rates and the patient or his insurer was expected to pay up. Medicare payments to hospitals increased more than tenfold from $3 billion to $37 billion nationwide. Ms. Graham remembers the panic in hospital boardrooms when insurers and employers started to complain about rising prices and pushed back, introducing payment plans more like Baylor's original price-per-week Blue Cross offering. Medicare had initially paid hospitals their "usual and customary charges," but in the mid-1980s it began paying according to a diagnosis related group (DRG). The payment for a hospital stay for an appendectomy or for pneumonia would be a fixed amount depending almost entirely on the diagnosis. The hospital would make money on patients who healed more quickly and efficiently—and lose money on those who did not.

Most commercial insurers never adopted Medicare's DRG system with its immovable cost constraints. But they also balked in other ways at paying for long, expensive, procedure-filled hospital stays: they hired care managers to review and approve elective surgery as well as negotiators to determine what proportion of the bill they would agree to pay.

That's how the gap between the big numbers on hospital bills and what any insurer actually pays, which began as a small crack and has evolved into a gaping chasm, came about. The crazy-quilt phenomenon of some patients paying less and some more for exactly the same care evolved the same way: hospital business departments realized if Medicare or a powerful insurer wouldn't agree to pay a big enough proportion of the rate they wanted, they had the leverage to insist that smaller insurers—and people with no insurance—pay more. (See **Rule 8: There is no such thing as a fixed price for a procedure or test. And the uninsured pay the highest prices of all.**)

In the early 1990s, with prices and health insurance premiums sometimes increasing 20 percent a year, many employers and the insurers they hired desperately sought to move patients into health maintenance organizations (HMOs) to contain costs. HMOs often received a fixed payment per patient per month. A primary care doctor who served as a gatekeeper for tests, specialists, and hospital care, all within an HMO's closed network, was assigned to each patient. With business falling off as a result of this "care management," hospitals could only make money if they were streamlined and cost-effective, and most were not.

In response, hospital CMOs and newly hired business advisers in the late 1990s began pulling together a "chart of accounts"—financial data from the inpatient group, the outpatient group, radiologists, and even, for example, some one-doctor specialty centers for diseases like cancer that had been founded by a grateful patient. Hospitals were finally heeding the warning from Berman and Weeks's 1982 textbook: "The hospital's administrator, controller and finance committee need accurate cost finding" just like "the executives of . . . a giant supermarket or a chain of discount department stores."

HMOs succeeded at containing costs at least for a while. The 1990s were the only decade since the 1940s when U.S. health spending did not increase faster than the cost of living. But most hospitals dragged their heels in creating quality cost-effective care to attract managed care contracts, and these lackluster offerings tarnished the HMO concept in some parts of the country, perhaps forever. Successful HMOs took permanent root in a few markets, most notably Kaiser Permanente in California. But overall patients hated them, in part because so many were hastily designed and poorly managed. The central office of HIP, the largest HMO in the New York market, routinely left patients on the hook for payment by failing to reimburse hospitals in its network. By the turn of the century, many HMOs had died out, but hospitals and doctors had become far more adept at the business of medicine. Many healthcare management companies have their origins in that era.

Within a few years, the position of the chief medical officer would itself seem out-of-date. According to a 2011 article in the newspaper published by the American Medical Association, more business experience was needed to be a hospital executive: "The chief medical officer remains a common leadership position, but hospitals are creating positions such as chiefs of physician relations, integration and medical informatics. . . . Some physicians may find it worthwhile to receive additional training, such as an MBA or other advanced degree. But on-the-job mentorship or training could be sufficient."

Enter the Consultants

To ensure that the U.S. healthcare system would grow in a cost-effective way, Congress passed a law in 1974 requiring state health-planning agencies to grant approval before hospitals could build new facilities or indulge in the purchase of expensive technology. The agencies granted a "certificate of need" indicating that the community would benefit from the new investment, for example. The goal was to avoid the duplication of services and overbuilding, which studies had indicated would increase cost.

But in 1987 that federal law was rescinded and over the next decade many states ended or watered down their review programs so that hospitals could buy or build whatever they wanted, so long as there was enough revenue to support it. Medical purchases became an "investment." "At that point the medical arms race between hospitals was on," remembers Paul Levy, a former longtime CEO of Harvard's Beth Israel Deaconess Medical Center.

Kristen Zeff, a young consultant at Deloitte & Touche in those years, watched the firm's hospital business grow. At first, hospitals ran on such thin margins that consultants had to offer a pay-for-results model. Deloitte would take a percentage of the increased revenues that were generated through its advice about "strategic pricing": "We came to them with this proposal that at little up-front cost you can increase the amount you bring in just by manipulating how you bill."

In 2005 Deloitte hired Tommy Thompson, who had been George W. Bush's secretary of health and human services for the previous four years, as chairman of its global healthcare practice, thereby lending a big name to its outreach in the new sector. Restructuring a hospital as if it were a steel mill or a chicken processing plant seemed uncouth to some boards, but second-tier hospitals and those straining under financial pressures opened their doors wide to consultants.

Deloitte used teaser projects to entice new clientele: for example, it offered free advice to New York–Cornell Medical Center on how to move up in the "Best Hospitals" rankings. (It declined.) In those days Cornell perennially lagged behind Columbia-Presbyterian Medical Center, with which it later merged (it's now known as NewYork-Presbyterian). "You could analyze the metrics and see what was the lowest cost and easiest way to do it," Ms. Zeff recalled.

Hospital reimbursement is essentially a strategic puzzle. Medicare has assigned to every hospital a specific overall cost-to-charge ratio that it deems reasonable to participate in government-sponsored insurance. Raising list prices for one thing means lowering them for another. All hospitals have a master price list—a chargemaster—and adjusting it to maximize income was the focus of Deloitte's strategy. To squeeze more money from the purse, Deloitte advised hospitals to stop billing for items like gauze rolls, which insurers rarely or never reimbursed, and to boost charges for services like OR time, oxygen therapy, and prescription drugs. It was all about optimizing payment by raising prices on certain items. "While it's legal, it felt ethically dubious and not good for patients," reflected Ms. Zeff, who is no longer in the business. "And it certainly increases the cost of healthcare."

For the business departments of hospitals and doctors on staff, the discovery was transformational. The billed price of an item could be completely decoupled from its actual cost. Items that had previously been included in the charge for the operating room or a hospital day could be billed separately.

Patricia Kaufman was born with a congenital spinal condition that has required multiple upper back surgeries at Long Island Jewish Medical Center, another hospital that worked with Deloitte. She has always been happy with the results. But the bills for her last procedure included a $250,000 fee from an outside plastic surgeon to close up the wound, a service that had always been performed by residents at no charge before.

Some absurdities of strategic billing are well known, such as those $17 charges for a Tylenol pill, but there can be far worse consequences: In one instance, a family was billed for $21,000 after the father had a heart attack in the living room of his home. He was driven by relatives to the hospital only to be declared dead in a wheelchair in the lobby before a single test was done. In another case, a Canadian who wintered in Arizona was charged $210,000 for a failed attempt to take out a hip implant that had become infected. (That total doesn't include the $28,000 he had to pay for an air ambulance to get him back to Canada, where a successful surgery was performed for free.)

Today just about every hospital employs strategic billing, which is enabled and supported by consultants and healthcare advisory firms, large and small. Deloitte is ranked number one by revenue in all areas of healthcare consulting—life sciences, payer, provider, and government health. In 2014 it announced record revenues of $34.2 billion, fueled by more than 17 percent growth in the sector.

Strategic Billing 101: Upcoding and Facility Fees Lead to a $3,400 Needle Stick

Dr. Randy Richards, a surgeon in Tennessee, didn't think much about the bills his patients received until 2014, when he got stuck with a needle in the operating room. Before the era of HIV and hepatitis, gloves were worn primarily to protect the sterility of the operation. In the 1980s, doctors became far more cautious and by the 1990s all hospitals had strict protocols for reporting such incidents, partly for safety concerns and partly because of the expansion of "risk management" teams whose job it is to make sure hospitals don't get sued. Today, a needle stick requires a report and an immediate blood test. That is partly to consider starting medication to prevent an infection from taking hold, and partly to document whether the doctor or nurse had hepatitis or HIV already at the time of exposure, so that disability insurance will be clear about its obligations.

After getting stuck, Dr. Richards reported to the ER in keeping with protocol. But some months later he was shocked by the $1,137 bill from the ER doctor, not to mention the $48 charge to put an oxygen meter on his skin, and a $2,198 fee for hospital services. The brief blood draw had been coded as a level 5 visit, the most intensive, which according to guidelines of the Centers for Medicare and Medicaid Services (CMS) requires a detailed history, extensive management or lab results, and examination of multiple body systems. Dr. Richards wrote to me: "What is written down and what was actually done bear little relation. The net charges are just dissociated from reality. All I needed was a blood draw, nothing else. I have discussed this with ER docs and with the Hospital Administration but they stand by their practices." The phenomenon known as "upcoding" didn't come into existence overnight.

Around 2000, the hospital where an internist named Dr. W. had long worked became worried that some doctors were not seeing enough patients or bringing in enough revenue. (Dr. W. cannot use his full name because he is worried about losing his job and health insurance.) The hospital decided it would no longer pay these physicians a fixed salary; instead, they would be compensated in proportion to the relative value units (RVUs) of the care they dispensed. RVUs are a measure of productivity used to determine medical billing.

Generalists like Dr. W. are assigned RVUs primarily according to the complexity of their exams and treatment plans, which are coded on a scale of levels 1 to 5. A simple level 2 visit may yield $60; level 3, $120; level 4, $210; and so on. "What started to happen is lots of pinkeye was billed at a level 4," he explained. "It may not sound like much—but it adds up."

There was financial incentive: colleagues who were coding expansively could make twice as much—over $300,000 instead of $170,000.

Because many prestigious medical centers have all their medical staff on a salary, they contend that their physicians and surgeons therefore have no incentive to upcode or perform unneeded tests and procedures. But many of the well-known health systems (including the Harvard-affiliated Partners HealthCare, the Henry Ford Health System, Duke Health, and Baylor Scott & White Health) tie those salaries to physicians' RVUs or sometimes offer "productivity bonuses" based on them. A small number even deduct money from a doctor's salary if his or her RVUs are too low. In 2015, 71 percent of physician practices supplemented salary with productivity bonuses. Bonuses can motivate doctors, just as they do bond traders.

Insurers, particularly Medicare, tried to prevent upcoding by spot audits of charts, but hospitals provided helpful assistance to doctors. "It's like a candy store—all you have to do is check the right boxes," one doctor told me. "We had software for dictation, and it would even say, 'You need to check two more boxes for level four.'" A questionnaire filled out by a patient can be labeled as a "health needs assessment," which is a billable item. Injecting a patient's bum knee with steroids can be coded as "surgery" costing $1,200. If the doctor uses an ultrasound machine to guide the needle (an unnecessary step because it's easy to enter the knee space), that's another $300.

Coding creep grew ever bolder—until it made no sense at all. If needle sticks and eye infections are coded as level 5, what was a crushed chest from a car accident or a heart attack? A Center for Public Integrity (CPI) investigative series in 2012 found a huge increase between 2001 and 2008 in Medicare billing for levels 4 and 5 visits among emergency room patients who were sent home, from a quarter to nearly half of all patients. Meanwhile, the proportion of level 2 visits decreased by about half, to just 15 percent. More than 500 of the 2,400 hospitals in the database billed the two most expensive codes for more than 60 percent of patients. Dr. Donald Berwick, a former Medicare administrator, told the CPI that he believed most doctors were not breaking the law, just "learning how to play the game."

Dr. Richards's bill also included a $2,198 "facility fee," which would not have been there two decades ago. Upcoding by doctors has a multiplier effect on hospital profits, because this hospital-imposed charge for the use of its rooms and equipment—the facility fee—rises with the level of service.

Facility fees were a logical outgrowth of a period of rapid scientific progress in medicine, which allowed many treatments to move to an outpatient setting. Improvements in anesthesia, pain medicine, minimally invasive surgery, and biopsy techniques meant that many procedures and operations could be safely performed without an overnight stay. New medicines to quell the severe nausea of chemotherapy meant patients could receive treatment at an infusion center. Because hospitals had traditionally charged a day rate for inpatients, it made some sense that insurers (including Medicare) had largely accepted their new practice of charging facility fees for major outpatient care as well by the turn of the century.

Then abuse (and sometimes fraud) crept in, since facility fees proved easy to manipulate for gain. There is a lot of leeway in the pricing of something as nebulous as two hours in the endoscopy suite (some fees are billed in fifteen-minute increments). What's more, facility fees provided a great incentive to stop performing any and all procedures in doctors' offices and instead use a surgicenter or a hospital outpatient department.

Dr. Ronald Anderson, a Pennsylvania rheumatologist, can inject a bursa with painkillers in his office for about $80. (Bursas are fluid-filled sacs that reduce friction around joints. When they become temporarily inflamed it is called bursitis.) But when one of his patients had the condition treated by an orthopedist at a surgicenter with ultrasound guidance, the bill was almost $5,000, most of which the insurance company paid.

Facility fees are a unique construct of American healthcare and its business model. Hospitals in Europe don't have them. Nor do other types of businesses in the United States. As Yevgeniy Feyman, currently of the Harvard T. H. Chan School of Public Health, observed in *Health Affairs Blog,* "When you buy anything—a watch, a car, even groceries—you pay a single price for the goods. The Walgreens down the street doesn't add a separate charge to cover its rent, utilities, or the cost of refrigeration units."

Closing Departments: Make Money or Die

The new hospital consultants were experts not just in raising revenues with strategic pricing but also in corporate restructuring. Hospitals traditionally had departments that perennially lost money: emergency rooms, labor and delivery, dialysis centers, drug treatment programs, and outpatient clinics in poorer neighborhoods that served Medicaid populations. These were part of their mission and a moral obligation (importantly, they also receive federal funding to subsidize them). But by the early 2000s, every department had to carry its own weight. The chief medical officer and his advisers were expected to find new profitable lines of treatment and to reevaluate the old money-losing departments to see if they could be "turned around." If not, the department or the service often had to go. "I have worked in an ER for the past ten-plus years and the administration was very frank that the ER was expected to generate revenue," said Jacqui Bush, a nurse in California.

As departments underwent serial financial review, hospitals did away with loss leaders and enhanced their most profitable offerings: orthopedics, cardiac care, a stroke center (revenue from expensive scans), and cancer care (revenue from infusions). They erected electronic billboards promoting the short wait times in the ER—a bizarre notion if, as they all aver, people shouldn't use high-priced emergency rooms to get elective care.

As obesity rates climbed, medical equipment companies devised new operations using new products to help combat the condition, and bariatric surgery was a boom field. Companies, hospitals, and doctors' groups lobbied successfully to have insurers pay for it all. Being overweight was rebranded as a disease. Dr. Alfons Pomp, a weight-loss surgeon from Canada, was recruited first by New York's Mount Sinai Medical Center in 1999 and then by NewYork-Presbyterian / Weill Cornell Medical Center just two miles away in 2003. Each hospital invested heavily to create lucrative bariatric wards: buying new beds, lifts, wheelchairs, and OR tables that could accommodate the bulk of the patients. The returns were exceptional.

New machines were purchased based not on medical necessity or even utility but according to financial calculations. Proton beam therapy was developed to treat the small number of tumors that were hard to reach by other methods. Low-energy proton beam machines have long been used at a few centers to treat rare tumors of the eye. But manufacturers of newer high-energy machines, costing over $100 million, had a bigger market in mind. Originally experts predicted there would be at most a handful of these behemoths scattered around the country, which patients could fly to if their tumors could not otherwise be treated. Since it was a complicated new therapy with unpredictable finances that few patients would need, Medicare reimbursed generously. In short order proton beam therapy was being used on a far wider range of tumors than had ever been intended, despite little evidence that it was superior to cheaper options. Every hospital wanted one and new machines came with billing tips as well as elaborate calculations about how long it would take to recoup the investment. (See **Rule 1: More treatment is always better. Default to the most expensive option.**) The National Cancer Institute and the American Cancer Society tried unsuccessfully to tame the frenzy with science, to no avail, even though one study of thirty thousand patients with prostate cancer found that "proton beam therapy provided no long term benefit over traditional radiation therapy, despite far higher costs," according to a report in the *Wall Street Journal.*

Bankers, who regarded the purchase as a safe investment, were approaching hospitals and offering to finance the machine. Companies sprang up to help smaller hospitals broker, build, and install proton beam centers. One such company, ProCure, received more than $100 million in equity funding. The result: The British National Health Service sends the few patients whom it deems suitable for high-energy proton beam therapy to the United States for treatment (paying for travel and eight to ten weeks of lodging). There is one proton beam machine in all of Canada, but with plans for aggressive construction under way in the United States, there should be three in Washington, DC, four in Florida, and two in Oklahoma City by 2018.

At the other end of the care-profitability spectrum, many hospitals started outsourcing services like dialysis, which is largely financed by Medicare and therefore less amenable to billing legerdemain. According to a 2006 survey, 31 percent of hospitals said they were already outsourcing dialysis, a trend that has only accelerated.

Typically, the hospitals sold their dialysis practices to large for-profit chains of dialysis centers, like DaVita and Fresenius, which were better able to make do with Medicare reimbursements because of their huge economies of scale. But they also, patients complained, cut costs by using poorly trained technicians to administer treatments rather than nurses. In deals brokered by consultants like Innovative Health Strategies (and backed by private equity investors), hospitals "sold" their patients for $40,000 to $70,000 per head to the big commercial players.

Innovative pitched its appeal to hospitals by underlining the economic advantages: "Today's challenges require successful healthcare entities to establish new revenue sources to fund new technologies and initiatives. High-functioning dialysis units, often having reached economic maturity, are prime candidates for spin-off to independent dialysis companies." Dozens of health centers from the University of Pennsylvania to Emory have bought in.

But some corners of medicine yielded little revenue no matter how hard consultants squeezed. Dr. Gene Dorio, a geriatrician, was practicing at a small California hospital that went bankrupt in the early 2000s. Business professionals were brought in to "turn it around." In 2006 the hospital announced plans to close its transitional care unit, where elderly patients could gain some strength before discharge. The unit was popular and provided invaluable healthcare, as far as patients and doctors were concerned. Dr. Dorio, a member of the Medical Executive Committee, organized a protest by the hospital's elderly patrons in the lobby, to no avail. There was no revenue stream to support it, and it closed in 2008.

The Business of Medical Training: Hospitals and Cheap Labor

My three years of medical residency were the most stressful of my life. I was on call every third night, arriving at the hospital at 7 a.m. for rounds and leaving about thirty-six hours later, having perhaps caught a few hours of sleep on a gurney. Life was a seemingly endless cycle of blood draws, deaths, and IVs that needed to be replaced in the middle of the night. I learned how to treat someone with heart disease who was having chest pain; how to stitch up wounds so that they would look pretty when healed; how to snake a central line into a deep vein near the heart through the neck. But I often worked outside my comfort zone and at the very limits of my competency.

Residents have long been the worker bees that keep hospitals going, and debates about who should pay for their training and how much have evolved in tandem with our profitable medical system. Before the 1940s hospitals paid trainee stipends by building their costs into patient charges. After World War II, the GI Bill subsidized training and then the creation of Medicare, in 1965, established that federal and state funds should "to an appropriate extent" cover the purported cost of training future doctors, which was viewed as a public service.

By 2014 hospitals received about $15 billion a year in government subsidies to support graduate medical education, a number that had been "increasing for decades." These payments include "direct payments" for salaries and supervising physicians, as well as "indirect payments" to compensate for the theoretical inefficiencies and institutional sacrifice involved in training new doctors, such as longer hospitals stays and the need to order more tests for teaching purposes.

The trouble is that studies haven't provided proof of those purported inefficiencies and sacrifices that merited special compensation. Stays in teaching hospitals are no longer than those in hospitals without residents, for example.

In fact, there is much to suggest that hospitals have turned residencies into another profitable business. The senior supervising doctors, called "voluntary faculty," are often not paid for their time. The residents are the primary teachers of the medical students assigned to their wards, relieving hospital staff of that burden. What's more, residents provide much of the hospital's on-the-ground medical manpower by seeing patients in the ER, assisting in the OR, and drawing blood, to name just a few of their duties. They are learning, yes, but are also effectively low-wage labor.

The median cost to a hospital for each full-time resident in 2013 was $134,803. That includes a salary of between $50,000 and $80,000. Federal support translates into about $100,000 per resident per year. Researchers have calculated that the value of the work each resident performs annually is $232,726. Even without any subsidy having residents is a better than break-even deal.

That explains why, even though the Balanced Budget Act of 1997 placed a cap on the number of residents supported by Medicare subsidies, between 2003 and 2012 the number of residents rose by about 20 percent. The recent growth has been particularly large in subspecialty fields where there are generally already (by many estimates) sufficient numbers of doctors, such as urology and pathology.

The Medicare Payment Advisory Commission (MedPAC) estimates the indirect subsidy hospitals receive for medical trainees may be $3.5 billion higher than deserved. The 2010 National Commission on Fiscal Responsibility and Reform recommended downward adjustments that would save an estimated $6 billion in 2015. President Obama's 2015 budget called for cuts to education payments of $14.6 billion over ten years. Congress has never acted on any of these proposals.

The American Hospital Association (AHA) has lobbied to hang on to this pot of money and the cheap labor and is even lobbying to facilitate the entry of foreign medical graduates since there are not enough U.S. grads to fill the Medicare-subsidized residency slots in less traditionally lucrative or glamorous specialties, such as nephrology, and in underserved communities.

The AHA, along with the Association of American Medical Colleges, avers that cuts would "jeopardize the ability of teaching hospitals to train the next generation of physicians" and "directly threaten the financial stability of teaching hospitals."

If Republicans were disingenuous in evoking death panels to discredit the Affordable Care Act, Democrats have been equally so in heeding their local hospitals' calls for more residents. Senator Bill Nelson (Florida), along with cosponsors Senators Charles Schumer (New York) and Harry Reid (Nevada), introduced the Resident Physician Shortage Reduction Act of 2015, to *expand* the number of subsidized training positions by fifteen thousand, or 15 percent.

One reason why hospitals have been desperately fighting to get still more residents is that, over the past fifteen years, states and medical societies have passed laws, regulations, and recommendations curtailing the work hours of doctors in training, largely to reduce the rate of medical errors that resulted from fatigue. That may be good for everyone's well-being, but it creates a staffing problem.

Some hospitals responded by reducing educational activities, such as elective rotations and seminars, so they could have more hours of cheap labor. Many also hired moonlighters. In some instances, the doctors whom hospitals pay at a rate of $10 per hour as residents or fellows (more senior doctors in specialty training) can receive $100 per hour to do the exact same job after hours.

Any physician in practice will attest to just how valuable (in terms of medical knowledge and finance) these doctors in training are. Dr. Paul Aronowitz was the director of training at a highly regarded private hospital in California in 2012, when he decided that several attending doctors should no longer be allowed to have residents care for their patients. He cited "repeated serious complaints" concerning their patient care—one resulted in a death—as well as the failure to adequately supervise the student doctors. The hospital CEO overturned the decision. Without the services of residents, the quality of patient care for the doctors' patients would certainly suffer, the executive said. Moreover, those doctors would likely leave the hospital and move to another if they couldn't avail themselves of the residents' services—taking the $1.5 million they generated annually with them.

The Emergence of Hospital-Hotels

The idea that hospitals can't afford to train residents without subsidies is hard to believe as their buildings have become ever more opulent and their executives earn Wall Street–size salaries.

Twenty-five years ago, rooms with four beds were common. Private rooms were rare and traditionally reserved for patients with contagious diseases or who were vulnerable to infection. Now, singles have become the norm despite the fact there is little medical justification and many insurers won't cover them, leaving patients who had no choice stuck with "single supplement" charges. Private rooms may be more pleasant for patients, but even if an insurer covers a private room, we all pay higher prices and premiums in the future to fund building them.

As healthcare became a business, hospitals could have spent their operating surpluses on raising pay for nurses and orderlies, or reducing list prices for patients. But there was not much commercial incentive to do that. "There are an infinite number of ways to spend: amenities, scanners, higher salaries," said James Robinson, a health economist at the University of California, Berkeley. "So they build more. They're like Four Seasons Hotels, with valet parking and chandeliers. Then they go to Congress and say Medicaid and Medicare aren't paying us enough, my margins are low, the CEO doesn't make much money compared to the private sector."

Three years after Nancy Schlicting, MBA, took over the helm of Detroit's Henry Ford Health System in 2003, she hired a hotel industry executive, Gerard van Grinsven of the Ritz-Carlton Group, to be CEO of its new hospital. Henry Ford West Bloomfield Hospital has all private rooms, including in the emergency department, and patients are assigned a concierge who "guides you from check-in to check out." In the name of medical care, it provides health coaching and acupuncture through Vita, its wellness center. In the late 1990s, the Henry Ford Health System was losing tens of millions of dollars annually, but by 2013 it was comfortably in the black, with revenues of over $2 billion. "We focused on people and service excellence," Schlicting said. "Patients ask their docs to admit them here, because they want a hospital that treats them this way."

The hospital is a perennial top scorer in the Press Ganey ratings, a survey tool that rates the "patient experience" at hospitals. Founded in the 1980s by a medical anthropologist and a statistician, Press Ganey bills itself as continuing "to lead the patient experience industry," hired by an estimated 50 percent of all U.S. hospitals. In 2015 it filed with the Securities and Exchange Commission for an initial public stock offering.

Customer satisfaction is important and predicts repeat business, but it does not necessarily indicate medical quality. Studies have determined that such surveys have only a "tenuous" link with patient outcomes. Physicians hate them. But Medicare pays hospitals a bonus for performing well on patient surveys. "So if a patient asks for a test and it won't hurt, they'll get it," one doctor told me. "It's good for Press Ganey scores. It takes more time and trouble to explain why they don't need the X-ray."

As hospitals became lavish, executive salaries did too. Top brass of hospitals received packages that included golden parachutes, cars, and funding for their kids' education. More than two-thirds of the country's hospitals are not-for-profit, and IRS rules state that nonprofit CEOs should receive only "reasonable compensation," which it advises should be determined in part by considering salaries at similar organizations. But, as also occurs in the corporate world, the CEO typically picks the compensation consultant and controls who is on the board.

In most cities the highest-paid nonprofit executive by far runs the local hospital. In 2012 Jeffrey Romoff of the University of Pittsburgh Medical Center earned almost $6.1 million, far more than the university's president. Delos Cosgrove at the Cleveland Clinic earned $3.17 million. Thomas Priselac at Cedars-Sinai earned $3.85 million. Steven Corwin at NewYork-Presbyterian earned $3.08 million. But salaries are very large even at small community hospitals in New Jersey. In 2012 Audrey Meyers, the CEO of Valley Hospital in Ridgewood, earned $2.18 million. Michael Maron, the CEO of Holy Name Medical Center in Teaneck, was paid $1.83 million. In fact, the CEO of one small nonprofit suburban hospital almost certainly earns more today than Darren Walker, the CEO of the Ford Foundation, which operates in more than one hundred countries and has assets valued at about $12 billion.

Total cash compensation for hospital CEOs grew an average of 24.2 percent from 2011 to 2012 alone, which increasingly includes bonuses as well. No surprise. Those bonuses are typically linked to criteria such as "finance," "quality," "profit," "admissions growth," and "increase in net funds," not medical goalposts like reducing blood infections or bedsores and avoiding unneeded procedures.

The Most Profitable Nonprofits: The Evolution of Hospital Charity

In 2014 I spoke at the commencement of the University of Pittsburgh School of Medicine, a revered institution and the home base of Dr. Thomas Starzl, a pioneer of transplant surgery, who has been at the University of Pittsburgh Medical Center (UPMC) since 1981.

I was startled to see the place in the city occupied by the University of Pittsburgh Medical Center, with which the medical school is affiliated. To me Pittsburgh was a steel town, a gritty place associated with Andrew Carnegie and manufacturing. Today, it is a gleaming temple of healthcare. UPMC, with nearly sixty thousand employees, is the largest nongovernmental employer in Pennsylvania. It is by far Pittsburgh's largest employer, almost six times larger than Mellon Bank. It aggressively markets its services not just in western Pennsylvania (where there are few alternatives) but all over the country and internationally—at least to wealthy paying patients. But like nearly all prestigious American medical centers, the UPMC is nonprofit, so it pays almost no U.S. property or payroll taxes.

Until the 1960s, most hospitals and doctors had to do charitable work. Laws and codes of ethics said sick people should be treated even if they couldn't pay. By 1969 most Americans were insured, so the IRS defined a new standard for hospitals that wanted to keep their tax-exempt status: these institutions had to provide "charity care and community benefit."

The government placed the value of the tax advantage to hospitals at $12.6 billion in 2002 and in 2011 at $24.6 billion. How to keep that tax benefit while spending the least amount possible on "charity care and community benefit" has become the job of some hospital accountants and consultants in the business of medicine.

Not-for-profit hospitals are now just as profitable as capitalist corporations, but the excess money flowing in isn't called "profit"—it's "operating surplus." Charity Navigator, a group that rates nonprofit organizations based on their governance and use of donated funds, doesn't even rate not-for-profit health systems because they function on such a different model.

That is why the city of Pittsburgh wrangled for years with UPMC to get it to pay more taxes. In 2013 the then mayor Luke Ravenstahl filed a lawsuit in the Court of Common Pleas demanding six years' worth of back payroll taxes and a removal of UPMC's tax-exempt status. He said it was a case of "the David versus the Goliath," where the second-largest city in Pennsylvania was David, the underdog.

Cities across the nation nervously watched how the legal action played out. Hospitals tend to have more high-priced legal counsel than cash-strapped cities. In addition to avoiding property taxes as well as federal, state, and local payroll taxes, hospitals can issue tax-exempt bonds for building projects. They can collect tax-deductible donations (a boon when a big donor wants to underwrite a new wing or hand over a valuable piece of art to adorn a lobby).

It's probably fair for hospitals to be able to count services for low-income patients (Medicaid or uninsured) as "charity care and community benefit," because that practice brings in less than the cost of treatment.

But since 1986, hospitals that care for large numbers of low-income people have already been compensated in other ways. They buy all their pharmaceuticals at a discount, through a federal program. Likewise, Medicare gives them so-called disproportionate share payments, essentially bonuses for treating higher numbers of poor people, who tend to be sicker and less able to pay bills. At least three of the twenty hospitals in the UPMC system collected these payments in 2014.

But beyond that, there is little agreement and much gaming surrounding what can or should count toward the IRS requirement of charity care and community benefit. Before 2010, there was little pretense of specific accounting—hospitals could just attach some brochures to their tax returns to illustrate what they were doing. But in 2010, despite fierce hospital protests, a provision of the Affordable Care Act started requiring the IRS to collect each hospital's quantitative enumeration of charitable activities and their value.

Every year, on a form called Schedule H (Form 990), they now have to list how much money-losing care they dispense—and how they calculate that number. They also have to list and value what they've done gratis to better their communities. And that has given scholars and consumer advocates a window and an opportunity to assess whether they deserved their huge tax breaks.

Recent research shows that many are providing nowhere near the amount of charity care and community benefit that would justify the value of their tax exemption. A survey of the forms conducted by the California Nurses Association concluded that 196 hospitals received "$3.3 billion state and federal tax exemptions and spent only $1.4 billion on charity care—a gap of $1.9 billion." Three-quarters of the hospitals got more dollars in tax breaks than they spent on benefiting the communities they serve.

UPMC had more than $11 billion in revenues and $10 billion in assets in 2014 and an average 12 percent growth rate in revenues over the last fifteen years. It has demonstrated "strong, consistent financial performance" and has a superior credit rating. "UPMC is a nonprofit that melds an unwavering community mission with entrepreneurial business models," its Web site says. It is "building a global health care brand." It provides "world class care to private-pay patients" in agreements with hospitals in Qatar and China, among other countries.

Many medical centers have strategies for exporting their brands, if not always their standards. NewYork-Presbyterian Hospital has outreach offices in capitals in Asia and the Middle East—kind of like the U.S. Army recruiting station in Times Square—where paying patients can sign up for operations and treatment in New York. Zhang Lei, a Chinese venture capital billionaire, announced that he was teaming up with the Mayo Clinic "to bring one of America's best-known health care institutions to China."

The *Pittsburgh Post-Gazette* has uncovered many of the relevant numbers on UPMC: it is "Allegheny County's largest property owner, with 656 acres," 86 percent of which is tax-exempt. If it were not classified as a nonprofit, "UPMC would owe the city $20 million more in taxes every year." On its 2014 IRS Form 990, UPMC claimed that about 11 percent of its costs went to charity care and community benefit. But it took credit for vague notions like "spurs the economy," via direct construction jobs, a commitment to diversity through the hiring of minority contractors, and environmental improvement because it had created an award-winning "healing garden." It avers a shortfall from treating Medicare patients, which it counts as charity, even though Medicare calculates that it pays hospitals more than it should reasonably cost to dispense care.

But the question of UPMC's service to Pittsburgh never got a public airing. UPMC quickly responded to Mayor Ravenstahl's lawsuit with a federal countersuit claiming the city had "violated its right to due process." Then, in 2014, after a year of court wrangling, a judge dismissed the city's suit on narrow technical grounds, saying that it should not be suing UPMC as an entity, but instead the health system's individual member hospitals, which dispense the paychecks, since the major issue centered on payroll taxes.

In July of that year, a new mayor, Bill Peduto, decided the city would abandon its legal efforts and instead try to wrest UPMC's "fair share" of contributions from the hospital in other ways. He said his team would meet privately with UPMC representatives to determine what that might be. Many other cities have avoided protracted court battles by adopting a similar approach.

In 2001 San Francisco passed its Charity Care Ordinance, in large part because there was a suspicion that one of its major hospitals, California Pacific Medical Center, was not providing care commensurate to its size. That ordinance, which mandates review of charitable performance in conjunction with approval for new hospital construction, provides a stick the city uses to demand more of its high-end health providers.

Before California Pacific Medical Center could break ground on a new flagship hospital on Cathedral Hill a few years ago, Sutter Health, its parent company, had to negotiate for months about what it would contribute to San Francisco in return. Sutter agreed to continue to operate St. Luke's, an old hospital in its system that served mostly the poor and uninsured. It agreed to spend at least $86 million per year on charity care, Medicaid, and services for the poor. It would spend $20 million to create a Healthcare Innovation Fund to help the city's community clinics and $60 million for various programs in affordable housing. It would also spend tens of millions on transit upgrades and pedestrian safety programs. The final package even included a bone that was probably particularly tasty for city budget planners: it agreed to not raise rates charged to health insurers that covered city employees by more than 5 percent annually.

All in all, California Pacific Medical Center was willing to spend $1.1 billion to hang on to its tax-exempt status.

Observation Status: A New Financial Purgatory in the Hospital

The idea of admitting a patient for "observation" has long been an important medical tool. Indeed, it was likely far more useful a few decades ago when getting results of cardiac enzymes to see whether someone was having a heart attack took twenty-four hours or before CT scans could determine whether a patient with belly pain had an inflamed appendix and needed a trip to the OR.

But as observation has become less important for diagnosis, it has become more important as a lucrative billing construct, manipulated by hospitals, insurers, and nursing homes. The easy money for Medicare patients is not in inpatient admissions. Medicare pays a bundled rate for those. But outpatient care has no similar limits—the till is open for testing. For hospitals there were other advantages as well: For example, Medicare penalizes hospitals if patients bounce back thirty days after discharge—the "readmission penalty." But if they were never officially admitted but were merely under "observation" they couldn't bounce back!

At first Medicare tolerated the sleight of hand and only pushed back when it noted that, by 2011, 8 percent of people under observation were in the hospital for more than two days. (Observation status does not count toward the three days of inpatient care required for Medicare to pay for a subsequent nursing home or rehabilitation stay.) Beginning on April 1, 2015, it said that observation status could not persist for more than "two midnights." That ruling prompted articles from consultants with titles like "How Your Hospital Can Succeed Under the Two-Midnight Rule"— meaning in terms of money, of course.

For hospitals and insurers, observation status has benefits. For patients it is a disaster. After Jim Silver, a retired software engineer in Indiana, had a brief fainting episode after a medication change, he was sent via the ER to a hospital room on a hospital ward, under "observation status." In twenty-four hours, he had an array of tests, including scans, all of which were normal. Only later, he discovered the financial implications. Since the terms of outpatient insurance apply, observation status typically means far larger co-payments. Mr. Silver's insurer negotiated a rate of $12,000 for the stay. If he had been an inpatient, his insurer would have had to cover the entire amount. With his "observation" status, he said he was on the hook for about 20 percent, or $2,300.

In 2015 President Obama signed a bill requiring hospitals to notify patients receiving more than twenty-four hours of observation care of their status as outpatients and its varied implications. But that notification will come after the fact, when patients are already supine in their hospital bed and can do little about it.

3

THE AGE OF PHYSICIANS

D r. Michael Canning, a Florida general surgeon, sent me the official pledge he took when he was admitted into the American College of Surgeons in 1990. In elaborate calligraphy, on faux parchment, it had a couple of clauses that caught my eye (emphasis is mine):

> I promise to deal with each patient as I would wish to be dealt with if I were in the patient's position and **I will set my fees commensurate with the services rendered.**

> I will take no part in any arrangement **such as fee splitting or itinerant surgery** which induces referral or treatment for reasons other than the patient's best welfare.

It was hard to believe that some of the surgeons I've met would commit to such a declaration. Every doctor who is a part owner in a surgery center where he operates engages in a form of fee splitting (where a physician gets financial advantage from referrals). In 1990 the American College of Surgeons felt that it was immoral to be an itinerant surgeon—moving from place to place collecting fees for surgery but not being there for the follow-up. Today many surgeons operate at a large number of hospitals, collecting fees for the revenues they generate at each.

The current version of the American College of Surgeons pledge, adopted in 2004, has been amended to remove those pesky ethical limitations:

> I promise to deal with each patient as I would wish to be dealt with if I was in the patient's position, and I will respect the patient's autonomy and individuality.

> I will take no part in any arrangement or improper financial dealings that induce referral, treatment, or withholding of treatment for reasons other than the patient's welfare.

Surgeons are not the only group of doctors watering down their moral commitments. The American Medical Association's code of ethics has been similarly diluted. Through the 1960s and 1970s it said that physicians' fees "should be commensurate with the services rendered *and the patient's ability to pay*" (emphasis mine). But this latter exhortation did not survive into the 1980s.

What Is a Doctor's Work Worth?

Being a doctor is a tough job, deserving of reasonable compensation. But the idea of what's reasonable has escalated to unusual heights in recent years. Doctors make more in the United States than in other countries. The gap is particularly striking in the specialties. While primary care doctors in the United States make about 40 percent more than their peers in Germany, American orthopedic surgeons make more than twice as much as similar German specialists. In fact, U.S. doctors who are best compensated are often not the ones who undertake the longest training or work the hardest. They are the ones who are best at the business of healthcare. The average U.S. physician is more likely to be in America's 1 percent (27.2 percent fall into that category) than the average lawyer or manager. Doctors' salaries have been consistently rising since 2009, which isn't true of any other profession, not even hedge fund managers.

Medical school is expensive and long, generally four years after an undergraduate degree. It costs between $120,000 at a state school and $220,000 at a private university, including tuition and fees. (It is free or cheap in many other countries.) Medical students graduate with a mean debt of about $170,000, including some carried over from undergraduate years.

Medical residencies—the required apprenticeship before becoming an independent doctor—run between three and seven years. Residencies in intense patient care specialties, such as general surgery or internal medicine or OB-GYN or cardiology, require many long hours and sleepless nights in the hospital. Those in niche fields—such as dermatology or ophthalmology or ear, nose, and throat (ENT) surgery—do not, which is part of why they are popular. At every medical school, there is a small coterie of students who suddenly find the skin or the eye or the ethmoid sinus so fascinating that they study the basic pathophysiology of these organs in a research lab, because demonstrating your scientific commitment is part of the drill to secure a coveted residency in one of those specialties.

The first and second years of residency are the hardest. By third year many residents are working mostly from 7 or 8 a.m. to 5 or 6 p.m., with only the occasional backup call from home. (I spent three months of my third year working at hospitals in Kenya.) Some subspecialties require a couple of extra years of training as so-called fellows. Miriam Laugesen, a researcher at Columbia University, has found that the extra debt incurred to pursue specialty training is about $21,300 in total and, since specialist compensation is proportionally far higher, "they pay that off quite readily."

Huge debts no doubt influence medical students' choice of fields. In a recent survey 56 percent of residents said it was slightly or somewhat influential and 36 percent said it was very or extremely influential. Dr. Logan Dance, who recently completed a residency in radiology in Rochester, New York, said that debt was "one factor" that influenced him to choose radiology over pediatrics, which he loved as much, perhaps more. "I have $240,000 in debt, but I'm not that worried—I plan to pay it off quickly," said Dr. Dance, who has three children.

There are likely easier paths to get really rich than entering medicine. But every profession involves its own form of hard labor to establish position. Lawyers have clerkships. New investment bankers work around the clock. Aspiring writers wait tables or write blog posts without pay. Few paths are as secure as medicine. I know unemployed lawyers; I know unemployed bankers. I know lots of unemployed journalists. I've heard of few, if any, unemployed doctors. "I'm not terribly sympathetic to the argument that healthcare costs so much because of medical school debt—I think it's a red herring," said Dr. Joanne Roberts, sixty-four, chief medical officer at Providence Hospital, Everett. "Even if it's two hundred thousand dollars, that's easy to pay off on a doctor's salary. What I do see is new doctors straight out of training buying million-dollar homes because suddenly they're making all this money."

And yet practicing doctors seem to view themselves as exceptionally burdened. Even medical students—the people actually facing the debt now—seem perplexed and disheartened: "On rotations I've sat and listened to dermatologists, plastic surgeons, orthopedic surgeons, neurologists and oncologists all tell me they don't make that much money," wrote one student from the University of California at San Francisco, one of America's most prestigious medical schools, speaking of her "cognitive dissonance." "There is a bizarre martyr complex that permeates medicine—people think they are working harder and longer for less money than everyone else in America."

When I left medicine in the 1990s doctors commonly complained that they made less per hour than plumbers. Today, they seem more inclined to compare (negatively) their compensation to that of sports stars like LeBron James or titans of commerce like Lloyd Blankfein, the CEO of Goldman Sachs. But perhaps in this age of industrialized medicine, they're merely looking for dollars to compensate what has been lost from the profession, the joy of getting to know your patients. Anyway, as the numbers and salaries of hospital administrators were vaulting upward, the doctors wanted in on the profits.

The Price of a Cure: A Brief History of Doctors' Finances

Physicians have struggled with the issue of income for centuries. Hippocrates, a wealthy physician of noble birth who eschewed fees, noted that since physicians save people from death, "no fee, not even a large one, is adequate for the physician, but it is with God Almighty that his remuneration rests." But Hippocrates realized that some doctors needed to charge to survive, so he wrote in his *Precepts* that the doctor should be kindhearted and do his best to accommodate fees to the patient's circumstances.

For the first half of the twentieth century, American patients were mostly paying for doctor's visits out of their pockets, and so that noble tradition largely continued. Many patients paid on an informal sliding scale, in proportion to their income. Paying a doctor's bill was not really a commercial transaction. Every child who had a doctor for a parent in the early 1960s remembers the gifts of booze, chocolates, and artwork from grateful patients. My brother had to have his stomach pumped after imbibing some "thank you" bottles of ouzo my father had stored in the living room closet. I spent many happy hours poking my finger into the underside of fancy chocolates to determine the contents. In those days, physicians were comfortably middle-class but not rich.

In the years after World War II, more workers acquired insurance through their employers that covered hospitalization and later physician visits. The trend accelerated dramatically with the increasing popularity in the 1960s and 1970s of Medicare Part B, the program that covers physician payments. (Part A covered hospitalization at no cost, but Part B was optional and required paying a small premium.) For a time, as with hospitals, those Part B insurance plans paid essentially whatever was asked or nearly so, making the 1980s a Golden Age of physician payment, which is why some older doctors nostalgically hark back to that era.

"Employer provided insurance plans produced a significantly higher rate of growth, and Medicare blew the walls out," wrote Dr. Richard Patterson, a surgeon, describing the gold rush. Doctors, he recalled, "suddenly had the wherewithal to invest heavily in the stock market and shopping centers, to buy airplanes and island retreats."

Physicians collected 98 percent of the charges they billed and insurers, including Medicare, went on paying "usual and customary" fees by locality for years after—hardwiring high payments into our bills. Many still do.

"Usual and customary" quickly became inflationary: If only five doctors in a zip code performed gallbladder surgery, "usual" was defined as the mean charge of the five surgeons and "customary" was defined as the level that insurers would typically reimburse (which was then 75 to 90 percent of the bill). Since future payments depended on current charges, the incentive was for doctors to perpetually increase rates; the five doctors would benefit and they likely knew one another. (See **Rule 6: More competitors vying for business doesn't mean better prices; it can drive prices up, not down.**) That led to price divergence that made no sense at all. By 2014 the "usual and customary" fee for gallbladder surgery in Queens, New York, could cost $2,000, but twenty miles east in Nassau County, Long Island, where more doctors are in private practice, it was $25,000. By the 1980s, just as in the hospital sector, Medicare responded to runaway bills by trying to define what it should and would pay, regardless of what the doctor might bill.

In 1986 Congress, in cooperation with the American Medical Association, commissioned a respected health economist, William Hsiao of Harvard, to create what was ultimately called the resource-based relative value scale (RBRVS). The goal was to scientifically determine what each physician service was really worth. The researchers on Dr. Hsiao's team would assign a work value to each of the seven thousand codes then in the American Medical Association's *Current Procedural Code Manual.*

Dr. Hsiao's team calculated a work value in a new currency called relative value units (RVUs), based on (1) the work/time spent by a doctor for the visit or intervention, (2) the overhead incurred in rendering the service, (3) the cost of training required to learn to perform the service, and (4) the malpractice expenses involved. That RVU score was then multiplied by a conversion factor that was adjusted annually and varied slightly by location to determine a dollar payment. It was an elegant but complicated algorithm and—it turned out—one ripe for manipulation.

In 1992 Medicare began using that scale as the basis for its physician payments. Unlike payments to hospitals, however, overall payments to physicians under Medicare would have a legal cap to more or less maintain budget neutrality. If Medicare's valuation for one procedure went up or a new highly valued procedure was approved, other costs had to decrease. If payments to doctors went up more than $20 million in a year, Medicare would decrease the conversion factor, so the price of all procedures dropped. (While the RBRVS technically applied to only Medicare, many commercial insurers turned to the agency's judgments to scale and revise their own payouts.)

As intended, many doctor payments initially tumbled. Dr. Richard Patterson wrote about a colleague who "was disposing of some records after his father's death around 2000 and he came across what Blue Cross paid his father for gallbladder surgery in the 1980s. It was about 150% more than BC was paying my colleague in 2000."

Despite that start, through the next decade and even through the Great Recession, many doctors, particularly some specialists, did very well. According to the Medical Group Management Association, median physician income for all primary care doctors increased by 9.9 percent from 2000 to 2004, compared with a 15.8 percent increase for all non–primary care specialties. Median income for hematologists and oncologists increased 35.6 percent to $350,000, and median income for diagnostic radiologists increased 36.2 percent to $407,000. Average real income for all Americans dropped 3 percent during that time.

There were of course winners and losers as a result of Dr. Hsiao's new payment scheme. Because Dr. Hsiao's algorithm tied the amount of time it took to perform a medical intervention and how long it took to learn a new skill to reimbursement, it tended to reward procedures more than visits that relied on a physician's "cognitive skills." It's much easier to quantify how long it takes for a radiologist to learn to snake a catheter into the brain than to quantify the slow process by which neurologists learn to put together the complex bits of evidence that suggest an impending stroke. (Neurology is one of the most challenging corners of medicine, and yet today neurologists are often poorly paid compared to their medical colleagues.) Who won and who lost under the new system was determined as much by figuring out how to exploit the RBRVS for financial gain as by developing medical expertise.

Doctors Get the Key to the Vault

Within the new system, constant updates were needed to determine fair value and payment. In a decision that might today seem ill advised, Medicare assigned that task to a multimillion-dollar organization, the American Medical Association (AMA), medicine's most powerful industry group, which at the time still possessed more of a veneer of wise professional association with commendable ethics than it does today.

Three times a year an AMA committee called the Relative Value Scale Update Committee (RUC) meets to adjust the value of codes in a highly vituperative meeting. Medicare and insurers inevitably suggest that codes are valued too generously and the doctors who perform a service inevitably protest that the valuation is not high enough.

Each specialty has a representative on the RUC who tries to defend and expand its piece of the pie. Dr. Brett Coldiron, a former RUC member for the American Academy of Dermatology, described the RUC meetings as "26 sharks in a tank with nothing to eat but each other." (He blocked many attempts by Medicare to reduce payments for skin cancer surgery during his time.) Allowing the AMA to determine doctors' payments is akin to letting the American Petroleum Institute decide what BP and Shell and ExxonMobil can charge us not just for gas but, somehow, for wind and solar power as well.

The AMA says that the RUC "represents the entire medical profession," but it is not really representative of practicing doctors. It is more akin to the U.S. Senate. The RUC apportions each specialty society equal representation, although in recent years a few extra generalists have been added. That means the eight thousand urologists and eight thousand otolaryngologists in the United States have more or less the same sway as the eighteen thousand general surgeons and hundreds of thousands of general doctors. Specialists tend to make their money by doing procedures, which results over time in a strengthening of the bias toward paying for them. "It's not about science—it's often a product of lobbying," said Dr. Christine Sinsky, a leading academic primary care doctor who has watched the payment system evolve. "It was supposed to fix inequities but it has exaggerated them in many ways."

Researchers have determined that the all-important "time" component assigned to procedures is often wildly inaccurate. Better surgical approaches, computerized equipment, and more effective anesthesia mean that surgical times have often declined dramatically since the RBRVS was first used in 1992. But the RUC determines the time it takes to perform a service by polling several dozen specialists who actually do the procedure, which is essentially asking them whether or not they want to be paid more.

One study demonstrated that the 2014 estimates were longer than actual times in twenty of twenty-four procedures, sometimes by as much as double. The biggest gap was for a host of common simple operations: deviated septum, prostate surgery, upper GI endoscopy, hysterectomy, and cataract removal. For two decades, the RUC meetings were held behind closed doors, but as of 2013 the AMA bowed to pressure to publish its minutes, which revealed the kind of bargaining that goes on. The urologists are granted two additional minutes of prep time before one type of surgery. The orthopedists and trauma surgeons get twelve additional minutes of pay for positioning before operations to fix rib fractures. (Never mind that in most hospitals the residents or techs typically do this work.)

What's more, the RUC often values new procedures by using the best-paid existing interventions as a yardstick. To assign work units for a new technique using injections to kill the nerves of the bladder, for example, the urologists suggested comparing it to upper GI endoscopy, an unrelated but highly lucrative procedure.

Attempts by Medicare to rein in inflation at the meetings are resisted. After Medicare decided to pay surgeons an all-inclusive rate for spine surgery (rather than paying separately for each step), representatives from the

American Academy of Orthopaedic Surgeons and the North American Spine Society saw to it that the valuation of the bundle increased at the RUC meeting in April 2013.

The RUC does not always give the appellants their way. After many years, for example, it reduced the relative value units for immunological tests done by pathologists, noting that in the past the doctor had to prepare a separate slide for each antibody, but now many can be tested on a single slide. The RVUs dropped from 1.7 to 0.84. (Pathologists tend to be quiet, antisocial types and have never been very good at forming alliances or lobbying.)

The sense of desperation at RUC meetings over the past twenty years stemmed in part from the fact that the profession felt it was under siege because of a long-standing government proposal to reduce Medicare payments to doctors by as much as 21 percent, called the sustainable growth rate, which was originally part of the Balanced Budget Act of 1997. Medical groups spent hundreds of millions of dollars over nearly two decades to warn doctors of the impending doom and to lobby Congress each year to postpone any actual reductions, until it was finally defeated once and for all in 2015.

But even if Congress didn't appreciate the value of the medical profession, there were many other revenue streams that doctors, particularly specialists, could turn to, and, in short order, many did.

Strategy #1:
Doctor-Entrepreneur-Owner

Ambulatory surgery centers (ASCs) became increasingly popular over the course of the 1980s and 1990s and into the new century. More and more were owned and run not by long-established hospitals but by individual doctors and investors. ASCs were popular because patients were generally thrilled to be sleeping in their own beds. Health economists and policy makers approved because—at least theoretically—treating disease in an outpatient setting that does not involve a hospital's huge overhead should be much cheaper.

But doctors saw new income potential, because they could charge "facility fees"—essentially room rentals for the suites where they plied their trade. With Medicare physician payments decreasing after the imposition of the RBRVS, doctors started investing in or opening surgery or other treatment centers. Each specialty gravitated to the kind of outpatient business that grew out of its practice; it was a challenge for some, but most eventually found a niche. ENT doctors opened sinus centers. Orthopedists opened arthroscopy centers. Gastroenterologists opened colonoscopy centers. Neurologists opened sleep centers, where patients could have their brain activity measured and breathing monitored for sleep apnea. Insurance was often billed $5,000 to $10,000 a night.

Regulators tried in vain to curb the practice by requiring that physicians disclose to the patient in advance if they had an ownership stake. But those disclosures typically came in a pile of other paperwork to sign in the minutes before heading into the procedure room when patients had no option to leave. Minor interventions doctors had once performed in the office were moved into their centers for financial benefit. Nueterra Capital and other private equity firms actively recruited doctors as partners.

Dr. Michael Zapf, an office-based podiatrist in California, has been approached by at least four surgicenters in his area to buy in as an investor/owner. "They guarantee a return on investment of more than one hundred percent," he told me. How? The doctors sign up with insurance plans, but the centers themselves do not participate in any insurance networks, so the facility fees are not constrained by insurers' negotiated rates. That allows them to bill $40,000 to $50,000 for what Dr. Zapf called "a simple surgery" like a bunion removal, when the standard office fee would be $3,000 to $4,000.

Strategy #2: The Hidden Doctors and Their Mysterious Bills

There are physicians who contribute to your care whom you may never see and whose names you're unlikely to ever know: pathologists, anesthesiologists, radiologists, and emergency medicine docs. The first three are often referred to as the NPC ("no patient contact") specialists.

Their skills are crucial, but they're not the docs who patients bond with, praise, or even get to choose. Traditionally, doctors entered these fields for a variety of reasons. Some were just not very social people. Others liked the more scientific nature of lab work (pathologists) or the challenge of mastering new technology (radiologists). Historically, these physicians were hospital employees, and their services were embedded in hospital charges just like bandages and beds. They were paid decent salaries but no more. So it's surprising that today they account for some of the highest, most confusing doctors' bills you're likely to get.

Because radiologists could most easily ply their trade outside the hospital, they likely initiated the migration to a private practice business model. In the 1980s most still had hospital jobs, but they also started opening office-based practices that were precursors to surgicenters, focusing on elective procedures like mammograms or sinus scans. Over the next two decades their business strategy would continue to evolve.

Groups of pathologists, anesthesiologists, radiologists, and ER physicians (PARE) followed, creating limited liability companies (professional LLCs) and becoming corporate contractors who sold their "physician services" to their former employers. Many did so even as they continued to work within the hospital. Emergency room physicians were the last to jump on board. When I worked as an ER doctor in the mid-1990s, we were all hospital staff. By 2014, 65 percent of the nation's five thousand hospitals had contracted out their emergency department staffing/management function, according to Merritt Hawkins, a physician staffing company.

For those in the industry, it was a win-win situation: hospitals no longer had to buy malpractice or health insurance or figure out how to staff vacations. Doctors could charge what they felt they were worth. But for patients, this meant the proliferation of separate bills for these doctors' services, from companies with mysterious return addresses in distant states. Then, around 2010, many of these doctors' groups, who worked at in-network hospitals, simply stopped contracting with any insurers at all, leaving unsuspecting patients with tens of thousands of dollars in surprise medical bills.

Patients will typically only visit hospitals in their network. Few patients can afford hospitalization otherwise. But patients are less attentive to whether doctors are in their network, particularly doctors they've never met. "The game with the PARE specialists is that they began to refuse to contract with any plan or insurer," said Dr. Seth Lewin, who was senior director of a health plan in central Massachusetts from 2008 through 2012. "These guys decide not to contract, so they can charge whatever they want. The patient is over a barrel." Most insurance plans limit your financial liability only if you remain in the network of hospitals and doctors with which they have contracts.

The latest group of physicians to join the out-of-network trend is neonatologists, who care for ill newborns—the friendly doctors with fuzzy bears clipped to their stethoscopes.

Lee Schaefer has great federal employee insurance through Blue Cross Blue Shield, but she and her husband are "risk averse," she says, so they researched the costs of her pregnancy, went to an in-network hospital, and thought they'd figured out fees before she delivered her daughter, Etta, in 2010. After Ms. Schaefer was induced at thirty-seven weeks for high blood pressure at New Jersey's Overlook Medical Center, the baby stopped breathing in the nursery and so was transferred to the neonatal intensive care unit. The hospital charge for eight days of ICU observation was fully covered. But "we got billed for ten thousand dollars from MidAtlantic Neonatology—the pediatricians—and they don't take our particular insurance," she said. (The neonatology group staffs four intensive care units in suburban New Jersey.) The Schaefers negotiated that down to $5,000 but, she said, "despite our insurance and all our research, we ended up on a long-term payment plan."

Strategy #3: The Pacts Doctors Make

Olga Baker's twenty-something daughter went to a California emergency room in 2012, complaining of a severe headache. A scan showed a tumor growing in her brain. She was seen by a neurosurgeon who had been called in to consult, and told that she had brain cancer, "potentially dangerous and type unknown." He advised that she should stay in the hospital to have surgery ASAP.

I have at one time received much the same information: In 2005 my healthy thirteen-year-old daughter, Cara, had a seizure in school and was taken by ambulance to a New York City emergency room. A brain scan revealed a large fluid-filled tumor. The neurosurgeon on call advised that she stay in the hospital to have emergency surgery. But my and Olga Baker's stories are different.

The mother of a young child and an MD, I called around to neurologists and neurosurgeons and learned that it is often possible on a scan to get a good idea if a tumor is malignant and aggressive. Neurosurgery to remove a tumor is never an emergency. The symptoms, such as seizures and headaches, can be treated with medicines as the surgeons learn more about the tumor and plot a more deliberate course of action. We signed Cara out of the emergency room "against medical advice." Two weeks later, she had surgery to remove the benign tumor, after that hospital's tumor board had reviewed her case, and after we'd selected a pediatric neurosurgeon who is on staff at both NewYork-Presbyterian and Memorial Sloan Kettering Cancer Center.

In contrast, Olga Baker's daughter was in the OR the very next day. Only after the surgery had failed did Ms. Baker, who practices law in San Diego, discover that the on-call surgeon was an out-of-network "subcontractor" who had an exclusive deal with the hospital but no particular expertise in brain tumors. "He opened her skull, meddled with her brain, and stapled her skull flap back, leaving most of the tumor intact," said Ms. Baker. A billing service then sent an invoice for $97,000 for the ninety-minute procedure, and insisted that her insurer should pay in full because it was an "emergency."

Traditionally, individual doctors were proudly and devotedly affiliated with one and only one hospital system—part of a team. But as doctors and hospitals have gone their separate financial ways in the last two decades, more of a business relationship evolved. The docs brought in their patients, the raw material; the hospitals provided the physical workshop for care.

In 1986 a statute called the Emergency Medical Treatment and Labor Act (EMTALA) was designed to force hospitals to remember their long-standing obligations in an era of more commercialized healthcare. All patients who turned up at the emergency room had to be treated, regardless of their ability to pay. Hospitals couldn't turn away sick patients or pregnant women who were poor. But EMTALA doesn't apply to physicians, who are free to pick and choose which patients to accept.

Hospitals were in a quandary. If a desperately ill poor patient turned up at the emergency room after a car crash or a gunshot wound in need of a neurosurgeon or an orthopedist or an ophthalmologist, who would get out of bed to treat him? By law, hospitals had to offer the service, but high-paid specialists could just sleep. Many hospitals and groups of specialists signed contracts, like the one that Olga Baker said governed her daughter's care: the neurosurgeons would cover the ER and, in exchange, get the exclusive right to see new, well-insured patients and bill them however they chose. Ms. Baker said that people like her daughter, "with good insurance and money are kept in, conditioned with fear, upsold on questionable procedures in a hurry, in order to create undisclosed, and unconsented, exorbitant 'emergency' bills."

Strategy #4: One Doctor for the Price of Two

In 2014 Robert Jordan, seventy-one, a semiretired foreign service officer, had an outpatient heart procedure at Virginia Hospital Center in Arlington, with the anesthesia provided by Dominion Anesthesia, a PLLC. The anesthesia was administered by a nurse-anesthetist, but an anesthesiologist "did a drive by" as Mr. Jordan lay on a stretcher prior to the procedure, saying "Hi. How you doing? Do you have any questions?" Mr. Jordan heard the doctor mention to the nurse-anesthetist that he had to be at another hospital before his procedure was scheduled. Nonetheless, he ultimately saw bills from both the doctor and the nurse using the same billing codes for the same amount, each somewhere between $2,000 and $3,000.

On a busy day, have you ever thought, "I wish there were two of me"? Over the last twenty years many doctors have managed that feat, at least for billing purposes. They do it with physician extenders. *Physician ex-*

tender is an umbrella term that refers to the trained ancillary personnel who help doctors and surgeons care for patients, including nurse-practitioners, surgical technicians, physician assistants, and midwives. In many countries they practice independently, but in most of the United States, according to law, they typically work under the auspices of an MD.

Many of these professionals have long rejected the term *extender*, which they feel implies that they require physician guidance for interventions they are perfectly equipped to do. The AMA and other medical societies long applauded the moniker, because it reinforces the hierarchy. But more recently, it has also become a useful billing construct, enabling doctors to bill for work done by the extenders who work for and with them, as if the doctors themselves were personally dispensing the care. A dermatologist can do biopsies in two or three offices at once. An anesthesiologist can supervise four to six operating rooms at a time.

The use of physician extenders in the United States has its roots in the late 1960s and early 1970s. There was a perceived shortage of doctors, particularly in the area of primary care, as many more Americans got insurance and more doctors trained as specialists. At the same time, a new labor pool presented itself: combat medics returning from Vietnam needed employment and possessed practical skills. Universities started physician assistant training programs.

Into the 1980s, physician extenders tended to assist doctors who were on duty 24/7/365 in solo outpatient settings, or to take care of tasks a resident would perform in a teaching hospital—holding the retractors during surgery, checking in on a patient who was short of breath, or sewing up a cut in the emergency room. The goal was improved patient care and to give doctors a break to attend lectures or training courses. The good ones were great at what they did; however, slowly but surely the idea that extenders' work constituted "billable hours" became commonplace. The idea to give physicians the time to bone up on advances in medicine had morphed into a business strategy to maximize revenue.

In 2014, when Peter Drier, thirty-seven, was being wheeled into the operating room for neck surgery at Lenox Hill Hospital in New York, he was asked to sign his consent forms by a technologist/extender from Intra-Operative Monitoring LLC, a doctor-owned company. The company would be responsible for monitoring the delicate nerves of Mr. Drier's spine to make sure they were not damaged. After the technologist told Mr. Drier that he would be responsible for the $5,000 fee since the company didn't accept his insurance, Mr. Drier asked to speak to the doctor. That wasn't possible. Intra-Operative Monitoring is based in Covington, Louisiana, and the neurologist was checking the data at some unnamed distant locale, simultaneously following many operations.

Neurologists can make a base pay of $200,000 to $250,000 in this way, as a job on a recruiting Web site describes: "WORK FROM HOME POSITION. CAN BE LOCATED ANYWHERE IN THE US. NO TRAVEL. . . . This position will supervise certified NIOM [neurophysiologic intraoperative monitoring] technologists in the operating room to help in the prevention of neurological problems during surgeries." By billing for the work of extenders, a single MD could amplify his or her billing potential exponentially.

Doctors traditionally had one office or, perhaps, two locations where they practiced on different days of the week, but once the work of extenders became billable it made economic sense to rent a number of satellite offices and keep them open whether or not the doctor was in. The Arkansas Skin Cancer and Dermatology Center, a fairly typical dermatology practice, is owned by three dermatologists but has full-time offices in seven "convenient locations" staffed much of the time by physician assistants.

Sometimes the substitution could be rationalized as medically acceptable because there was no harm done to patients. But the widespread use of extenders at the very least eroded the face time with doctors that had long inspired patient confidence. And it led to legions of trade wars that had nothing to do with their care.

Doctors often say that anesthesiology is 95 percent boredom and 5 percent terror. For cardiac surgery or a liver transplant or an operation after trauma, the anesthesiologist is constantly intervening to make sure the delicate balance of chemicals in the blood and the blood pressure are stable. But much of today's practice is about monitoring patients during day surgery or procedures like endoscopy, which requires only light sedation and which in other countries isn't done by anesthesiologists at all. Much of that work, done by extenders called nurse-anesthetists, is so routine that anesthesia personnel read magazines or check e-mail in the OR. For the past twenty years, anesthesiologists and nurse-anesthetists have been haggling over how to divide up the money that flows in.

At one point, Medicare declared that anesthesiologists could not bill for supervising more than four operating rooms at once. It briefly decreased payment for each subsequent room, but lobbying undid the plan. Next, for a time, it determined that paying for the services of both an extender and an anesthesiologist was worth at most 140 percent of the rate it would pay to the doctor alone—"split 50-50 between the two parties"; the percentage was ratcheted down in the following years. (Many bills still include full freight charges for both the anesthesiologist and the extender because doctors know that commercial insurers aren't as vigilant or as parsimonious as Medicare.)

Such business models have made anesthesiologists some of the best-compensated doctors in American medicine, though their training is not terribly difficult. It galls others in hospitals. As one wrote to me: "The ability of the anesthesiologists to 'monitor' multiple patients and bill for this monitoring (while sitting in the lounge monitoring their portfolios) is damaging our society. To pay a nurse near $150k and the ghost doctor another $500k to do the same task is just an example of how the medical community is pilfering." Though a few states allow nurse-anesthetists to practice independently, anesthesia societies have fought vigorously to prevent that, citing safety, of course. In 2000 a press release from the American Society of Anesthesiologists targeting members of Congress ominously declared that "seniors will die" if nurse-anesthetists are not supervised by anesthesiologists.

On the other hand, a number of studies, generally done by nurse-anesthetists' trade organizations, have predictably determined that it is safe for these practitioners to practice—and bill—independently, even for complex operations like heart surgery, when the patient is on cardiac bypass. The problem, as the death of comedian Joan Rivers illustrates, is that when things go wrong in the operating room, they go very, very wrong very, very fast, requiring quick intervention and even emergency surgery. Nurse-anesthetists study for twenty-four to thirty-six months after obtaining a nursing degree, less than half the time as a doctor. The anesthesia food chain became even longer in 2008 when nurse-anesthetists, themselves extenders, obtained the right to bill for extenders working under them, according to a provision of the Medicare Improvements for Patients and Providers Act.

In Mr. Jordan's case, Medicare at first paid both the anesthesiologist and the nurse-anesthetist, each getting the approved rate of about $700. When he called Medicare auditors to complain about what seemed like double billing, they rescinded the physician's payment. So Old Dominion sent him a bill, which he refused to pay, adding, "Either they wrote it off or they've sent me to collection and I don't care which it is."

Consultants advise doctors and extenders about how to walk the legal line in billing twice. In "Maximizing Reimbursement for Physician Assistant Services," an article that appeared in the *Clinical Advisor*, an online magazine for nurse-practitioners and physician assistants, Michael L. Powe, vice president of reimbursement and professional advocacy at the American Academy of Physician Assistants (AAPA), recounted that he told a conference audience in 2013: "I hear people ask 'How can I do that?

The doctor never saw the patient, never had any interaction with the patient, and yet I can still bill this service under the physician?'" According to the article, "Under many private payers, it is not fraud."

In the last few years the concept of billing for extenders seems to have spread like a chain reaction to surgeons as well, who began billing for assistants during operations like joint replacements.

Medicare again tried to curtail the practice, having long said that if surgeons were going to bill in their own names, they had to be present for the "key parts" of an operation. If a physician assistant was helping with surgery, his or her services could be billed at about 15 percent of the surgeon's rate. But providers parsed each such restriction for loopholes to use to their advantage, and they proved difficult to police in thousands of operating rooms and offices.

And if an orthopedist could become two people for billing, why couldn't a heart surgeon? At the 2014 meeting of the American Association for Thoracic Surgery, Dr. Kenan W. Yount presented a review of cases showing that one cardiothoracic surgeon could run surgery in two operating rooms simultaneously, without harm to the patients. "The results imply that the policy of having one attending surgeon for every operating room is too narrow," he said.

Strategy #5: Selling Stuff— Buy and Bill

Dr. Gerald Weisberg, an endocrinologist, was an executive at TAP Pharmaceuticals from 1992 to 1996, when the company began deploying what became a trendsetting business innovation for the United States. TAP was a joint venture between an American firm, Abbott Laboratories, and a

Japanese drugmaker, Takeda Pharmaceutical Company. In Japan, doctors have long made extra money by selling the drugs they prescribe.

In the United States oral prescription drugs are legally dispensed only in pharmacies. But there are an increasing number of intravenous and injectable drugs that, with outpatient medicine flourishing, could now be administered in doctors' offices for a fee and with a markup. TAP manufactured Lupron, a medicine that could potentially be sold using such a scheme.

Lupron had been approved by the Food and Drug Administration (FDA) many years before, in 1985, to treat late-stage prostate cancer. Before drugs like Lupron, men with advanced prostate cancer had their testicles removed, because prostate cancers sometimes grow in response to male hormones. Lupron blocked those hormones, providing a chemical form of castration. In 1985, when it first came to market, Lupron's approved formulation was a daily subcutaneous injection that could be self-administered at home. Dr. Weisberg recalled, "Sales essentially went nowhere."

Researchers at Takeda then developed Lupron Depot, a longer-acting formulation, to be delivered once a month, but tested it via a deeper injection into the muscle. That route is trickier and requires a bigger needle; therefore, it can justifiably be administered in a doctor's office. That was crucial for TAP's new business strategy: giving doctors a new "procedure" to bill for in the office, and the chance to make money by charging for the drug.

Urologists, who had ignored the drug for years, suddenly loved Lupron, and gynecologists began enthusiastically prescribing it to treat endometriosis as well. (See **Rule 1: More treatment is always better. Default to the most expensive option.**)

When other drugmakers came up with similar but cheaper medicines, TAP devised a program to sell doctors discounted Lupron and even provided free "bonus" samples that the physicians could administer and bill for full charge. The company sent doctors promotional material called "the Lupron checkbook," and calculated how many vials a urologist had to prescribe to earn as much money as from performing a surgical castration.

The president of the American Urological Association sent out an advisory reminding his fellow urologists that billing for free samples could render them "afoul of the law." After Dr. Weisberg raised concerns he was fired and, later, labeled a "disgruntled employee." "Thousands of physicians were involved—it was a kickback scheme and there were huge rewards," Dr. Weisberg said, noting that within the company executives referred to physicians as "drug whores." Some were making hundreds of thousands a year just from prescribing and administering Lupron.

After years of investigations and lawsuits prompted by a whistle-blower, TAP pleaded guilty to a "nationwide conspiracy" surrounding Lupron sales. It paid $885 million in restitution, fines, and interest.

But there were no criminal penalties for the company or doctors and, in other slightly modified forms, the practice continued. For example, instead of providing free samples, TAP paid doctors an "administration fee" for injecting its drug, Dr. Weisberg said.

TAP's success with its Lupron scheme "opened the door to lots of bad behavior," he added. Whistle-blower lawsuits filed against makers of drugs and devices, alleging bribes and kickbacks to induce doctors to use—and overuse—high-priced products, have since become a staple of legal dockets. In one typical case, former drug reps for Novartis said that the company gave doctors free samples and secret rebates on an expensive intravenous asthma medicine called Xolair, to induce them to use a niche drug that was not medically indicated in many cases.

Oncologists prospered buying chemotherapy drugs from manufacturers and infusing them in the office, generally with a hefty markup, a practice known as "buy and bill."

As the wholesale price of the new drugs jumped again and again, doctors had little motivation to complain, because they were allowed a markup that was often a set percentage of cost. Doctors who used more expensive drugs earned far more. The practice of buy and bill increased dramatically in the late 1990s and into the new century.

With it, the median compensation for oncologists nearly doubled from 1995 to 2004, to $350,000, according to the Medical Group Management Association. One study in 2013 attributed 65 percent of the revenue in a typical oncology practice to such payments. "Drugs and biologicals make up approximately 80% of all medical oncology charges submitted to Medicare each year. In 2010, submitted charges soared to $13.3 billion for cancer-related pharmaceuticals," according to Ben F. Holland, then vice president of Oncology Solutions, a consulting firm that advises cancer doctors on billing—and how to avoid Medicare audits.

Medicare and insurers again tried to push back, creating elaborate guidelines defining the circumstances under which oncologists could bill for administering chemotherapy, prompting an elaborate tug of war: To bill, doctors had to be present in the office for the first fifteen minutes of the infusion, though they didn't have to hang it themselves. Since high payments were often tied to the length in time of the infusion as well as the dose, Medicare ruled that doctors couldn't simply slow down the infusion to clock up the minutes. But when the agency announced there would be one payment for the first hour and a half (many chemotherapy medicines can be easily administered in this time), with a second for any part of each hour thereafter, it started receiving bills for lots of infusions that lasted ninety-one minutes.

Doctors' offices and hospitals were all buying and billing, and patients generally had little idea about markups, what was reasonable, or what their lifesaving drugs actually cost. Betsy Glassman's insurers agreed to a rate of $23,900 for the infusion of three drugs to treat her breast cancer (negotiated down from a billed rate of over $40,000); her co-payment and deductible for each of the first two rounds was $3,564. The most expensive drug, oxaliplatin, was billed by the New Haven infusion clinic at nearly $22,000.

In a 2012 study, Italian researchers placed the cost per cycle of the same trio of drugs at €546, or about $750. In 2000 Britain's National Health Service calculated the cost of oxaliplatin at about £500 per infusion, or about $1,167 today. (See **Rule 4: As technologies age, prices can rise rather than fall;** and **Rule 5: There is no free choice. Patients are stuck. And they're stuck buying American.**)

Strategy #6: Upgrades

Active and still driving into her eighties, Barbara Bennion decided to get her slowly progressive cataracts fixed. She was referred to an ophthalmologist near her home in the suburbs of New York. "It was much more impressive than doctors' offices I was used to, with lots of assistants and nice prints on the walls," she noted.

The eye surgeon explained the three "options" for her surgery. The most expensive involved "using a laser and a special lens," though he warned that this choice would not be covered by Medicare. With good Medigap insurance and enough income, she was undeterred by the finances. "Which is safest?" she asked. The doctor said option three, and so without thinking much she said, "Fine, I'll do that." She was sent to the business office for a longer consultation. "I got glossy brochures and signed lots of forms. I wouldn't say they pushed me but they were very encouraging." The *extra* out-of-pocket price per eye beyond what her insurance would cover was over $4,000.

The average price paid per eye for cataract surgery (doctors' and hospital fees combined) in 2013 was $1,038 in Argentina, $1,610 in the Netherlands, $2,016 in Spain, and $3,384 in New Zealand, according to the International Federation of Health Plans. It was $3,762 in the United

States, and Medicare now pays about $1,600 to $1,800 per eye, including fees for the facility and the surgeon (who gets slightly less than half).

Ms. Bennion's eye surgeon was asking patients with the means to pay nearly double or triple what government insurers in the United States and everywhere else in the world have determined is a reasonable price for the cataract operation.

Over the last quarter century technological medical advances have made cataract surgery progressively more effective, precise, and efficient. A surgery that once required enormous skill and took an hour to complete is now so simple that it is performed by technicians instead of doctors in some poorer countries. In twenty minutes or less, the aged, clouded lens is removed and replaced with an artificial one. And, in the United States, because the Medicare pay scale sets doctors' reimbursement standards according to the length and complexity of the procedure, payments have come tumbling down.

In 2013 Medicare payments for both simple and complex cataract surgeries were cut by 13 percent and 23 percent, respectively, after studies by the Centers for Medicare and Medicaid Services determined that operation times had decreased to an average of twenty-one minutes from thirty-five minutes at the last review. (Medicare also determined that it had previously overestimated how much ophthalmologists had to pay for malpractice insurance, which led to a 1 to 2 percent reduction in payments.) The American Society of Cataract and Refractive Surgery protested, to no avail. The 2012 inflation-adjusted physician fee for cataract surgery was just 10.1 percent of what eye surgeons were paid for the same procedure in 1985. Medical progress had proved great for patients but not for ophthalmologists' incomes. The doctors have done their best to fix that shortfall.

In the 1990s, the breakthrough technique of Lasik surgery was able to compensate for eye surgeons' dropping revenues. Initially, it was priced at thousands of dollars for each eye, and patients often paid for it out of pocket. But the initial flood of those who desired the surgery waned. By

2010 demand was way down, and the price had dropped from $2,000 to $5,000 per eye to $500. More new business was needed.

One option was encouraging more operations. Cataracts can be detected during an eye exam long before they become a real bother to patients, so there is much discretion about when to perform surgery. Studies have shown that the rates of cataract surgery are highly dependent on how much doctors are paid to do the procedure. In one study in St. Louis, the number of cataract surgeries performed dropped 45 percent six months after a group of doctors went on salary and were no longer paid per surgery.

Many eye surgeons made up for Medicare's increasingly stingy cataract payments by charging commercially insured patients more, leading to some staggering prices. Wendy Brezin, a Web designer in Jacksonville, Florida, had cataract surgery billed at $17,406. John Aravosis, a political blogger, was stunned to be billed over $10,000 for each eye. Still, there were simply not enough cloudy lenses in people under sixty-five to make up the deficit.

In 2007 a customized asymmetrical lens called Toric, meant to free patients with astigmatism from needing to wear glasses after cataract surgery, came on the market. Medicare wouldn't pay the extra cost because it considered a lens included in the price it paid for cataract surgery, and it does not cover normal corrective glasses or contact lenses. Also, many studies indicated that Toric lenses did not completely correct astigmatism. Glasses, though perhaps with a weaker prescription, were often still required.

Eye surgeons and Toric lens manufacturers lobbied for permission to sell the lenses directly to patients slated for cataract surgery, as an "upgrade" or a "deluxe" item—like an offer to fly business class. Medicare acceded, so cataract surgeons purchased the Toric lenses for under $500 and resold them for lots more.

Manufacturers of the lenses provided business guidance to doctors who wanted to exploit the opportunity. Firms like Corcoran Consulting Group instructed them on how to market the Toric lens and what codes to use, and even included forms that would keep them on the right side of the Medicare law. Corcoran suggested a sales price to patients of $1,670. But, it cautioned, the surgeon should determine the actual charge "taking into account what the local market will accept."

In 2011 another new product was introduced: the femtosecond laser, essentially a precision scalpel. Thanks to acquisition costs of $500,000 per machine, its use was initially limited to academic hospitals. In 2012 Dr. William W. Culbertson, a professor of ophthalmology at Bascom Palmer Eye Institute in Miami, Florida, opined that it was impractical to add the femtosecond laser to office practice, saying: "You would lose money on every procedure."

There was little if any evidence that the femtosecond laser actually improved outcomes for the vast majority of patients undergoing an already straightforward and successful operation. Even though a standard scalpel worked just fine, "few products have captured the imagination of ophthalmologists as much as femtosecond-assisted cataract surgery," according to Riva Lee Asbell, an ophthalmology billing consultant.

After discovering that ophthalmologic practices were advertising laser cataract surgery, Medicare issued a "guidance." Making an incision—whether by scalpel or laser—was considered part of the surgery fee and could not be billed separately. If patients really wanted "laser" surgery they would—once again—have to pay for it themselves.

Manufacturers of femtosecond lasers circulated charts advising practices how much to charge in "upgrade fees" to pay off the machines. At the 2011 International Conference on Femtosecond Lasers in Ophthalmology Dr. Kevin Miller presented a "hypothetical break even scenario." For doctors who were reluctant to take the plunge with an actual purchase, companies delivered portable machines that could be used for a morning, charging a "click" fee for every time the doctor activated the laser. Ophthalmology journals ran articles titled "Are Lasers Good for Business?" as many physicians were seemingly unconcerned about whether they were good for people with cataracts.

Some expressed their misgivings. Dr. Thomas A. Oetting, associate professor of clinical ophthalmology at the University of Iowa, wrote, "Sure, in several years you may be able to pay off the laser, maybe even before it becomes obsolete. But . . . which procedure is better for the patient? That is not clear."

Ms. Bennion paid for the "upgrade" to a Toric lens to correct for astigmatism and is happy she did. But she decided against the femtosecond laser. Ms. Bennion's daughter-in-law is a surgical nurse who works for an ophthalmologist in another state who performs cataract surgery. He advised against it. (See **Rule 3: Amenities and marketing matter more than good care.**)

Strategy #7: Adopt a Surgical Procedure—Money, Money Everywhere

On April 10, 2014, I gave a talk to six thousand attendees at the annual meeting of the American College of Physicians in Orlando, Florida. This happened to be an awkward landmark day in modern American medicine: the day before, in response to a lawsuit filed by the *Wall Street Journal,* Medicare for the first time had released data showing how much it had paid every individual doctor.

Thousands of physicians made more than $1 million each from Medicare in 2012 and dozens more than $10 million. Of course, doctors have expenses like office overhead, but these were still tidy payments from an insurer that doctors often complain is stingy.

I decided to look up the big billers in Orlando and found a bunch of predictably highly paid specialists, but I also saw that one of them was a kidney doctor, Florin Gadalean, who billed over $2 million that year. Many of his more than two dozen partners at Nephrology Associates of Central Florida were also doing remarkably well, with individual revenues from Medicare, at the bottom of the practice, of nearly $400,000 per doctor.

Nephrologists' central task is treating patients with kidney failure using dialysis machines, which approximates the natural miracle of functioning kidneys. Theirs is hard, unglamorous work that had never been very well paid, which is why the ranks of nephrologists are populated by foreign medical graduates and so many hospitals have outsourced the task.

Patients with kidney failure are generally covered by Medicare, under a 1972 act of Congress that allows them to join the federal insurance program earlier than the standard age of sixty-five. (The somewhat miserly idea was that the expense wouldn't be great because patients couldn't live very long.) Because Medicare payments are typically far lower than those of commercial insurers, kidney doctors often look to supplement their patient income by investing in dialysis centers and forming partnerships with or collecting directorship fees from dialysis companies.

But the Medicare data dump indicated that Dr. Gadalean was making $2 million from actually seeing patients. Curious, I took a cab out to see his office. His $2 million kidney practice was in a small, half-empty one-story yellow stucco building at the back of a parking lot near a highway crossover. Inside was an empty waiting room with linoleum floors and brown plastic chairs. The only person present was a receptionist in scrubs behind a sign offering flu shots.

The nephrologists at Nephrology Associates, it turns out, don't do dialysis at all. That low-margin activity is left to high-volume for-profit commercial chains like DaVita and Fresenius. Instead, Nephrology Associates has apparently found a lucrative niche: performing procedures related to "vascular access." Dialysis is done through a surgically created merger of a vein and an artery on the arm, called a fistula. Even after creation, fistulas need a certain amount of maintenance to keep the blood flowing—they have a tendency to clog. Uniting arteries and veins requires delicate microsurgery, which is why these structures have traditionally been created by vascular surgeons, who train for seven years after medical school.

But today nephrologists are performing the delicate operation and taking in the revenue, though they often have little or no formal surgical training, vascular surgeons note, decrying what they see as a risky incursion. Once doctors are licensed, they can pretty much offer whatever services they choose. Dr. Rick Mishler, an Arizona nephrologist who went to Germany to receive instruction from a surgeon in fistula creation, pioneered the idea that nephrologists could themselves offer the procedure. Today, four doctors have joined him in practice, three other nephrologists and a Chinese orthopedic surgeon.

MEDICINE IS A BUSINESS. It won't police itself," said William Sage, a doctor and a lawyer who is a professor of health law at the University of Texas. "People had a lot of faith in the American medical profession—that they would act differently than other businesses—but they were wrong."

Meanwhile, doctors who have not commercialized their practice are today at risk of extinction. Dr. Robert Morrow has had a family practice in the Bronx, New York, for more than thirty years. He never invested in labs or scans or sold his practice to a hospital to add facility fees. By 2013 his rates from Medicare, which paid him $82 for an office visit, were the best he got, compared with about $45 from Aetna and Cigna. If medicine continues on its current trajectory, the kinds of doctors whom Americans say they value and want could very well become, in his words, like "dinosaurs."

4

THE AGE OF PHARMACEUTICALS

Hope Marcus has spent much of her adult life on mesalamine, an affordable decades-old drug used to control ulcerative colitis. Mesalamine was identified in the 1970s as the active component of an even older aspirin-related medicine long used to treat chronic bowel disease, but was better because it had fewer side effects. But mesalamine was unstable in the human gut, so scientists developed coatings that would protect it from attack by stomach acids so it could get to where it is needed. For full effect, patients like Ms. Marcus often used both oral and rectal versions of the drug. All of the medicines Ms. Marcus takes and has taken are different versions of mesalamine, packaged in various patented delivery forms.

Ms. Marcus started paying attention to the pricing in 2005, when her husband lost his job. Now covered under COBRA (a form of health insurance extension), she was paying for more of her health expenses. While researching the cost of the oral form of mesalamine, called Asacol, she discovered that its polymer coating process had been patented by two Welsh scientists in 1983. Asacol had been sold from one drug company to another until it ended up with Procter and Gamble, which was charging $500 per month for the brand drug at the time. Solvay Pharmaceuticals was the sole (and brand) manufacturer of Rowasa, the rectal formulation in the United States. Although the price was initially $700 when she inquired, the generic drug manufacturer, Teva Pharmaceutical Industries, had just gotten approval to sell its version in the United States, so by year's end she was paying $167 per month for the generic.

In 2011, Ms. Marcus was thrilled to find a Florida Medicare managed care plan that covered the cost of all generic medicines without a co-pay. She looked forward to the end of her struggles to come up with hundreds of dollars each month for her drugs: Asacol, by then priced at over $750 a month, was slated to lose its patent protection in 2013.

Unfortunately, the generic didn't materialize.

By 2009, a different drug manufacturer, Warner Chilcott, had acquired the rights to Asacol, and just a few months before the eagerly awaited patent expiration, the new owner introduced two "new, improved products": Asacol HD, a once-a-day long-acting version of mesalamine, and Delzicol, a gel-coated version of the old 400 mg pill. Both were covered by new patents. Then Warner Chilcott stopped manufacturing the 400 mg version of Asacol that Ms. Marcus and many others had been taking, removing it from the market.

The patients who must take this lifesaving medicine every day were stuck paying whatever was asked for the "new" branded products, which were not really new or improved. They complained that Delzicol, with its thick gel coating, was hard to swallow—and so well protected that it sometimes came out of their other end whole. When one man attempted to remedy the situation by prying off the gel, he discovered the familiar old 400 mg tablet of Asacol inside. The research and development to create Delzicol had apparently involved slapping on a new layer to obtain continued patent protection. The new products "offset the generic threat to Asacol," wrote one financial analyst. "Generic competition for the company's mesalamine-based Ulcerative Colitis (UC) franchise remains highly unlikely over the next few years."

Other branded mesalamine products on the market used different types of delivery systems, but were all equally or more expensive. So, in July 2013, Ms. Marcus began buying generic mesalamine pills for about $55 a month from India via Canada. "I was scared to do it, but I had little choice," Ms. Marcus said, because the branded products were approaching $800 a month in Florida. "I needed mesalamine to live."

Dr. John Mayberry, a professor of gastroenterology at the University of Leicester in England, is an expert in this class of drugs. "It is very hard for me to understand why these medicines are so expensive" in the United States, he told me. In the United Kingdom, people with private prescriptions pay about £40, or about $55, a month, full price, for coated mesalamine, although most patients get their drugs for the standard National Health Service prescription charge of £9, or about $12. Many versions of mesalamine are available, with different coatings or delivery systems, different names and patents. Hospitals in Great Britain usually choose a couple to dispense according to which pharmaceutical manufacturers offer the best deal. Pharmacists dispense them interchangeably. "Technically results should be similar, but there are very few head-to-head trials because no one wants to demonstrate that theirs is worse or—God forbid—that the cheapest one is better," Dr. Mayberry explained.

At the end of 2014, Ms. Marcus saw the monthly price of the generic rectal preparation she'd been using for years suddenly go haywire: up to $230 in November, down to $49 in December. In January 2015 it soared to $775—where it has largely stayed since. A decade after Ms. Marcus started using generic rectal mesalamine for $167 a month, the generic enema now costs $700 and the brand version over $1,200.

The Pharmaceutical Research and Manufacturers of America (PhRMA), the industry's powerful trade group, calls pharmaceuticals our country's most competitive industry. But, in the case of mesalamine, the

intense competition has not been about making a better or more affordable drug: it is a fight by mesalamine manufacturers to get the hundreds
of thousands of Americans with ulcerative colitis to use their particular
medication. (See **Rule 6: More competitors vying for business doesn't
mean better prices; it can drive prices up, not down.**)

Manufacturers' sales tactics quickly came under scrutiny from the
FDA, which repeatedly censured them for practices like overstating benefits and encouraging use when the drug was not helpful. One manufacturer, Alaven Pharmaceutical, was reprimanded after sending doctors a
2008 "Holiday Promotion Postcard" for Rowasa (mesalamine) Rectal
Suspension Enema that urged physicians to give their patients a "gift kit"
containing the enema to guard against flares that might interrupt Christmas celebrations, noting: "They can enjoy the holidays (and so can you!)"

For the past decade of Ms. Marcus's life, manufacturers of her lifesaving drug have cycled in and out of the market, depending on their calculations of potential profits and propelled by shifting corporate deals in a
consolidating international pharmaceutical industry. In 2011, without
warning, Teva stopped making its generic mesalamine rectal formulation.
Rowasa, previously owned by Solvay, was now in AbbVie's stable. Alaven
was acquired by the Swedish drug firm Meda. Another manufacturer of
generics, Michigan-based Perrigo, started production.

Through that evolution, the price of Ms. Marcus's old drug, long off
patent, had increased 500 percent, even as its price decreased for patients
in other developed countries. (See **Rule 4: As technologies age, prices
can rise rather than fall.**)

Adding insult to literal injury, in that very same time period, nearly all
of the American manufacturers of mesalamine products figured out ways
to move their tax base overseas, using a controversial practice called an
inversion that many legal experts regard as tax evasion.

One of the last to move was Perrigo, which bought an Irish drug company, Elan Pharmaceuticals, in 2013 and relocated to take advantage of

Ireland's 12.5 percent corporate tax rate, resulting in more than $150 million in recurring savings, the company boasted to investors. Shortly thereafter AbbVie tried to do the same, in a planned merger with another Irish drugmaker. The $55 billion deal was only scuttled when the Obama administration revised tax policy in September 2014 to make the deal somewhat less rewarding.

The Modest History of Making Medicines

Most modern pharmaceutical firms grew out of nineteenth-century small businesses, which sold tonics and potions of often-dubious benefit. They relied on a little bit of science and a heavy dose of marketing.

Warner Chilcott is the descendant of a company founded by William Warner, a Philadelphia pharmacist who had earned a fortune in the mid-nineteenth century by inventing a sugar coating for pills. Perrigo was started in 1887 by the owner of a Michigan general store, who packaged and distributed patented medicines and household items. Meda, the Swedish firm, first acquired a mesalamine preparation when it merged with the American firm Carter-Wallace, whose original product was a mysterious "liver pill."

In 1906 Congress passed the Wiley Act (also known as the Pure Food and Drug Act), which entrusted the U.S. Bureau of Chemistry to monitor and regulate drug safety, though in an era when so few medicines actually did much, the focus was on preventing harm from dangerous chemicals mixed into the pills and elixirs, rather than ensuring that they worked. It was replaced in 1938 by the Food, Drug, and Cosmetic Act, which enhanced and expanded the protections of the Wiley Act, as well as required testing before drugs could be marketed. The bill had languished in Congress for many years before being rushed into law after a disastrous episode in 1937 that involved a preparation of an early antibiotic used to treat strep throat.

Though sulfanilamide had been used for many years in pill and powder form, the sales force for a Tennessee drug company suggested that a liquid version would be popular and profitable. A company chemist quickly responded by mixing up a raspberry-flavored concoction after discovering that the medicine dissolved in a sweet smelling liquid compound. Bottles were shipped all over the country.

Somehow no one registered that the compound, an analog of today's antifreeze, was highly toxic. More than one hundred people in fifteen states who took Elixir Sulfanilamide died. One doctor, A. S. Calhoun, wrote: "To realize that six human beings, all of them my patients, one of them my best friend, are dead because they took medicine that I prescribed for them innocently, and to realize that that medicine which I had used for years in such cases suddenly had become a deadly poison in its newest and most modern form, as recommended by a great and reputable pharmaceutical firm in Tennessee: well, that realization has given me such days and nights of mental and spiritual agony as I did not believe a human being could undergo and survive."

The new law required that drugs be labeled with adequate directions for safe use. For the first time false therapeutic claims were prohibited. Manufacturers were required to prove to a young government agency, the Food and Drug Administration, or FDA, that a drug was safe before it could be sold. To distinguish itself from the dodgy elixirs of past, the new industry branded itself "ethical pharmaceuticals." From early on, the moniker was an uncertain fit. A congressional investigation and subsequent hearings launched in the late 1950s by Senator Estes Kefauver raised many questions. Seeing medicines as a public good, he proposed price limits and restrictions on marketing, among other measures. He pointed out that there was not enough effort to ensure that the actual performance of drugs matched manufacturer's assertions.

But the need for such thoughtful consumer protections was quickly eclipsed by another medical tragedy. Though it had never been marketed in the United States, thalidomide was producing grotesque birth defects in the babies of mothers in other countries who took the drug during pregnancy to combat morning sickness. Thanks to the thalidomide scare, the 1962 Kefauver-Harris Drug Amendments to the Food, Drug, and Cosmetic Act were enacted. The FDA promulgated guidelines detailing approved methods for clinical testing, enforced a strictly quantitative approach for evaluating drug applications, and began using its new authority to approve, postpone, or reject new drugs, initially within a two-month time frame. Concerns about value vanished; in any case, drugs were cheap.

To get products approved, firms had to create applications to prove that medicines were "safe and effective," meaning more effective than doing nothing at all. That standard was never refined to include the more modern question: Is the product more effective than the dozens of other treatments for a particular condition that are already on the market? Equally important, the FDA yardstick for approval did not include any consideration of price or measure of cost-effectiveness—a metric that virtually all other countries now use as they consider admitting new drugs to their formulary.

In its haste to respond to the thalidomide scare, Congress missed an opportunity to short-circuit some of the most vexing financial questions that haunt our healthcare today—cost, cost-effectiveness, and comparative utility—by giving the FDA tools to deal with them in an era when the pharmaceutical and lobbying industries were far less potent.

Early inventors of drugs often made at most only halfhearted attempts to gain patent protection for their discoveries. When Edward R. Murrow asked Jonas Salk who owned the patent for his new polio vaccine, which eliminated a crippling disease, he famously replied, "Well, the people, I would say. There is no patent. Could you patent the sun?" In fact, according to the legal thinking at the time, the problem was that the vaccine was deemed unpatentable: the research had been done by many people, with both public funding and millions of contributions to the March of Dimes. More to the point, lawyers at the University of Pittsburgh, where much of the research was performed, concluded that there wasn't anything novel enough about the manufacturing process to merit intellectual protection.

Today, the University of Pittsburgh would almost certainly have made the opposite decision. For one thing, the Bayh-Dole Act of 1980 permitted scientists, universities, and companies to obtain patents on products that evolved from research funded by the government. But more than that, the whole concept of what was legitimate intellectual property in medicine was transforming.

In the past twenty-five years, the long-standing notion of "one drug, one patent" (focusing on the chemical composition) has evaporated. The average number of patents per drug rose from 2.5 around 1990 to 3.5 in 2005, a number that has only increased since. Many bestselling medicines are today covered by more than five patents, and some by more than a dozen. They protect not just the molecule but also the processes that create each particular formulation and the delivery systems as well.

Part of the patent explosion was thanks to the perverse unintended consequences of another well-intentioned piece of legislation, a 1984 amendment to the Food, Drug, and Cosmetic Act, known as Hatch-Waxman (the Drug Price Competition and Patent Term Restoration Act). With new drugs pouring into a competitive market and trying to make their way through an overwhelmed FDA approval system, the pharmaceutical industry complained that the elaborate testing and approval process in the United States meant that manufacturers often missed out on the financial benefits of a huge chunk of their twenty-year period of patent protection. At the same time, patients and policy makers noted with alarm that drug prices were beginning to rise.

The goal of Hatch-Waxman was to clarify for pharmaceutical makers the length and extent of their patent protection, as well as to offer makers of generic drugs financial incentives so they would be motivated to bring cheaper versions onto the market the moment that patents expired. It set up what seemed like a smart new set of rules that would benefit patients— but even smarter businessmen would soon learn to manipulate the legislation for financial gain.

Hatch-Waxman codified the notion that a valuable pharmaceutical product could be protected in a multitude of ways and required drugmakers to provide a list of all the patents on each new medicine. To speed the arrival of generics, the act dictated that applications from makers of copycat drugs to sell their products no longer had to include fresh clinical trials to demonstrate safety and efficacy, but could rely on prior studies done by the makers of the brand drugs. The generic manufacturers' abbreviated new drug application (ANDA) merely had to show that the chemical compound was the same as the branded drug at the same dose, produced the same levels of medicine in the body (bioequivalence), and violated no patents, which had to have expired.

To appease the brand manufacturers, Hatch-Waxman provided them with a host of new ways to extend their patents, some beneficial for patients and some not. For example, it allowed for a three-year extension for manufacturers who did new clinical trials to support a change in "dose form." It gave manufacturers a seven-year period of exclusivity for orphan drugs, defined as "medicines with a single indication for diseases that had a population of less than 200,000 in the United States." It gave them a six-month extension of patents for doing pediatric trials. More broadly, Hatch-Waxman allowed up to a five-year extension for claims of "time lost in regulatory review" during which makers of generic drugs could not even submit an application.

Hatch-Waxman had attempted to define the moment when it was fair business practice for generics manufacturers to jump into the fray. But brand makers' new ability to claim extended patent protection, coupled with generics competitors' constant challenges to weak patents, meant that the amendment instead ushered in an era in which multimillion-dollar court battles over patents now precede (and delay) each generic entry, driving prices up in the process.

A few years after Hatch-Waxman's passage, the pharmaceutical manufacturers' egregious business practices prompted federal investigations. As a result, legislation was passed to address the issue. The Generic Drug Enforcement Act of 1992 gave the FDA the right to "temporarily refuse to approve an Abbreviated New Drug Application submitted by a person under active federal criminal investigation within the 5 prior years and (1) if the person has been involved in an attempted bribe of a federal, state or local official in connection with an ANDA and (2) a significant question has been raised regarding the approval process related to the drug or the reliability of the data."

By the mid-1990s, the basic rules of engagement, determined by the FDA and the U.S. Patent and Trademark Office, had been settled to the lasting benefit of business: a strong patent system and no pricing restrictions led to a profound shift of pharmaceutical investment into the United States and away from Europe, where government price setting was increasingly common. By 2002 global drugmakers were spending 82 percent of their money in the United States. The U.S. pharmaceutical industry has grown twice as fast as the economy at large since 1990.

The character of the drug discovery endeavor had changed. "In the 1980s people running pharmaceutical companies were still interested in social impact as well as the money," Dr. Marcus Reidenberg, a former editor in chief of *Clinical Pharmacology and Therapeutics,* told me. Pharmaceutical executives were often culled from the ranks of respected academics. They focused research on big medical needs and kept making unprofitable drugs because they were useful. "Now," he continued, "money managers are in charge and these are pure business decisions."

By 2015 the industry's poster child was Martin Shkreli, a thirty-two-year-old former hedge fund manager who bought rights to a cheap generic drug to treat parasites that had been on the market for years and overnight raised the price from $13.50 to $750 a pill. Though unusually brazen, as we'll see, he was not alone in such efforts. (See **Rule 5: There is no free choice. Patients are stuck. And they're stuck buying American.**)

New Policies Transform an Industry

For much of medical history and into the 1980s, drugs were cheap. Vaccines cost pennies. Antibiotics and epinephrine shots were a few dollars. Even the most exotic medicines couldn't list for more than a few hundred dollars a dose. But the emergence of successful drug therapy in response to the crisis of HIV/AIDS permanently shifted the long-standing business paradigm of drug approval, pricing and value.

It is difficult to convey the devastation and despair on hospital wards in the late 1980s: Scared young men (mostly), whose immune systems had been destroyed by the HIV virus, would arrive in the emergency department gasping for air from pneumocystis pneumonia or hallucinating from fungal infections that had invaded the brain. They would often be dead a week later. The only medicines that could even theoretically combat the unusual infections that afflicted people with AIDS were so toxic that people sometimes died from the treatment.

Because these ailments were so rare prior to the epidemic of HIV/AIDS, there had been little pressure or financial incentive to identify better drugs to fight many of them. Treating viruses had always been a financial nonstarter because the vast majority caused only colds and transient digestive ills. (See **Rule 2: A lifetime of treatment is preferable to a**

cure.) But with the advent of AIDS, activists like Larry Kramer changed the pharmaceutical landscape by loudly demanding action. Rapidly, molecular genetic techniques helped scientists identify the cause of AIDS as a so-called retrovirus. Dr. Samuel Broder, head of the National Cancer Institute, put out a call for manufacturers to test all the shelved and stockpiled compounds they'd previously created against the new germ.

One such compound was AZT, which had been synthesized in 1964 by Jerome P. Horwitz of the Michigan Cancer Foundation. Little used because it wasn't effective against tumors, AZT proved to be active against viruses in preliminary tests, and specifically to suppress replication of the AIDS virus. With people dying amid public outcry, AZT was approved by the FDA in March 1987 after only one human trial (instead of the usual three) that lasted just nineteen weeks.

AIDS was transformed from a death sentence into a potentially treatable chronic disease. But the world gasped when Burroughs Wellcome, the drug's owner, revealed what a blistering *New York Times* editorial called AZT's "astoundingly high price," the "most expensive prescription drug in history." It cost about $670 a month ($1,343 adjusted for inflation in 2016) or $8,040 annually. Other drugs that soon followed proved equally important because it turned out that AZT alone did not hold the virus at bay for very long. By the late 1990s, patients were taking three drugs, each of which prevented the virus from duplicating in different ways and each of which was, by the standards of the time, hugely expensive.

These miracle drugs changed not just the acceptable limits of pricing for new medicines but the approval process as well. There was enormous public pressure to get even potentially useful drugs to patients. With the race to treat HIV, a virus that had infected more than a quarter million Americans by 1991, the FDA relaxed its rules for what constituted proof that a drug was effective, allowing for greater use of what are called "surrogate measures": Drugmakers no longer had to show that their product actually cured the symptoms of illness over months or years or extended life. Instead they could measure things like blood markers that were felt to correlate with such benefits.

That made good sense for HIV, because the virus attacked CD4 immune cells, so measuring their levels was a great proxy for the patient's condition and the drug's success. But it made little sense for trials of drugs to treat many other conditions for which surrogate endpoints are now the norm, such as type 2 diabetes, providing a fast track to approval.

Within a decade, researchers complained that such so-called accelerated approval (AA) measures were being abused for financial advantage rather than used to address health emergencies. "Often, sponsors of drugs and biologics view the AA process as the easiest way to get their products onto the market," wrote Thomas R. Fleming, professor of biostatistics at the University of Washington. "Not only does the AA process allow sponsors to get marketing approval much sooner and with much less research expenditure, but also, quite frankly, it allows them to market products that likely are biologically active but less likely to provide truly important effects."

The drug companies that used interim measures to prove the success of their products often made empty promises to do follow-up studies to make sure products approved through these proxy targets actually yielded long-term improvement for patients. (For example, there is conflicting evidence that merely lowering blood sugar in type 2 diabetes significantly impacts longevity.) But there were no punishments for failing to carry out the subsequent research. Nor was there a mechanism to revoke FDA approval or take drugs off the market if scientific studies by academics proved them to be without benefit. An in-depth data investigation by the *Milwaukee Journal Sentinel* and MedPageToday in 2014 revealed that, thanks to surrogate endpoints, 74 percent of cancer drugs approved by the FDA during the previous decade ultimately did not extend life by even a single day.

But accelerated approval wasn't the only novel practice the FDA permitted. In the early 1990s, the agency first allowed what were called "help seeking ads," in which pharmaceutical manufacturers were permitted to mention the name of either the drug or the disease it was intended to treat but not both. For the sake of greater accountability, the FDA laid out conditions in 1997 under which drugmakers' advertisements could specify both the condition and the medicine, most notably by including in the ad "a brief summary of all necessary information related to side effects and contraindications." At first, the industry fought the disclosure on the grounds that requiring a laundry list of scary warnings would prevent direct-to-consumer advertising from taking hold, but eventually it found artful ways to embrace the demand.

Direct-to-consumer drug advertising rose from $166 million in 1993 to $4.2 billion in 2005, and by 2006 it made up nearly 40 percent of total pharmaceutical promotional spending. For some drugs, the lion's share of promotional spending was for direct-to-consumer advertising. In 2000 Merck spent more advertising its new painkiller, Vioxx ($160 million), than Budweiser ($146 million), Pepsi ($125 million), or Nike ($78 million). That year drug sales for Vioxx topped $1.5 billion and twenty-five million people took the drug. In hindsight that over-the-top success proved tragic: Even before formal FDA approval, a reviewer had raised concerns about data suggesting that Vioxx might be tied to increased risk of heart attack, a hunch that later studies confirmed. Researchers ultimately concluded that the drug caused eighty-eight thousand heart attacks, nearly half of them fatal. In 2004 Merck withdrew Vioxx from the market. The company ultimately paid a criminal fine of $950 million for its marketing and sales tactics.

Despite episodes like these, drug advertising is now a constant in our lives. The Supreme Court has protected drug advertising under the guise of free speech. We are one of two countries that allow it, along with New

Zealand. Media companies, and particularly cable television stations, are ever more dependent on it for survival; healthcare advertising stayed robust even through the Great Recession.

Pharmaceutical companies like to say it takes well over $1 billion to bring a new drug to market: the costs of the basic science, developing a new compound, figuring out the right dose, and the FDA process of human testing for safety and efficacy. (Many companies also include opportunity costs—the profits that could have been made by investing the money elsewhere—in the estimate.) In some cases, that is likely true. But academic studies have placed the actual average scientific research and development costs for a new drug at between $43.4 million and $125 million. It is unclear how much of PhRMA's typical $1 billion estimate is for testing markets, advertising, and promotion.

Non-24; or, It Pays to Advertise

Dr. Robert Sack's late-night gardening show was interrupted by one of a series of television advertisements that ran widely in 2015 and 2016 describing a malady called Non-24. The ads featured active, attractive blind people with guide dogs and canes, traveling on business or welcoming kids home from school. One had lost his sight in Afghanistan, another to cancer.

The ads were made by Vanda Pharmaceuticals and described an obscure sleep disorder that befalls mostly totally blind people who can't perceive light, so their body gets out of sync with circadian rhythms. The condition affects at the very most one hundred thousand Americans.

Dr. Sack knows a lot about Non-24 because he was one of the sleep researchers who originally characterized the condition—in the early 1990s. In 2000 he and Dr. Alfred Lewy, at Oregon Health & Science

University, published a landmark study in which twenty blind people with the disorder were entrained to a normal sleep pattern with carefully timed doses of melatonin.

Nearly twenty years later, Vanda, a boutique drugmaker based in Washington, DC, had developed a new molecule, called tasimelteon, which resembled melatonin and attached to a melatonin receptor, producing a similar effect. The brand name of the new drug, which is built on decades of federally funded research by scientists like Dr. Sack, is Hetlioz.

The FDA granted Vanda's Hetlioz the green light in January 2014. To his consternation, Dr. Sack was an expert on the panel that had unanimously recommended the approval a few months before. "I came out thinking our system of drug approval doesn't make any sense," he told me two years later. "Because of the FDA's criterion we were following to determine efficacy, I was forced to vote yes, but it made me deeply uncomfortable." It was not demonstrably better than melatonin itself.

FDA panels don't consider the cost of the products they review. When Hetlioz received approval, Dr. Sack assumed it would be maybe $10 or $15 a pill. In fact, Hetlioz was later priced at $96,000 a year, $8,000 a month, or $267 per dose. "So now we have a prescription medicine for over two hundred dollars a day that is not as effective as melatonin used properly—which you can buy for six dollars over the counter for a bottle of one hundred," Dr. Sack said. "It is eye-popping that we could get in this situation. And that it would be advertised on TV."

Because melatonin is a product of nature the molecule can't be patented. No company will go through the expensive testing and application process to get melatonin formulated as a prescription drug. It's sold as a nutritional supplement, and not regulated or tested with great exactitude. The proper dosing of melatonin has never been studied to FDA standards. But the chemically created analog tasimelteon can be patented.

Vanda had been doing drug trials on tasimelteon as a general sleep aid for people with insomnia since 2005. It "may have therapeutic potential for transient insomnia in circadian rhythm disorders," according to a 2009 study. But with such lackluster results, it couldn't compete with Ambien and Sonata, blockbuster sleep aids already on the market. One pill that targeted the same melatonin receptor, Rozerem by Takeda Pharmaceutical Company, had already flopped.

Determined and creative, Vanda adopted a strategy for expedited approval as a first-in-class drug to treat Non-24, an orphan disease. Instead of testing tasimelteon rigorously in the general population, the testing could involve dozens rather than tens of thousands of patients, and could last six months instead of years. It could more readily focus on highly fungible surrogate endpoints.

"Vanda's Sleep Disorder Drug Is a Nightmare" declared Adam Feuerstein of TheStreet.com in 2013. He pointed out that the company's study size of sixty-two patients had shrunk from the original plans, and, "by Vanda's own admission," the majority of them "did not suffer from non-24 according to the 'textbook definition' of the disease." Vanda and the FDA originally agreed that nighttime total sleep would be the proper metric of success for the study, but Vanda had backed away from that. Instead of focusing on all nights, they included only the 25 percent of nights when subjects' sleep times were lowest. On those nights, patients who took the drug slept fifty-three minutes more.

Vanda also selected two other surrogate measurements to prove its drug's efficacy: a urine test of melatonin and a "Non-24 quality of life scale," designed by Vanda, which measured only days 112 to 183 of the study. "Changing the endpoints of an ongoing clinical trial—especially without the FDA's blessing—is a sign of trouble," Mr. Feuerstein wrote. "The story Vanda tells of its sleep-disorder drug doesn't have a happy ending."

But it did.

In front of Dr. Sack's committee, Dr. Charles Czeisler, a Harvard expert and head of Vanda's scientific advisory board, explained why the proxy measurements were valid. Blind people, flown in by the company, told how Hetlioz had solved their sleep problems as nothing before. As one said, "Blindness is easy. My disability is non-24." For a small number of people, the drug seemed to be truly invaluable.

Despite such testimonials, the other panelists expressed reservations about the drug's effectiveness and necessity. Dr. Robert R. Clancy of the University of Pennsylvania questioned Vanda's defining "success" as an extra forty-five minutes or so of sleep during that worst 25 percent of sleep nights. "They may go from 3.2 hours to 4 hours," he said. "That's still pretty dreadful." Why not just give melatonin? others asked.

When one questioner asked why not use existing sleep aids and an alarm clock, Dr. Mihael Polymeropoulos, Vanda's CEO, made him seem like a heartless lout. "A suggestion of, 'Get another drug,' or, 'Get an alarm clock,' really does not match the pain and suffering. What we are trying to do is we're trying to address this unmet medical need for patients."

In the end, the eleven-member committee had no choice but to approve the product because it was, strictly speaking, safe and effective. The agency's criteria for efficacy stipulate only that a new drug has to be shown effective when compared with a placebo, so Hetlioz was never compared with melatonin.

This practice of comparing new drugs with placebos rather than other currently available treatments as a criterion for licensing has also led to both a plethora of expensive me-too drugs and a dearth of trials and published efficacy studies. "In the old days the NIH used to fund a lot of trials comparing drugs like Stelazine and Thorazine, but those don't happen very often anymore," Dr. Sack, a psychiatrist by training, said. Now that we rely on the profit incentive to motivate drug research, we learn only what the industry deems it profitable for us to find out.

Hetlioz went on sale on January 31, 2014. At $8,000 for a thirty-day supply, one analyst calculated that Vanda needed to sell just fifteen hundred annual prescriptions to break even. But selling drugs is not the only way for a pharma start-up to profit. By October Vanda announced a stock offering of $50 million worth of common stock.

Anyway, blind people with Non-24 are likely not the primary target of the company's ads. As Dr. Czeisler noted at the approval meeting, disturbed circadian sleep cycles—aka jet lag—are a huge problem for frequent fliers and that is a much bigger target market. By 2016 the company was conducting trials for that indication. Once a drug is approved for one use, doctors can prescribe it for others, as they see fit. Vanda is endeavoring to expand the boundaries. The things Vanda says you should consider before "talking to your doctor about whether Hetlioz is right for you" are as general as "I have trouble falling asleep or staying asleep."

Patent Plays

Playing in accordance with the federal rules established during the 1980s and 1990s, pharmaceutical companies progressively tested every frontier of price and propriety. In a congressional hearing in late 2014, Stephen Schondelmeyer, a leading pharmaceutical economist at the University of Minnesota who has collaborated with drugmakers on many projects over his long career, described the current situation as the "Wild, Wild West of drug pricing." He added, "I believe in markets, but this market is broken; it's failing."

In the early 2000s almost all aerosolized products in the United States—from hairsprays to spray paints to asthma inhalers—had to eliminate their CFC propellants under the Montreal Protocol, a global treaty to protect the ozone layer. The price of paint and hairspray didn't change much, if at all. But drug manufacturers seized on the opportunity to get new patents for asthma inhalers with new propellants, removing from the market generic inhalers that had long been available. The usual price of the most common inhaled asthma medicine, albuterol, rose from about

$10 to over $100. It costs $7 to $9 in Australia, where it's still generic and even sold over the counter. Some inhalers in the United States now top $300.

(The conversion to inhalers with new propellants was not bad business for the Food and Drug Administration either, because each new application brought in millions of dollars in application fees. The FDA says the fees, permitted under the 1992 Prescription Drug User Fee Act, allow it to staff up to keep drug reviews moving expeditiously through the approvals system. Critics say the half a billion dollars in fees it collects annually makes the FDA beholden to pharma.)

There proved to be endless ways to extend your product's value through manipulating FDA policies and patent law.

File a lawsuit. To receive a secondary patent on an off-patent molecule (like mesalamine) drugmakers merely had to show that any new modification was "non-obvious" and also useful, although the latter was so loosely interpreted that it is rarely a barrier. Getting a patent costs only $20,000, and applications are unlimited. "If you're persistent you can usually get one, so there's a strong motivation for the drug companies to file weak patents," Stanford law professor Lisa Larrimore Ouellette said.

Brand makers take out weak patents, generics makers challenge them, and the brand makers answer back with an objection. Under Hatch-Waxman, that objection alone sets off a mandatory thirty-month halt in the FDA's consideration of the generic entrant.

In 2013 the world's bestselling brand of insulin was Lantus, owned by Sanofi Aventis, which was scheduled to lose U.S. patent protection in 2015. Lantus is taken daily by many type 1 diabetics along with short-acting insulin to dampen the high and low swings of blood sugar. Sanofi had a virtual monopoly on this market, worth billions, and increased U.S. prices by 25 percent in 2013. Patients had trouble affording the $300 a month jacked-up price. So many American diabetics were ordering Lantus from Canada that the FDA sent warning letters to firms like CanaRx informing them that the practice was illegal; it noted that the drug must be shipped cold and could be harmed in transit. (One skeptical diabetic noted, "Why is it I can order steaks and seafood from California that'll arrive frozen and cold from over 3,000 miles away, yet I can't get 52° insulin from Canada?")

When I asked Susan Brooks, a spokesperson for Sanofi, about the price increase, she was open about the strategy to optimize profit with cheaper generic products on the horizon, *"which might result in lower prices for all products within a given therapeutic class"* (emphasis mine). Eli Lilly, another giant in the world of diabetes, had created a "biosimilar" (e.g., generic) version of Lantus and was prepared to launch as soon as Lantus's U.S. patents lapsed. Indeed, Lilly's Lantus biosimilar was already in use in many developed countries, where intellectual property laws are less business-friendly and patents less litigated.

In 2014, to eke out a little more time with patent protection for Lantus in the United States, Sanofi sued, claiming that the Lilly product violated four patents, which triggered the automatic thirty-month Hatch-Waxman "waiting period." "So the biggest thing that will affect patients with type 1 diabetes here is being decided legally not medically," David Kliff, editor of *Diabetic Investor* and himself a person with type 1 diabetes, told me. "I know that sounds crazy but it's true. The only people who win are the lawyers and the patent holder." After some further backroom business deals between the two companies, the legal action was "settled" and the patent was set to expire in December 2016.

Modify the delivery. In the summer of 2014, Dr. Laura Schiller, an obstetrician-gynecologist in New York City, suddenly began getting frantic calls. Patients had gone to the pharmacy to pick up their usual prescriptions for the birth control pill Loestrin 24 Fe, only to be told it was no longer available.

Oral contraceptives are not much different today in their essential ingredients than they were thirty years ago. But they have been repackaged and marketed and, often, repatented in new (but not necessarily improved) forms. The dozens of options offer slightly different hormonal mixes and dosing schedules. Women choose a particular pill because for them it produces fewer side effects like bloating, or comes in a more convenient dispensing pack, or just because it has nicer advertising.

Warner Chilcott's Loestrin 24 Fe was one of the most popular contraceptive pills. It combined a low dose of estrogen in a twenty-four-day cycle and iron; periods were light but predictable. It sold for about $90 retail in the United States and $20 elsewhere in the world. Nonetheless, with U.S. purchases covered largely by insurance, sales of Loestrin 24 Fe climbed 25.4 percent to $89 million in 2012.

Under Hatch-Waxman, Warner Chilcott had sued a few drugmakers who planned to make a generic for patent violation in 2011, thereby gaining that thirty extra months of protection. The suit never went to court, because Warner Chilcott used a tactic called "pay for delay" to settle: the company gave two drugmakers, Watson and Lupin, various financial incentives in exchange for agreeing to delay their applications to make a generic. The arrangement suited all the manufacturers just fine, but it was clearly bad for patients. According to industry analysts, every six months of delay before generics hit the market can be worth billions in profits or added spending.

By 2014 that strategy had played out, and the first patent for Loestrin 24 Fe was finally slated to expire soon. But before it did, Warner Chilcott had another trick up its sleeve.

It conducted research and development to invent a new *chewable* form of the pill with a new name, Minastrin 24 Fe, and a new patent. Then Warner Chilcott stopped making the old favorite, Loestrin 24 Fe. There were no generic versions of the pill on the market yet, so patients who wanted to stay with the same formulation of birth control pill had no choice but to switch to the chewable brand.

The advertising for Minastrin touted its benefits; for example, the pill could now be taken even if there was no water available. Most adult women, however, had no desire to chew a birth control pill. Some objected to the artificial sweeteners. The new version cost between $130 and $150 when paying cash with a discount card, depending on the pharmacy—about 30 percent more than the old.

The industry name for this maneuver is "product hopping," and Warner Chilcott was, historically, a master artist. A lawsuit filed by Mylan Pharmaceuticals alleged that Warner intentionally moved its acne medication Doryx from one form to another three times in order to stymie the launch of a generic. It swapped a capsule for a tablet; developed a version that could be broken up and sprinkled on applesauce; and introduced a new scored pill. Since generics must be identical in dosage and form to the brand-name drug for a pharmacist to substitute, each move succeeded in delaying competition from generics for years.

Play to the FDA's weaknesses and blind spots. Sprays, lotions, and creams don't have to play legal games to fend off competition from generics, since these formulations are hard to replicate according to the FDA's exacting standards. For pills, it is relatively straightforward to show that the chemical composition is equivalent to the brand and to measure that it produces the same level of medication in the blood. But because equivalence is much harder to demonstrate for an inhaler that delivers medicine into the lungs, or a cream that needs to be absorbed, many manufacturers of generic versions of such products are hesitant to enter the U.S. market.

The FDA has at other times offered up market opportunities. In 2006 it announced it would no longer permit the sale of drugs that had not undergone formal FDA approval, mostly long-used compounds that predated the agency and its mandate. One was colchicine, a cheap treatment for gout used for hundreds of years that was made by many generics manufacturers and was not associated with risks. To ensure that the drug would remain available to those who needed it, the agency offered drugmakers a deal: test the drug for safety and efficacy and be granted three years of exclusivity on sales, a monopoly. Studies by URL Pharma, a small industry player, showed (no surprise) that the drug worked well with few untoward reactions. Colchicine, which had cost pennies a pill, was now covered by five patents, rebranded Colcrys, and sold for about $5 a pill. All generics were banned. URL was acquired by a big pharmaceutical firm, Takeda, for $800 million in 2012. Colchicine is still sold in Canada for a list price of 9 cents per pill.

Take it over the counter. Changing a drug's legal status so that it can be sold over the counter is sometimes a profitable patent play for pharmaceutical companies. But what is called an "OTC switch" is a risky decision. Prescriptions are key to charging high prices (because insurers pay) and holding a pharmaceutical monopoly intact. In much of the world, products go over the counter when they are deemed safe enough to take without a doctor's intervention. In the United States it is more of a business calculation.

When Flonase was patented in 1994, it joined a number of shorter-acting nasal steroid sprays that provided new relief for allergy sufferers. There was talk of selling the many new anti-allergy products over the counter, rather than by prescription, nearly from the get-go, even pressure to do so. In 1998 insurers petitioned the FDA to have three nonsedating prescription allergy pills sold without a prescription, noting they were all safer than Benadryl. An FDA advisory panel overwhelmingly agreed, but the agency did not have the authority to force manufacturers to switch. (See **Rule 1: More treatment is always better. Default to the most expensive option.**)

An OTC switch makes products available to a wider audience of buyers. But manufacturers have to lower prices dramatically because insurance is no longer involved; they also have to establish brand recognition with consumers. Many pharmaceutical firms lacked expertise in selling an off-the-shelf product. Schering-Plough had notoriously lost market share when it took the vaginal antifungal cream Gyne-Lotrimin over the counter some years before, in competition with Monistat.

By the early 2000s, many allergy medicines were slated to lose their patents. Schering-Plough did some further testing of Claritin on children, which gave it a six-month patent extension, until December 2002. It developed a new version, branded Clarinex, that slightly changed the chemical composition, but users didn't switch because the old pill worked just as well as the new one. In 2000 Schering-Plough even took the effort to Congress: extending Claritin's patent was written into an appropriations bill—the drugmaker claimed that it had taken the FDA so long to approve its initial application that it had lost valuable time on the market. Two years later, a judge rejected Schering-Plough's last-ditch attempt to gain another thirty months, and it took Claritin over the counter.

But the nasal steroid sprays were able to cling to their "by prescription only" status for years more in part because they are much harder than pills to copy exactly to the FDA's satisfaction. Also, the sprays were steroids, a class of medications that doctors are leery of prescribing because they have many theoretical side effects—though all are "dose dependent," significant mainly when steroids are taken by mouth, at higher doses, and for longer periods of time. By 2012 one branded prescription spray, Rhinocort Aqua, was selling for $250 a month in the United States, but for about $7 off the shelf at Boots in London.

A generic equivalent for Flonase had cleared FDA hurdles and entered the market by 2006. GlaxoSmithKline did its best to protect its brand, by means both legal and, apparently, unlawful. On May 7, 2007, the FDA sent a warning letter, chiding the company for disseminating materials to doctors containing "unsubstantiated superiority claims" about Flonase. In 2015 purchasers of the drug filed a class action suit against Glaxo to recover money they had overpaid as a result of Glaxo's "brand maturation strategy" designed to prevent or delay less expensive generics from entering the market. The lawsuit accused the company of filing bogus "citizens petitions" to protest the entry of generics, for example.

By 2010 a bottle of generic Flonase, whose chemical name is fluticasone, was selling for about $20, and it was occasionally turning up on the list of $4 prescription specials featured at stores like Target.

But Glaxo had one last strategy in its playbook: a masterful OTC switch that allowed it to maximize profit on both its prescription and over-the-counter allergy medicines, and wipe out generic competition with one stroke.

According to U.S. law, the same product cannot be on the market as both a prescription and an over-the-counter product. So once Flonase was sold off pharmacy shelves, the generics manufacturers had six months to use up supply and close their factories, even though generic Flonase had been the market leader among steroid nasal sprays for years. Moreover, the FDA grants any company that takes a prescription drug to OTC status three years of market exclusivity for that sales route, during which other manufacturers are forbidden from making store-brand copies. With no direct competition, a little bottle of Flonase was priced at $40.

Glaxo's prescription drug business benefited as well: In 2008 the company had introduced Veramyst, another branded nasal spray with the same essential ingredient as Flonase, but whose minor differences allowed Glaxo to receive new patents. With competing generics off the market in 2010, Glaxo's Veramyst got a new lease on life as a choice for people who wanted to buy a steroid nasal spray using insurance. Glaxo's sales of OTC Flonase and branded prescription Veramyst could both prosper.

Create a combination. In 2011 Horizon Pharma—a small five-year-old company—received approval for its first product, Duexis, a painkiller. Duexis is a combination of two familiar off-the-shelf drugs: ibuprofen (an anti-inflammatory, brand names Advil and Motrin) and famotidine (a stomach-lining protector, brand name Pepcid). The price at Costco for the two drugs separately is about $9 monthly, but Duexis is covered by five patents and costs over $1,600.

In 2012 some industry analysts criticized Horizon's business model. "There really is no benefit to using DUEXIS over generic ibuprofen and Pepcid," remarked Patrick Crutcher of Chimera Research Group. But by the end of that year, Horizon had deployed a team of 160 sales representatives, and with a little promotion and marketing, the gross sales of Duexis quickly rose to $85.5 million.

Manufacturers sued to be allowed to make a generic version of the drug, challenging patents and averring that the drug was not really new. Horizon "vigorously" defends "patent challenges in order to protect our innovation," according to its CEO, Timothy Walbert. In 2013 Horizon and the generics manufacturer Par Pharmaceutical entered into a pay-for-delay settlement. Horizon will pay Par not to produce a generic version of Duexis, a drug of questionable utility, until January 1, 2023.

The number of pay-for-delay arrangements has increased dramatically since 2010, and the result is no generic drug competition to produce cheaper alternative versions for a growing number of brand-name drugs. The Federal Trade Commission (FTC) says these anticompetitive agreements cost consumers and taxpayers $3.5 billion in higher drug costs every year, but the agency has not been able to halt them.

Mike Wegner, a former Texas comptroller who was prescribed Duexis in 2015, was outraged when his insurer requested a $110 co-pay. After exploring the medicine's provenance, he refused to buy it, saying it felt like "extortion."

Patient outrage over the high price of patent plays was the last business barrier drugmakers had to resolve. As pharmaceutical prices increased, insurers imposed co-payments that were a percentage of the bill to encourage the use of cheaper alternatives. With some medicines, that meant hundreds or even thousands of dollars in out-of-pocket payment, which caused patients to balk. And so the pharmaceutical industry invented co-pay coupons.

Desperate Patients and Bribes, or Charity?

Two decades ago Mary Chapman, now in her forties, a consultant and competitive dressage rider, began experiencing dizziness, numb limbs, and a burning pain down her side. She was diagnosed with multiple sclerosis (MS). Since then, her disease has progressed despite a string of different drugs. When her disease is flaring, she has suffered leg paralysis, lost her sight, and been delirious. Even when it is relatively quiescent, she lives with a multitude of chronic problems, including the inability to urinate, incoordination, and extreme fatigue. She is no longer healthy enough for full-time employment, and for most of the past five years her nearly full-time job has been doing whatever she can to afford her ever-more-expensive medications.

In 1998 she started taking Avonex, which cost $1,200 a month; it was covered by commercial insurance. When that stopped working well, and better drugs were developed, she moved on to Copaxone; though "covered" it required monthly co-pays of $1,500. After Ms. Chapman spent about five years injecting herself daily with Copaxone, her scans showed it was no longer effective and her neurologist prescribed a newer drug, Novartis's Gilenya. When yet another new drug, Tecfidera, entered the market with a price tag of $5,000 per month, the cost of all MS drugs, including the one Ms. Chapman was taking, moved up to that price point. (See **Rule 6: More competitors vying for business doesn't mean better prices; it can drive prices up, not down.**)

Treating MS is a bit like dealing with forest fires in a long, dry summer: you treat with maintenance therapy to keep things quiet, and when symptoms flare you act aggressively. You can't stop. You don't put down the hose if the water becomes more expensive. "All drugs were ten thousand to fifteen thousand dollars a year a decade ago; now in the United States they're all fifty thousand dollars. I don't know what happened," said Dr. Mark Gudesblatt, a Long Island neurologist who has a large MS practice. Many of the same drugs in Europe still cost $15,000 a year because countries there bargain with the pharmaceutical companies for a national price, which Medicare is not legally allowed to do. (See **Rule 10: Prices will rise to whatever the market will bear.**)

By the early 2000s, co-payments for MS drugs could total tens of thousands of dollars a year; few patients could afford that (including Ms. Chapman, who had switched to a less demanding job, with a lower salary, to accommodate her condition). As a result, drug companies invented "co-pay assistance," a unique form of self-interested corporate charity to cover patients' co-payments—a "donation"—so that the manufacturers can continue to submit bills for the full price of the drug to insurers. A direct payment by the drug company could be considered a kind of bribe, so foundations with noble-sounding missions like "ending healthcare disparities" were often created to cut the checks. On paper, these charities are among the most generous in the country. The AbbVie and Johnson & Johnson Patient Assistance Foundations each "give" more than $700 million each year. By donating $1,250 to cover a patient's 25 percent monthly co-payment on a $5,000 drug, companies are still making a hefty profit. (The $1,250 is also tax-deductible.) It costs the U.S. healthcare system huge amounts of money.

Physicians are not permitted to waive patient co-payments because they are part of insurance contracts: if a doctor routinely "forgives" patients' required 20 percent co-pay, insurance law considers that fraud. Following similar logic, Medicare forbids its beneficiaries from accepting pharmaceutical co-pay offers. But private insurers had a hard time saying no to programs that were advertised to sick patients. Novartis asked: "How does a $0 prescription co-pay sound to you? Most eligible people paid a $0 prescription co-pay for GILENYA." If a commercial insurer didn't allow patients to take advantage of the offers, its customers would leave in droves for a competitor that did.

The problem for Ms. Chapman, as for many people with progressive diseases, is that many end up disabled and insured by Medicare as their health declines, setting off a financial crisis because they can no longer accept drugmakers' largesse. Even relatively well-off patients need outside financial help. A 2016 survey of nearly eight thousand MS patients found that 38.9 percent reported difficulty paying for medication: 30 percent reported skipping doses or stopping treatment due to cost; 40.3 percent were enrolled in pharmaceutical company financial assistance programs.

In 2011 Ms. Chapman wrote to her senators, Barbara Boxer and Dianne Feinstein: "As it stands currently, I pay $1200/month out of pocket for medical expenses, COBRA, medications, etc. Once I go onto Medicare, it appears that the number would be closer to $2,000+, which is not possible for me. This past week, I cried for several hours as I considered that I might be looking at a much higher level of disability due to a health care system flaw. I am bewildered and devastated."

Suddenly, Ms. Chapman's medicines alone involved monthly co-pays between $900 and $1,350. She remembers that time as the darkest of her decades of living with her disease. "I was perpetually panicked," she said. "If you can't afford your meds, you can't walk." A frugal person already, she drained her savings, replaced one used car with an even older one, and, when she felt healthy enough, did odd jobs like helping a nearby stable owner tend to stalls in exchange for riding time. In early 2014 she sold all her jewelry to pay for her medicine.

Each year she also spent weeks filling out applications for grants from "patient assistance funds," yet another newly evolved type of charitable organization with mysterious benefactors. With names like the Patient Access Network Foundation (PAN) and the HealthWell Foundation, they offer applicants stipends to defray the cost of medicines and treatment. She'd wake up at 6 a.m. to get organized to start making calls. "You'd keep calling back each to check on the status. And then you'd get a letter saying something like 'We regret to inform you that the Patient Access Network doesn't have any more MS funding this year.' Or maybe you get a notice that, yes, you've been covered for the year, and you'd relax. But the whole thing is crazy and super unnerving."

On its IRS Form 990, the Patient Access Network defines its mission as "a society where every individual can access needed medical care." It describes its method as "helping underinsured patients access needed medical treatment through copay assistance." PAN brags that it does almost no fund-raising, but it received *more than $300 million* in donations in 2013. PAN does not disclose its donors, but says they include "pharmaceutical companies, medically related organizations, individuals and foundations." Four gave more than $25 million and one over $100 million. It is administered by the Lash Group, a healthcare consultancy whose major clients are pharmaceutical companies.

According to a report by the U.S. Department of Health and Human Services (HHS), most of PAN's funding is provided by manufacturers of the drugs covered by the foundation's programs. Donors are permitted to earmark funds for particular diseases—presumably the ones their drugs treat. PAN's financial report shows that 85 percent of its "grantees" are on Medicare, which means they can't legally accept co-pay assistance directly from a pharmaceutical firm's foundation.

Pharmaceutical firms are skirting the spirit if not the letter of the Medicare antikickback law. The Patient Access Network even asked the Office of the Inspector General (OIG) of HHS to render an opinion on the legality of their practices. In 2007 Lewis Morris, the HSS OIG's chief counsel, wrote that the arrangement as described "would not constitute grounds" for civil monetary penalties or administrative sanctions. But like the doctors on the FDA panel tasked with evaluating Hetlioz, Mr. Morris expressed skepticism about the arrangement, noting that such assistance "could be misused as conduits for pharmaceutical clients to provide remuneration to Medicare or Medicaid beneficiaries who use the client's products."

Late in 2014 Ms. Chapman's condition deteriorated. She ended up delirious and semiconscious in the hospital, with multiple sclerosis flaring in her brain. She survived. The silver lining of her harrowing experience was that the next treatment option prescribed for her was an intravenous medicine called Rituxan. Because Rituxan is administered in a clinic or a hospital every six weeks, it is billed as a medical procedure, drugs included. Medicare paid $27,568.50 for each of her first two monthly infusions. Her co-payment was zero.

"I have money in retirement accounts and I'm a problem solver, but I'm always panicked about the future because I know I'm incredibly vulnerable, living in the U.S.," she said, noting that stress is one prominent factor known to set off flares of MS.

The Rise of Invisible Robber Barons

It's hard for patients like Ms. Chapman to know whom to blame for their travails, though the drugmakers and insurers are the most visible culprits. But a different class of backroom mercenaries that entered the medical fray in the late 1980s and early 1990s has consolidated its influence more recently: the pharmacy benefit manager (PBM). Today, there are only a handful of huge PBMs—Express Scripts, CVS Caremark, OptumRx—and they have enormous sway over your care.

Hired by many employers and insurers as middlemen to negotiate drug purchases with pharmacies, the PBMs occupy a place of business advantage. According to antitrust law and under contractual gag clauses, insurers cannot compare prices they pay for medicine. But PBMs, who each represent large swaths of the healthcare industry, know all the deals and have huge negotiating power.

The PBMs are for-profit companies that make money by pocketing a percentage of the discounts they negotiate. The items that end up on the formularies of covered drugs and devices aren't always the ones patients need most or those that work best, but rather the ones on which the PBM has wrangled the best deal, with the best negotiated profit margin.

The ever-changing business deals explain the perpetual churning of the products available through insurance plans. The PBMs may, for example, drop a drug from coverage as a negotiating tactic in order to bring pharmaceutical manufacturers back to the table with a better offer next year. For example, in 2014 Express Scripts suddenly dropped Advair, one of the most popular but most expensive asthma inhalers, from its formulary, sending millions of patients scrambling to find alternatives.

Bad for patients, but good for revenue: the fourth-quarter profits of Express Scripts increased 16 percent in 2014 compared with a year before, to $581 million. That was true even though it filled 7 percent fewer prescriptions during that period, suggesting it made more on each one. "As Express Scripts Attacks Costs, Investors Profit," *Barron's* noted.

"We Regret to Inform You That the Generic Isn't Available . . ."

As prices for newer drugs trended skyward since the early 2000s, patients were progressively losing one of the few solutions that had provided America some relief from high pharmaceutical prices: plentiful generic drugs.

For much of the past decade, Dr. James Larson, an ER doctor in

Northern California, has been struggling to treat patients who are vomiting. Prochlorperazine (brand name Compazine) and droperidol (brand name Inapsine), two generic antinausea drugs, had long been a mainstay of ER care, medicines physicians deployed every day for things like food poisoning and migraines. Suddenly, about a decade ago, these time-honored drugs became hard or impossible to get, sometimes for months or even years at a time. Not having prochlorperazine available in an emergency room is like not having acetaminophen (Tylenol) in a drugstore.

Initially, their disappearance meant that ER doctors had to rely on a newer, far more expensive brand-name nausea medicine manufactured by GlaxoSmithKline called Zofran, which had been approved by the FDA in 1991 to treat nausea during chemotherapy. Zofran revolutionized cancer care. Around 2005, the manufacturer began encouraging its use in other situations, for so-called off-label indications. At that moment, "our two best generic injectable antiemetics for emergency use suddenly became unavailable within months of each other," said Dr. Larson. "A lot of us felt it was suspicious." Rumors circulated that a major pharmaceutical industry player had purchased the plant that was making all the generic Compazine and shut it down. Prochlorperazine shortages have plagued the United States ever since, although supplies remain plentiful in other countries.

Around the same time, the FDA issued a black box warning linking droperidol, the other generic injectable antinausea medicine, to life-threatening arrhythmias. Hospital risk managers became reluctant to stock it. Anesthesiologists were stunned, complaining that the drug, the one they most often prescribed for postoperative nausea, had been used safely for decades. They noted too that the cost of preventing postoperative nausea and vomiting was $149 for Zofran, compared with $2 to $3 for droperidol, which studies showed worked equally well. Some doctors went so far as to file a Freedom of Information Act request to secure the documents that had led the FDA to issue the warning, which effectively handed over a very lucrative market to Glaxo. When the doctors reviewed the evidence, they discovered that the abnormal heart rhythms that prompted the warning had occurred at doses fifty to one hundred times higher than those typically used in the United States, and that the same arrhythmias resulted when newer antinausea drugs like Zofran were used.

In ERs and recovery rooms, Dr. Larson recalled, "suddenly there was no other option except Zofran." No wonder that by 2006 Zofran was the twentieth bestselling drug in the United States, and American business accounted for 80 percent of its $1.3 billion in global sales.

It is unclear exactly how active Glaxo was in getting prochlorperazine and droperidol, the two long-used, cheaper generic antinausea drugs, off the market. By the early 2000s, many hospitals had hired yet another new type of middleman, called a group purchasing organization (GPO), to bargain with drugmakers on their behalf. Since GPO fees are based on a percentage of sales, they have little incentive to promote the use of the cheaper drugs because that decreases their revenues.

But some paranoia about Glaxo was justified, given that the company had previously been caught undertaking dubious market interventions to promote Zofran: In 2008 the company was taken to court for an elaborate Lupron-like scheme in which it lied about Zofran's wholesale price in order to give doctors who prescribed it in their offices more profit. Glaxo listed the drug's average wholesale price as $128.24, when it was actually charging doctors $22.61, the Kansas attorney general, who spearheaded the case, said.

Around the same time, regulators in several countries ended up suing the company over its underhanded—and illegal—efforts to keep competing nausea drugs off the market, resulting in massive fines. South Korea sued Glaxo after it struck pay-for-delay deals with drug manufacturers to keep generic Zofran—or any other anti-nausea medicine—out. In 2012 the U.S. Department of Justice reached a record $3 billion settlement with Glaxo covering a variety of misdeeds, including promoting Zofran's use in pregnant women with morning sickness, for which it had not been approved.

Between 2008 and 2013 the number of Zofran prescriptions written in the United States for pregnant women more than doubled to over one hundred thousand—a trajectory interrupted only when the findings of a huge Danish study indicated that pregnant women who took the drug had a twofold risk of having a baby with heart defects.

Zofran lost its patent in 2008 and there are now cheaper generic versions on the market, but they are still far more costly than the older drugs. In the United States, generic Zofran now runs about $10 and branded Zofran about $60 per IV dose. A pill is still $23. The same pill is 75 cents in New Zealand. Meanwhile, the supply of the older, cheaper antinausea drugs remains erratic. Zofran and its generic offshoots by now have long-standing contract deals with hospitals. Makers of prochlorperazine and droperidol saw little chance to compete, so they simply stopped producing them.

Shortages of cheaper, affordable essential medicines in hospitals have become the new normal. Dr. Larson said that each week he and the staff of the emergency room where he works in California get a list of drugs that are unavailable.

Generic Sticker Shock at the Pharmacy Counter

Hospitals and their proxies negotiate ferociously over drug contracts and prices, but individuals picking up their prescribed antibiotic or heart medicine at the drugstore are not in a position to bargain.

Well over 80 percent of prescriptions in the United States are filled with generics, a higher percentage than in most developed countries. Competition in the generics sector was typically fierce, leading to medicines that often cost just pennies a pill, typically 20 percent or less compared with the brand-name drug. The Generic Pharmaceutical Association estimates that generics saved U.S. consumers $1.68 trillion between 2005 and 2014, a relief from sky-high brand prices.

But some generics are no longer a bargain.

Dr. John Siebel's adult son and his young family were experiencing another outbreak of pinworm, a parasitic infection that causes an itchy rash. It's a common problem that often afflicts the whole family, so Dr. Siebel called in the standard treatment: four days of a long-used prescription medicine called albendazole for his son, daughter-in-law, and grandson.

He was shocked to discover that the sticker price in the United States for the twelve pills of albendazole was now $1,200, or $100 per pill. "For cancer drugs, research is an arguable excuse. Here, we are talking about an old, off-patent, generic worm medicine that sells profitably in most of the world for a nickel a tablet. No research or marketing costs. Why does it cost $100?" He ordered the treatment for $1 a pill from an online pharmacy in Canada.

Medicaid data show that spending on albendazole had increased from less than $100,000 per year in 2008, when the average cost was $36.10 per prescription, to more than $7.5 million in 2013, when the average cost was $241.30.

The explanation was simply the business strategy of one company, Amedra Pharmaceuticals, to corner a niche market for a pharmaceutical agent and then to raise prices for captive patients to once-unthinkable levels. Other companies were doing much the same: A dose of doxycycline, an antibiotic used to treat a wide variety of infections from bronchitis to Lyme, rose from 6.3 cents to $3.36 between 2012 and 2014. Doxycycline became the single biggest drug outlay for the Pennsylvania Medicaid program in 2013.

Intense competition among manufacturers of generic drugs in the early twenty-first century had resulted in some rock-bottom prices for consumers. But the smaller profit margins, plus the lure of easier money to be made by producing more lucrative items, drove some of these manufacturers to quit making older cheap drugs, thereby handing near monopolies to those who remained in the market.

Dr. Aaron Kesselheim, a Harvard expert on drug pricing who has studied the albendazole case, told me that to really bring down prices through market competition, probably four or five generics would need to be on the shelves, and that level of competition was increasingly rare. As a result, after 2010 generics often settled into a price point just slightly lower than that of the brand-name drug.

And some executives of companies making generics discovered a newfound ability to do what the brand makers had gotten away with for years: to charge whatever the highly dysfunctional U.S. market would bear. In February 2014 Arthur Bedrosian, president and chief executive officer of Lannett Company, a small obscure drug manufacturer and distributor that made generic heart medicine and thyroid and pain pills, proudly announced record-breaking sales "driven by price increases." Though the Connecticut attorney general and a congressional committee investigated, Lannett maintained it had done nothing illegal. When Mr. Bedrosian was asked to testify before a congressional committee convened by Senator Bernie Sanders and Representative Elijah Cummings to explain his firm's pricing in 2014, he declined the invitation. He was meeting with investors in Europe. In 2015 Lannett was by some measures the fastest-growing company in the United States.

A Myth: At Least We Get Drugs First

> The United States leads the world in the introduction of novel drugs, and Americans have first access to new treatments and cures.
>
> —THE U.S. FOOD AND DRUG ADMINISTRATION, "TARGETED DRUG DEVELOPMENT: WHY ARE MANY DISEASES LAGGING BEHIND?"

America pays double, sometimes triple, what other developed countries spend on drugs but takes comfort in getting new treatments and cures first. That's often true: drugmakers like to introduce novel products in the United States, where the sky's the limit for setting an initial price point. In 2015 a British friend of mine with late-stage lung cancer was considering two expensive new immunotherapy drugs—brand names Keytruda and Opdivo—that might help. Although they were not yet available through the National Health Service, they were being used in the United States. Opdivo, which costs $150,000 for the initial treatment and then $14,000 per month, was being advertised on TV—even though it is indicated only for the small group of patients in whom certain conventional chemotherapies have failed, and extends life on average ninety days over other, cheaper treatments, according to studies. In Great Britain, the drugs were still being administered only via an NHS trial, and the government was assessing their worth over existing regimens—though my friend could get Opdivo for $24,000 a month if he paid privately. (British health regulators ultimately decided that covering Opdivo was not a "cost-effective use of resources.")

It is true that we sometimes get cures first in the United States—but only if the treatment has a good business model.

Two small but deadly outbreaks of meningitis B centered on Princeton University and the University of California, Santa Barbara, in 2013–14. My daughter was a student at Princeton at the time, so I paid careful attention. The outbreaks spread over the course of many months. Ultimately, one student died and several others suffered permanent disabilities; one lacrosse player lost both feet. Students were given crash courses in infection control: no sharing of water bottles in the locker room, frequent hand washing, no communal punch bowls of booze at those Eating Club Friday-night parties.

About halfway through the year, I realized a vaccine for meningitis B, called Bexsero, was in use in England, Australia, and Canada. Novartis, its Swiss-based manufacturer, had not applied for licensure in the United States because it seemed unlikely to be used enough to offset the high cost of approval the FDA imposes. There was no business model. In the United Kingdom, where rates of meningitis B are higher, all babies get vaccinated, rendering the product inherently profitable. The incidence of meningitis B is low in the United States, affecting mostly college students in rare, scattered outbreaks.

Novartis knew that the vaccine would only be used occasionally on American college campuses, and the FDA said it would have to repeat testing in the United States rather than rely on already completed European studies for licensure. The U.S. market just wasn't worth it. So for nearly a year, thousands of students at two universities lived with the threat of a deadly disease, until the FDA and the Centers for Disease Control (CDC) could clear the hurdles for the emergency importation of Bexsero. Early on in the outbreak, one infectious disease specialist I spoke with recommended what seemed like an extreme measure: put my daughter on a plane to get the shot in London. After students were fully vaccinated, there were no further cases.

Likewise, cost-saving new treatments have had a maddeningly hard time finding their way into the American medical bazaar, because lower prices for patients often translate into loss of income for someone with greater clout. Here are a few examples of how entrenched interests in the healthcare market are pushing back against innovations for the patient-consumer.

A promising new noninvasive stool test for colon cancer, called Cologuard, is now on the market. You can imagine how the colonoscopy industry is fighting acceptance.

Tens of millions of Americans have allergies, and studies in the last ten to fifteen years have shown that sufferers can be desensitized by taking a daily preparation that is dissolved under the tongue. The World Allergy Organization endorsed sublingual therapy in 2009, and it has become the standard of care for patients with allergies in Italy and Great Britain, for example.

But in the United States, the under-the-tongue treatment will cost a patient $600 out of pocket because the clinical trials have never been done to secure FDA approval. Every allergy sufferer responds to different triggers, so there is no mass market, and no incentive to do trials because doctors would lose money if they stopped giving patients the familiar expensive series of desensitizing shots.

Dallas Buyers Club tells the story of patients smuggling AIDS medicines from Mexico that were not yet available in the United States because of a sluggish regulatory system indifferent to patient suffering. Today, patients employ the same strategy for far more trivial diseases and for a different reason: money. That has led to the somewhat incongruous spectacle of elected politicians in border states like Maine and Minnesota culling votes by organizing bus tours to Canada to buy prescription drugs illegally. One of my readers, who feared having her name associated with drug trafficking, obtains diabetes medicine over the border: "Januvia is more than $300 per month—$6 a day—and I cannot afford to buy it in the United States. Therefore, I travel twice a year to San Diego, walk across the border to Tijuana where the IDENTICAL pill of Januvia costs about 40 CENTS—thanks to Mexican government regulation of pharmaceutical companies and drugs!"

5

THE AGE OF MEDICAL DEVICES

n 2006 Robin Miller's forty-eight-year-old younger brother, who was uninsured, had a heart attack and needed an implantable defibrillator. Robin, a small business owner, flew from Florida to Arizona to take financial charge. Mr. Miller asked the hospital how much the defibrillator would cost. "They said, 'We don't know.' I said, 'Why not?' They said, 'OK about thirty thousand dollars.'" Mr. Miller called the manufacturer to check on the wholesale price to see if he could buy it himself, but they wouldn't or couldn't tell him how much it cost. (See **Rule 8: There is no such thing as a fixed price for a procedure or test. And the uninsured pay the highest prices of all.**)

THE MEDICAL DEVICE SECTOR has quietly matured, devising new financial models and methods that have escaped in-depth scrutiny. The relative insulation makes sense. You likely don't know the name of the catheter that delivered the wire-mesh stent into your heart, or which company made it, and are even less likely to have any idea about its price. Yet these pieces of hardware are frequently the single biggest item on your medical bill, costing many thousands, if not tens of thousands, of dollars. They are often more than the surgeon's fee, the three nights in the hospital, or the "pharmacy charges" for all the medicines dispensed during an inpatient stay.

Medical devices essentially have no real price at all. These pieces of sterilized equipment could rationally sell for a few hundred dollars but sometimes cost more than a small house. That huge, notional number on your bill is the result of serial negotiations by a long list of intermediaries and their business decisions. For a hip implant, the chain includes joint implant manufacturers, joint brokers, joint distributors, joint device salespeople, and the purchasers at the hospital or surgery center. Each year, more people seem to get involved, and each takes a commission or adds a markup as the device moves along the long road from the factory into your body. The sales representative takes 16 to 18 percent, the distributor 30 percent, and hospitals then raise the charge by 100 to 300 percent more, according to a doctor who owned a small private surgery hospital.

Dr. Blair Rhode, an orthopedist who is trying to kick-start an industry for generic devices, estimates it costs about $350 to manufacture a hip or knee implant in the United States, and about half that overseas. Compare that with these prices (from my collection of patient bills): $36,800 for a metal alloy knee implant at New York University's Hospital for Joint Diseases; $4,000 for the screws used in a back operation at Lenox Hill Hospital in New York City; $32,900 for an external fixator, a stabilizing rod screwed into the bone to help heal a child's leg fracture after he was hit by a car in Atlanta.

If device makers' sales representatives, who often work on commission, open the wrong-size device for a total hip replacement, they are charged a couple of hundred dollars for the wastage. "A defibrillator costs $40,000, even though it's just a battery, two wires, and pads," said Peter Cram, a doctor and an MBA at the University of Toronto who studies health economics. "I've often asked why couldn't we make hip implants in China. The answer gets into regulatory policy and patents, and companies defend these ferociously."

Device manufacturers are a tight-knit oligopoly with nearly absolute control of distribution. There are dozens of large drugmakers and hundreds of small ones. But only a handful of huge device manufacturers dominate the global market. For some devices customers have only one option. Stryker, Zimmer Biomet, DePuy Synthes, and Smith & Nephew make virtually all knee and hip implants available in the United States. Experts jokingly call them "the cartel."

Medtronic is the primary supplier of insulin pumps and—with St. Jude Medical and Boston Scientific—also of implantable defibrillators. These three behemoths are based in Minnesota and Massachusetts, which is likely why Al Franken, Amy Klobuchar, and Elizabeth Warren, some of our most liberal senators, have all "worked across the aisle" with Republicans to support repeal of the medical device excise tax, a 2.3 percent tax on all medical devices that was meant to finance the Affordable Care Act. Senator Franken said the tax would "stifle technological innovation," even though a report by the Congressional Research Service said the effect would be "negligible."

Companies in the device industry spent $32.8 million on lobbying in 2014 to get rid of the tax, with top individual donations going to Senators Franken ($47,249) and Klobuchar ($39,900). It was a success. Congress suspended the tax for two years in December 2015, saving the industry an estimated $3.4 billion on revenues that are currently estimated to be in the range of $150 billion.

Most voters are likely suspicious of the Pharmaceutical Research and Manufacturers of America (PhRMA), the drugmakers' trade association that is a frequent target of criticism in the media. But they've likely never heard of the Advanced Medical Technology Association (AdvaMed, started in 1975) or the Medical Device Manufacturers Association, (MDMA, created in 1992). That's partly why the idea of including a medical device tax in the ACA was anathema to the industry, shining a spotlight on a dark, highly lucrative corner of medicine that had previously escaped any attempt at cost control or scrutiny. One analyst who tracks devices for investors worried that price pressure from the ACA would "hamper the growth of the growth" that device makers had long enjoyed.

The Secret History of Medical Devices and Their Regulation

Decades ago, laws intentionally provided an easier path to market for devices than for drugs. Before the second half of the twentieth century, "device" meant a tongue depressor or a syringe. But as the number and complexity of devices increased over the decades, it became clear that stepped-up scrutiny was needed.

Many device makers had humble origins in hardware, consumer electronics, or the general store. Medtronic was founded in 1949 as a medical equipment repair shop, but progressively evolved from making cardiology devices to supplies for spinal surgery and diabetes care. Zimmer Biomet, the largest orthopedic device maker, was established in 1926, when Justin Zimmer, a salesman for an Indiana company that made wooden splints, decided to strike out on his own and manufacture instead with aluminum.

In 1960, when Dr. Albert Starr coinvented the first artificial heart valve, he conducted clinical trials, including an informed consent procedure and long-term tracking of patients, to make sure the process was scientific and conformed to medical values. But others were less circumspect: in 1969 Dr. Denton Cooley caused a stir by implanting the first artificial heart in a patient, for three days, without FDA approval. By the 1970s, a number of similar heart devices were progressing through successful animal studies and headed for humans.

In 1976, amendments to the 1938 Food, Drug, and Cosmetic Act defined three different classes of devices that needed various levels of approval to ensure their effectiveness and safety before sale.

Class 1 included equipment like tongue depressors that required little if any scrutiny. Devices whose impact was "life-threatening or life sustaining" or that "present[ed] unreasonable risk of illness or injury, and required extensive testing," such as pacemakers, were included in class 3. Class 2 devices were those in between, which were governed by a new program called 510(k). To gain access to the market via the 510(k) route, companies had only to claim that their new device was "substantially equivalent" to a product already sold in the United States and used for the same purpose. The program defined "substantially equivalent" in vague terms that device company lawyers would come to love and exploit: "Not intended to be so narrow as to refer only to devices that are identical to marketed devices, nor so broad as to refer to devices which are intended to be used for the same purposes as marketed products."

The boundaries of the three device categories seemed easier to define four decades ago, and the government likely never anticipated a world in which those categories would be gamed for profit. The revolutionary Starr-Edwards heart valve had a relatively simple ball-and-cage design. There was no microprocessor, no genetic engineering, no Internet. But as the device industry got more sophisticated—both medically and financially— it began to tussle with the FDA over defining "substantial equivalence" and which devices should fall into which category.

It was obviously far more profitable to be in class 2—and gain speedy approval through the 510(k) program—than to be in class 3, which required far more testing and red tape. In a court decision in the 1990s, it was revealed that investigators discovered the FDA spent about twenty hours evaluating 510(k) requests, compared with 1,200 hours for class 3 devices. According to another report, only about 8 percent of 510(k) applications were scrutinized by outside reviewers and only 10 percent contained clinical data. Suddenly, most applications were submitted as class 2 products.

The surprising result is that today there is generally far less careful scrutiny of new devices than of new drugs, even though most drugs can be stopped in an instant if problems emerge and many devices are permanently implanted in the body. Many devices are not even tested in animals before they are placed into humans; in fact, there are often no clinical trials at all for devices. When claiming "substantial equivalence," manufacturers don't have to prove that their class 1 and class 2 products are "safe and effective."

Although the Food and Drug Administration Modernization Act of 1997 sought to clarify which products fell into class 3, the industry lobbied successfully to minimize its effect. Companies were permitted to apply to have products reassigned from class 3 to class 2. The agency created a fast track for the 510(k) clearance process, cutting the deliberation period to ninety days, sometimes shorter, making it even more appealing.

Quick approval under the class 2 substantial equivalence paradigm was good for the bottom line of the device maker, but didn't do much to protect patients. The FDA's ability to evaluate the software in devices was likely inadequate because the idea of software barely existed when the 510(k) process was born. The tracking of complications related to devices that had been cleared through the process relied on various registries to which doctors and manufacturers could voluntarily report problems—or not. The program allowed companies to keep selling cleared class 2 products even if the "predicate device" to which their device was "substantially equivalent" had been recalled because it had proved harmful.

When vaginal mesh came on the market in the 1990s, it was used to help resuspend the bladder and uterus of older women whose organs had "dropped," causing symptoms like incontinence. The first offering was Boston Scientific's ProteGen Sling, which became the predicate device for all others that followed. After evidence of a growing number of internal injuries and lawsuits related to the sling, it was recalled in 1999 and taken off the market in 2002. But its descendants continued to sell, with other manufacturers contending that it was the sling's particular design or the surgeons' poor skill that had resulted in problems.

By 2011 class 2 submissions numbered between three thousand and four thousand, but there were only thirty to fifty class 3 applications. A report by the Institute of Medicine that year concluded the former pathway was mostly a rubber stamp: "Many significant-risk devices go to market via [the] 510(k) route, including implants and life-sustaining and life-supporting devices."

During the period studied, the FDA "cleared" 85 percent of devices that applied under the "substantially equivalent" clause. Of the 15 percent it rejected, only 3 to 4 percent of the applicants went on to do additional trials. The rest withdrew their application if extra work was required. In the wake of the damning report, the FDA held a public meeting to discuss reforming the program. Doctors spoke about how 510(k)-approved devices had failed their patients.

Dr. Lisa Lai, a surgeon in upstate New York, described how a patient bled to death after she inserted a new balloon-tipped device into his intestine. The device's packaging said it could be left in place for twenty-nine days, but pressure from the inflated balloon caused an ulcer in the man's colon after just twelve. She later discovered that the device, which had been approved through 510(k), had only been tested on several dozen patients for a mean of under six days.

Dr. Amy Friedman described how a newfangled surgical clip that was used to close off a major blood vessel during a kidney transplant had come loose, causing her patient to bleed out. She did not know at the time that other patients had also died because the device failed. "What seems like a trivial medical device, a simple vascular clip, has the potential to be every bit as deadly as a far more complex high-end medical device," she said. "It too required, but never received, appropriate testing for safety and effectiveness before use in humans."

From 2005 to 2009, 70 percent of the high-risk-device recalls involved products that had gone to market through the 510(k) program, said Dr. Diana Zuckerman, a health researcher who testified at the hearing. Many of these devices should never have been in class 2 at all, she said.

Device companies have become the darlings of venture capital and there has been a proliferation of device patents. In 2012, 16,537 U.S. patents for medical devices were issued, surpassing the previous record of 13,699, in what analysts have compared to a gold rush. At the FDA hearing, device manufacturers and investors turned out in force to contend that any tightening of regulation would slow the pace of medical progress.

Joints Are a Big Business (but Don't Expect a Warranty)

Barbara Baxter lives in San Diego and has a business lecturing about the history and culture of wine. She is constantly on stage and on her feet, but unfortunately was born with bad hips, both of which needed to be replaced in her fifties. Joint replacements are truly miraculous. That said, neither of Ms. Baxter's joint replacements worked out quite as planned. Orthopedics is not a high science like neurology. It is frequently something more akin to precision carpentry. Well-controlled long-term studies in the specialty are not always the norm. Ms. Baxter had her left hip replaced at Scripps Health in San Diego in 2009, using a Stryker Rejuvenate hip prosthesis. She went back to work and, for a few years, was happy.

By 2013, however, she had pain in her right hip too. This was a more complicated proposition because the nearby bone already contained three screws from years before. She returned to Scripps, where an orthopedist predicted she'd have a "92 percent chance" of success with surgery (*note to patients: such precise probabilities are always a red flag*). He didn't mention that the bone was weak and so she was vulnerable to problems or discuss what that might mean. "I can't really go on stage with a walker. I trust these guys. So I go ahead," she explained. (See **Rule 5: There is no free choice. Patients are stuck. And they're stuck buying American.**)

Initially, the surgery was declared a success. But just two weeks later she heard a very loud "pop" as she leaned over. The pain was awful. Stress from the implant had fractured a crucial bone structure of the hip, the greater trochanter.

Doctors, device manufacturers, and drugmakers worry endlessly about the fear of huge payouts for malpractice suits. But more often it is patients who not only live with but also bear the financial consequences of bad results and problematic devices. For patients like Ms. Baxter, who had a health insurance policy with a $10,000 deductible, those consequences can be big.

One orthopedist suggested that he operate on this hip again to put a titanium sling around the bone, but Ms. Baxter was leery. (See **Rule 1: More treatment is always better. Default to the most expensive option.**) That would mean another big surgery and twelve weeks away from her work. Another suggested a bone growth stimulator, a small electronic device placed on the skin to deliver current that might help heal the fracture more rapidly. Her insurer wouldn't cover the device, but the hospital would lease it to her for $10,000. The doctor quoted $7,000. She called the manufacturer, who proposed $5,000. When she explained she couldn't afford it, that she had only $1,778 in her health savings account, the reply was: "We'll take it!" (The bone never healed properly and she has progressively lost half the strength in her hip.)

In the months that followed, the fracture healed slowly. Things seemed to be on the mend. So she was surprised when, during an office visit, the doctor handed her a printed letter with an ominous warning about the device in her other hip, the one repaired half a decade before. It read: "The purpose of this letter is to reinforce our recommendation to you for continuing close follow up of you and your hip replacement. . . . Some recent design innovations in hip replacement implants have led to increasing concerns about the potential for adverse reactions."

Ms. Baxter's Stryker Rejuvenate implant is not mentioned by name. Nor does the letter mention that the Stryker Rejuvenate had been recalled six months earlier, which Ms. Baxter only later discovered on Google. The company was under no legal obligation to notify patients; the letter, she noted, "does not even say 'we're sorry.'"

The Rejuvenate had been recalled because growing numbers of patients were experiencing problems with its novel patented metal-on-metal design, composed of chromium, cobalt, and titanium. When first marketed in 2008, the Rejuvenate implant had been touted as a new, more durable device, worth its higher price. It turned out that when the implant's components ground against each other, the metals leached into the surrounding muscle and into the blood, leading to joint failure, local tissue and bone death, and, potentially, damage to other organs.

The Rejuvenate had come on the market through the 510(k) program in 2008, cleared as "substantially equivalent" to prior implants. There were 123 other substantially equivalent hip implants in the same category ("Prosthesis, Hip, Semi-Constrained, Uncemented, Metal/Polymer, Non-Porous, Calicum-Phosphate"), though all had their own unique patents. "The Rejuvenate wasn't even put in a dog before it was put in humans," said C. Calvin Warriner, a malpractice attorney in West Palm Beach, Florida. "If your car had a faulty carburetor you can just change it but what do you do with a hip?"

In fact, the 510(k) program has led to a number of medical disasters. In 2014 and 2015, at Ronald Reagan UCLA Medical Center, after doctors used a newly designed intestinal scope that proved hard to disinfect, two patients died and five others fell gravely ill after being infected with a drug-resistant superbug. After creating the device in 2010, the manufacturer, Olympus, had decided not to seek FDA approval because it considered its design to be not "substantially different" from that of older models. "Can you imagine a prescription drug getting out on the market that didn't go through the approval process?" asked Dr. Steven Nissen, chief of cardiovascular medicine at the Cleveland Clinic, who has testified to Congress about device safety problems. "This is really disturbing."

Because of these lax policies, Ms. Baxter has a potential ticking time bomb in her body.

Equally troubling still, she was expected to lay out the cash for blood tests and scans to monitor the defective hip implant in perpetuity. The MRI at Scripps to make sure the joint hadn't loosened was billed at $1,150. Her insurance contributed just $150, leaving her a bill for $1,000. She has had three tests for cobalt, and the last two were high. When she asked why she should pay, Scripps sent her account to collections, who in turn said she should pay and get reimbursed from Stryker. In 2013 and 2014 alone, she spent $10,000 dealing with the follow-up. (See **Rule 9: There are no standards for billing. There's money to be made in billing for anything and everything.**) As she put it, "If I bought a BMW and it threw a rod, you'd expect the dealer to fix it for free. They wouldn't say 'send it to Germany.'"

Though she had filed to be part of a settlement fund that Stryker created to help pay for claims related to Rejuvenate, she had seen only $200 back after more than a year. That too is just another profitable medical business. Each patient hires a malpractice law firm, and the firms deal with Broadspire, a huge multinational company, which is paid to administer major implant recall claims in the United States.

"This is bogus—they're grinding me down. I called Stryker and said, 'Where's the money?' They say you have to deal with the attorneys. And they tell me to call Broadspire," Ms. Baxter said. By late 2014, the payments from Broadspire started to trickle in, $450 here, $26 there.

"What if I need surgery? What if Stryker goes out of business? It's not just that some chick in California has to spend time and money," Ms. Baxter said. "It's the principle that the device makers and the hospital and the doctor who chose this device for me are taking no responsibility. Right now this is coming out of the bank of Barbara Baxter."

Joint implant makers have been particularly creative and successful in exploiting the FDA's 510(k) program. Their business success is all the more striking because many of the original hip and knee implants placed in the 1970s and 1980s worked very well, so there wasn't a great need for hundreds of new models.

"They are largely interchangeable—the older implant worked great. It has one percent failure," said Dr. Rory Wright, of the Orthopaedic Hospital of Wisconsin. "We had the gold standard. The majority of our patients should be getting tried-and-true method. We're not oncologists—there's no benefit to the newest. In fact, it's often worse."

Medically, there were some worries that the earlier devices would not hold up in younger, more athletic patients, who were increasingly seeking hip and knee replacements. But the business case for designing new implants was more compelling. To gain new patents and raise prices, manufacturers needed something cool and new to promote. Following drugmakers' leads, device manufacturers tried a bit of direct-to-consumer advertising and marketing, promoting "women's knee implants" and hips designed for sports with names like Pinnacle and campaigns like Forever hip.com.

But the most effective way to make sure that the newest, most expensive products ended up in the highest number of patients was in forming tight, codependent relationships with orthopedic surgeons. "Manufacturers marketed heavily to the doctors—'We have this great new thing!'" Dr. Wright recalled. "And a lot of us took a bite of the apple."

Device makers start courting young orthopedists during their residencies and fellowships and fight to get their brands into the major training programs, because doctors get accustomed to the products they learn on. In many ways the device manufacturers followed pharma's practices in sidling up to physicians, but they took them many steps further.

They formed alliances with doctors they considered "influencers." At one prominent Massachusetts hospital the longtime department head collaborated with Zimmer in modifying implants and designing new ones. With the 510(k) programs, device makers could readily reward the surgeons with patents and profits or funding for pet research projects. All the young orthopedists who trained at the hospital learned on and became comfortable installing that one brand's products.

By the 1990s, many hospitals and doctors' offices had banned pharmaceutical salespeople or limited their access, but device makers couldn't be ejected so easily. Part of the sales deal is that the reps typically serve as unpaid assistants in the OR, helping surgeons install the devices they sell, a new tool at the ready to adjust a knee implant, for example. It was free help, and the good reps made operations go more smoothly.

With the device makers' clever business models, such assistance was rendered almost essential because each implant is installed with brand-specific tools and screws, and often even on a brand-specific operating table to help ensure, for example, that the legs are the same length once the implant is in place. Like Apple and Microsoft, Zimmer and Stryker each had its own complex operating systems, which were constantly being "upgraded," creating yet another reason to have the company rep at the ready.

Until the 2010 Physician Payments Sunshine Act prohibited the largesse, the relationship between surgeon and company sales rep was cemented with golf outings, meals, and tickets to sporting events. Even without that glue, today "it's nearly impossible to break into the market—it's all about these relationships," said Dr. Rhode, the orthopedist who is developing generic implants.

With the introduction of the ACA, Medicare—and, increasingly, some big insurers—started paying hospitals an all-inclusive price for a joint replacement (often in the range of $20,000 to $35,000). That meant the escalating prices the "cartel" charged for those pieces of metal and ceramic became a problem, since their purchase was often eating up more than half of Medicare's fee.

No surprise, then, that in recent years, hospitals have begun fighting back against the industry, suddenly demanding that device reps, like lobbyists, be registered and get permission each time they enter the premises. But the only thing this effort to limit the influence of money has led to is yet another business opportunity, which seems to define the circle of life in medicine. Novel business ventures like Reptrax and Vendormate "credentialed" drug and device representatives, offering access to "networks" of hospitals whose gates they control. Using systems similar to E-ZPass at hospital entrances, some even charge device reps each time they make a sales call.

Doctors began fighting back too. Having watched implants rise in price from $2,000 to $4,000 to $10,000, Dr. Wright and his colleagues at the Orthopaedic Hospital of Wisconsin changed their center's policies: no marketing, no personal choice of implant for each surgeon. The center now generates requests for proposals (RFPs) and negotiates deep discounts for the two implants it stocks. The HMO Kaiser Permanente likewise narrowed the range of implants it uses to gain bargaining power, achieving discounts of more than 60 percent. The surgical results were just as good.

But other orthopedists, disgruntled by the pricing, simply found a way to reap more of the profit themselves. A number of group practices formed physician-owned distributors (PODs), a new type of company to cut out the layers of middlemen. Then they bought implants and resold them to the hospitals and surgery centers where they practiced, where they installed them in patients for twice as much, yielding a hefty, predictable profit. An active practice of orthopedic surgeons could do $4 million to $5 million in implant sales a year.

Dr. Larry Teuber said he decided to cash out his partnership in a doctor-owned surgical hospital in 2014 when the physicians decided to form a POD. "We're already making eight hundred thousand dollars," he explained. "Then we have assistants and bill two hundred thousand dollars for them. And we get a six-hundred-thousand-dollar payment for our ownership stake in the hospital. It was never enough."

How to Get into a Patient's Heart? Follow the Money

Dr. Nalini Rajamannan had referred her thirty-eight-year-old patient Antonitsa Vlahoulis for an operation to buttress her leaky heart valve by implanting a synthetic device called an annuloplasty ring. The operation was many generations beyond putting in that historic Starr-Edwards ball-and-cage heart valve, but it solved a similar medical problem.

The heart is basically a simple pumping device, with four chambers separated by delicate valves that are easily damaged by infections or just wear and tear. They must function with exquisite precision for human health. If they leak, blood can back up into the lungs and cause symptoms such as shortness of breath.

The famed Dr. Albert Starr declined his patent rights on the original artificial heart valve he coinvented. But his partner, M. Lowell Edwards, a fluid engineer, went on to found a company that evolved into Edwards Lifesciences Corp., which still specializes in cardiac devices, from defibrillators to valves. One of them was sewn into Ms. Vlahoulis's heart, as she learned from the warranty card that arrived several days after surgery: Edwards Lifesciences' McCarthy Annuloplasty Ring.

In annuloplasty, the surgeon refashions a heart valve's damaged leaflets and then sews in a ring at its base to stabilize the outlet. The McCarthy ring was somewhat different from other offerings at the time because the springy ring had a slightly more triangular shape than the norm and was composed of some new materials, which its seller said made it an easier fit on insertion.

Ms. Vlahoulis had trouble almost immediately after surgery: fluid accumulated around her heart. She developed inflammation that led to scarring, which narrowed the valve opening so severely that she was referred to the Mayo Clinic for possible heart transplantation. She ended up going to the Cleveland Clinic for further surgery in which the device was removed.

Medical interventions don't always go as planned, but this one had an unusual twist: The surgeon who performed the operation was Dr. Patrick McCarthy, chief of surgery at the hospital and the inventor of the eponymous new product and the original holder of its patent. Dr. McCarthy received royalties on sales of the device (though he said he donated them to a food bank).

In Dr. Rajamannan's view, the device was "experimental" and Ms. Vlahoulis—only the eighth human to receive the device—should have been informed and required to consent. In interviews with the *Chicago Tribune* at the time, Dr. McCarthy said that Edwards had assured him that the device was legal to insert according to FDA standards and he had relied on its judgment.

In 1997 AdvaMed, one of the industry trade groups, had successfully applied to have annuloplasty rings downgraded from class 3 to class 2, meaning that rings could hit the market without prior human trials, through the pro forma 510(k) route.

The *Chicago Tribune* found out "that the internal memo outlining the reasoning behind the agency's decision [on such products] lists a single reviewer: a hydrodynamics and acoustics engineer," who lifted much of his verdict word for word from the industry's petition. The FDA approved the switch, but seemed somewhat anxious about the implications, immediately issuing a "guidance" that listed all the "risks" of new annuloplasty rings and suggested that testing companies voluntarily proceed with caution. Between 2006 and 2011, more deaths were associated with annuloplasty rings than any other class 2 device.

But as the bar for device approvals sank lower and lower in the early 2000s, Edwards had not even bothered to seek 510(k) clearance for Dr. McCarthy's newly patented modified ring, maintaining that it required no green light from the FDA at all.

In 2004, when Edwards went to the U.S. Patent and Trademark Office to protect Dr. McCarthy's new annuloplasty ring, it touted its entirely "novel" shape and larger size compared with previous entrants; these features would simplify the surgery and make it available to more patients. But when it came to seeking FDA approval, Edwards averred the device was so "substantially equivalent" to other rings that the company initially didn't even tell the FDA about it.

On March 7, 2006, Edwards Lifesciences unilaterally cleared the new ring for use in patients. Dr. McCarthy used it in Ms. Vlahoulis's operation just a few weeks later, and Edwards began marketing what it called the McCarthy Myxo ring. It tracked patient outcomes by requesting that surgeons voluntarily report their experience. Federal regulators did not hear about any problems until Ms. Vlahoulis and Dr. Rajamannan reported them in 2008 to the FDA's database. Another patient had suffered disastrous leakage around the ring after surgery, also in 2006. But the adverse event was not reported to the FDA until 2009, when the patient read about the valve's travails and wrote to the agency himself: he had suffered severe heart failure and life-threatening arrhythmias that had required an implantable defibrillator.

By August 2008 the FDA informed Edwards that it should have sought FDA clearance, but imposed no punishment. Edwards compiled the application and, a year later, received a green light from the FDA, though the device had perhaps been modified by then, according to Dr. Raja-mannan, who published a fascinating monograph, *The Myxo File: The Tale of Three Rings,* about her experience and a subsequent congressional investigation. In granting its clearance, the FDA used the weak 510(k) metric: the product was "at least as safe and effective as other annuloplasty rings being sold in the U.S." —however safe or unsafe that might be.

In 2010, the wholesale price was about $4,000.

Like drugmakers, device manufacturers have another big line of business to invest in, one that has nothing directly to do with serving patients: suing over intellectual property. Between 2010 and 2014, Edwards was embroiled in a lengthy suit with Medtronic over a new prosthetic aortic valve that is placed in the heart via a catheter snaked through the blood vessels instead of through open-heart surgery. Medtronic's CoreValve device infringed on its patents, Edwards protested in court. (These patents were important to defend, since this type of truly transformative artificial valve that could be placed without open-heart surgery had gone the class 3 route, requiring a huge investment in human testing to meet the FDA's requirements.)

In 2014 a jury agreed with Edwards. But before Medtronic paid the mandated award and its device had to be removed from the market, the two companies reached an agreement: Medtronic paid Edwards $750 million and said it would continue to pay royalties on a percentage of sales from its CoreValve devices. Who really pays the price for all the legal maneuvering? Patients, of course.

Dr. Elliott's Lonely Crusades

In 2011 Dr. Daniel Elliott, a urologist at the Mayo Clinic, contacted the FDA about those mesh kits to suspend women's pelvic organs that had been approved through the 510(k) program. "On a weekly basis, either I or my colleagues evaluate and treat patients suffering from the consequences," he wrote. The polypropylene mesh—a material similar to fishing line—tended to break free and migrate around the pelvis, damaging nerves, burrowing into the bladder and vagina, causing severe pain, bleeding, and infection. The only treatment was another surgery to remove the embedded mesh, and that was not always possible.

"No small confounding factor in the widespread acceptance and use of the mesh kits comes from the immense industry pressure on physicians to adopt 'the latest technology' without proper prior surgical training and independent scientific evaluation," Dr. Elliott told the FDA. "All too frequently, industry knowingly targets less experienced surgeons, knowing these mesh kits have not, and never will be accepted by more experienced surgeons who are fully aware of their inherent risk without benefit." He recommended banning the mesh kits until they'd been properly studied by research groups not funded by the industry. The manufacturers' one-day training courses should end.

In 2012 the FDA ordered the makers of transvaginal mesh products for the first time to systematically track what happened to recipients. Within two years, it received twenty thousand reports of adverse reactions. By 2014 the FDA's tracking efforts had collected enough evidence of risk—thousands of injuries and a small number of deaths—to propose moving the mesh from class 2 to class 3. (The switch was enacted in 2016.) By 2015 there were about one hundred thousand mesh lawsuits filed against multiple manufacturers in different states, and judges advised the companies to settle to avoid many billions in trial costs and awards.

But Dr. Elliott's actual subspecialty is implanting artificial sphincters in men whose ability to control their urine has been damaged during prostate cancer surgery, and he has fought his battle with industry on that small front as well. He does more sphincter implants than any other American doctor. When the artificial sphincters, or valves, came out in the 1970s, they revolutionized life for men who needed them to prevent incontinence. Over the next decade or so, until 1986, there were some tweaks in designs and materials—and, of course, increases in price. For the next twenty years, nothing changed. The sphincters are made by one company, American Medical Systems.

In 2008 the company said it was coming out with a new, improved product: the old sphincter infused with antibiotics to stave off infection, a technology it named InhibiZone. "There was a promise that it was better so everyone jumped on the bandwagon," Dr. Elliott said. But when Dr. Elliott didn't notice any reduction in infection rates after a few years, he discovered the company had no good data to back up its claims.

He decided to do a study comparing infection rates and success of the old and new devices: they were identical. But Mayo was paying an extra $1,300 for each InhibiZone sphincter. "With the new valve, my hospital spent $276,000 more for 213 devices with no added value," he said.

When he began presenting the results at meetings, American Medical Systems asked if he could do anything to "soften our presentation." He refused—"I said the data is the data"—and published the study in the *Journal of Urology*. The company complained to Mayo, saying, "If Dr. Elliott is unhappy with our device he can go elsewhere," he recalled. But no one else makes this device.

He vowed to use only the older, cheaper valve and urged his colleagues to do the same. American Medical Systems parried by raising the price of the older valve by $1,300 so that it was no longer more cost effective. One surgeon's "little attempt" at cost control proved "futile," Dr Elliott told me, adding, "If there was a generic valve I'd be there tomorrow." (See **Rule 5: There is no free choice. Patients are stuck. And they're stuck buying American.** Doctors are too.)

6

THE AGE OF TESTING AND ANCILLARY SERVICES

n 2013 Jerri Solomon was scheduled to undergo a routine colonoscopy at Albany Medical Center. Her gastroenterologist submitted an electronic order for some blood tests at the hospital lab. Ms. Solomon's bill was $1,400 for "labs" after her insurer's negotiated discount. When she called UnitedHealthcare for an explanation, a customer service representative explained that the hospital lab charged $772 for a vitamin D test. Only three weeks earlier, the exact same test at a commercial lab had cost just $16.70. In 2014 UnitedHealthcare paid laboratories between $17 and $618 for vitamin D tests, and those done in hospital labs were by far the most costly—Albany Medical Center receives the highest payment in New York State, three times as much as any other hospital. (See **Rule 8: There is no such thing as a fixed price for a procedure or test. And the uninsured pay the highest prices of all.**)

Jason Makowski's outpatient foot surgery in New York City to correct his "turf toe" took less than an hour. He was home by lunchtime, in what he called "a Percocet fog," when a machine that his doctor's office had arranged for him to lease was delivered. Resembling "a small portable air conditioner" and manufactured by a company called NuLife, it was essentially an ice pack that vibrated. As he signed forms, a representative explained that he should wear the pack for several weeks and NuLife would "fight for you" to make sure his insurance would cover the therapy. They won 99 percent of the time, she said.

More than a year later he got a letter from a billing and collection agency called American National Medical Management, informing him that the insurer had rejected the claim and he owed more than $10,000. "Suddenly I'm on the hook for eleven thousand dollars for a machine that I could buy for about nine hundred dollars." After calling and writing everyone and anyone he could think of to complain, he got a formal apology from NuLife, saying that it had ended its contract with the billing service and collection agency.

Testing, medical equipment, and what doctors call "ancillary services" (for example, a physical therapy session) were long considered to be the stepchildren of medical care. For the most part, these incidentals generated modest income. But to hospitals and doctors resentful of insurers' trying to trim their rates and in search of fresh lines of business, they offered new revenue streams. Suddenly, a half-hour office visit could prompt a mechanized blood test that cost three times as much as the consultation with the doctor. It was as if the baggage fees cost more than the plane ticket from New York to Paris.

Part of the explanation is that American patients desire this kind of high-priced exploration and treatment; they want their illnesses fixed on the spot. Doctors worry about missing something and getting sued. Runaway testing and ancillary treatment are not only culturally desirable and, perhaps, legally prudent but also lucrative.

Over the course of the past decade, testing, medical equipment, and ancillary services became to hospitals and clinics what booze is to restaurants: high-profit-margin items that can be billed for nearly any amount. Better still, many insurers require no co-pay for these items once patients have met their deductible, so most patients don't care how much they cost.

A 2012 article on Medscape, a Web site for physicians, urged practices to offer tests and ancillary services to counteract insurers' stingier reimbursements, in order not to "miss out on a lot of opportunities." It described a five-physician general practice that had done so, noting "the new income from them has started to roll in."

An Experiment in Billing

In 2013 some radiology residents at a large Arizona hospital were troubled by all the MRIs they were being instructed to order. Radiologists in training spend much of their days in dark rooms giving preliminary interpretations of scans. If the findings are somewhat indeterminate, they can recommend a further test.

The senior radiologists on the hospital staff had instructed the residents to recommend what their textbooks and lectures had defined as unnecessary follow-up: "My boss is ordering me to get more MRIs, at great cost to patients. I can't say no, but I find this ethically and morally troubling," Dr. Spencer Hansen told me.

Nationwide, data on Medicare payments for MRIs in recent years suggest something exceptional has been happening in Arizona. Prior to 2007 imaging was the fastest-growing component of healthcare costs all over the nation. After Medicare and other insurers cut payments, spending on radiology services decreased dramatically beginning in 2008, including on MRIs. But in 2011 Medicare payments for MRIs suddenly spiked impressively upward in Arizona (uniquely compared with other states); they simultaneously dipped in Georgia. That year, a group of radiologists, who specialize in MRI and whose research focuses on exploring new uses, moved cross-country to preside over the radiology department at that Arizona hospital.

Many factors, of course, impact the ordering of tests, and Medicare data are for the entire state, not just for that particular medical center. Some of the testing was likely ordered to figure out if MRI was useful for diagnosing conditions for which it is not commonly deployed. (Though it's not clear why insurance should pay for such tests, which are essentially research.) But equally important, the doctors (perhaps) and the hospital (definitely) directly profited from the ordering of more MRIs.

In an effort to understand the actual economics behind the tests, Dr. Hansen called the hospital's billing department to find out the charge for an MRI: $3,470, about $500 more than the price of a CAT scan. (Medicare limits what it will pay for the tests—well under $1,000—but hospitals could try to make up for low Medicare revenue by charging everyone else more.) "The hospital's in the red and ordering more of these tests will help, but this is running up hundreds of thousands of dollars a day," said Dr. Hansen, who is no longer in the field.

In Japan, where the price for tests is determined by a panel of doctors, economists, and policy makers, an MRI costs $160 using the most advanced machines; $133 on a machine with moderate resolution; $92 for the most primitive version. That allows for a decent profit on a technology that is a quarter century old. It doesn't include the radiologist's $45 fee. (See **Rule 10: Prices will rise to whatever the market will bear.**)

A resident at another prominent medical center, this one in upstate New York, similarly noted that when his hospital hired a new radiologist, the volume of a sophisticated and extremely profitable test called CT angiography suddenly quadrupled. Everyone noticed this shift, and understood the motivations. He was told to keep his mouth shut.

Many such tests pose no direct physical danger to patients, which contributes to the canard that overtesting is a victimless crime. There are cases, however, where generous revenues from testing, equipment, and ancillary services have predisposed hospital executives to overlook danger-ous medical practices. Dr. Yasser Awaad, a neurologist, was a favorite at Oakwood Hospital and Medical Center in Dearborn, Michigan, in the early 2000s. He had a knack for discovering previously undiagnosed sei-zures in kids, whom he would evaluate every few months with follow-up electrical brain wave testing. Hospitals make thousands of dollars off this kind of test, called electroencephalography (EEG), because it involves wir-ing a patient's head with electrodes for twenty-four to seventy-two hours and close monitoring of the tracings. Dr. Awaad became the top-paid doctor at Oakwood, making more than $600,000 a year: $250,000 in base pay and the rest a "productivity bonus" tied to EEG ordering.

He was a rainmaker. The only problem was that most of Dr. Awaad's patients turned out not to have seizures. Early on in his reign, pediatri-cians reported suspicions about the sudden epidemic of epilepsy. Patients who got second opinions were told that their tracings were normal. But Oakwood executives for years stood behind their doctor, even as the state investigated and more than three hundred patients filed a class action suit. Dr. Awaad eventually moved back to Saudi Arabia.

Making Money with Bad Medicine: Test First, Examine Later

When I injured my hand on a reporting trip in Europe in 2006, I was referred to a prominent orthopedist at one of Stockholm's best hospitals. He saw me and sent me for an X-ray, which showed a broken bone. He even splinted it himself. (The cash price for it all was about $400.) When, a few years later, I was referred to New York's Hospital for Special Surgery to evaluate a similar injury, I could not see the doctor without getting an X-ray or a scan first. No test, no appointment, the receptionist informed me.

In emergency rooms today, physician assistants and even nurses at the triage desk are permitted to order tests before a doctor has a chance to prescribe more judicious procedures, or even becomes aware of a patient's existence. A study by the Harvey L. Neiman Health Policy Institute, which researches the use of imaging, showed that physician extenders were about 50 percent more likely than primary care doctors to order a test for the same set of problems. When Björn Kemper of Cincinnati took his son to the ER at Florida Hospital Celebration Health for a stomach bug during a family vacation to Disney World, he was surprised to find the boy whisked away for a CAT scan—and even more surprised when he learned that it cost $7,000, nearly half the total bill. "The hospital would not negotiate; it was the most expensive Disney World vacation we ever took," said Mr. Kemper, who ended up paying over $5,000.

Some hospitals automate ordering based on the patient's initial complaint, such as abdominal pain or a headache. ProMed, a popular electronic medical record software used in emergency rooms, can order a generous list of diagnostics based on a patient's complaint without human intervention. While efficiency may have been the reason why some hospitals adopted ProMed, the scattershot technique is often simply bad medicine for patients. But hospitals are likely wont to tolerate that flaw, because such programs are good for the bottom line. According to Jacqui Bush, a former ER nurse in California, salespeople and administrators told the staff where she worked that one such product would "capture charges" (but—as she noted—"nothing about capturing actual patient assessments").

Extensive preoperative testing is a particular boon for hospital budgets because those tests are often done on an outpatient basis, prior to admission, so they can be billed separately even if an insurer pays an all-inclusive rate for the hospital stay. Particularly popular are sonograms of the pumping heart (echocardiograms) because private insurers typically pay thousands of dollars for an exam completed by a technician in twenty minutes. At many hospitals it has become routine to require one prior to any surgery, even for minor procedures like cataract surgery that require no anesthesia at all.

Melanie Dukas of Boston, a healthy sixty-year-old with no risk factors for heart disease, had two echocardiograms done a year apart prior to a carpal tunnel operation and another minor outpatient surgery procedure at Massachusetts General Hospital. The American Society of Echocardiography says the test is not appropriate for routine preoperative screening of healthy patients, but Ms. Dukas couldn't say no: "The offices refused to allow any type of surgery without this test," she said.

One of the most common blood tests, an electrolyte panel (also known as a CHEM-7), measures sodium, chloride, potassium, bicarbonate, blood urea nitrogen, creatinine, and glucose. It is a single test performed simultaneously on one red-topped tube. When I most recently checked in my area, the commercial labs were charging $17.25 to $22.69 for an electrolyte panel. But on hospital chargemasters the same single test is now often billed as seven separate tests—about $50 to $70 apiece, for a total of $350 to $490.

A Snip and $1,000: How Pathology Evolved into Big Business

Biopsy tissue is removed by gastroenterologists, urologists, dermatologists, and other specialists. It is then studied for diagnosis in a variety of venues: hospital pathology departments, huge international commercial labs, small private labs run by pathologists, or even a specialist's office by an individual pathologist hired to do the interpretation. With ever more money at stake, there is intense competition for these specimens.

In 2012 Dr. Jeffrey Crespin, a Manhattan gastroenterologist, suddenly began getting calls from patients about big pathology bills. Dr. Crespin, who had performed colonoscopies at a number of different hospitals and surgical centers during his career, had started using a new center affiliated with a major New York City academic medical center. "These are tiny specimens that are not hard to prepare and looking at them takes a minute," he said.

The medical center's pathology lab was charging $500 to over $1,000 apiece for that service, two to four times as much as other hospitals he'd worked with and ten times the $40 to $100 charged by commercial labs. Insurance typically reimbursed at most $80. The hospital, he said, was "ripping off my patients."

Patients typically have no choice over where their tissue fragments get sent and doctors frequently have no idea of the charges. The destinations have changed.

Ten or fifteen years ago most doctors sent the specimens to a hospital pathology lab or to one of the big commercial companies like Quest Diagnostics or LabCorp. But since then "new business models" have popped up, said Dr. Jean Henneberry, a staff pathologist at Baystate Medical Center in Springfield, Massachusetts.

Dr. Henneberry joined Baystate straight out of her residency and fellowship at Johns Hopkins in 1998. Even then, she realized quickly that some specialists affiliated with the hospital were balking at giving away the revenue associated with biopsies.

The Stark Law of the 1990s had sought to limit doctors from referring patients for testing, X-rays, or ancillary services to facilities that they or close family members owned or from which they would otherwise profit. But over time, doctors' groups had argued it was an unwarranted intrusion into the practice of medicine. In 2002 Congress established an "exception" for certain types of care rendered in the physician's office. Orthopedists could own in-office X-ray machines and offer in-office physical therapy, for example. Many specialists, including urologists and gastroenterologists, hired a pathologist and technicians to process samples in-house. It was a natural business evolution occurring all over the country. "That's where the money is and the more you do, the more you make," Dr. Henneberry said.

So they made money from each biopsy they performed. A report of the Government Accountability Office estimated that among Medicare patients in 2010 there had been 918,000 extra pathology specimens taken by physicians who stood to profit, amounting to $69 million in excess charges to Medicare. Ninety percent of the extra tests were from dermatologists, gastroenterologists, and urologists.

Pathologists began leaving hospitals and forming their own small LLCs. The successful ones were generally bought out by one of the increasingly powerful national pathology companies as the industry consolidated. Profits could be enormous. In 1997 Dr. Lisa Cohen started Cohen Dermatopathology in Boston. A decade later she sold it for $80 million *cash* to Caris Diagnostics, which was in turn swallowed up by Miraca Life Sciences, an international behemoth.

These big players could undercut the hospitals on price and, like any big business, they outsourced to cheaper vendors. Today, the biopsy from a local doctor's office that once might have gone to Baystate's pathology department perhaps travels to Florida to be prepped and then on to Tennessee to be read. The commercial companies courted hospitals to send them specimens by "sponsoring" fellowships and paying the salaries of doctors in training. Some practices would pay national labs to read their specimens for a low fee, but bill the patient directly for far more, as if they had performed the interpretation in-house. Soon once-busy hospital pathology departments no longer saw enough biopsy business to train residents. "We just lost our prostates," Dr. Henneberry told me in 2015, explaining that her department used to see dozens a day, a number that had dropped to the equivalent of forty a year in 2015, though it has since rebounded somewhat.

But tissue specimens don't travel well—and, of course, the stakes for an inconclusive biopsy result are much higher than buying a bunch of tulips sourced from South America that wilt the next day. If the biopsy report suggests that an operation is needed—say, for a melanoma or colon cancer—hospitals frequently require their own pathologists to reread the slides. Interpreting specimens is a highly specialized art, and surgeons don't trust the cheaper contractors at industrial-scale national labs. That leaves the patient with two bills from different pathologists for one snip of an organ.

Taken for a Ride: Private Equity Ambulance Care

Kathleen Williams, fifty-nine, fractured her arm bike riding in the suburbs of Cincinnati. She could have taken a cab or called someone to drive her to the hospital, but when an ambulance arrived, she rode it to nearby Bethesda North Hospital, but refused any pain medicines. She has good insurance through Humana, so she assumed it would cover the ambulance from the Hamilton County Fire Department. Six weeks later, she received a bill for $835, which she'd have to pay herself.

The Hamilton County Fire Department puts out fires for free but runs the ambulance service with charges. It did not have a contract with Humana, one of the largest insurers in the area. Ms. Williams tried to negotiate over what she considered an "excessive charge for such a short ride."

The billing service offered to allow her to set up a payment plan and, outraged, she agreed to pay $10 a month for the next eight years, she said, adding, "It was all I could do to protest."

Professional ambulance services are relatively new to American healthcare. In 1966 half of ambulance calls in the United States were still handled by morticians. But ambulance companies occupy an indispensable position in the hospital supply chain and one that proved easy to monetize: they bring in the paying customers.

Some ambulance companies are run by cities, some by hospitals, and some are private, but all crews get most assignments through a central municipal dispatcher. They have great leeway in deciding where to take patients. To compete, hospitals need their own ambulances to guarantee arrivals, but a generous stock of pizza and a comfortable lounge for paramedics help ensure the arrival of a good stream of patients with insurance.

Until recently, few ambulance companies exploited their position of power. Being a "first responder" was a passion that combined adrenaline and public service. Crew members worked crazy shifts, did their training after school or work, and were either volunteers or paid minimum wage. That latter fact has not changed.

But around 2000, nearly all of the once-free ambulance companies began collecting fees for their service.

The increasingly sophisticated medical equipment was expensive: an ambulance cost $100,000 to $150,000, they explained. In the late 1990s, the Bensonhurst Volunteer Ambulance Service of Brooklyn sent out a missive: "We found ourselves struggling to operate twenty-four hours a day even on the days we had available crews, let alone seven days a week. We have had to vacate, to some degree, a part of our Founder's vision to provide our services at no cost." While the company would not bill patients directly or ask for donations at the time of the call, it said, it would "have to participate, as many other volunteer ambulance services do, in third party billing as a way to help fund the Service."

By 2011 ambulance transport was no longer primarily a charitable service but such a good business that America's two largest private sector providers, Rural/Metro and American Medical Response, were both bought by private equity firms that year.

Buoyed by the potential for ambulance revenues, cities and counties also began billing insurance and charging more. Los Angeles's receipts for ambulance services rose from about $33 million in 2000 to $49 million in 2005 to an estimated $79 million in 2015, only about $4 million of that from Medicare. Some of that increase, the city's annual revenue report notes, resulted from "improved billing practices."

"The Fire Department's attitude, which the City Council bought, was that we could keep raising the ambulance transportation rates because the private insurance companies always paid," said Richard Dickinson, who worked as a budget analyst for the city for decades before his retirement in 2006. "For individuals who had no insurance, often the council member would tell them to ignore the bills. After three or four bills were sent, LAFD would write off the account receivable."

Specialized professional billing companies in turn sprang up to help ambulance companies produce more ambitious "revenue capture"—and they were not so forgiving. Enhanced Management Services, founded in 2001, touts itself on its Web site as "a leading ambulance billing company dedicated to maximize our Emergency Medical Service clients' income through proven EMS billing processes, technology solutions, and knowledgeable support teams."

As in all the other sectors of medicine, ambulance companies progressively "unbundled" their bills. In Los Angeles, which sets charges for all ambulance providers, the base rate for a basic ambulance ride in 2014 was $1,033.50 ($1,445 if an advanced life support team is on board), plus $19 per mile and $51.50 for every fifteen minutes of waiting. And that didn't include extras, such as $84.75 if it's after 7 p.m., $65.75 for the use of an oxygen tank, and $27.25 for each ice pack and bandage, and the oxygen mask.

In 2012 the Fire Department of the City of New York raised its base charges for a ride from $515 to $740, even though Medicare determined it was worth only $243.57. Medicare patients could not be billed for the difference, but if a commercial insurer balked and refused to pay the whole amount, the FDNY could charge the patient. Ambulance rides generate more than $200 million for the city each year.

Like the PARE doctors, many ambulance companies now refuse to contract with any insurers because they consider their negotiated rates too low. That leaves patients like Ms. Williams with big bills. Some ambulance companies now bill separately for the ambulance (the facility fee) and for the paramedics on board (the professional fee)—although many insurers as well as Medicare do not recognize the billing practice as legitimate.

No Pain, Big Gains: The Business of Physical Therapy

I visited Therese Ciesinski in 2013 when she was recovering from a hip replacement. After her discharge from the hospital, a physical therapist conducted sessions at her home for a brief period, and she was then prescribed twice-a-week outpatient physical therapy at a center that was part of the Lehigh Valley Health Network. Each session was billed at about $750, or a total of $5,470 per month.

In New York during the 1990s a physical therapy session was likely under $100. PT was sometimes covered by insurance and sometimes not.

But as ancillary services became increasingly commercialized—profit centers that hospitals and doctors looked to for new revenue—physical therapy practices fought for insurance coverage, charging minute by minute and item by item.

In her typical postsurgical appointment, Ms. Ciesinski spent the first ten minutes walking on the treadmill, followed by side steps against resistance from an elastic band, some squats and other exercises, and finally sometimes icing. "It was very informal—once you knew the exercises you did a lot on your own," she said. Those appointments were billed in fifteen-minute segments of, for example, "therapeutic exercise" ($183.41), "neuromuscular education" ($189.37), and "gait training" ($168.96). That did not include supplies, such as the $94.09 ice pack.

Lehigh Valley Rehabilitation Services is a small gym in a redbrick building with several offices affiliated with Healthcare at Macungie. Nothing fancy or out of the ordinary. When I drove along East Main Street in this small Pennsylvania town still recovering from the recession every little strip mall has a few shuttered businesses . . . and a new physical therapy center. There was Keystone Physical Therapy, Good Shepherd Physical Therapy, and Physical Therapy at St. Luke's. In a town with a population of 3,102 there were four PT centers.

In 1979 Medicare limited the amount it would pay for outpatient physical therapy to only $100 per year. That increased to $500 in 1982, $900 in 1994, and $1,500 in 1999. But the American Physical Therapy Association (APTA) considered that too low and has spent much of the last seventeen years successfully lobbying for a series of moratoriums and exceptions to limits on PT spending, which have been written into countless pieces of unrelated legislation.

The Medicare Prescription Drug, Improvement, and Modernization Act, signed by President George W. Bush on December 8, 2003, was a landmark bill because it provided for the first time prescription drug coverage for seniors. But its fine print also extended the moratorium on a cap for physical therapists (as well as speech and occupational therapists) from 2003 to the end of 2005. In early 2006, the Deficit Reduction Act included a provision that allowed Medicare "to develop an exceptions process for beneficiaries needing coverage above the therapy caps." The physical therapy trade association then promoted the cleverly named SENIORS Act (Securing Effective and Necessary Individual Outpatient Rehabilitation Services) to "extend the therapy cap exceptions process beyond 2006."

By 2010 the therapy cap had officially been raised to $1,860, but the industry managed to further postpone the actual imposition of any limit. Indeed, every law even vaguely related to healthcare in the last five years seems to have contained this pork-barrel extension. APTA also lobbied hard for the right of patients to see physical therapists without a physician's referral and, in 2008, the right for physical therapists to deploy extenders—physical therapist assistants. The assistant could deliver therapy in the physical therapist's stead so long as the latter was accessible "by telecommunication" and within one hundred miles of the treatment location; the physical therapist could supervise no more than three physical therapist assistants at any time.

By 2014 physical therapy was a $26.6 billion enterprise, worth almost 50 percent more than it had been in 2004 and expected to grow 7 percent a year. In national breakdowns of health spending, the amount paid to "other health professionals," the category that includes physical therapy, rose 5 percent in 2012 and 4.5 percent in 2013, more than any other heading.

When Dr. Rebecca Bechhold's husband had a hip replacement, the bill for his thirty-six-hour stay included $245 for physical therapy evaluation, $245 for occupational therapy evaluation, and $111 for a physical therapy session. The only intervention that fit those descriptions was when someone arrived the day after the surgery with a walker and watched her husband get out of bed and walk down the hall. "At this point the procedure is so good, you really don't need it," she said. "It was outrageous but it was awkward for me to say anything."

A physical therapy consultation and prescription for follow-up has become a precondition of nearly every hospital discharge. Heart surgery patients are prescribed weeks of cardiac rehabilitation at the hospital's outpatient center where they mostly walk on treadmills. Hip replacement patients like Ms. Ciesinski get long pricey courses of PT, though that is not the norm in other countries or at America's few really cost-conscious providers. Research has shown that extended outpatient physical therapy is important to recovering from a knee replacement, but irrelevant after the replacement of a hip.

Preying on the Elderly for Profit

Pam Farris's eighty-seven-year-old father was recovering from a major stroke when he was encouraged to have a screening colonoscopy by doctors in Terre Haute, Indiana. They asked him five or six times to schedule the test, assuring him that it would be covered by Medicare. "Why would you put him through this? Even if he had a precancerous polyp, isn't it likely he'll be taken by a stroke first?" her brother snapped at the doctor. (Her father died about two weeks later.)

A radiation oncologist told me about a dermatology practice that bused in elderly priests, many of them demented, from a nursing home for biannual skin cancer checks and aggressive treatment. In a study, Dr. James Goodwin, a geriatrician at the University of Texas, determined that people on Medicare tend to get more colonoscopies than guidelines recommend. "This procedure kills people, especially old people. It knocks them off for several weeks," he said. "They have incontinence. They can't get to the bathroom. It's humiliating."

When Dwight McNeill went to visit his ninety-two-year-old father at his upscale retirement community outside Boston, he saw an odd notice on the dining room table that declared his father to be in excellent health. His father explained that he'd gotten a call from someone representing his Tufts Health Medicare Advantage plan asking if he'd like to have a free in-home physical. "He was a bit puzzled and flattered. He remembered having a house call many decades ago and was nostalgic about doing so again," Mr. McNeill told me. His father was urged to accept the invitation quickly as "doctors are in the area now" and "this is a limited time offer."

He told his son that "a very nice doctor came by and gave me some tests and examined me and told me I was in excellent health," but suggested he might benefit from some testosterone to combat fatigue. Mr. McNeill called Tufts to inquire and was referred to a company called CenseoHealth, which explained that it had subcontracted with health plans like Tufts to perform home visits. "Who is this doctor? Where is he from? What's Tufts got to do with it?" Mr. O'Neill asked, noting that his dad already had an excellent primary care physician whom he saw frequently.

Home evaluation companies like CenseoHealth are a new kind of investor-owned healthcare business that has thrived in the past five years. The companies say their home visits are good for the elderly and that they report problems to patients' primary care doctors. Their business model also increases reimbursement. Medicare Advantage plans are paid a fixed monthly fee to take care of their members, but that fee varies according to each patient's "burden of illness." More than seventy conditions can push up "risk scores," from depression to back pain. Plans can profit by adjusting the score upward, and a host of new companies are there to help them.

In his pitch to the insurance plans that hire his company, Dr. Jack McCallum, a cofounder of CenseoHealth, says they typically can count on getting $2,000 to $4,000 more per person from Medicare, because home visits may uncover a new illness or tease out a new complaint that will send the risk score upward (although he adds that they should be conducted for the good of patients). According to the company, insurance plans pay about $300 for a physician or a nurse-practitioner to conduct the home exam, which more than pays for itself. Censeo, founded in 2009, is one of the fastest-growing companies in Dallas. Tufts also contracts with Predilytics, a data company that works to identify people who will accept in-home exams, which is likely to generate 25 percent more coding value with the same resource investment, according to a venture capital firm that backs that company.

Medicare Advantage plans, offshoots of traditional Medicare that work on an HMO model, were intended to provide more coordinated care for seniors at a lower cost; 31 percent of Medicare beneficiaries were enrolled in 2015. But 2012 payments for patients in Medicare Advantage plans were in fact 8 percent *higher* per patient than in fee-for-service plans, where patients could visit any physician or hospital. That excess is likely at least in part the result of coordinated efforts to raise risk scores, extracting billions in dubious billing.

Uninsured and underinsured Americans often get less testing and fewer services than they need. Poor Americans are less likely to get crucial recommended screenings for colon cancer and blood pressure. But well-insured Americans suffer often from too much treatment—particularly as they age—with tests and services meted out not for health but for money.

7

THE AGE OF CONTRACTORS: BILLING, CODING, COLLECTIONS, AND NEW MEDICAL BUSINESSES

The crisis that led the Norfolk, Virginia, sheriff to hammer a summons onto Wanda Wickizer's front door in January 2015 began thirteen months earlier on Christmas Day, with a random explosion deep within her skull.

A healthy, energetic fifty-year-old widow, with two teenage children, Ms. Wickizer had been complaining of headaches and throwing up. Her teenage son was alarmed enough to call an ambulance. The paramedics advised that she had food poisoning and didn't take her. When she became confused and groggy at 3 a.m., her fiancé raced her to Sentara Norfolk Hospital, where a scan showed she was suffering from a subarachnoid hemorrhage. A vessel had burst, and blood was leaking into the narrow space between the skull and the brain. The clock was ticking.

If the pressure in the head isn't relieved by emergency surgery, blood accumulates in the closed space, pushing the brain down into the narrow conduit of the neck. Vital nerves that control breathing and vision are compressed. Breathing slows; the eyes cease to move in tandem. Death is imminent. She was whisked by helicopter ambulance to a bigger hospital 160 miles away.

After emergency surgery to repair the vessel, she hovered semicomatose for days. But slowly, one faculty after another, she recovered, and by mid-January, was sent home, lucky and grateful to be alive. Nevertheless, by April 2014, she found herself writing to President Obama: "I survived, and other than some pain in my back and everyday headaches, I am doing well. My children, my parents and my fiancé are all happy. I am not."

Soon after Ms. Wickizer returned home to her loving family, she started receiving a torrent of bills: $16,000 from Sentara Norfolk (not including the scan or the ER doctor), $40,000 for the air ambulance. By the end of January, there was also one for $24,000 from some doctors at the bigger hospital. "I thought OK that's not so bad," Ms. Wickizer recalled. But then the next one, for $54,000, came a month later from the same physicians' group, including a $240 "late charge." Then the hospital bill arrived: $356,884.42.

The months after discharge from a subarachnoid hemorrhage are trying at best. While surgery clips off the leaking vessel, the blood that had already oozed out is only slowly absorbed and the bruised nerves take months to fully recover. Ms. Wickizer barely remembers anything before February. Afterward, she had trouble concentrating and finding words; more than a year later she still spoke deliberately, slowly.

Living in a navy town, Ms. Wickizer had always been a law-abiding, bill-paying citizen, so she tallied her resources. She received about $2,000 a month in Social Security survivor benefits since her husband's death (he'd worked for the city of Norfolk), and had about $100,000 of death benefits from an insurance payment in a retirement account. While raising kids she had occasionally worked for a print shop and a fraternal lodge but had never made more than $15,000 a year. With medical bills totaling nearly $500,000, the numbers didn't add up. "My dad said they'll never expect you to pay that," she told me. "But they did."

Ms. Wickizer was uninsured due to circumstances well beyond her control. When her husband died, she continued to cover her family, including two school-age children, with an extension of his health insurance. (COBRA allows employees or their families to pay out of pocket to continue on a company policy after certain life-changing circumstances, such as firing or death.) It cost $400 per month, a stretch, but she paid by taking odd jobs, none of which offered their own insurance.

In 2010 her extension plan ran out and she tried to get insurance on the commercial market, but was denied by several companies, she said, because of a preexisting condition: she had once taken medicine for mild depression. (This would no longer be legal since enactment of the ACA!) That left her in the state's high-risk pool, where she would pay $800 per month for a policy with a $5,000 deductible and 80/20 coverage thereafter. She couldn't afford it. She quit her job so her kids would qualify for Medicaid. She was determined to save the retirement account for their college fees. She did her best to control her borderline high blood pressure through healthy eating and exercising because she couldn't afford medications. In her own words, she "was doing pretty well, until a vessel in my head burst."

Foggy-brained and faced with staggering medical charges, Ms. Wickizer acted logically: as a sign of good faith, she paid $1,500 to the hospital and $1,000 to the doctors and asked for the itemization of her bills. A month later, on March 19, the hospital finally sent a list of charges. Despite being sixty pages long the tally was incomplete, and many charges made no sense. There was a room charge for one day of $4,762 (presumably when she was in intensive care) for January 12 and for $1,509 for another day, January 15. No charges were indicated for the other nineteen days she was in the hospital. A CAT scan on January 12 was billed at $1,579, but there was no record of her many other scans. Two stool softener tablets on January 12 were billed at $12.18 despite costing about $5 for a bottle of one hundred in a drugstore. (See **Rule 9: There are no**

**standards for billing. There's money to be made in billing for any-
thing and everything.**) Just imagine if your monthly credit card bill
arrived as a haphazard list of some random meals and clothing purchases,
accompanied by a demand that you pay for everything, including the
items you couldn't see.

She also received the actual bill demanding payment of $356,884.42
for the hospital portion of her care, broken down only into broad categories: $111,162 in room charges, $34,755.75 for pharmacy, $19,653 for
labs, $8,640 for the operating room, $8,325 for anesthesia, $1,143 for the
recovery room, $44,524 for medical supply, $40,489 for radiology services, and more. The bill informed her that the medical center was prepared to offer her its standard 20 percent discount for patients who are
uninsured, leaving a "what you owe now" fee of $285,507.54. It noted that
the hospital could offer some additional financial assistance, but only if
her household had assets of less than $3,000 ("such as bank or retirement
accounts"), which disqualified Ms. Wickizer and likely most Americans
who have ever had a job. "Thank you for choosing our hospital for your
health care needs," the notice read. "We hope to serve you again if a health
need arises."

Less than three months earlier Ms. Wickizer had been in intensive care
babbling that she was going down to the river to feed horses, so impaired
that the hospital had granted her father power of attorney for life-and-
death decisions. Nonetheless, the forms she had signed upon arrival in the
emergency room were deemed proof of her consent to pay.

After scanning Internet chat rooms on helicopter ambulance services,
Ms. Wickizer negotiated with the air ambulance company, which agreed
to take $8,000 for their $40,000 bill. The company operator made her
promise not to tell anyone about the discount—as if she were getting the
bargain of the century—after it had taken nearly 10 percent of her life's
savings.

She did her best to find out what Medicare would have paid, hoping to offer the hospital that sum from her retirement account. In 2013, for a subarachnoid hemorrhage (coded as an "intracranial hemorrhage or cerebral infarction disorders, DRG 021, with procedures and major comorbidities or complications"), Medicare would have paid between $65,000 and $80,000. Had a member of the armed services experienced the same condition, Tricare, the military insurer, would have paid $72,127.19. (See **Rule 8: There is no such thing as a fixed price for a procedure or test. And the uninsured pay the highest prices of all.**)

(A few states use Medicare rates as a yardstick for what hospitals can charge uninsured, low-income patients. In New Jersey, for example, the bill for an uninsured patient with an income up to five times the poverty level cannot be more than 115 percent of what Medicare would pay. No such protection exists in Virginia.)

When the hospital billers called insisting on payment of the full $285,507.54, she patiently explained, "I don't have this kind of money." She offered her $100,000 retirement account, but the hospital declined, and suggested that she sign up for a payment plan of $5,000 a month—an untenable amount.

She drove to the hospital to visit financial services. "The officer said we can put a lien on your house," she recalled. When I asked her to confirm that the hospital had threatened to take her property, she replied, "No, I wouldn't say she threatened. I'd say she was offering that as a good solution." On the three-hour drive home, she decided that she'd be willing to drain the retirement account, but would declare bankruptcy before giving up the house. (She and her children were living in a rental and leased out the small home, her only property.) It was an emotional time. "My kids got really upset because I said—and I meant it—if I'd just died, you'd have money for college. It would be better."

The hospital pursuing Ms. Wickizer like one of those predatory lenders who were shut down during the financial crisis was the University of Virginia Health System in Charlottesville. It is the hospital of one of the most eminent public universities in the country, founded by Thomas Jefferson in 1819 to educate leaders in public service. Like most medical centers, it pays few taxes in exchange for providing "charity care and community benefit."

Also, like many medical centers, the University of Virginia has turned at least some of its billing and debt collection over to professionals, third-party contractors who have no pretense of charitable mission because they are often paid a percentage of what the patient owes. Ms. Wickizer's bills were ultimately handled by Daniel & Hetzel, a law firm in Winchester, Virginia, specializing in debt collection.

Studies have showed that hospitals charge patients who are uninsured or self-pay 2.5 times more than they charge those covered by health insurance (who are billed negotiated rates) and three times more than the amount allowed by Medicare. That gap has grown considerably since the 1980s.

After Ms. Wickizer posted about her plight on the Internet, a dream team of billing specialists, patient advocates, and healthcare lawyers from other states offered to help her pro bono, but encountered roadblocks at every turn. Multiple requests to review Ms. Wickizer's complete bill were refused by the hospital. The billing snippets that the hospital had previously sent along to Ms. Wickizer were "error laden," said Nora Johnson, a billing specialist in West Virginia who was involved. There was a charge of $82,640 for "ambulatory surgery," a clear mistake: Ms. Wickizer arrived in a coma for an emergency intervention. By referring to the cost report estimates the University of Virginia hospital must file with Medicare, Christine Kraft, another billing expert, estimated that even by its own calculations the medical center spent only about $77,000 treating Ms. Wickizer.

Ms. Wickizer's offers to pay the university more than that, by cashing out her retirement fund, were rebuffed, often in an insulting way, using blistering language. "Your client may feel that she will never be able to pay the bill and she may not feel truly well after going through the experience of a cerebral hemorrhage," wrote Peter Hetzel, a partner, insinuating that Ms. Wickizer was not mentally fit to appreciate the grim reality of her predicament. He noted that judges in the area were known to side with the hospital. (See **Rule 7: Economies of scale don't translate to lower prices. With their market power, big providers can simply demand more.**) In April 2016, more than two years after her surgery, Ms. Wickizer was nervously awaiting her face-off with the University of Virginia and its lawyers in court.

A Brief History of Medical Coding

To troubleshoot Ms. Wickizer's bill, her dream team needed the hospital to turn over not just her chart but also the billing codes it had used. "Without proper coding the charges are not valid, not correct, complete fiction. UVA could be charging Ms. Wickizer anything," the advocates wrote. "Codes are critical to understanding the fair and reasonable value of the charges and required by all third party and governmental payers. NO CODES=NO PAY."

Medical coding is a cryptic and constantly evolving numerical language through which the things that are done to you in a hospital or other medical office are expressed on claims and bills. (In one version called Current Procedural Terminology, or CPT, CPT 35476 means "repair venous blockage using a balloon catheter" and CPT 35475 means "repair arterial blockage," for example.)

Medical coding and coders like ours essentially don't exist in any other healthcare system. And, like an Uber driver or a solar panel installer, a medical coder really didn't exist as a profession here twenty-five years ago either.

A detailed itemized bill for a hip replacement in Belgium takes up about three pages, and is not hard to understand, even though it is in Flemish: "Twoopersoonskamer [two-bedded room] = 329 Euro / Implantaten [implant parts] = 1621, 1195 and 209 Euro."

An itemized bill for the same operation at many hospitals in the United States would likely total over $100,000 and run dozens of pages, each filled with medical terminology and numerical codes you couldn't possibly comprehend. Trade groups representing billers and coders like to tout the centuries-old pedigree of their profession, but that is a half-truth: the historical purpose of coding was strictly epidemiologic—to classify and track causes of death and prevent the spread of infections among populations that spoke different languages.

Medical coding systems originated at the time of the bubonic plague. In the 1890s the French physician and statistician Jacques Bertillon further systematized death reporting by introducing the Bertillon Classification of Causes of Death, which was adopted and modified in many countries. It became an official global effort, which was periodically revised by an international commission. During the first half of the twentieth century, the number of entries naturally increased with improved understanding of science, and many countries began tabulating not just causes of deaths but also the incidence of diseases.

In 1948 the World Health Organization took over stewardship and gave Bertillon's system a new name to reflect a new broader focus: the International Statistical Classification of Diseases, Injuries and Causes of Death (ICD). The codes became an invaluable tool, a common language for epidemiologists and statisticians to use when tracking the world's afflictions. But in the United States, the codes gradually took on a bedrock financial function as the basis for medical billing. In 1979 the U.S. government decided to use ICD codes in adjudicating Medicare and Medicaid claims, with some modifications added specifically for that business purpose, so the U.S. version is called ICD-CM. Other insurers followed. In multiple volumes, the U.S. version not only categorized and number-coded diagnoses but also introduced codes for procedures.

The financial stakes in coding are high. If you code for "heart failure" (ICD-9-CM code 428) when you could code for "acute systolic heart failure" (code 428.21), the difference is thousands of dollars. According to a coding professional, "In order to code for the more lucrative code, you have to know how it is defined and make sure the care described in the chart meets the criterion, the definition, for that higher number." (For "acute systolic heart failure," the criteria include the patient's heart being able to pump out less than 25 percent of its blood with each beat, undergoing an echocardiogram, and taking a water pill to lower blood pressure.) Submitting a bill using the higher code without meeting those criteria could constitute fraud. The coders who work for hospitals strive to get money. The coders employed by insurers try to deny claims as overreaching. Coders who audit Medicare charts look for abuses that need to be punished.

Suddenly coding meant big bucks and a new industry thrived. For-profit colleges began offering medical coding degrees, and required internships soon followed. There are three different alphanumeric coding languages—CPT, HCPCS (Healthcare Common Procedure Coding System), and ICD—and each is as different from the other as Chinese is from Russian and Russian is from French. As a result, different degree tracks were necessary, along with professional exams, certifications, and licensure offered by competing professional organizations.

At these professional schools, students spend six months learning about anatomy, physiology, and pharmacology before the language training begins; "coding concepts" are taught by major disease category. Highly skilled coders have contributed to higher costs for patients, because the salaries of this new layer of professionals and their years of education are reflected in our medical bills.

The international ICD system has created codes for novel diseases— Lyme disease, AIDS, and SARS—as well as for conditions like obesity, which was not considered a disease state until 2013. Until obesity was labeled a disease and had codes assigned to it, insurers in the United States could not be obligated to pay for its treatment as a medical condition. Because, in the United States, codes define not just disease states but also the procedures and treatments that the medical profession can sell, providers, insurers, and regulators lobby for and fight over each code rule and revision. Having your code as part of the lexicon matters.

In 1996, Medicare's National Correct Coding Initiative made it clear that certain CPT codes couldn't appear on the same bill because they were inherently part of the same procedure. (While ICD codes indicate diagnoses, CPT codes indicate medical services.) As a rule, an anesthesiologist could not, for example, separately bill for anesthesia and checking your oxygen level during your surgery. One subsumed the other. But the government created modifier 59—a code that could be appended to other codes to allow doctors to take exceptions to that rule in rare cases. Modifier 59 could be deployed to allow for two payments in certain situations, such as when an oncology nurse needed to insert two separate IVs—one to administer chemotherapy and another because the patient appeared to be dehydrated.

And the games began.

An investigation by the HHS OIG in 2005 found massive evidence of modifier 59 abuse. Forty percent of code pairs billed with modifier 59 in 2003 weren't kosher, resulting in $59 million in overpayment. The OIG explained that "most of these services were not distinct because they were performed at the same session, same anatomical site, and/or through the same incision as the primary service." It promised a "Medicare Learning Network (MLN) Matters" alert to clarify how to appropriately bill modifier 59.

Instead of resolving the problem, such attempts at clarification simply created a secondary business of even more advanced coding consultants, who advised other coders as well as healthcare providers and taught courses that covered the nitty-gritty of insurers' reimbursement policies. For example, an ER doctor learned that insurers would accept a better-reimbursed code for the examination and treatment of a patient with a finger fracture (usually 99282) if a narcotic painkiller was prescribed (bump up to 99283).

With that type of guidance, some surgeons stopped suturing wounds shut after their operations and instead handed off to another doctor, say, a plastic surgeon, who could therefore code and charge separately.

Coders became so fluent in a particular language that they would specialize in particular disciplines—joint replacement or ophthalmology or interventional radiology, for example. Some, like Riva Lee Asbell, an ophthalmology coder, even received academic appointments: she has served as a clinical assistant professor of surgery (ophthalmology) at the University of Medicine and Dentistry of New Jersey, Robert Wood Johnson Medical School at Camden, as well as a member of the American Society of Ophthalmic Administrators and the Association of University Professors of Ophthalmology—Administrators' Section (past president).

Coding debates often eclipsed medical controversies about optimal treatment. In April 2015 the Business of Spine, a coding consultancy that serves spinal surgeons, issued an urgent "Coding Alert": Medicare had just issued a new set of modifying codes to modify modifier 59 for 2015 that it expected doctors to use. Modifier XP, for example, meant a part of a procedure that was distinct and could be separately billed "because it was performed by a different practitioner." Companies like 3M began selling encoder programs to help coders track the latest shifts and optimize payment. Coders often work off-site, even from home, with no knowledge of what actually occurred in the surgical suite or at the patient's bedside. They make many assumptions. Thomas Goetz of San Francisco, cofounder of Iodine, a company that uses digital tools to provide patients with information about their medicines, discovered a charge on his newborn's hospital bill for a circumcision his son never had.

The latest iteration of international disease codes, ICD-10, was completed in 1992 and has been used by the rest of the world for decades. Why did it take the United States until 2015 to fully deploy it? The problem was that the United States' medical billing system, and how to game it, evolved based on ICD-9. Changing to the new system, which identifies medical conditions more specifically using new numerical codes, was good for international epidemiology—but terrible for the business of American medicine.

Physicians' groups mocked the new system, noting that it contained codes like W56.22, "struck by Orca"; or V91.07, "burn due to water-skis on fire"; or W55.21, "bitten by cow." (Remember, in most of the world this is primarily a scientific system for tracking disease, injuries, and deaths; codes were unconnected to practice and finance.) Because adopting the new system in the United States would require new billing software and require every coder to go back to class, the medical industry convinced Medicare to delay adopting ICD-10 year after year. Doctors' groups warned that switching to the new system would lead to a "catastrophic" number of "unpaid Medicare claims."

When it finally came into use—uneventfully—in late 2015, it created some headaches for doctors and a burst of new business for coding consultants.

The Verifiers and Certifiers

In 2014 Dr. Richard Hayes, a Manhattan cardiologist, decided to leave the private practice of medicine. In solo practice for over two decades, he had found himself dealing with twenty-one different insurers, each of which is an umbrella for a host of plans with different benefits and rules.

Because he was affiliated with NYU, he was eligible to join its independent physicians' association, the University Physician Network (UPN), for $1,500 a year, which negotiated rates with each plan and kept track of insurers' procedures for getting paid. To keep up with coding in his corner of medicine, Dr. Hayes had to take seminars from UPN as well as courses from E/M University, which offers special classes tailored to physicians. As federal rules required medical offices to become more digital, he transferred to an electronic medical record system known as Practice Fusion (there are many others), which he also used for electronic prescriptions (e-prescribe). To make sure a patient was currently covered by an insurance plan that he accepted, he sometimes used an online service called Availity.

Though tech savvy, he was struggling. "I have to check if we participate. I have to check if we're on the panel. Then you have to figure out if a particular procedure is covered and if you need authorization." He got frequent bulletins from the UPN regarding the comings and goings of different insurance products. Since the memos are confidential, Dr. Hayes wouldn't share, but another doctor I know in the group showed me the kind of perplexing notices he received: "You must terminate your Oxford Liberty participation—it will terminate your Liberty Products, but not impact your Oxford Freedom or United commercial participation."

When I visited his office in 2014, Dr. Hayes needed to get precertification, also called prior authorization, for a nuclear medicine stress test (CPT code 78452) for a patient covered by a Blue Cross Blue Shield plan. His patient, a man with heart disease, diabetes, high cholesterol, and new chest pain, clearly needed the test. But Dr. Hayes's office manager was not proving that to the insurer itself, but instead to a proxy company called CareCore National. Like most insurers, the plan had farmed out precertification to a contractor/middleman, who might work "for free"—but is compensated by keeping a portion of the money "saved" by making getting a test really difficult or denying care outright. That's how such firms make the business case for their services.

The original intent of precertification when it arrived in the 1990s was to review a small number of really expensive procedures and determine whether they were truly needed. Because precertification has become such a vibrant business in and of itself over the years—and remains a great way for insurers to save money—the requirement for precertification has trickled down to the most trivial medical needs. When Dr. Barry Lindenberg, another New York cardiologist, received a form requesting prior authorization for a patient's refill of an old generic heart medicine, he faxed back "ARE YOU KIDDING ME?"

The chain of for-profit businesses now involved in precertification magnifies the basic indignity and the errors made. As Dr. Hayes's office manager tried to get approval for the nuclear medicine stress test, the insurer's Web site said Dr. Hayes was in the Blue Cross network, but CareCore said he was not. Dr. Hayes himself had to get on the phone to request a peer-to-peer review with a CareCore doctor. After more than a half hour of waiting, and relaying a dozen pieces of information (patient's name, test code, provider's code, facility or doctor's office, diagnosis of chest pain, electrocardiogram finding, lab tests, ICD code, and more), the office manager got approval for an hour-long test, for which Dr. Hayes would be paid anywhere from $600 to $1,200. These wasteful bureaucratic processes have been a lucrative job creator for the business of healthcare. They also siphon hours away from what patients want from their doctor and what good doctors want to provide: human contact.

Patient Advocates: On Your Side?

Until a few years ago, Southwestern University in Georgetown, Texas, arranged for its employees' insurance through a local insurance broker. But as healthcare in central Texas became more complicated, with much of it joining the expanding empire of Baylor Scott & White Health, Southwestern hired Arthur J. Gallagher & Co., a national consultant, to help design and bid out its health insurance plans. It also hired Compass Professional Health Services to provide patient advocates for its employees, paying about $50 a head.

By sifting through prior insurance claims and using proprietary algorithms, Compass estimates local prices for procedures and treatments, in order to advise Southwestern employees about where to go for reasonably priced care. Employees can send Compass a list of their medications to review to see if something cheaper would suffice. Compass will review hospital bills, help patients understand them, and assist in fighting overcharges.

Employers hire services like Compass (or its large competitors Castlight Health and Change Healthcare) because such companies promise that the investment of, say, $50 charged per head can save them money on the average patient, without harming quality. Compass says that it has saved its clients $375 million as of late 2016. (But when Steven Davidson, a professor who was on Southwestern University's budget committee, asked Compass for a statement to see how much money was actually being saved, the request was refused.)

Patients, however, are often not the only, or even the primary, customers of such "trusted" guides. Many companies that advocate for patients also make good business by providing price information to hospitals, doctors, and insurers, who want to know how much their competitors are receiving for medical encounters, after negotiations. Companies that promote healthcare price transparency generally start by collecting claims, either purchasing huge claims databases from other companies that own them or crowdsourcing prices in some way. Each employer that hires a company for "patient advocacy" or transparency provides a cache of insurance claims, which help determine what prices are achievable in an area.

Mr. Davidson said that some employees had found the services useful in a health system where prices are often obscured. When he needed an

MRI before the university hired Compass, he had been unable to get a price quote from local radiology centers, even with the help of his orthopedist; he ended up paying $3,000, and only later discovered another provider would have charged $1,200. But he was frustrated that Compass wouldn't just provide employees with price lists and the patient contributions at various local providers, especially for common items like vaccines and scans.

There is, perhaps, one important reason why: because afterward, Southwestern and its employees would have less need for Compass.

8

THE AGE OF RESEARCH AND GOOD WORKS FOR PROFIT: THE PERVERSION OF A NOBLE ENTERPRISE

The Web site called on supporters to help raise $25.2 million through donations and fund-raisers to underwrite a clinical trial being run by a research group at Massachusetts General Hospital, one of America's preeminent academic institutions. The request was from Dr. Denise Faustman, a tenured professor at Harvard Medical School for a quarter century, who has been researching a potential cure for type 1 diabetes, with promising results. Dr. Faustman's cure could be a game changer, preventing disability—and saving a huge amount of money in the process. But few of the usual funders of medical research wanted to pay for her work, not even some of the major foundations dedicated to diabetes research. There will be no commercial profit if she succeeds.

Dr. Faustman began researching diabetes in the late 1980s, at a time when transplant surgery was revolutionizing medicine. She joined a team that was transplanting insulin-producing cells into diabetics. Their efforts failed. The experience sent Dr. Faustman on a decadelong detour into basic science, funded largely by government grants, to develop a more precise understanding of the cell types and errant immune pathways involved in the genesis of type 1 diabetes.

She concluded that the pathway error might be fixed with an immune modulator called tumor necrosis factor (TNF), which was known to also be involved in the body's natural defense against cancers. While clinical studies in the 1980s had determined that TNF was too toxic to give directly to patients, there was fortunately already a drug on the market that stimulated its production: bacillus Calmette-Guérin (BCG), a vaccine against tuberculosis that was so old it had long been generic. It was very safe.

Dr. Faustman discovered that BCG was powerful enough to reverse established type 1 diabetes in genetically predisposed mice. More exciting still, she found that mice with diabetes of long duration would start producing insulin once again after treatment with BCG. The results were heralded as thrilling and widely circulated when published in 2001, but further testing was obviously needed with human trials. "When we first discovered this, we went to pharma and they said, 'It's really interesting but we've got a problem: Tell us how it will ever make us money?'" she recently recalled. "'You're working with a generic drug.'" (See **Rule 2: A lifetime of treatment is preferable to a cure.**)

From the manufacturers' standpoint, if diabetes could be cured there would be no need for insulin, pumps, and monitors, all lucrative products. If it worked, it would ruin their business, which is why they suggested that she turn to philanthropy.

Unfortunately, JDRF (formerly the Juvenile Diabetes Research Foundation), the world's biggest charity devoted to diabetes, which spends more than $100 million a year on research, has also consistently rejected her requests to help fund BCG trials. She has also been turned down by the largest private foundation funder, the Helmsley Charitable Trust. (The Iacocca Family Foundation chipped in, but fully funding the project was beyond its means.) The problem is that many charitable foundations no longer see themselves as funders of research for knowledge propelled by donor dollars to cure a disease, but instead as investors in new treatments. BCG had been used for so many decades in generic form that there was no way to make money selling the drug. "Now they all want equity in the product and a product that will give back," Dr. Faustman said.

Ten years ago, Dr. Faustman—with the support of Lee Iacocca and a dedicated band of volunteers—raised $9 million to fund a Phase I "proof of concept" trial, which suggested that even people with long-standing diabetes had started to make some insulin after receiving BCG. When her results were published in 2012, interest in BCG spiked. Studies by research groups in Italy and Turkey lent support to the finding. A group at the National Institutes of Health looked at its use against a glandular disorder called Sjögren's syndrome.

Now she's crowdsourcing the estimated $25 million+ needed for a larger trial on her lab's Web site. "Donate Today!" "Host a Special Event or Fundraiser!" "Sign up for our e-mail updates and newsletter!" She noted: "Before the age of Facebook and Twitter, I couldn't have done this." The trial got under way in 2015.

A New Model: The Changing Vision of Medical Charity

After Frederick Banting and his colleagues discovered and isolated insulin in the early 1920s, they licensed the patent for only a dollar as "a gift to humanity." Type 1 diabetes, which had previously killed children only months after onset, was suddenly transformed into a chronic disease. To this day insulin is the alpha and omega of type 1 diabetes treatment.

Disease-specific charitable foundations emerged in the early twentieth century to fund basic research. The March of Dimes, focused on polio, raised money from hundreds of thousands of donors who paid much of the cost of developing both the Salk and the Sabin vaccines. The foundation never sought to make money from either inoculation. After World War II the Cystic Fibrosis Foundation (established in 1955) supported the scientists who identified the defective gene for that disorder. The National Multiple Sclerosis Society (founded in 1946) funded the Columbia University scientist who discovered the abnormal spinal fluid proteins associated with the disease. The Juvenile Diabetes Research Foundation was founded in 1970 by the parents of diabetic children to promote research into a cure, bemoaning the slow pace of the older, established American Diabetes Association.

Through the 1990s, these foundations and their patients often held the increasingly prosperous U.S. pharmaceutical and device industries at arm's length. Groups like ACT UP, activists for AIDS treatment, saw drugmakers as adversaries. But in recent years, patient disease groups and pharma have found common ground, as the industry wooed disease foundations and their members with corporate money, by sponsoring patient conferences and retreats and underwriting support groups and newsletters. It taught patients how to blog and hired them as disease spokespeople or "ambassadors."

In 2015 hundreds of kids with type 1 diabetes and their families convened at the Children with Diabetes Foundation's weeklong Friends for Life meeting, at Disney World in Orlando, Florida. It is a joyous and useful annual event for the participants. The kids go to dances and visit the amusement park. Parents and grandparents attend lectures about managing the disease and new treatment developments. Academics and manufacturers recruit kids for clinical trials. At a booth in the exhibition hall, kids earn beach balls or tattoos for answering a simple question on a white board: "What Is Your Wish for the Future of Diabetes?" The words are mostly all the same: "A Cure." But almost all of the dozens of exhibitors and sponsors who help underwrite the conference are focused on something else: selling ever-costlier treatments and supplies.

In the past quarter century, Banting's noble discovery of insulin has been used for profit by manufacturers who sell lucrative insulin modifications and treatment devices, with a hefty bump in cost for each innovation: Simple syringes have been replaced by penlike injectors, which in turn have been supplanted by tiny pumps that clip to a belt and contain tiny catheters to deliver insulin under the skin. Instead of measuring blood sugar levels by pricking a finger, new monitors that sit flush on the skin give patients an accurate moment-by-moment readout. Many of these advances allow people with type 1 diabetes to live a fuller, active life. But, for their price, some are not all that helpful.

Moreover, between 2010 and 2015, the cost of insulin and other products used to manage diabetes skyrocketed, despite few significant advances in treatment. The recommended wholesale price of different forms of insulin rose between 127 and 325 percent. The monthly wholesale price of Humulin, the most popular insulin, has risen to nearly $1,100, up from $258 for the average patient between 2012 and 2015. (See **Rule 4: As technologies age, prices can rise rather than fall.**)

Co-payments for expensive pumps and meters and test strips add up to thousands, often tens of thousands, of dollars a year. "It looks like a beeper," said Catherine Hayley of Memphis, a thirty-six-year-old diabetic whom I got to know during my reporting in 2014, describing the pump on the waistband of her jeans. "It's made of plastic and runs on triple-A batteries, but it's the most expensive thing I own, aside from my house."

The Invention of
Venture Philanthropy

The mind-set and mission of many disease foundations underwent a sea change in 2014, when the Cystic Fibrosis Foundation (CFF) received a

$3.3 billion windfall as the result of its decision to invest over the years in a small Massachusetts biotech firm. A total of $150 million invested in Vertex Pharmaceuticals ultimately helped produce Kalydeco, the first blockbuster drug against cystic fibrosis (CF), which was approved by the FDA in 2012. Two years later, the foundation sold its rights to drug royalties to a venture capital firm and received over $3 billion in an instant, about thirty times the amount the foundation had typically raised in a year.

Suddenly foundations had an enticing new business model: "venture philanthropy"; that is, investing money in drug, device, and biotech companies with the expectation of financial return. From the very start of the arrangement the folks at Harvard Business School were unsettled: "How could the board of Vertex and the CFF fundamentally align the objectives of a for-profit company with those of a non-profit institution?" How would the arrangement impact actual patients and prices for the new drugs? Through such investments, medical foundations would be reaping corporate profits, albeit indirectly.

Kalydeco attacked a biochemical defect underlying cystic fibrosis, which causes the lungs and other organs to clog up with thick secretions, leading to repeat hospitalizations and early death. Vertex set a high price on its discovery: $300,000 per year, which twenty-nine prominent CF experts immediately branded "unconscionable." Venture philanthropy had successfully propelled the innovation, but there was mixed motivation to make sure it was affordable, because the CFF gained royalties on sales. John LaMattina, a longtime pharmaceutical executive, said that the foundation's no-strings-attached deal surprised him, and wondered why there were no "price restrictions for these new medicines." Robert J. Beall, the chief executive of the Cystic Fibrosis Foundation at the time, said that he had "expressed concern" to Vertex over the price, but did not control it. Mr. Beall was paid $1.1 million a year.

For Vertex and its investors, Kalydeco was the beginning of unalloyed success, even though it was approved for use in only the 4 percent of patients with CF who had a particular gene mutation, a rather circumscribed market. In 2015 Vertex sought approval for another drug, Orkambi, which combined the active ingredient of Kalydeco with another closely related medicine. The company said that its studies indicated that the combination would be useful for about half of all patients with CF. The data did not entirely convince FDA statisticians: Vertex had tested the combination drug against a placebo. It improved lung function by only about 3 percent, not really that impressive or statistically different from Kalydeco's effects, they noted. But Orkambi was approved anyway and the familiar drill ensued: Vertex supplied patients to testify, and they pleaded with the committee to endorse the drug. "While on paper, Orkambi may not have given me drastic improvement in lung function, I'm here to tell you under no uncertain terms this drug has saved my life," said thirty-six-year-old Jeff Masters of Ann Arbor, Michigan, who noted that he was now running 5K races. The committee had little choice: Orkambi was "safe and effective."

The *Boston Globe* noted that Vertex, which "moved from Cambridge to a new $800 million campus on Boston's Fan Pier [in 2014], has become one of the state's largest biotechs, with a market value of more than $30 billion—despite having lost money in all but one of its 26 years. The new drug regimen is expected to help provide more than $53 million for a dozen Vertex senior executives who were granted one-time bonuses."

As other disease foundations pivoted toward the venture philanthropy financing model, a new breed of medical foundation executives took over. Fund-raising rather than curing disease often seemed like the first metric of success.

In 2010 JDRF appointed Jeffrey Brewer, a technology entrepreneur and philanthropist whose son has diabetes, as its CEO. Its new executive vice president, Dr. David Wheadon, was a psychiatrist whose previous job had been as a vice president at the Pharmaceutical Research and Manufacturers of America. The foundation undertook an official "rebranding" campaign "to more accurately represent its work": its founding purpose had been to find a cure for type 1 diabetes, but the new mission was "not only toward curing, but also toward treating and preventing T1D." In 2012 the foundation appointed its first director of research investment opportunities. "The purpose of the organization shifted from collaborating with academia to collaborating with industry," a former official of the organization who left around that time told me.

By 2015 JDRF had twenty-eight industry partners listed on its Web site. It had given Medtronic $17 million to develop a glucose sensor, partnered with Tandem Diabetes Care to make a new dual chamber pump, and invested $4.3 million in BD, a New Jersey–based medical device manufacturer, to fund projects like creating smaller needles that reduced pain. In late 2013 JDRF announced that it was "going the equity route," joining with PureTech Ventures, a for-profit venture capital firm, to create a fund to fuel new diabetes start-ups.

With only about thirty thousand sufferers in the United States, cystic fibrosis is an extremely rare disease. By investing in a tiny drug company with few assets to make a novel drug that no one was certain would work, CFF had provided support for an exceptionally high-risk undertaking. But type 1 diabetes affects millions. Medtronic—the most profitable device maker in the world—doesn't need a few million from JDRF to come up with serial improvements on its glucose pumps and monitors. But by sharing in the profits, the foundation has little incentive to advocate for more affordable prices.

By 2013 JDRF research grants hit a ten-year low, down 30 percent since 2008, while nonresearch grants increased. Dr. Faustman's work didn't make the cut.

"If the March of Dimes was operating according to today's foundation models, we'd have iron lungs in five different colors controlled by iPhone apps, but we wouldn't have a cheap polio vaccine," said Dr. Michael

Brownlee, the Anita and Jack Saltz Chair in Diabetes Research Emeritus at the Albert Einstein College of Medicine in the Bronx, a JDRF critic who himself has type 1 diabetes. Today, every piece of good work in medicine, it seems, needs a promising business model.

A Bible with Ads

Every year for almost a century, to ensure his or her knowledge of prescribing drugs was current, nearly every doctor got a new *Physicians' Desk Reference (PDR)*. The *PDR* cataloged doses, side effects, half-lives, interactions, chemical structures, and results of clinical trials for all approved medicines.

The advent of the Internet and the acceleration of pharmaceutical marketing posed great challenges for the venerable bible of prescribing, which was published by a company called Medical Economics and underwritten in large part by drug manufacturers. The publication had been sold at a reasonable price and its distribution to doctors was a kind of public service. It was ad-free, with the straightforward mission of providing doctors with accurate, up-to-date information that would get the right medicines to patients who needed them.

In 2012 Medical Economics hired Stephen G. Buck, a Silicon Valley entrepreneur and healthcare executive with a background in pharmaceuticals, as its senior vice president of strategy and innovation, to help usher the *PDR* into the digital age. "It didn't have the skill set to make the transition," he said.

Drugmakers had also become extremely ambivalent about the *PDR* in the previous decade, with its dry, objective information. With all the new promotional tools at their disposal, manufacturers themselves could go directly to doctors and patients and offer information in much sexier (if not always as accurate) packages.

Sophisticated new business ventures offered pharmaceutical manufacturers new opportunities to influence doctors: On some popular electronic medical office software, physicians were peppered with drug company advertising and promotion as they prepared to write prescriptions. Physicians tolerated the electronic incursion of marketing and drug coupons into their office software because it subsidized their government-mandated conversion to electronic records and e-prescribing, which could cost tens of thousands of dollars. One version of Practice Fusion, a software package designed to appeal to small practices, was totally free.

Mr. Buck thought that the *PDR* could survive by incorporating into its program the price of a pharmaceutical product when purchased through insurance and the exact patient co-pay. The entry for a medicine could provide a list of similar drugs and their prices in patients' zip codes, allowing their doctors to choose the cheapest alternative. "*PDR* had a great footprint in electronic medical records for safety information," said Mr. Buck. "What if we added the price? We felt that would drive a lot of interest."

Some prescribing programs were touting price transparency, but the information was vague and not "actionable," Mr. Buck pointed out, meaning not specific enough to allow a patient to make a different purchase. Surescripts, an e-prescribing network, for example, lists drugs in three colors: red, green, and white. Red means it's really expensive (How much? Compared with what?). Green means there's a lower-cost alternative (but gives no indication of what it might be or where to buy it). White means a good choice.

When trying to gather information to integrate real price information into the *PDR*, Mr. Buck hit a wall: all the parties in the pharmaceutical supply chain knew exactly how much they were paying, but no one was willing to give him their data. "The pharmacy benefit managers, the pharmacies, the drug companies, the insurers all have a vested interest in keeping this secret," said Mr. Buck.

Mr. Buck was soon out of a job. In 2014 Lee Equity Partners, a New

Jersey firm that had a majority stake in PDR Network, merged it with the LDM Group, a leading pharmaceutical marketing company, and put the latter's executives in charge. Instead of surviving by helping doctors and patients embrace price transparency, the *PDR*'s future would depend on drug advertising, "providing the right messages at the right time to prescribers, *supporting pharmacy marketers, payers and others*" (emphasis mine). A little more than a year later, Lee Equity sold the *PDR* to the private equity firm Genstar Capital and its affiliate, PSKW, a company that distributes co-pay cards supplied by pharmaceutical manufacturers.

For nearly a century the *PDR* name had been "synonymous with credible, comprehensive drug information for prescribers." From now on that trusted brand will be deployed in the service of drug marketing and promotion.

In the Service of Medicine— and Money

In 2014 a luxurious three-bedroom, 2,600-square-foot condominium at the Ayer Building in downtown Philadelphia was put up for sale for just under $2 million.

The owner of this property was the foundation of the American Board of Internal Medicine (ABIM), an offshoot of the nonprofit back-office group whose official task is certifying medical doctors.

In 1998 the American Board of Internal Medicine declared $17 million in revenue. By 2015 its revenues had increased to $58 million, almost all of it earned by testing and certifying physicians. Each year, a hefty chunk of that revenue was passed on to its affiliate, the ABIM Foundation (the condo's owner), a nonprofit foundation that the nonprofit ABIM created around 2000 to promote "medical professionalism." It has become common in the world of healthcare that nonprofit hospitals and medical societies set up secondary nonprofit foundations. These foundations sometimes do good works: the ABIM Foundation initiated a campaign called "Choosing Wisely" to encourage doctors to be more judicious in their use of expensive and unneeded medical interventions. But they often seem like outposts for vanity projects or just places to keep cash.

The officers of the ABIM and the officers of its foundation were the same, and received salaries from both organizations. The exact details of how the money is earned and spent are opaque, said Charles Kroll, a forensic accountant who investigated the links, because the two Philadelphia-based nonprofits were long curiously reported by both organizations as domiciled in Iowa, "which does not require submission to the state not-for-profit board, nor public access, to the audited financial statements of either organization," he said. (Shortly after Mr. Kroll began his investigations and posting results on the Web, the foundation officially changed its domicile to Pennsylvania.)

By 2013 the ABIM Foundation had funds on hand of $76 million, almost all of it passed along from its parent. The lux condo was an investment property of the foundation, officially used for purposes like housing visiting officers of the ABIM and an IT team from India as well as communications meetings, ABIM officers told Dr. Westby Fisher, a physician blogger who has been a frequent critic of the organization.

In fact, many physicians had become suspicious of the ABIM though it was headed by Dr. Christine Cassel, a highly respected geriatrician and one of the doyennes of American medicine. Charged with organizing periodic recertification to make sure doctors stay current, the ABIM was requiring more and more testing, as well as the completion of online modules, courses, and "maintenance of certification" programs, charging high prices for all of it. "Lifelong learning and education are what I love about medicine, but that's not really what ABIM is about anymore," said Dr. Christopher Dibble, who practices cardiology in upstate New York, noting that primary care modules could cost $1,500 and specialist modules $2,500.

In addition, doctors needed to accumulate one hundred credits of learning each year by doing ABIM courses or attending ABIM-approved conferences in order to receive bonus payments from Medicare; many hospitals require the ABIM's "maintenance of certification" seal of approval for admitting privileges. Dr. Dibble said that conferences and webinars not approved by the ABIM don't count toward the total. "It's a conflict of interest and feels like extortion," he added. When a prominent California cardiologist started an online petition against the ABIM's "onerous" and "expensive" requirements, ten thousand physicians rapidly signed on.

With a little sleuthing, Mr. Kroll discovered one reason this apparently rich organization might be so aggressively raising its demands on doctors and its fees. The lavish spending habits of the ABIM and its executives had in fact left the organization tens of millions of dollars in debt. It had been counting doctors' payments for future modules as income before they'd even taken the tests. It was a kind of testing Ponzi scheme: the ABIM had to keep adding evaluations and raising fees to break even, said Mr. Kroll, the forensic accountant.

In early 2015, after Dr. Cassel left the ABIM to take another job, the new president and CEO, Dr. Richard Baron, issued an apology to doctors and said that the organization was rethinking its certification programs and would hold fees at 2014 levels for several years; he also suspended the requirement to complete some modules. Increasing the heat, in June 2016, at a forum sponsored by the Pennsylvania Medical Society held at the American Medical Association's annual House of Delegates meeting, Dr. Westby Fisher recommended that the ABIM Foundation be shut down.

Around the same time, the $2.3 million condominium was sold at a big loss for $1,650,000.

Entering the Gilded Age

But if real estate is a proxy for the financial trajectory that American medicine has traversed over the last quarter century, there is perhaps no better symbol than 330 North Wabash Avenue, Chicago, Illinois. A fifty-two-story Ludwig Mies van der Rohe tower with sweeping views of Lake Michigan, this architectural landmark and engineering feat was built for IBM in 1972 and was for decades a corporate headquarters.

Eventually IBM moved, and in 2010 Langham Hotels took over the lower eleven floors to create a luxury five-star hotel. At the end of 2011, management announced that it would rename the building after a new prime tenant that was moving its entire workforce into 330 North Wabash: AMA Plaza, in honor of the American Medical Association.

The American Medical Association was founded in Philadelphia by 250 doctors in 1847 with stated goals like "scientific advancement, standards for medical education, launching a program of medical ethics, improved public health." The AMA has long pursued other interests, of course, artfully representing the profession in politics. In 1962 Milton Friedman called the AMA "the strongest trade union in the United States," which restricted competition, for example, by controlling the numbers of medical schools and training slots, as well as filing suits to circumscribe the ability of nurses and osteopaths to practice.

But traditionally, the AMA's scientific and professional activities were also central to its identity. It published the *Journal of the American Medical Association*, which is still the most widely circulated weekly general medicine journal in the world. It publicly weighed in on medical causes: in 1985 it helped create history by urging Congress to take widespread action against cigarettes, including eliminating federal price supports for tobacco farmers and increasing taxes on tobacco. For years, most doctors joined the AMA, paying dues to get the journals and in solidarity with their comrades.

But by the late 1990s, as the solidarity within the profession—and membership—waned, the AMA was trying on more commercial models. In 1998 it signed a deal with Sunbeam to put its logo on the company's medical devices in exchange for cash and the privilege of including AMA literature in packaging. The deal was abandoned only after it was condemned by an ethics task force, which opined at the time: "As a professional association the AMA is not and cannot function as a profit-maximizing business interested in perpetual growth."

But just fifteen years later the AMA is a multiheaded hydra that is, in many respects, as much a diversified corporation as a nonprofit professional group. Only 25 percent of doctors join. Between 2002 and 2011 membership dropped from nearly 278,000 to 217,000, although it is now ticking up again.

While it still formulates policy that concerns all types of physicians, such as whether to support the Affordable Care Act (it did), the AMA no longer relies on dues or advertising in journals for income. It now has "seven, eight, nine different revenue streams," the most lucrative of which involve business, Dr. James Madara, the AMA's current CEO, told me when I visited its pin-drop-silent headquarters filled with expensive art and breathtaking views of Lake Michigan (and a Trump Hotel), which most resembles a first-class airport lounge.

Most notably the AMA owns the copyright for those CPT codes, which are essential for billing. It sells books of the code to doctors, hospitals, and researchers. It requires companies that use the codes in their products—such as collection agencies—to pay royalties and licensing fees. It derives money and power from that ownership. The AMA's seventeen-member CPT editorial panel must decide to create a CPT code for any new procedure or interaction between doctors and patients before it can be billed.

Though the AMA set up guidelines about corporate relationships after the Sunbeam fiasco, that deal now seems in some ways just ahead of its time. The AMA has now formed many business ventures. It has an alliance with TransWorld Systems, a billing and collection agency that "offers today's medical practices the opportunity to increase their revenue on unpaid insurance claims and overdue patient balances." It has tried its hand at developing smartphone applications targeting weight loss and compliance with taking medicine, for example. It has what Dr. Madara called "a relationship" with Matter, a tech incubator that funds seventy companies in healthcare.

The AMA Foundation is today supported by a Corporate Roundtable, "a group of key stakeholders," who meet with the AMA to discuss their shared "commitment to public health in America." Its platinum, gold, and silver members are all from the pharmaceutical or healthcare industry.

The AMA spends over $20 million on lobbying each year. In the first three months of 2015 it ranked third in spending on lobbying in the United States, after the Chamber of Commerce and the National Association of Realtors. Its political action committee (AMPAC) contributes millions to campaigns and holds workshops for physicians who aspire to political office.

The AMA's primary focus in the past ten to fifteen years has been medical finance—filing lawsuits against insurers over how to calculate "usual, customary and reasonable" and opposing Medicare's public release of payments to physicians, for example. Its biggest single lobbying effort has been the two-decades-long fight against the sustainable growth rate, the government proposal to cut physician payments; each year it averted enactment with its so-called doc fix.

It's hard to imagine today's AMA spearheading an all-out assault on the tobacco industry, for example. One gold member of its Corporate Roundtable is Walgreens, which has refused to stop selling cigarettes even after other giant drugstore chains, notably CVS, have done so as a matter of principle. Still, now that the need for the annual doc fix is history, the AMA seems once again a bit more socially inclined, working on programs to prevent type 2 diabetes, for example, as well as speaking out against pharmaceutical advertising, which it says promotes useless, expensive treatments.

Turf Battles and Trade Wars: Medical Societies Form Super PACs

A big part of the reason why AMA membership has dwindled is that there are now so many separate specialized medical groups, each spending prolifically to promote its particular interests. Collectively, the medical industry has become the country's biggest lobbying force, spending nearly half a billion dollars each year. In 2015 the oil and gas industry spent $130 million, securities and investment firms about $100 million, and the defense/aerospace industry a mere $75 million.

Specialty medical societies are rich. Though many are less than fifteen years old, some of the specialty PACs now give as much or more money to candidates than AMPAC. There is RADPAC (radiologists), BrainPAC (neurologists), the Orthopaedic PAC, ACC PAC (cardiologists), FamMed-PAC (family medicine), SkinPAC (dermatology), NEMPAC (emergency medicine), and more. The Orthopaedic PAC raised more than $3 million in the 2009–10 election cycle, from more than 4,500 contributors.

The American College of Radiology's RADPAC, one of the largest, spends close to $4 million annually. The American College of Radiology changed its tax status from 501(c)(3) (a charity) to 501(c)(6) (a nonprofit business league) in 2002 so it and its members could more directly make political contributions. The goal of such groups "is toward the betterment of business conditions for a particular trade or community. Contributions to 501(c)(6)'s are not deductible as charitable contributions, but they may be deductible as a trade or business expense."

In the face of cost-cutting healthcare reform, and realizing that doctors were fighting the forces of big business, medical societies started becoming much more aggressive about knocking on politicians' doors. "The societies recognized that the hospitals and pharma were spending a lot on the Hill and we wanted to be the person the congressman turns to when they have a question about a bill," said Dr. Alexandra Page, an orthopedist in San Diego, who is chair of the American Academy of Orthopaedic Surgeons Health Care Systems Committee.

But the efforts were not always noble. Anesthesiologists have fought successfully to have the label for the sedating drug propofol state that it must be administered only by "persons trained in the administration of general anesthesia." Meanwhile, gastroenterologists have argued and lobbied ferociously to get that label restriction removed, noting that nurses working under their supervision could do the job as well.

At the state level, medical societies and *their* PACs have pushed "scope of practice" laws, regulations that define what type of professional may do what kind of work. Doctors fought to prevent drugstores from giving shots other than influenza vaccines. They required schools that stock epinephrine pens to follow protocols developed by a hired physician. In 2007 the North Carolina State Board of Dental Examiners wrote a cease and desist order to salons and spas offering teeth whitening using peroxide preparations, accusing them of the unlicensed practice of dentistry and asserting they could be subject to criminal penalties. What was good for patients often seemed to be an afterthought.

It seemed like a shoo-in when Illinois state representative Daniel Burke proposed a bill in 2012 requiring physicians to inform patients whether they were in a patient's insurance network before rendering treatment to avoid surprise out-of-network charges. It didn't pass. A parade of doctors, called into action by the Illinois State Medical Society, blocked the legislation, testifying that it would burden office staff and "could harm patients as care would often times have to be delayed."

In the same legislative session, the Illinois State Medical Society helped defeat acts that would allow physical therapists to treat patients without a doctor's referral and psychologists to prescribe medicine, as well as another that would effectively protect physicians from enhanced scrutiny for Medicaid fraud. On the other hand, the society successfully championed legislation allowing doctors to supervise up to five full-time physician assistants and bill as if they delivered the care themselves. A doctor in Illinois can now be in six places at once.

Who Writes the Guidelines?

Dr. Scott Norton, a distinguished academic dermatologist who had spent years as chief of dermatology at the Walter Reed National Military Medical Center and with the National Institutes of Health, was eager to serve on a panel convened by the American Academy of Dermatology and other professional dermatology societies in 2012 to evaluate the appropriate use of Mohs surgery, one of his specialty's most expensive treatments. In the last decade, Mohs surgery, one of many procedures to remove benign skin cancers, has occupied the number one spot on Medicare's list of "potentially misvalued" CPT codes. (Medicare considers it a red flag if use of a procedure increases dramatically, an indication that it is reimbursed at too high a rate.)

Mohs surgery, developed in 1936 by a general surgeon named Frederic Mohs, involves the sequential removal of tissue specimens from a lesion until the entire growth is gone. Mohs is used primarily to treat basal cell carcinomas, benign lesions that grow slowly and do not metastasize beyond their original location. The sequential technique can prevent disfigurement and preserve vital functions, like the closing of an eye. Most doctors agree that Mohs is advisable in such cases. But it is now deployed in a far wider set of circumstances.

The rate of use of Mohs surgery among Medicare beneficiaries in the United States grew 700 percent between 1992 and 2009, though there was little evidence to suggest in many cases that Mohs was superior to cheaper treatment options, which include scraping, snipping, or even applications of a cream to create a chemical burn. The big difference between these more pedestrian treatments and Mohs is the price tag: hundreds of dollars versus more than $10,000 or even $20,000 for Mohs. Mohs surgery is often followed by plastic surgery to correct the skin defect. (See **Rule 1: More treatment is always better. Default to the most expensive option.**)

For most benign skin tumors, "the decision to utilize MMS [Mohs Micrographic Surgery] is likely to reflect the economic advantage to the provider rather than a substantial clinical advantage for the patient," wrote Dr. Robert Stern, a Harvard dermatologist, noting that in 2012 America spent more than an estimated $2 billion on Mohs surgery, with wide variations in its use: even for sensitive locations like the face and the hands, it was used 53 percent of the time in Minnesota versus only 12 percent in New Mexico. Dr. Stern estimated that nearly 2 percent of all Medicare recipients had Mohs in that year.

The panel's mandate was to form a unified scientific expert opinion about when it was to the patient's advantage to use Mohs. Unfortunately, Dr. Norton said of the exercise: "The questions and the methodology were designed to capture the largest range and the biggest market." Dr. Norton and his colleagues on the panel were given a huge number of different scenarios—cancer type, size, and body location—and asked to rate whether Mohs could *ever* be an appropriate treatment for each on a scale of 1 to 9. Scenarios that scored in the 7 to 9 range were deemed appropriate. (Some people voted 9 on every situation but were still allowed to serve.) Many of the scenarios ending up being scored in the 3 to 7 range, but the panel was ordered to take serial votes to force a middle result into the "appropriate" or "never" end of the spectrum. Once that occurred, the vote was labeled "unanimous."

At the end of the meeting, it looked as though "we were unanimous" in about 90 percent of the situations, Dr. Norton said, adding, "A lot of us were surprised to see that many things that were quite controversial going in now looked positive and unanimous. How did that happen? It made us really uncomfortable."

The American Academy of Dermatology and the American College of Mohs Surgery then published the new guidelines in academic journals and circulated them to insurers, giving dermatologists the patina of scientific support for doing Mohs surgery on nearly anything; they could demand reimbursement. Dr. Norton felt as if he had been used: "They say, we fight to protect patients, but what they really mean is we fight to get exorbitant fees for unneeded procedures. This was not a medical issue; it was a trade issue."

Doctors who identify themselves as Mohs surgeons are paid about as much as cardiologists and general surgeons, though the average dermatologist works only thirty to forty hours a week and has no emergency cases or night calls. In 2014 both John Boehner and Nancy Pelosi got $10,000 checks from SkinPAC, and dozens got smaller amounts.

Dr. Norton's experience highlights a flaw in how we pursue evidence-based medicine. The specialists who make money from procedures create the guidelines for when and how often they should be performed. Medical societies argue that the experts are best poised to evaluate optimal treatment, but there is an obvious conflict of interest. Once a dermatologist equips his office to do Mohs surgery, his patients are more likely to get it.

Dr. Stern would like to see large randomized studies to compare Mohs with simpler procedures for relative effectiveness. But he says that is unlikely. The Mohs surgeons, who would need to participate, have little interest in proving that a cheaper treatment would suffice.

In other fields, similar guidelines have been written by specialists: Urologists suggested that all men be screened for prostate specific antigen (PSA) to detect prostate cancer, creating a huge industry for testing and surgery. Radiologists advised women to get mammograms every year. Orthopedists felt that cartilage injuries in aging knees should be treated with arthroscopy to "clean up" the joint space. Dentists tell us to get our teeth examined and cleaned every six months.

Many such recommendations have been upended: PSA screening has resulted in men's getting surgery that often leaves them incontinent or with sexual dysfunction, just to remove slow-growing prostate tumors that would never lead to problems. The test is no longer recommended for routine use by the U.S. Preventive Services Task Force. Yearly mammograms proved in many studies no better at detecting significant breast abnormalities than an every-other-year regimen, as the same task force now advises. Studies have shown that arthroscopy to shave cartilage in arthritic knees doesn't help pain.

But some specialists themselves are disturbingly wont to ignore those findings. In late 2014 the head of urology at New York's Lenox Hill Hospital, Dr. David Samadi, kicked off what he called "the Samadi Challenge," patterned after the viral "Ice Bucket Challenge." He asked women to record a video message telling "the man in their lives" to get his PSA and testosterone levels checked and then post a video of their message on the Internet. Dr. Samadi, who runs the hospital program in robotic surgery to treat prostate cancer, makes around $3 million a year.

The Samadi Challenge is at odds even with current recommendations from the American Urological Association, which advises that men should be told of the risks and benefits of the PSA test and then decide about whether to be tested, said Dr. Gerald Chodak, one of the country's leading experts in prostate cancer, who has been critical of profiteering in his field. The idea that there is a "normal" or "abnormal" level of testosterone for older men is controversial, experts say, because levels decline with age.

And some studies in the last few years have linked testosterone supplements to an increased likelihood of heart disease, prompting a new FDA review of the risk.

Many patients can't shake the idea that the one-on-one relationships with doctors that once earned the profession our respect and allegiance may no longer be medicine's driving force. When Dr. Norton's own father was dying of liver cancer several years ago, his dermatologist performed three Mohs surgeries. "I told him 'don't!'" Dr. Norton recalled, with a sigh. "But he said, 'I'm getting these calls from my doctor and he says I need it and I've been with him for twenty years.'"

9

THE AGE OF CONGLOMERATES

Susan Foley and her husband long operated Foley & Foley, a mom-and-pop law firm. In their midsixties, the couple has lived the American dream: four successful adult children and, now, a happy retirement. In 2009 Susan Foley had her knee replaced at Mills-Peninsula Medical Center just south of San Francisco. "The knee surgery was a miracle—it gave me my life back," she told me, noting that she was barely able to walk a block in the year leading up to the operation and now rides bicycles and horses.

Before the joint replacement, she had tried arthroscopic surgery, a knee brace for which her insurer paid $1,000, and an injection with a gooey fluid called Synvisc, made from chicken combs, a kind of WD-40 lubricant for human joints—costly and unsuccessful interventions that she now regards as probably unneeded and definitely overpriced. (One injection of Synvisc costs over $1,200 for the drug alone.) She had expected the bills from her surgery to be large, but what she received made no sense.

Her explanation of benefits statement from Blue Cross showed that the hospital bill alone came to $122,600 for four nights, although the insurer had negotiated it down to about $54,000, or still more than $10,000 a day. That did not include the fee for the implant, the surgeon, or the anesthesiologist. "For that I could have taken the doctors and nurses to Maui," she noted.

At her request, Mills-Peninsula sent her an itemized bill. "It says $849 for oxygen in the days after surgery. It didn't happen. $75.82 for a warming blanket. It doesn't make any sense. There were four different charges for parts of the implant though I only got one new knee." Although Blue Cross picked up the lion's share of the bill, "I did pay really because my premium is two thousand dollars a month and keeps rising. I'm angry at this system because it seems predatory." (See **Rule 9: There are no standards for billing. There's money to be made in billing for anything and everything.**)

A knee replacement is a fairly standard procedure. One big reason Sutter Health's Mills-Peninsula Medical Center is able to charge so much in what is supposedly a market-based system is consolidation. While hospitals have long been allied in loose networks, the trend has accelerated in the last five or ten years, leaving patients and companies trying to get a good price in a terrible negotiating position with the new behemoths. And Sutter Health is a grand master, envied by some less powerful hospital networks, criticized by insurers for its prices and negotiating tactics—as well as studied by economists and business professors for its business success.

There are dozens if not hundreds of hospital systems across America roughly following a similar playbook, though with varying intensity, motivations, and results.

By 2016 the NewYork-Presbyterian healthcare network consisted of eight acute care hospitals from lower Manhattan to far up the Hudson River. It has more than six thousand affiliated doctors and ambulatory care clinics scattered throughout the area. One of the more aggressive consolidators in New York, the North Shore–LIJ Health System (which emerged from a partnership between two community hospitals), contained nineteen hospitals, three skilled nursing facilities, more than twenty-five hundred physicians, four hundred regional ambulatory locations, and international affiliates by 2015. In 2016 it rebranded itself Northwell Health.

Reflecting a new era of "hospital conglomerates," there were ninety-five hospital mergers in 2014, the highest yearly number in over a decade. An analysis of 306 geographic health markets in the United States showed that none was "highly competitive" and more than half were "highly concentrated," often with one system dominating healthcare.

Healthcare systems typically characterize the mergers as a means to provide more seamless, coordinated care. But the impetus is more complicated and partly commercial. At first joint purchasing gave hospitals economies of scale and reduced redundancy as they negotiated with manufacturers for devices, drugs, and supplies. But over time the consolidated alliances meant primarily inordinate sway to demand high rates from corporations, insurers, and HMOs. Large medical centers could use the smaller hospitals and practices they absorbed as feeders for patients.

At a certain point, the major effect of consolidation was simply a huge rise in prices, economic research has now shown, because hospital conglomerates that have driven out competition can raise prices with abandon. The existence of one dominant healthcare system in a region can result in price increases as high as 40 to 50 percent. A study in California established that premiums are 9 percent higher in San Francisco, Sutter Health territory, compared with those in Los Angeles, even though LA boasts high-end hospitals like Cedars-Sinai and Ronald Reagan UCLA Medical Center, because there are more players in the LA market. Also, a 2012 study in California determined that hospital mergers were associated with more cardiac procedures and an increase in inpatient deaths, suggesting that the patients had been subjected to "suboptimal care" and "overtreatment"; hospitals without competition could more easily get away with rendering only profitable services, the authors suggested.

"There's a big flurry of consolidation and the result depends on what the objective of the health system is," said Orry Jacobs, a former healthcare executive and now a leading healthcare consultant and president of Orry Jacobs LLC. "If the intent is to improve care and bend the cost curve, networks can do it. If the objective is to corner the market and negotiate higher rates, that's what will happen."

Pioneers: Sutter or Bust

Sutter Health largely comprises what were originally community hospitals, many of which were established more than a century ago, to tend to California's growing population of prospectors and miners. It is part of the company's Wild West foundational myth: "Although Gold Rush–era San Francisco beckoned with tales of fame and fortune, she was anything but a healthy host. Malnutrition, plague, scarlet fever, meningitis, typhoid, and tuberculosis were among the scourges that ravaged the rough and tumble Barbary Coast." (The latter was the nickname of San Francisco's red-light district.)

By 1996 the growing sophistication of healthcare made it beneficial for two consortiums of local hospitals, Sutter Health of Sacramento and the California Healthcare System, based in the Bay Area, to formally ally to form the nucleus of what is currently Sutter Health. Sutter Health rapidly created an empire, as hospitals and other medical providers joined willingly or opted in because they felt they had no other choice from a financial standpoint. It was Sutter or bust.

Forces like rising costs and declining payment for services have made it difficult for hospitals and physicians to continue operating on their own. In a little over a decade at the beginning of the twenty-first century, more than seventy California hospitals had to close. Small hospitals that tended primarily to poor patients and those on Medicaid were particularly vulnerable.

Against this backdrop, Sutter could offer strategic business deals, buying a financially troubled hospital and reversing its fortunes by restructuring and charging patients far more for services. Or it would acquire the only maternity ward in an isolated region, forcing insurers and large employers with even just a few workers in that particular area to accede to Sutter's high prices. Sutter favored all-or-nothing deals: purchasers who wanted to include any of Sutter's facilities in their networks had to include all of them. (Capturing maternity care is also a smart marketing strategy, because studies show that women have great loyalty to the hospital where they give birth, even at somewhat extra cost.)

By its own accounting, in 2014 Sutter Health has assembled twenty-four hospitals, thirty-four outpatient surgicenters, nine cancer centers, and, most recently, thousands of affiliated doctor practices. In many areas of California there is now no other choice. Employers and insurers with "covered lives" in areas where Sutter operates pretty much have to accept all of its hospitals and doctors into their plans, along with its charges.

Its success has emboldened facilities outside its system to raise their prices as well. Therese Meuel was nonplussed by the $15,000 price for her kidney biopsy at John Muir Medical Center in Concord, California, but she knew that the bill at the Sutter hospital in her area would have been 20 percent higher. Glenn Melnick, a professor of health economics and finance at the University of Southern California, describes the behemoth this way: "Sutter is the tallest Sequoia and everyone goes up just underneath them."

The Doctors' Faustian Bargain

In 2010 Sutter invited Dr. Alexander Lakowsky to join its growing physician network, offering to buy his practice with a generous package and a promise to "keep community medicine whole." His office is right across the street from Sutter's Mills-Peninsula Hospital, where he admitted patients anyway, so it seemed a good fit. (Sutter enticed older doctors to join by suggesting they wouldn't have to work so hard, he said.) "It was a sweetheart deal—twenty-five to thirty percent more than what you'd made before, and I had two young kids," Dr. Lakowsky, forty-one, said. "It turned into a pumpkin pretty quickly."

A few months later, with Sutter in command of his billing, the charges for a physical at his office jumped from $150 to $450, for example. Sutter wielded such market power that insurers and employers had to agree to the fee. "But that was a big burden for patients with high co-pays," Dr. Lakowsky said. "I didn't like the fact that my patients were being taken for a ride."

Over the next two years, he encountered pressure to place the good of the conglomerate over the good of his patients. "There was heavy pressure to refer patients for testing and surgery within the Sutter system, which was overpriced," he said. "I wasn't really able to be my patients' advocate." By 2012 Dr. Lakowsky severed ties with Sutter. He joined an upstart alliance of a few remaining independent physicians in the area called Private Practice Doctors of the Peninsula (he is now its president) promising patients better care for a fraction of Sutter's cost.

But independent doctors have struggled for financial survival in a region where Sutter owns so much of the healthcare infrastructure and has so dominated insurance negotiations that independent doctors found themselves excluded from many patients' insurance networks—especially plans that paid well. An alliance of independent physicians to which Dr.

Lakowsky belongs, the Mills-Peninsula Medical Group, signed an agreement with one of Sutter's busy large group practices, essentially agreeing to take its overflow. Sutter's own doctors kept the more profitable, commercially insured patients in-house and sent patients covered by lower-paying HMO plans to Dr. Lakowsky and his colleagues. He still tries to refer patients to independent centers for endoscopy and radiology, where the prices are much cheaper. But each year they are fewer, and the obstacles multiply.

The Electronic Medical Record as a Business Weapon

Growing health systems often effectively protect their market by controlling electronic medical records (EMR), a tool originally intended to improve communication between hospitals and physicians: the idea of digital record keeping in healthcare was considered so beneficial that the American Recovery and Reinvestment Act of 2009 included $19 billion in incentives to develop and deploy the technology, "one of the largest publicly funded infrastructure investments the nation has ever made in such a short time period, in health care or any other field."

The first step under President Obama's HITECH Act was to require doctors and hospitals to go electronic with their record keeping. The second step, required a few years later, was termed "meaningful use"— prodding doctors and hospitals to deploy the new technology for the good of patients: sending records to another hospital or doctor with the click of a mouse or allowing patients to review lab results at home without waiting for a doctor's call.

Sutter spent $50 million to develop and install an EMR system. Whether intentionally or not, that system—Sutter Community Connect—

became a barrier blocking competitors from well-reimbursed tests and ancillary services.

Naturally, doctors employed by Sutter would direct tests and surgeries to Sutter labs and surgery centers. But the system also effectively encouraged independent doctors to do the same. Because Dr. Lakowsky continued to send patients who needed hospital admission to Sutter's Mills-Peninsula Medical Center he had to use the Sutter EMR system to follow their progress and see their labs. Sutter charged independent doctors only several thousand dollars to get its system, a fraction of what it would have cost to install an EMR system that complied with the government's requirements on the open market.

But when doctors used Sutter Community Connect to order a blood test or a scan, the default destination was a Sutter-owned lab or radiology office. When they clicked to order physical therapy or a knee brace, those too were dispensed through Sutter unless otherwise indicated. For motivated doctors who wanted to direct a blood test to Quest, for example, the system allowed an override to the default settings. But Sutter was subtly doing its best to hang on to important revenue streams, while costing patients and their insurers millions of dollars. (Some commercial labs have employed a similar strategy: installing free EMR software in doctors' offices that is programmed to order any tests selected from their own labs.)

The setup was also threatening to drive Sutter's few competitors out of business. Peninsula Diagnostic Imaging, a thirty-year-old radiology practice located near Mills-Peninsula, is at risk, said Dr. Beth Kleiner, a partner. That is true, even though its prices are one-sixth to one-half those charged at Sutter. Susan Foley's knee scans, billed at $3,000 before her surgery, would have cost $1,200 if billed to insurance at Peninsula Diagnostic, according to Dr. Kleiner, or $500 for patients who had to pay themselves.

Also, smaller outside testing and radiology centers like Peninsula had no way to input results into the Sutter EMR; they had to fax results or call them in to the doctor. Sometimes those extra steps made a huge difference in care—for example, when a doctor needed the results of a scan to decide if urgent surgery was required. Sometimes the extra steps were just a hassle. There was a 90 percent decline in referrals from certain areas and for particular tests. "Some internists and OBs still refer to us because they know that we're good value," Dr. Kleiner said, but theirs is the last remaining independent radiology office between San Francisco and Palo Alto.

Peninsula Diagnostic Imaging tried to join Sutter Community Connect, but Sutter told them it would cost $100,000.

The government invested heavily in EMRs as a tool to enable good patient care, with the idea that they would allow the sharing of medical records between a sick person's physicians. But competing health systems have little financial incentive to do so. Instead, they have frequently become tools for conglomerates to protect market share or dominate their market.

Dr. Lakowsky said that the electronic medical records of health systems in the Bay Area have gotten better at interacting, so he can readily get records and results electronically from Stanford or UCSF, for example. (They all rely on the same vendor, Epic.) But that isn't true in many places. Beth Israel Deaconess Medical Center and Brigham and Women's Hospital are two prestigious Harvard hospitals literally a couple of blocks from each other, and many patients visit both for their care. But they use different EMR systems that don't interact, so that an MRI scan has to be downloaded to a CD and walked over or mailed.

Hospitals blame the shortcomings of EMRs on the companies that sell the software. But like Apple and Microsoft, Cerner and Epic—the two giants—are naturally not inclined to make it too easy for their systems to talk to each other. But successful businesses build products their customers want.

Epic is currently building a new $1 billion IT system for a large part of Denmark, where the ability to share patient data among hospitals and doctors is an essential requirement. Patients will have direct access to their medical data and the system will allow referrals, discharge summaries, data, and prescriptions to be shared securely among all providers.

In the United States, EMRs have evolved to put business before patients. Disjointed and siloed, they have not delivered on their promise. Dr. Joanne Roberts, chief medical officer at Providence Regional Medical Center in Everett, Washington, recently completed a master's degree in health administration. The professor teaching a course on medical information systems began the class with an apology: "On behalf of the informatics industry I just want to say 'I'm sorry.'"

What Happens to Small Hospitals After Consolidation

When Sutter Health first invited Coast Hospital in Crescent City, California, to come under its umbrella in 1985, it seemed like a perfect union. At that time, Sutter merely offered management assistance, the service it typically performed at affiliated hospitals. Coast remained community owned, serving a lightly populated swath of the far northern reaches of California's redwood forests. According to Dr. Greg Duncan, then a young orthopedic surgeon, "They made sure we had good equipment and were very supportive of the docs. For eighteen years, I was happy."

But in 2009 Sutter Health ended its role of supporting locally owned hospitals and embarked on a statewide merger strategy it called "regionalization." The plan was to transfer ownership of the affiliate hospitals, many of which were the sole providers for hundreds of miles around, to Sutter-controlled regional corporations.

Regionalization led to higher charges: At one point, Blue Cross Blue Shield refused to sign with Sutter, noting that its rates were 60 percent higher than the statewide average. But it ultimately had to surrender because it could not leave patients stranded in huge areas where Sutter was the only option. By 2013 Sutter hospitals represented seven of the ten most expensive hospitals in California, according to California's Valued Trust, a public employees group focusing on benefits.

AT COAST HOSPITAL, prices kept rising. By 2012 an MRI of the knee at Sutter Coast cost $3,383, more than double the rate at the three closest hospitals not owned by Sutter—though none was close enough to provide a practical alternative. In 2013, it was billing patients nearly $6,000 for the first thirty minutes of operating room time under general anesthesia—not including drugs, IVs, sterile supplies, or the fees of the surgeon and anesthesiologist. By 2011 Dr. Duncan "had patients come to [him] after minor surgery with bills in excess of twenty thousand dollars. The financial stress among working families was too profound to ignore."

A negotiating stalemate over rates between Sutter and Anthem Blue Cross, one of the region's big insurers, prompted Anthem to ask physicians like Dr. Duncan to obtain admitting privileges at a non-Sutter hospital. Dr. Duncan started to drive to a hospital in Arcata, about one hundred miles away, to operate on patients who needed more affordable care, although the elderly and poor couldn't make such trips. When Dr. Duncan pointed out to a Sutter executive that commercially insured patients were leaving town to avoid the conglomerate's high charges, the response, he says, was that Sutter said it would consider lowering the charges for elective services to gain back the business, but not for emergencies—since patients in extremis couldn't travel.

In 2011, according to Dr. Duncan, a Sutter Health representative rewrote the hospital's bylaws with more than a thousand changes, which included a clause requiring the board to be "loyal" to Sutter Health. That same year, Sutter drew up a plan to replace the Sutter Coast Hospital board, then made up largely of locals, with a "community committee" that had no decision-making authority, as had already taken place at Sutter's twenty-three other affiliates under regionalization.

In 2012 Dr. Duncan was elected medical chief of staff by his colleagues and attended board meetings in an ex officio capacity: "It was really an eye-opener. Regionalization is OK if it brings operational efficiencies," he told me. "But an executive even told us there are no efficiencies in this. It's about control, pricing, contracts, profits." (One longtime healthcare executive who was recruited by Sutter but took a job elsewhere told me, "They pay their administrators an enormous amount of money and the appetite for acquisition was enormous.")

In December 2013 Sutter announced that Coast was not financially viable and would be converted into a "critical access hospital"—downsizing from forty-nine to twenty-five beds.

Sutter had already closed Coast's surgical care unit and hospice program, when a directive arrived announcing that the corporation was studying discontinuing obstetrical care as well because it was losing money. "I was truly beside myself," Dr. Duncan said. "We were all shocked. There's no other place around here to have babies." When he divulged the proposal to the medical staff, the board formally censured him at the recommendation of a Sutter Health attorney. Following physician backlash, Sutter Health left OB services in place.

The critical access program was created in 1997, to ensure the survival of small remote hospitals of not more than twenty-five beds. Medicare pays these hospitals more for their services, which are exempt from many of the government insurer's cost-saving measures. They can, for example, bill full hospital rate for "swing beds," for recovering patients who might have been discharged to cheaper rehabilitation facilities in urban centers.

The critical access program was being manipulated for profit, in the opinion of many Sutter Coast staff doctors. Sutter had already used the program to downsize Lakeside, another Sutter hospital in Lakeport, California, to critical access status, taking advantage of the higher payments. But because of bed shortages at the smaller hospital, emergency transfers from Lakeside increased 300 percent, and patients or their insurers, including Medicare, were left paying massive bills—including charges for air ambulances to fly patients out. The hospital's twenty-five beds were often filled with elective admissions, patients with nonurgent problems, as well as patients who merely needed rehabilitation occupying swing beds.

In 2015 the HHS OIG found that billing for such swing beds at critical access hospitals had risen rapidly, costing Medicare an extra $4.1 billion from 2005 to 2010. Sutter Lakeside's charges to Medicare were the highest of all thirteen hundred hospitals in the program the year after its conversion to critical access status in 2008, 24 percent higher than those of the institution in second place. It was a model that others would follow, as bigger fish ate up smaller fish all over the country.

A Part-Time Emergency Room

New York State assemblyman James Skoufis represents five towns about fifty miles north of New York City in the Hudson Valley. Much of his first term in office had been consumed by preventing attempts to gut some essential services at the community's health provider, Cornwall Hospital, or St. Luke's Cornwall Hospital, as it is now called.

Cornwall Hospital, which opened its doors in 1931, was founded with a grant from a doctor, Ernest Stillman, who explained:

> Some years ago I was asked to see a sick child. As the patient was in dire need of hospital care to save her life, I rushed her in my car to an adjacent hospital. But the hospital would not admit the patient and the child died. That tragedy marks the starting of the Cornwall Hospital.

The little hospital prospered with its community, adding forty beds in the 1960s and thriving with the generous healthcare payments of the 1980s. In 1982 the hospital opened a ten-bed intensive care/coronary care unit; in 1986 it added an ambulatory surgery suite; and in 1990 it cut the ribbon on an endoscopy center.

But the HMO era in the 1990s hit the hospital's pocketbook hard, and, in 2002, it merged with a somewhat larger area provider, St. Luke's in Newburgh. At Cornwall, over the course of the next decade, services were slowly pared down: by 2013 inpatient care, the operating room, mental health, the maternity ward, radiology, and the labs had all been eliminated.

By the time Skoufis took office in 2013, St. Luke's had over two hundred beds, while the Cornwall campus was, in his words, "a ghost town"; the only services left were a cancer treatment center operated by a contractor and the hospital's emergency room. On September 9, 2013, St. Luke's management circulated a draft press release announcing that it henceforth planned to operate the Cornwall emergency room only part-time, closing it from 10 p.m. to 10 a.m. each day, since it was losing money by staying open at night.

In the past decades, emergency room care has been quickly commercialized, governed often not by patient needs but by finances. Many states—notably Texas and Colorado—have permitted the opening of freestanding ERs often owned by entrepreneurial physicians. If a patient arrives via ambulance and is seriously injured or really sick or has had a heart attack, a doctor checks him out and sends him to the nearest real emergency department connected to a hospital with facilities like operating rooms and a cardiac laboratory. Aside from the risk of delays in treatment, the sequence results in bills for two separate high-level ER visits and a charge for emergency transport.

Most states that allow freestanding ERs at least insist they stay open 24/7 and take all emergencies regardless of the ability of customers to pay—though they cannot accept Medicare or Medicaid, since government insurers insist that to qualify as an ER and bill ER rates, an emergency room must be physically connected to a hospital.

Management in Cornwall tried to take the freestanding concept further by closing at night. In presentations to state regulators who needed to approve the plan, St. Luke's executives said the hospital couldn't afford to run an emergency room during hours when it was only lightly in use. But the hospital's tax records showed St. Luke's had just awarded compensation bonuses to administrators totaling hundreds of thousands of dollars; Allan E. Atzrott, its CEO (now retired and an "aspiring golf pro" according to his LinkedIn profile), was making over $700,000.

A Catholic Hospital Conglomerate Makes Off with a Bequest

People were surprised when Harvey Pell, a parsimonious appliance store owner known for sensible old cars and polyester trousers, bequeathed $10 million to his local hospital in Cadillac, Michigan. The bulk of his donation to Cadillac Hospital was earmarked to start a foundation to help the hospital pay for important services it could not otherwise fund. He left his daughter $40,000. His housekeeper $10,000. His grandchildren nothing.

Most hospitals in America were established to meet very local needs, struggling valiantly to provide quality basic medical services: stitches, removing an infected gallbladder, setting a broken bone. If you needed a heart transplant or cancer chemotherapy, you might head to an urban medical center. But for everything else the local hospital was there. Patients like Mr. Pell were grateful.

In 1978, with revenues beginning to roll in from all the insured patients, Cadillac built a new hospital, "one of the finest facilities of its size in Michigan." Though for a time managed by the Sisters of Mercy, it ultimately came under the ownership umbrella of the healthcare conglomerate Trinity Health, which by the twenty-first century had become "one of the largest multi-institutional Catholic health care delivery systems in the nation," with ninety-two hospitals, coast to coast.

In May 2014 Trinity announced that it had decided to sell Cadillac Hospital to Munson Healthcare, another big medical corporation active in Michigan. Paychecks would come from Munson. The building, scanners, beds, and wheelchairs henceforth belonged to Munson. But Trinity would keep Mr. Pell's bequest.

Katy Huckle, a local banker and a friend of the Pell family, resigned as president of the foundation board in protest. She wrote to me: "People are behaving really badly and I think they thought it would fly under the radar." During months of secretive deal planning no one had advised Mr. Pell's children or grandchildren about the hospital sale, much less the fact that Trinity was keeping the family money—even though family members were on the hospital board. One month before the official transfer, a delegation from the hospital visited Ginny Mackey, Mr. Pell's now-elderly daughter, on New Year's Eve. In conveying notice of the plan, they brought along a nun.

The grandchildren were furious. Trinity said it would make sure the funds were spent "in the best interest of the hospital." His granddaughter, Helen James Lehman, wrote to the local bishop, Steven J. Raica, asking for help: "It was grandfather's intent to keep this money in Cadillac, to be managed, invested and spent in Cadillac." Bishop Raica sent an emotional letter to Trinity Health asking it to reconsider and invoking "the very principle of respecting the intention of donors."

In March 2015 I received a note from Ms. Huckle: "My beloved family got screwed. . . . To not even negotiate with us is hooey."

Consolidation: Rebranding Doctors' Offices

Eileen Debold, who lives in central New Jersey, visited her internist in late 2014 for an exam and a portable chest X-ray. She was surprised when she received a bill totaling over $500 for that single film, including an interpretation fee from a radiology group. It made no sense. Her chest X-rays had never cost nearly that much and her insurance required only a $25 co-pay for a chest X-ray performed in the office.

Soon her husband noticed similar mysterious and sudden increases in prices: an allergy test rose from $51.80 to $265; his diabetes blood test was up from $102 to $172; even the Medicare-set fee for an office visit had increased to $163 from $85.

When Ms. Debold called the number on the bill to inquire, she encountered not her doctor's longtime office staff, but "a surly billing supervisor" who informed her that the hospital had purchased her primary care physician's office. Her patient visits and tests were now billed as hospital charges; they now included a "facility fee."

In the last half decade or so, hospital systems have been aggressively acquiring not just other hospitals and X-ray centers but doctors' offices as well. Once your local hospital conglomerate has bought your doctor's office, it often unilaterally declares, for billing purposes, that the little office you've visited for twenty-five years is a hospital.

Some of the increased cost is borne by insurers, but patients also encounter larger bills. According to the terms of Ms. Debold's policy, X-rays done in a physician's office required only a $25 co-pay, or $50 at a radiologist's office. But services performed in a hospital require her to pay the first $2,000, a deductible. That's why she received a bill for $500.

Intuitively, insurers should be shutting down this sort of gaming if they want to save money. But big hospitals hold enormous leverage in setting the terms of insurance contracts, because insurers need them in their networks.

Dr. Mark Gudesblatt, an independent neurologist on Long Island, can no longer give infusions of drugs in his office to many patients with MS because their insurers' contracts require that those types of procedures be done in a "hospital," even though that location makes them three times more expensive. "These hospitals and these offices that pretend to be hospitals are charging a facility fee the patient doesn't need," he said.

Endgame

Conglomerates beget conglomerates. To maintain profits, huge insurers joined forces to strengthen their hands. In the world of medical device suppliers, Zimmer acquired Biomet in 2015 and Stryker considered purchasing Smith & Nephew. That would leave three mammoth companies supplying hip and knee implants in the U.S. market. In 2015 the insurance giants Aetna and Anthem announced deals to take over their rival colossi Humana and Cigna, respectively, thereby reducing the number of major insurers from five to three. The CEOs of Aetna and Anthem, Mark Bertolini (2015 compensation $27.9 million) and Joe Swedish (2015 compensation $13.6 million), lobbied for congressional approval. Though it initially waffled over whether the mergers should be labeled anticompetitive and prevented, the U.S. Department of Justice filed to block them in late July 2016. It looked to be an epic fight.

10

THE AGE OF HEALTHCARE AS PURE BUSINESS

Our healthcare system today treats illness and wellness as just another object of commerce: Revenue generation. Supply chain optimization. Minimization of tax liability. Innovative business modeling. Things sold. Services rendered. Bills to be paid. "As a consumer (formerly 'patient' or 'sick person') how cool it must be to find oneself on the innovative, enrollment-optimized upper specialty drug tier when sickness strikes and you face 20 to 30 percent coinsurance," quips Uwe Reinhardt, a Princeton economist who has been challenging the financial underpinnings of the American healthcare system for years.

Helen, a real estate professional in a major eastern city, had a history of ruptured disks in her back that required surgery. So when she developed severe pain in her neck and numbness and tingling in her hand and arm she knew she would likely need another operation. An MRI showed a piece of bone pushing on a nerve.

The first surgeon she consulted said he wouldn't see her because her Oxford Premium plan paid fees that were too low. The second, a surgeon she'd used twice before, agreed to take her on. His office would negotiate

224 AN AMERICAN SICKNESS

with Oxford to obtain a reasonable rate. "I begged them to get me on the schedule as soon as possible—I was in unbearable pain," she said. With neurological deficits that merited urgent intervention, he scheduled the surgery for a fortnight later. She drugged herself, canceling all work appointments.

But five days before surgery, the doctor's office called to inform her that Oxford wouldn't agree to more than $58,000, less than half the $130,000 the doctor usually charged. The office biller asked Helen to send in $23,000 to help make up the difference, in addition to the $12,000 co-payment. If she couldn't come up with the money, the surgery would be canceled, the biller explained: "We can't do the surgery for what your insurer's willing to pay."

From about 2010 on, new types of medical charges multiplied, just as priority boarding fees and fees for window seats appeared on airline bills. Doctors who considered themselves good diagnosticians began charging longtime patients annual retainers of $2,000 to remain in the practice, or $150 a month extra for customers who wanted same-day answers to medical questions, or $20 just to write each prescription. Some parents of children in New York City public schools began receiving $300 explanation of benefits statements generated for a child's trip to the school nurse's office (which had been outsourced to a contracted medical provider), even if for a scraped knee on the playground or a stomachache born of test anxiety.

Doctors and medical centers, who two decades ago might have worked hard to figure out an affordable payment, now rapidly turned over patient accounts to billing services and collection and credit rating agencies. By 2014, 52 percent of overdue debt on credit reports was due to medical bills and one in five Americans had medical debt on their credit record, impacting their ability to get a mortgage or buy a car.

There was money, money everywhere . . .

In my own years of medical school and practice, I never saw a single patient with hemophilia, whose victims lack an essential clotting factor (most commonly factor VIII) and so suffer from repeated internal bleeding. Treating this rare condition certainly didn't seem like a profitable proposition. So I was surprised to hear a medical marketing consultant I interviewed refer to hemophilia not as a devastating, debilitating illness if left untreated, but instead as a "high value disease state."

Improved treatment for hemophilia in the past fifty years has transformed the lives of patients with the disease, which is passed from mothers (who are silent carriers) to sons. Mark Skinner, fifty-six, a lawyer and a past president of the World Federation of Hemophilia, spent much of his early adulthood in a wheelchair, his joints decimated by bleeds that occurred at the tiniest bump. Today, thanks to joint replacements and— even more—the vials of clotting factor he packs in his carry-on, he leads a busy, active life working globally and traveling to all corners of the world. His great-nephew, who is nine, also has hemophilia but can run and play baseball and basketball just like every other kid his age. The treatment, however, has become manna for a very lucrative niche industry in which each patient is worth up to $1 million annually to a web of companies, doctors, and, often, ancillary home delivery services.

In the 1960s, factor VIII was partially purified from donated blood and concentrated in a form called cryoprecipitate, which could be infused for treatment when a patient was bleeding. Within a few years, life expectancy for people with hemophilia rose from twelve years in the 1940s to over sixty. There was little sense at the time that this life-giving "cryo," made mostly by blood banks, had great commercial value. But by the late 1960s, a nascent industry turned cryo into a profitable commodity by rebranding it as a pharmaceutical instead of a blood product and charging good money. With that innovation, Baxter, Bayer, and other pharmaceutical firms began manufacturing factor VIII, improving it by turning it into an easier-to-transport powder that stayed fresh even if not refrigerated. Other manufacturers moved into the market, but that greater competition didn't yield better prices, and families were outraged at medicine costs that amounted to more than $3,000 a year—a shocking number at the time.

Thus began what Dr. Glenn Pierce, a specialist in the disease who was born with hemophilia, calls "a long complex relationship between pharma, docs, and patients that has evolved over decades concerning pricing, supply, and demand." Each treatment advance yielded a new benefit—some larger, some smaller—but also a steep increase in price.

During the 1980s, the drugmakers and, later, specialized hemophilia treatment centers were presented with an opportunity of literally epidemic proportions. Because tens of thousands of units of blood plasma were needed to make a single dose of the new factor VIII concentrates, nearly all severe hemophiliacs contracted both HIV and hepatitis C. A community linked by one serious disease now battled three.

Over the next few years, pharmaceutical manufacturers quickly developed a variety of processes to kill any errant viruses in their concentrated clotting factor products, using heat or detergents, for example. The price of each treatment doubled and tripled. Oddly, there were no price wars to control inflation—just the opposite. When, in the late 1980s, Cutter Pharmaceuticals came out with a product that was purified using a chemical process, it decided to charge the same 40 cents a unit as the one made with a detergent process by Armour. "They said we can't charge less because we don't want to look inferior," a doctor involved told me. (See **Rule 6: More competitors vying for business doesn't mean better prices; it can drive prices up, not down.**)

In 1993, after the gene for factor VIII was sequenced, suddenly the medicine could be made using recombinant DNA technology rather than pooled blood plasma, making it much cheaper and simpler to produce. Despite that, the new recombinant products were priced still higher, at $1 a unit wholesale; that came to $4,000 for treating a typical bleed, with the treatment center's markup (which reflected, often, the even bigger markup introduced by various middlemen). In response, the older blood-derived products *raised* their wholesale price by 50 percent, to 60 cents a unit. (See **Rule 4: As technologies age, prices can rise rather than fall.**)

More important, with the gene inserted into cells (usually cultured from animals), drugmakers could churn out unlimited amounts of pure factor VIII, unconstrained by a limited supply of donated blood or sold blood plasma. Patients who had once used factor VIII only in a medical crisis could now take it as a preventive, three times a week, at a cost of sometimes over $300,000 to $600,000 annually. Use of factor VIII quadrupled. And with triweekly infusions, it was no longer as practical to trek to a doctor's office, prompting a rollicking expansion of the hemophilia home care industry, which delivered factor VIII, infusion supplies, and assistance to a patient's doorstep.

Though such intermediaries sometimes provided valuable services to patients in need, the idea quickly spun out of control. The industry developed a brilliant new business model, cleverly designed to skirt the law and scrutiny. Instead of charging patients or their insurers for their services, each home care company allied with a particular manufacturer and got paid by the drugmaker per unit of factor VIII delivered into patients' veins. The margin was so high that companies needed only a few "clients" to turn a nice profit. Companies wooed each "high value patient" with offers of rides to doctor's appointments, trips to amusement parks, tickets to baseball games, and even jobs—offers that would have been illegal for doctors, hospitals, or drugmakers to hand out. Reps of the home care companies would volunteer as counselors at summer camps for kids with hemophilia to entice campers to use their employers' services. "In this field you can't create a market—there are only a few hundred new patients a year," said Mark Skinner. "All you can do is cannibalize."

Prices were astronomical, but the industry made sure nobody directly felt them. One patient told me the cost of his drug is $600,000 a year and, because he has a 40 percent co-pay under the terms of his insurance, his share of the $50,000 January bill for factor VIII gets him over his $9,000 out-of-pocket maximum spending limit for the year. But of course he doesn't pay any of it himself, anyway: it is covered by the drugmaker's co-pay assistance plan.

There was trouble on the horizon for the hemophilia industry in the early 2000s, however, because most factor VIII products would lose their patents in 2008 and 2009. A number of companies were gearing up to manufacture generic versions, which could drastically lower prices. Countries where national authorities bargain hard with pharmaceutical companies, such as Britain, Canada, and Australia, were cutting deals for half or less of the $1 per unit price in the United States.

It was time for the industry to pull out a new "brand extension strategy." By attaching factor VIII to another molecule that lasts longer in the bloodstream, manufacturers created improved products that could be infused less frequently. Imagine the convenience of administering once a week, rather than three times, before school. It was a significant and much desired advance—one that probably could have and should have come before patent expiration induced companies to make the effort.

The development was so exciting that Dr. Pierce accepted a position at Biogen, a newcomer to the field, whose long-acting product was the first approved in 2014. Baxter, Novo Nordisk, and Bayer each soon developed its own version. A big market opportunity presented itself in the United States. Every patient with hemophilia would be choosing a new product. Manufacturers doubled their sales forces to prepare for the push. Because each of the eighteen thousand patients constituted a windfall, manufacturers hired dozens of full-time reps to sell the new drugs to them.

Manufacturing the new product would be relatively cheap, but the companies had spent heavily to get the new drugs to market: going through clinical trials and the full FDA approval process as well as setting up new production capacity. But Dr. Pierce and Mark Skinner, both highly respected leaders in the hemophilia community, advocated a novel idea for recouping the investment: lowering the price of factor VIII (as well as for factor IX, the other clotting protein that may be deficient in the disease). After all, research and development costs for the factors had been recouped many times over, so a lower price could expand demand in a functional market. Because of the exorbitant price, many insurers only cover full prophylaxis for children who do not yet have joint damage, meaning that only 35 percent of people with hemophilia are getting this full benefit. Current approaches to prophylaxis provide the minimum effective dose of medicine because it is so very expensive, allowing for some breakthrough joint bleeding and needless long-term damage. Some countries, such as Japan, refuse to approve factor VIII for wide deployment because of its high cost, so people are still crippled by a treatable disease. To Dr. Pierce's chagrin, Biogen's long-acting product was priced twice as high as the older versions of factor VIII per unit.

Hemophilia is a rare disease, but pricing for factor VIII is symptomatic of a nearly ubiquitous problem: we—and our employers and insurers—are shopping for healthcare in a market where everything is monetized to the maximum, without much regard for the implications for patient health. No wonder that by 2016, even some of the country's most admired, judicious health plans, like that offered by Pennsylvania's Geisinger Health System, were asking for some rate increases of 40 percent.

11

THE AGE OF THE AFFORDABLE CARE ACT (ACA)

At age fifty-five, Deb Ciszewski of Milwaukee scheduled a screening colonoscopy on the advice of her doctor. She had a family history of colon cancer and she'd had a tiny benign lesion that in rare instances evolves into cancer—a tubular adenoma—discovered and removed during a screening colonoscopy a decade before. It is an effective preventive intervention, the very reason screening colonoscopies are performed. (Another colonoscopy done five years later had been clean.)

One of the laudable requirements of the Affordable Care Act is that certain preventive tests, including colonoscopy screening, should be free to patients to encourage people to take advantage of early detection. But when Ms. Ciszewski called the clinic and her insurer, she discovered that both would categorize her procedure as "diagnostic" instead of as a screening procedure, as a result of the five-millimeter benign lesion that had been found ten years earlier. They estimated a charge of nearly $8,000, with an out-of-pocket expense of over $3,000. She canceled the test.

Even the well-intentioned provisions that managed to survive the tortuous congressional negotiations over the ACA have been in practice diluted and perverted, as providers find ways to maximize revenue by gaming its rules.

Obamacare, as it has come to be called, was supposed to build a first line of defense against the expenses of American medicine. It is, in some respects, revolutionary, a declaration that decent healthcare for every American is a guiding principle and government responsibility. It created some important incentives and rules to nudge the profit-oriented system toward better serving patients.

For example, the ACA barred insurers from denying insurance or treatment to people with preexisting conditions. Before the ACA, insurers had lowered the bar for their definition of "preexisting condition" to include a distant abnormal pap smear, a history of occasional allergic asthma, or the use of an antidepressant. The ACA banned lifetime limits on insurance payouts, which had been potentially deadly for patients with chronic illness.

Its policies capped annual out-of-pocket spending per person (at $6,850 in 2016) as long as the patient stayed in network, in an effort to avoid the extreme duress of bankruptcy.

It defined a list of "essential health benefits" that every insurance policy had to cover, including maternity care—which many policies had previously excluded—and the provision of free screening for certain conditions.

The ACA did little directly, however, to control runaway spending. President Obama had initially included several ideas in the bill that would have done so—like national negotiation for pharmaceutical prices. To get a healthcare bill passed and to win support from powerful groups like PhRMA, the AMA, the American Hospital Association, and America's Health Insurance Plans, the administration had to cave on anything that would directly limit the industry's ability to profit.

Given those political constraints, the ACA promoted some programs that might render the practice of medicine more cost-effective. It used financial incentives to encourage the formation of novel medical arrangements like accountable care organizations and patient-centered medical homes, through which providers create teams that respond to patients' health needs, receiving a variety of payments for coordinating care and bonuses for good results. Companies like Aledade, founded by Dr. Farzad Mostashari, a former government official, have worked hard to help primary care doctors improve care and lower costs through such models. But much of the industry deftly danced around the Affordable Care Act's well-intentioned edicts to minimize their financial impact on its business and maximize profit, arming Republicans who called for repeal.

"So much has happened that is anathema to the spirit of the ACA," said Brendan Williams, a lawyer who was a representative in Washington State and then a deputy state insurance commissioner as the Affordable Care Act was being enacted and implemented. "In healthcare, entrepreneurship outsmarts regulation every time."

Costs Take a U-turn: The Lesson of Medicare Drug Coverage

Medicare Part D, prescription drug coverage for Medicare beneficiaries, was enacted in 2006, under a Republican president, George W. Bush. Previously, the government hadn't offered prescription drug coverage for people over sixty-five because medicines were always relatively cheap. But as the costs of drugs began rising in the 1990s and reports of seniors forgoing vital medicine became widespread, the government added prescription drug insurance.

Medicare Part D was designed by health economists to cover the cost of necessary medicines, with incentives to prevent runaway spending and casual overprescribing. In 2015, for example, the patient paid the first

$320 as a deductible and then a 25 percent co-payment on up to $2,960 in retail costs for drugs. If costs exceeded $2,960 in a year, patients hit what is known as the "donut hole," when they had to pay 100 percent of the cost, making them think twice about taking very expensive medicines they might not really need. Once their outlays hit a retail cost limit of $4,700 for their medicines, Medicare kicked in again, paying 95 percent.

Medicare Part D worked just as intended to make drugs more affordable to seniors—but only for a very few years. The medical industry soon developed strategies to benefit financially from the policy, undermining its patient-centered ambitions. Basic drugs for common conditions in the elderly, such as high blood pressure and rheumatoid arthritis, had to be cheap in the decades before Medicare Part D picked up the tab. But once all seniors were guaranteed drug coverage and were paying only a co-payment, drug companies raised prices—a lot. Insurers then responded by charging higher-percentage co-payments to discourage use.

Steve Carlson's NovoLog insulin has become more and more expensive under Medicare Part D. It had previously been covered under another Medicare program and dispensed as a medical supply, at no cost. Now Mr. Carlson's insulin, which set him back under $20 a month in the 1990s, costs about $700, a part of which he pays himself.

With prices like that, far more Medicare patients end up in the donut hole, even if they have only two or three relatively ordinary conditions. Studies by Dr. Huseyin Naci, formerly of Harvard, and his colleagues showed that sicker patients, with four or more problems, are now more likely to stop taking medicines or have difficulty affording them than before Part D. "In the long run," he said, "costs come back to the system and they are even greater."

The ACA did its best to remedy the Part D boomerang effect on patients, mandating that patients would no longer have to pay 100 percent of the price for branded drugs in the donut hole, but instead 45 percent, with plans to close the donut hole completely by 2020. But until that hap-

234 AN AMERICAN SICKNESS

pens, there will be payment challenges for many seniors. The newer medicines for rheumatoid arthritis and type 2 diabetes have a retail cost of $20,000 a year. Across thousands of different Part D plans, the average cost-sharing requirement means that a Medicare patient has to pay many thousands of dollars in out-of-pocket costs each year for a single drug.

There is little reason to think that the rules and incentives created by the ACA (those that persist) will fare much better than those of Medicare Part D without vigilance to prevent their corruption—as well as modifications to close lucrative loopholes that the industry is already actively exploring to undercut the ACA's best intentions.

How Politicians Undermined the ACA

Health insurance cooperatives are a type of not-for-profit insurance—member owned and directed—that was established by the ACA. Strictly speaking, these plans are not really "new," but more a rebirth of the original not-for-profit Blue Cross Blue Shield–style plans. Their only real mission is to use their members' premiums to deliver higher-quality, cost-effective healthcare.

One reason the cooperatives formed by the ACA got little press was that many healthcare experts regarded them as a sorry stand-in for the "public option" that President Obama had initially promised. The "public option" refers to the notion that there would be on offer a national health insurance plan or that the government would allow anyone to choose Medicare as his insurer. That was jettisoned after the administration judged it would prevent the ACA's passage because of objections from the insurance industry. A public option would require commercial insurers to compete directly with the government program for patients' business.

The co-ops were, for many, a disappointing understudy, and were poorly prepared at that: formed in a hurry after the public option died, they were small start-ups—often operating in only one state—with none of the hefty bargaining power or financial reserves of big commercial insurers or Medicare. Moreover, Congress kept hedging its financial support for the co-op program, cutting seed funding by more than half and ultimately offering short-term loans rather than grants, as promised. Two of the plans went belly-up in the first year. Only one, in Maine, was on track to turn a profit. For many of these insurers the last nail was hammered in the coffin when Congress failed to come through with hundreds of millions of dollars in promised subsidies, called "risk corridor payments," to get them through their early tumultuous years of becoming an insurer. When Congress delivered only 12.5 percent of the money in 2015, many had to close their doors, leaving hundreds of thousands of customers without coverage. By July 2016 only seven of the original twenty-three co-ops were still in business.

How Insurers Undermined the ACA

Faced with more scrutiny of healthcare premiums, insurers' primary cost control plan has been to quietly transfer expense to the patient in the form of higher co-pays and deductibles. Outwardly, insurers put a good spin on what they aver is a strategy to tackle medical inflation: if patients have more "skin in the game"—those co-payments and deductibles—they will choose cheaper options. But, as we've seen, patients often can't get an upfront price anyway. And a $3,000 co-payment for a minor surgery when you're already paying $1,000 a month in premiums is not having a little skin in the game. It's more like having a kidney.

Most of the plans offered through the ACA are so-called high-deductible plans, and the law has helped spread this type of coverage. In the decade from 2006 to 2015, the number of Americans enrolled in such plans rose from 10 to 50 percent. Insurance doesn't kick in until the patient has paid a hefty sum, thousands of dollars. But a 2015 study found that when patients were switched into a high-deductible health plan, they didn't become smarter, more cost-conscious shoppers for medical care. The exorbitant prices demanded by the U.S. healthcare system meant that they mostly just avoided any interactions with medicine at all.

The insurers' second-line financial strategy has been to narrow networks, offering a limited selection of doctors and hospitals. If they are bringing a huge pool of customers to just a few doctors and hospitals, they have far more negotiating power to achieve lower payment rates and more profits for shareholders. Done well, this sounds like a reasonable strategy. But the choices available through many policies included only the less experienced doctors and second-tier hospitals, since the top-notch could afford to be picky in their contracting and demand better payments—or could opt out of insurance participation entirely.

While many parents welcome the fact that their young adult children can stay on the family health insurance until age twenty-six under the ACA, the benefit often proves useless because the narrow, hyperlocal networks include no doctors out of state. In some areas even in-state networks are so narrow that patients are unable to secure an appointment, and are forced to pay for out-of-network care themselves, particularly if they need a specialist. During the first year of the ACA, often all insurers had to do was provide a network name, and there was little further scrutiny of whether the choices contained were adequate or even real and accurate.

Fifty-nine-year-old Paul Schwartz of Nyack, New York, purchased a gold-level Emblem policy for 2016 to cover him and his wife, paying well over $1,000 a month for coverage because their longtime primary care doctor was on the plan's network list. (The ACA categorized plans according to different metal tiers—platinum, gold, silver, and bronze—depending on the proportion of medical expenses they were meant to cover.) Two months into that year, the doctor was dropped. "Now, they have my fifteen thousand dollars for ransom," he said. "It felt like a total bait and switch."

How Hospitals and Doctors Undermined the ACA

Providers—up and down the healthcare supply chain—rapidly devised ways to stay within the letter of the new law, while often flagrantly flaunting its quality-promoting cost-saving intentions. Business consultants offered advice about "Seizing Opportunities Provided by the ACA," as one article in *Physician's Weekly* indelicately put it.

"As health insurance exchanges go live, hospitals and emergency providers should take advantage of the protections provided by the ACA," the article maintained, finishing with a phrase that has seemingly displaced "First do no harm" as medicine's mantra: "Providers should not leave money on the table."

But the small financial incentives to encourage good behavior and coordinated medical care often paled compared to the profit that could be garnered by creative or aggressive billing that tested the boundaries of the law. Physical exams had to be free, for example, but not all the attendant blood tests a doctor might order. As Ms. Ciszewski discovered, the ACA benefit that required no-cost preventive screenings was distorted as doctors perverted the meaning of "preventive" and "covered" and "no cost" to no end.

There is no Supreme Court of the ACA to parse its original intent. The doctor's fee was covered, but the room rental or the anesthesiologist's charges were not. Fifty percent of colonoscopies involve removing a polyp, but if one was removed many doctors said it was no longer a free screening procedure. Logically, of course, the Affordable Care Act didn't mean that tests were no longer free if something was found and removed for scrutiny. That's the whole point. Connecticut's Office of the Healthcare Advocate said that getting billed for what patients had anticipated would be a free screening colonoscopy has generated more consumer complaints than any other ACA provision.

Under the ACA, the percentage of uninsured Americans dropped from 18 percent in 2013 to 11.9 percent in 2016. But there are still more than twenty million people without insurance. Despite the implementation of the Affordable Care Act, polls indicated that a growing number of Americans were having trouble affording medical care or avoided seeing a doctor for fear of the cost. In a *New York Times*/CBS News poll conducted a year after the ACA took effect, nearly half of respondents described affording basic medical care as a "hardship," up 10 percent when compared with responses before the act.

By 2016 some large insurers announced they would no longer offer ACA plans because they were losing money on them. Others sought premium rises of 40 to over 60 percent on some types of plans. Critics and pessimists wondered if such extreme events presaged an ACA death spiral.

THIS U.S. HEALTHCARE SYSTEM gradually evolved sector by sector, hospital by hospital, doctor by doctor. What the players are doing is, technically speaking, perfectly legal. Participants in the marketplace respond to the incentives and opportunities a market allows. That's what they're supposed to do. Each component of the system is genuinely convinced that it's not so bad, not responsible for our $3 trillion medical bill. Someone else is more to blame. Drug spending is only 10 percent of the national health budget! Nursing homes are only responsible for 5 percent of health costs! Payments to doctors only 20 percent! Dermatology accounts for only 4 percent of Medicare expenditures! Each segment of our medical system is convinced that its charges are reasonable. But put all the little excesses together and you get healthcare that is much worse and much costlier than the sum of its parts. We, the patients, are stuck in the middle, and it seems we've reached critical condition.

Part II

DIAGNOSIS AND
TREATMENT

PRESCRIPTIONS FOR
TAKING BACK OUR
HEALTHCARE

12

THE HIGH PRICE OF
PATIENT COMPLACENCY

The American healthcare system is rigged against you. It's a crap-shoot and from day to day, no one knows if it will work well to address a particular ailment. Unless you're part of the 1 percent, you're only ever one unlucky step away from medical financial disaster. Relatively well-off folks with insurance have lost hard-earned retirement savings paying for one serious disease. Twenty-somethings, just starting careers, have had their credit ratings trashed by unaffordable prices for a blood test or treatment of a minor illness.

We can't keep setting up payment plans, maxing out credit cards, and tapping into retirement savings. We're numb to statistics about medical debt being the single biggest cause of bankruptcy in the United States. When Americans talk about their battles with cancer or another serious disease, they often focus not on pain, fatigue, hair loss, and the odds of five-year survival, but on bills. We hate our healthcare system. And yet we've come to accept it as an inevitable burden of being American. But we patients have allowed this heist of our healthcare by commercial forces. More precisely, we didn't see it happening.

Now that you've read about how business stole our healthcare, you know we have the choice to stop it. This is a call to arms, as well as a road map for us to fight back personally, politically, and systematically. What follows is a blueprint and game plan for changing both our relationship with the medical system and the system itself, sector by sector, from doctors to hospitals to insurers to drugmakers.

The first part of each chapter lays out practical strategies you can implement right now and provides tools to make American medicine better and more affordable for you and your family. The second part describes some simple, concrete reforms that we can and should demand of the medical industry and all the elected and appointed officials responsible for regulating its practices. These are mostly basic measures that our representatives already have the power to put in place, which would not require an act of Congress. Just like us, lawmakers have been asleep at the wheel (or on the payroll), too often giving the healthcare industry a pass in the last quarter century.

These are ideas about how the citizens of the United States can better deploy and gain access to the amazing medical tools and machines that exist today. We have votes, and we have a voice—we must dare to raise it.

There is more than one solution to reverse the trajectory of our spiraling health costs. There are different actions we can take. The healthcare nonsystem we rely on is a product of a series of small steps over the past quarter century. We will most likely extricate ourselves in a similar gradual fashion, by a combination of strategies.

It is often only after Americans get sick in other countries that they understand just how broken their own system is.

When Michael Gibbons, a restaurateur from Portland, Oregon, developed a kidney stone at a spa in Gero Onsen, Japan, he saw a urologist, got an IV and pain medicine, blood and urine tests, and a CT scan in six hours at the local medical clinic—the same treatment he'd had before in the United States. The health center even assigned someone who spoke a little English, armed with Google Translate, to accompany him. After the stone passed, he was worried about how he would pay. The clinic didn't accept U.S. credit cards, but, it turned out, that didn't matter. Even though the doctors and health center were in private practice, the bills for absolutely everything totaled $281.

During Tiffany Spivey's second pregnancy, she was living in Turkey. She watched other pregnant women in her international playgroup depart one by one—to Canada, Australia, a host of European countries—to give birth at home. She told me she had "twenty-five thousand reasons" for not doing the same, referring to the price in dollars for her to give birth in the United States. "I am the only one who can't afford to have my baby near my family, because I'm American."

In researching this book I have encountered a growing population of middle- and even upper-middle-class American healthcare refugees who are departing to avoid unbearable costs in our profit-driven healthcare system: a graduate student with diabetes who is searching for academic positions in other countries because, even with insurance, she can't afford treatment here; a teacher from Oklahoma who moved to Brazil after a cancer scare made him aware of his financial vulnerability; a college professor in Michigan with a Canadian passport, who took his child back to Canada for complex cancer treatment because the costs would have been unsupportable where he works; a professional half-German, half-American family who with mixed emotions relocated with their three sons to Germany after well over a decade in Tucson, Arizona, because they were worried they wouldn't be able to afford healthcare (and university tuition) in the United States.

Every other developed country in the world delivers healthcare for a fraction of what it costs here. They use a wide range of tools and strategies that line up with each country's values, political realities, and medical traditions. Some set rates for healthcare encounters. Some negotiate prices for drugs and devices at a national level. Some have the government administer payments. Some mandate transparency. Some governments own hospitals and pay the doctors who work in them; others limit new hospital construction and the purchase of new machines. Most heavily subsidize medical school training. Although we tend to brand other countries as deploying "socialized medicine," almost all use unique hybrids of government intervention and free market forces. Let's look at a few basic tools that underpin their relative success at reining in cost.

1. Fee schedules and national price negotiations: Many countries—Germany, Japan, Belgium, and more—set national fee schedules for some combination of medical encounters or supplies and medicines. Those fees are negotiated by some combination of doctors, hospitals, governments, and academics; they can't be gamed or changed. If that sounds complicated, remember this is what Medicare already does. It's no more complicated than hundreds of millions of Americans and hundreds of thousands of doctors and their staff collectively wasting years haggling with insurers over individual payments and ending up with usurious rates.

National fee schedules inevitably yield prices that are far lower than those in the United States because a nation has far greater negotiating clout than a single insurer or an individual. But also because such a system doesn't waste time haggling over proper charges and bills. It is efficient. In the United States, doctors now spend one-sixth of their time on administration and medical practices to hire extra staff to wrangle with insurers. A sonogram of the heart costs anywhere from $1,000 to $8,000 in the United States. The 2014 negotiated fixed price in Japan and Belgium was under $150.

A national fee schedule doesn't preclude a private insurance market or a competitive industry. Japan and Germany have hundreds of insurers. In the Netherlands—where the government sets caps for some basic medicines and hospital services—everyone is required to buy private insurance that covers a set package of essential benefits. (These are somewhat different from those stipulated by the ACA. In vitro fertilization is covered, for example, but most physical therapy is not.) Within a regulated framework, these countries rely on market forces acting between hospitals and doctors and insurers to deliver cost-effective care.

2. Single payer: This is when a single authority, usually the government, dispenses most of the money paid to healthcare providers. Used in Canada, Australia, and Taiwan, as well as other countries, this system cuts private insurers out of most basic medical financial transactions. But doctors and hospitals are often still in business for themselves. Private insurance still exists to cover those who opt out of the national plan in favor of more upmarket care or for "extras" like eye care and dentistry.

In a few countries, like Denmark and Great Britain, a single payer system is combined with state ownership of hospitals and major healthcare infrastructure, creating true *nationalized or socialized healthcare,* a government-run medical system. Specialists and sometimes even general doctors are often government employees, although many take on extra private paying patients as well.

With its powerful, profitable private system, it is hard to imagine the United States moving to nationalized healthcare any time soon. But America's existing Medicare program is a pretty good single payer healthcare system, which could provide a gradual path to a more extensive one, if that's what Americans decide they want: for example, the program could be progressively opened to younger patients who were willing to pay by dropping the age for opting in every two years. During the 2016 U.S. presidential campaign, prodded by Senator Bernie Sanders's call for universal healthcare, the Democratic nominee, Hillary Clinton, proposed allowing people who were fifty-five and older to opt in to Medicare for a price.

3. Market-based tools of transparency and competition are deployed strategically by a number of countries to manage the cost of healthcare. Singapore is perhaps the prime example of this approach. The Singaporean Ministry of Health is the master conductor of that country's medical care, which award-winning scientist and philanthropist William Haseltine has called "highly calibrated capitalism." The political and philosophical emphasis on individual responsibility means that Singaporeans (and their employers) are required to contribute a portion of their salaries to a health savings account, which is dedicated to paying healthcare bills for their families. Basic medical interventions are considered a right, but patients make informed purchases about everything else.

In this system, most hospitals are public (state owned) and accommodations are tiered at four levels. Patients who choose the top level have private rooms with air-conditioning and can choose their doctors, but must pay the entire fee. Those choosing the lowest tiers reside in open wards and are assigned physicians, but the government pays 80 percent of the bill. There are also private hospitals, such as those operated by the high-end Raffles Medical Group, which offer faster service and still more amenities. But they compete with the top-level wards at the public hospitals, which effectively limits what they can charge.

The ministry ensures competition by publishing prices and bills from different hospitals and tiers of care on its Web site, allowing patients to make informed choices. It limits the purchase of expensive machines for pricey tests and treatments, because studies show that abundance leads to overuse. It seems to work: According to the World Bank in 2014 Singapore spent only 4.9 percent of its GDP on healthcare compared with the United States' 17.1 percent. Meanwhile, Singapore ranks sixth in the World

Health Organization's assessment of health system performance while the United States ranks thirty-seventh.

THE UNITED STATES will find its own particular healthcare solution. As you read on, you'll see that a wide array of tools is available for reforming and reclaiming our healthcare system for patients, building on the foundation of the ACA or its replacement. But we can't continue to choose "none of above"—that's not a plan. It's a $3 trillion cop-out.

13

DOCTORS' BILLS
(20 TO 30 PERCENT OF OUR $3 TRILLION BILL)

Part 1. What You Can Start Doing Now

Doctors traditionally praised "compliant" patients, individuals who did what they were told, followed instructions, and didn't ask too many questions. Medical journals used to publish papers profiling their opposite: "difficult patients," those who didn't just follow doctors' orders, who asked questions and expressed too many opinions. Today, in a world of data, consumer empowerment, and big bills, this is an outdated framework for the doctor-patient interaction. We all need to be more "difficult" patients to share in decision-making and to expect more discussion—and that is especially true about costs. You're entitled to a say about how your portion of our $3 trillion health bill is spent, especially since new insurance designs mean you'll be paying more of it. Ask why your doctor is ordering a particular test. Challenge those large numbers on your bill. Every patient can help to ward off unwanted healthcare costs by asking questions about care and its price tag beforehand. Do not wait until you're in the pre-op suite for same-day surgery wearing nothing but an open-backed gown or after you've cleaned out your intestine for a colonoscopy—you're not in a position to bargain or find a less expensive option then.

Some doctors may resist or resent being questioned especially because it will reduce their income and traditional sense of authority. John Gardner of Kirkland, Washington, was banned by a gastroenterology practice for being difficult when he took issue with its fees, arguing that with new technology and automation, prices should be cheaper, not far more expensive, than twenty years ago. (He could remember his father, a doctor, doing six to eight colonoscopies a day in his office in the mid-1990s for $600 apiece.) Another patient was labeled "difficult" after she'd asked to undergo two minor related surgical procedures in one trip to the operating room. The anesthesiologist derided her as "a two-for-one bargain shopper."

Choosing Your Doctor

When selecting a primary care doctor, there are some basic questions you should ask about the business structure of the practice that will impact your bills. It would be nice, someday, if such policies were required to be posted on the office walls. The office business manager should be able to answer most of them.

1. Is the practice owned by a hospital or licensed as a surgery center? If the answer is yes, you (or your insurer) may find yourself paying those outrageous facility fees—or caught in a battle about whether they're justified. You can ask specifically if such a fee will be added and how much it will be; however, many doctors' offices may not be able to answer the question correctly, because their bills come from the hospital or an outside biller.

2. Will you refer me only to other physicians in my insurance network, or explain why in advance if you can't? Many primary care doctors have long-standing relationships with specialists to whom they refer patients—a reflection of trust but also a type of business arrangement. If a doctor is employed by a hospital, there may be extraordinary pressure for him or her to refer patients to that hospital or its medical group. A doctor should take the time to look at your insurance network's list and pick someone he or she trusts within it.

3. If I need blood work or radiology testing, can you send me to an in-network lab? Blood processing is highly mechanized, so it doesn't matter where the tests are performed, but the prices at hospital labs can be one hundred times higher than at commercial labs like LabCorp and Quest. Electronic ordering programs keep such profitable testing in-house, when a few extra clicks of a mouse or a fax from the doctor's office can direct testing to cheaper outside providers. Any doctor should be able to do it, but will yours?

4. Will there be charges for phone advice or filling out forms? Is there an annual practice fee? It's good for you to know in advance about extra charges, and how your doctor views his commitment to medicine and his patients.

5. If I'm hospitalized, will you be seeing me in the hospital? What is your coverage on weekends? These services are an essential part of being a good doctor and most patients around the world expect to receive them. In the United States, despite physicians' high salaries, many practices have outsourced them. You don't want a doctor whose off-hour backup advice is to go to your local urgent care center or a hospital emergency room with which he has no contact.

In Your Doctor's Office

Here are some questions every doctor or healthcare provider should be able to answer for you at a doctor's appointment:

1. How much will this test/surgery/exam cost? "I don't know" or "It depends on your insurance" is not an answer. The doctor should give you a ballpark range or the cash price at the center where he or she refers. Many things that sound like simple little tests are now priced at many thousands of dollars. Before you schedule anything major, use one of the price calculators in appendix A to get a ballpark range of what your test or treatment should cost in your area. You may also want to consult one of the resources in appendix D that offer an independent evaluation of the scientific evidence behind your doctor's recommendation.

2. How will this test/surgery/exam change my treatment? If the answer is "It won't, but it might be good to know," take a pass. Doctors likely feel the need to do something or order something if you have a complaint, especially at a time when office visits can cost over $500. When a doctor begins a suggestion with "Why don't we just . . ." there's often no compelling reason for the test at all.

3. Which blood test are you ordering? What X-ray? Why? When doctors order blood work, they are frequently just ticking off boxes on a long electronic checklist, with no awareness of how much any might cost. Your questions alone will make them more discerning.

4. Are there cheaper alternatives that are equally good, or nearly so? If you go to a pharmacy or a lab and encounter a high price, call your doctor's office and tell him or her about it. Force your doctor to learn. He or she likely didn't know.

5. Where will this test/surgery/exam be performed—at the hospital, at a surgery center, or in the office—and how does the place impact the price? Doctors often practice and do procedures in different places on different days of the week. If you go on a Thursday and that happens to be your doctor's day at the hospital, it could double the price of your biopsy or colonoscopy. If he or she refers you to an ambulatory surgery center, ask, "Are you an owner?" A little shaming might encourage better behavior.

6. Who else will be involved in my treatment? Will I be getting a separate bill from another provider? Can you recommend someone in my insurance network? Avoid a lot of unexpected charges up front by making sure that whoever is involved in your care—doctor, physician assistant, pathologist, anesthesiologist—is in your insurer's network.

The Value of Waiting Before Seeking Treatment

American patients need to take back ownership of what it means to be healthy or sick. Commercialization has recast our health as a series of disease states: the cause of every symptom needs to be urgently diagnosed and treated. "Do something!" "Time is of the essence." The healthcare industry spends nearly $15 billion on advertising annually to encourage worry. That's good business, but not smart medicine. Complaints like chest pain, severe shortness of breath, or sudden double vision need to be evaluated urgently. But most problems—coughs, back pain, a rash—can be treated by waiting to see if they resolve themselves.

The value of so-called watchful waiting is taught in medical school, but it is terrifically underused in American medicine because it isn't at all profitable. The "Do something!" strategy prevails. But scans aren't always helpful. Each one sets off a cascade of treatment, and they often detect "junk"—incidental insignificant findings—unrelated to your symptoms. For example, MRIs of many middle-aged people *with no back pain at all* show bulging disks or some arthritis. These "abnormal findings" become a "disease" and a "diagnosis," which leads to treatment in the form of surgery or a steroid injection. The rate of spine surgery in the United States is about double that in Canada and Europe and five times that in Great Britain, calculates Richard Deyo of Oregon Health & Science University. One nationally renowned and respected back surgeon, who gets frequent requests for second opinions from patients who've been told they need an operation, told me that three-quarters don't need surgery at all.

Don't rush to the doctor. Give your body a chance to heal. Start with some advice from a pharmacist (their knowledge is terribly underutilized in our system). Expect your doctor or an assistant to talk you through the early stages of a potential medical problem by phone or e-mail rather than requiring you to come in.

Part 2. System Change: What We Want from Doctors

In 2014 Dr. Eric Scaife, a surgeon at the University of Utah, reported in the *Annals of Surgery* that when parents were informed that two types of appendicitis surgery were equally effective in children and given a price, two out of three picked the cheaper option—even if they had insurance that would cover either. (The more expensive choice involved using laparoscopic surgery, which sounds cool, but doesn't produce superior results in kids.) Ninety percent of parents said they liked having the choice, Dr. Scaife and his colleagues found. Medical journals contain endless studies debating whether patients can be effective shoppers. We can and we want to be. But we need information, and the first step in the process is doctors themselves learning and having far more access to information about medical pricing.

In training, doctors are generally taught little to nothing about the cost of healthcare. This ignorance has profound implications both for their future practices and for us. How can a doctor prescribe the best medicine for a patient if he or she doesn't know the relative costs of three classes of drugs? Cost and cost-effectiveness should be integrated into medical school curricula, and national medical boards should test this knowledge.

Individual doctors often have a hard time extracting prices from the finance departments of their hospitals and testing centers. The business side has encouraged, even enforced, this separation and, consequently, the ignorance it breeds. Because doctors don't know that receiving supplemental oxygen through the nose is billed by the minute—or that it is billed at all—they might habitually order oxygen therapy on every patient who comes out of surgery for the next twenty-four hours, whether or not it's needed. Prices should be included on order sheets or, at the very least, hospitals should provide medical staff with their master price list—the chargemaster—so they can educate themselves about what services the hospital charges for and how much.

Even in their own offices, doctors may feel they cannot share information about price or what the patient is expected to contribute. The discounted contracted rates that your doctor's finance people have negotiated with insurance carriers are protected by "gag clauses" or other nondisclosure agreements. Though some states have declared these illegal and they are of uncertain legal weight in court, doctors may still be afraid to divulge the information. Or they may be consciously hiding something that will make money for them: the high price charged by their in-office lab, for example.

It should be considered a doctor's obligation to provide you with financial information. That includes, at the very least, a cash price list of services rendered in the office. Your insurer may have a lower, contracted rate, but in an age of high-deductible insurance, you could still pay the first few thousand or have a significant co-payment. Unenforceable gag clauses in insurance-doctor contracts should be no excuse for blocking price transparency. You'll be paying at least part of that bill, after all.

An internist should also know, for example, the rates of labs and radiology centers in the geographic area and at the local hospital; he should direct you to the cheapest ones that deliver high-quality service. (Your doctor knows that, you don't.) Some centers routinely charge double or triple their nearby competitors' rates. I want my doctor to refuse to patronize the plastic surgeon who charges tens of thousands of dollars for a few stitches, or a radiologist who attempts to bill $5,000 for an MRI. Don't be afraid to push. Patients and doctors have long avoided these conversations, preferring a "don't ask, don't tell" approach until the bill arrives. It's too late then.

When Ann Winters's pediatrician's office referred her to a plastic surgeon to sew up a small cut on her toddler's face, Dr. Winters (an internist) didn't ask the price; the pediatrician's office staff certainly didn't ask the plastic surgeon's either. The bill for the three stitches from the surgeon was $50,000. (The plastic surgeon's office had greased the wheels for referrals by periodically dropping off trays of sandwiches for the office staff.)

At first, these will be tough, awkward conversations. A few years back, Dr. David Gifford, who was then director of the Rhode Island Department of Health, asked the more than one dozen labs in the state how much they were charging for some basic blood tests. "They all said it was confidential, they were protecting patients, everything under the sun," he said. "I was the commissioner of health who licensed them, and it took me a year and a half to get answers." For the same test, prices varied by a factor of twenty.

The chain reaction of price transparency begins with patients posing the same simple question: "How much does that cost?"

Price transparency is routine in many other countries and demands for it are growing in the United States. In France, where a public and a much smaller private health insurance system run in parallel, Dr. Fabrice Gaudot, an orthopedic surgeon, quotes a price to privately insured patients before each surgery. Basic price lists are posted on office walls. Dr. Gaudot and his patients sign a simple binding contract about what services will be rendered and what charges they will pay. His surgeon's fee in 2013 for a joint replacement was under $2,000.

In Australia, it is now considered every doctor's professional obligation to obtain informed financial consent as well as medical consent from patients. Here's the policy as stated by the Australian Medical Association: "Every medical practitioner is responsible for ensuring that their patient is aware of his or her fees and for encouraging open discussion with their patients about health care costs." The primary doctor for a procedure or a hospitalization is responsible for getting fees in advance from any ancillary doctors.

Don't we deserve as much?

Malpractice and Medical School Reform

The high cost of malpractice insurance and lawsuits is not a primary cause of expensive medicine in the United States. Still, studies show that about 80 percent of doctors will be named in a suit by the time they are sixty years old. Malpractice lawsuits are humiliating for hardworking physicians and result in many hours of depositions and testimony. Even though patients usually lose these suits, about three-quarters of doctors say that worries about malpractice suits at least occasionally influence their practice and encourage excessive test ordering. Reforming the malpractice system will also be good for patients. The most frequent beneficiaries of our current system are lawyers. Yes, patients on rare occasions get $10 million payouts—but only years after protracted legal action and settlements, or jury trials. On the other hand, the many patients who merely want the results they were promised and reasonable compensation to cover their costs often don't get them. Though the U.S. healthcare system is rife with mishaps and errors, studies show that a physician who committed an error leading to an injury has only a 4 percent chance of having to compensate the patient.

Malpractice reform is atop the wish list of every physician, and fair enough. Here are a few suggestions:

1. Place limits on noneconomic damages in malpractice lawsuits to dissuade patients from bringing frivolous suits in the hope of a huge payout. A small number of states have adopted this policy. In California, for example, patients can sue for the costs of past and future medical care as well as income lost as a result of injuries or poor medical outcomes. But there is a $250,000 limit on claims to compensate for less tangible things like emotional suffering. Though studies have shown that such laws do not, in fact, decrease the number of legal actions, medical societies are huge advocates of this solution, which does seem to decrease doctors' anxiety.

2. Encourage arbitration. Because malpractice lawsuits are typically long, drawn-out affairs that end in settlement, it makes sense to have a system of judge-directed arbitration or dispute resolution at the state level. In our current malpractice system, patients with serious injuries as the result of malpractice or defective medical products often wait years for a payment even as their day-to-day medical expenses mount. Barbara Baxter, whose defective hip implant was leaking cobalt into her blood, had to pay out of pocket for years for the follow-up of that failure.

3. Offer warranties and guarantees. Part of the reason why medical malpractice has grown into such a lucrative industry is because our medical system is terrible at responding to unhappy customers. Hospitals and doctors should offer patients warranties on certain predictable services. A few are already doing it. The Surgery Center of Oklahoma, for example, guarantees that if there are complications after your operation the center will take care of the problem at no additional charge. If your new hip dislocates two weeks after surgery, they redo it. There would be fewer malpractice lawsuits if providers were up front about acknowledging problems and took on responsibility to correct them.

Finally, if we want to train the best, most caring doctors to join the battle against costs, we need a fairer way to finance medical education. The huge expense of medical school may encourage some students to choose profitable specialties in order to easily pay back loans and deter others from entering fields where pay is relatively low, such as neurology, endocrinology, and family practice. It would be simple to set up a government program that forgives loan repayment for young doctors who go into lower-paying fields or set up practice in underserved areas—and keeps forgiving repayments as long as they stay there. If you choose to become a dermatologist or an ear, nose, and throat surgeon in suburban New York or Miami—fine, you pay back every penny you borrowed. But if you want to deliver babies in rural Oklahoma or practice pediatrics on the South Side of Chicago, then you get to keep your salary.

Doctors are, in fact, patients' best allies in any new quest to overhaul our high-priced system. Though some physicians are profiteering, many are today extremely distressed about the hijacking of their hard work and commitment for others' profit. Patients deal with the inefficiencies and absurd complexity of our medical system when they have an ailment. Doctors deal with it 24/7.

Here are two encouraging recent examples:

1. After a patient confronted Dr. Hans Rechsteiner, a general surgeon in rural Wisconsin, about a $12,500 hospital bill for a minor operation in 2013, the Tri-County Medical Society took on healthcare costs. "I had always felt good that I'd saved a patient's life by a simple act like taking out an appendix," said Dr. Rechsteiner, who was the society's president. "I realized right then I was bankrupting them too."

The doctors of the society, political neophytes all, took out an advertisement in the local newspaper to propose a list of bold cost-saving ideas. They should be music to many patients' ears. (1) Price transparency should be mandated: "The difficulty in obtaining the cost or price of medical care should end. These should be very easy to obtain. *Doctors are as ignorant as patients as to these prices and hospitals should teach doctors and patients these prices, not hide them.*" (2) Not-for-profit hospitals *"should be not-for-profit.* Period. These organizations currently hide large profits in excessive executive compensation, excessive lavish building projects, bloated foundations, and other 'shell games.' . . . If they invest in fancy new facilities that cannot be financed by more modest charges, they *should be allowed to fail.*" (3) "Physicians should be prohibited from owning medical care facilities of any nature that they could potentially refer patients to. Examples include surgicenters, laboratories, imaging equipment, etc. *This is clearly conflict of interest and should be illegal.*"

Like a growing number of doctors, they also support the expansion of Medicare to include younger patients, to create a simpler, more practical health plan: "We all bitch about Medicare but it covers my costs, and insurance companies now sometimes pay less," Dr. Rechsteiner explained.

2. Radiology, for decades one of the most aggressively business-focused specialties, is undertaking some serious introspection about how its practices have contributed to high medical costs. A few years ago, Dr. Richard Duszak quit private practice and left behind his years lobbying Congress for higher payments on behalf of the American College of Radiology. Instead, he took an academic job at Emory University and helped found the Harvey L. Neiman Health Policy Institute to study when scans were actually useful and at what cost. "We decided we'd look at the data and let the data inform the agenda," he said, "rather than the other way around." Already the Health Policy Institute has unearthed some fascinating findings: for example, radiologists in Florida perform five times as many tests per Medicare patient as those in Ohio, suggesting an epidemic of unneeded tests ordered strictly for profit.

Likewise, in the fall of 2015, the journal *Academic Radiology* devoted an entire issue to the overuse of radiology tests edited by Dr. Saurabh Jha, a professor at the University of Pennsylvania. Dr. Jha, who had practiced in Great Britain and Australia, said he was shocked at the batteries of tests Americans routinely received, many of them useless. Cost-effective, patient-centered, evidence-based care was often taking a backseat to generating as much revenue as possible, he said.

The journal's special issue is particularly critical of the now-accepted practice of routine radiological screening practices for various cancers: thyroid, lung, breast, and prostate. In some cases the scientific evidence that supports the practice is missing; in others—such as for thyroid cancer—studies have *proven* it useless. Some owners of radiology centers, particularly those whose business models center on screening, must have felt their hearts skip a beat when Dr. Jha called even mammography "one of medicine's marginal calls."

The best doctors will not be threatened by questioning, skeptical patients. They too are discomfited with the way we deliver medicine and the prices we pay. Their goals are the same as yours.

14

HOSPITAL BILLS

(40 TO 50 PERCENT OF OUR $3 TRILLION BILL)

Part 1. What You Can Start Doing Now

Patients are often incredibly loyal to a particular hospital. But, like loyalty to a sports team, this allegiance is often born of emotional history (I had my baby there) or based on amenities (good food and sweeping views from the rooms) rather than reflecting evidence or knowledge of good care. Doctors gossip in disbelief about people who could go anywhere, such as celebrities, politicians, and CEOs, who seek treatment from second-rate doctors or hospitals because of such bonds and the special VIP services they dispense.

Vet Your Hospital

Start before you are ill. Yes, you can go to Yelp for customer reviews, although many patients have told me they are reluctant to publicly criticize online a doctor or a hospital that they may need to consult for follow-up procedures. You can have a look at *U.S. News & World Report*'s Best Hospitals rankings, which rely on reputation within the medical community, as well as a published set of statistical metrics, such as nurse staffing ratios and the number of mishaps after seven common procedures. Keep in mind that business consultants offer to teach hospitals how to game these metrics. It pays to remember too that reputation is squishy, and physicians often know little about the warts and all of hospitals other than the ones they are affiliated with. But there are tools available that you can use as a barometer of hospital quality, although some are relatively young and still works in progress. (See appendix B for the tools to vet your hospital.)

First consider each hospital's general safety record: Does the hospital protect its patients from errors, infections, and injuries? Not all hospitals are the same, and some are much safer than others. The nonprofit Leapfrog Group grades all general hospitals on patient safety on a scale of A to F. It has a great reputation for objective measurement. An A or a B is probably all right, as it would be for a sanitary score for a New York City restaurant, but if your longtime hospital gets a C or a D year after year, you might want to ask your doctor why he or she is still there.

Leapfrog also offers information on the quality of different procedures offered at a hospital. Nearly half of all hospitals in the United States now answer Leapfrog's surveys on topics like C-section rates, the qualifications of intensive care doctors, and readmission rates after surgery for complications. If your hospital has declined to respond to Leapfrog's questions, ask why. Be suspicious of any hospital that believes it is above scrutiny.

There's also a wealth of information to help you assess your hospital through Medicare's young online Hospital Compare program, which provides data on all 3,600 hospitals that take Medicare payments. There you'll find measures of how often care was rendered in a "timely and effective" manner (did it provide state-of-the-art treatment for a stroke, for example) and hospitals' comparative records regarding complications (such as infections from deep intravenous lines). Hospital Compare was all set to release a five-star rating system for hospitals on April 16, 2016—it had even sent out the press release. But its debut was postponed by two months at the last minute after intense lobbying from the hospital industry, and a letter from sixty senators questioning its merit. Only 87 hospitals had been awarded a five-star rating and 142 got only one star, and they had been notified in advance of their performance. When the program finally went live in July, it faced intense political pressure, so it is perhaps no surprise that many hospitals are listed as "no different than the national average" in many specific categories.

To complete the picture with information about hospital pricing, check out Medicare's Provider Utilization and Payment Data for inpatient stays. Medicare publicly released data on hospital pricing for the first time in 2013, also over the vehement objections of hospitals. You can view the data on Medicare's Web site or in the more consumer-friendly formats that have been created by media organizations. Though Medicare itself actually pays hospitals a more or less fixed rate, which is a small fraction of the billed amount, some hospitals routinely charge two to four times more to treat a host of common illnesses. For example, in New York City, NYU Langone Medical Center was charging $74,000 to implant a cardiac pacemaker in 2011, twice as much as NewYork-Presbyterian, which charged $35,000. Both charged far more than $20,000, which is what Medicare deemed appropriate.

Depending on your insurance, you may or may not be paying any of this excess directly out of your own pocket. In any case, put all the information together and decide if your hospital deserves your continued patronage. Remember, scientific studies do not demonstrate a correlation between price and quality of care.

Finally, check one of several Web sites that provide free downloads* of your hospital's IRS Form 990 (only available for the approximately three-

---

*See appendix B.

fourths of U.S. hospitals that claim nonprofit status). It makes for eye-opening reading. One of the first sections lays out the compensation of the hospital's many executives. Elsewhere you'll find the hospital's "operating surplus," or profit. In Schedule H, the hospital lists the services it purportedly provides to the community to justify its continued non-taxpaying status. As you and your community press your hospital for change, you decide whether items like sending doctors in training on a mountain retreat or holding a greenmarket once a month in an unused parking lot is pork-barrel spending or genuine community service.

In the Hospital

You can protect your financial health while in the hospital by asking the right questions. Unless you are on Medicare or are a member of an HMO, your stay is (for now) most likely being billed intervention by intervention, visit by visit, item by item. Take these precautions:

1. Hospitals have built a huge oversupply of private rooms, though insurers frequently won't cover their cost. If you are assigned to a private room, make it clear that you did not request it and would be happy to occupy a room with another patient. Otherwise, you might be hit up to pay the "private room supplement" by your insurer.

2. In the pages of admitting documents you'll have to sign, there is inevitably one concerning your willingness to accept financial responsibility for charges not covered by your insurer. Before you sign, write in "as long as the providers are in my insurance network." You don't mind paying the required co-payments or deductibles but not out-of-network charges. For every medical encounter, Olga Baker, the San Diego lawyer, adds a "limited consent" clause to the chart, indicating that "consent is limited to in-network care only and excludes out-of-network care."

It has worked well for her and, at the very least, this annotation will give you a basis for arguing later.

3. Be clear on the terms of your stay in the hospital: Are you being admitted or held under "observation status"? Ask point-blank. The answer will have big implications for your wallet. Hospitals can keep you for up to three days (two midnights) on observation status. Though you will be in a hospital bed, you will be considered an outpatient and be responsible for outpatient co-payments and deductibles, which are generally far higher than those for an inpatient stay. (Recall how observation status cost Jim Silver several thousand dollars in chapter 2.) If you are on Medicare, the government insurer will not count days on observation status toward the three days of hospitalization required for coverage of a stay in a rehabilitation center or nursing home after discharge. Ask why you cannot be fully admitted. If there's not a good answer, insist on going the admitted inpatient route.

4. If you're feeling well enough, ask to know the identity of every unfamiliar person who appears at your bedside, what he or she is doing, and who sent him or her. If you're too ill, ask a companion to serve as gatekeeper and guard. Write it all down. Beware the nice doctor who stands at the foot of your bed each day and asks if everything's going OK. That pleasantry may constitute a $700 consultation. There's an epidemic of drive-by doctoring on helpless inpatients. These medical personnel turn up whether you need or want them, with the intent of charging for their services. Remember that you can say no, just as you can refuse a hotel porter's offer to take your bag. Did an internist stop by, even though you had already seen yours? Does the hospital send a physical therapist to help you out of bed after surgery and then bill for the service when a nurse could offer the same assistance? Did someone call for a dermatologist to examine a rash that has nothing to do with your present illness? Tell them all to go away. Everything done to you or for you in the hospital will be billed at exorbitant rates.

5. If the hospital tries to send you home with equipment you don't need, refuse it, even if it's "covered by your insurance." This is a particular concern if you've had an orthopedic procedure. Avoid $300 bills for slings you could buy for $10 at a pharmacy, $1,000 knee braces, and $2,500 wheelchairs, all billed to insurance and cluttering up your front closet.

Dealing with Bills

1. If you receive an outrageous bill from a hospital, a testing center, or a medical office, don't wait—negotiate! Prices are so inflated that even low-level clerks are often authorized to approve major discounts. If you haven't met your deductible and are paying out of pocket, make an offer. I've heard from patients who've had bills for a $3,000 emergency visit for a broken ankle and a $25,000 hospital stay more than halved *on the spot*. If a hospital has to refer your payment to a debt collector, it will likely lose way more than half anyway. The comedian John Oliver purchased (and forgave) nearly $15 million worth of medical debt for less than $60,000 as a stunt to illustrate the excesses of the collections industry.

2. When a hospital bill arrives in the mail, request complete itemization. Many hospitals will use umbrella headings like "pharmaceuticals," "room," and "surgical supplies" on their bills to try to fudge full disclosure of costs. You want to know exactly which medicines and implants were used by the surgeons in the OR, for example, and the charge for each. In hospitals these days, every pill, every piece of surgical equipment, every splint is bar-coded; the hospital knows exactly how much will be charged for each item.

The hospital may resist answering your inquiries and tell you that privacy regulations governing healthcare—such as those under the Health Insurance Portability and Accountability Act of 1996 (HIPAA)—prevent such revelations. That's wrong. Some hospitals say they don't discuss billing with uninsured patients "as a matter of policy." But that's not their choice. An itemized bill is your right.

Appendix C provides a glossary of billing terms and abbreviations that will help you decode the entries. You may not be able to do much to reverse the lofty $2 charge for one Tylenol pill because hospitals are allowed to set whatever prices they want, but you can protest large, particularly egregious charges. We all need to send the message that hospitals and other health centers can no longer act with impunity.

3. Check the bill against the notes you made while you were in the hospital. Make sure you received the services for which you are being charged. In an age of automated billing, errors are highly likely. One study found that over 90 percent of hospital bills contained mistakes, and others have detected errors in 50 percent of bills or more. The sooner we all start scrutinizing these statements and demanding some answers, the quicker this nonsense will stop. Hospitals will be forced to account for their billing practices.

Many patients have complained to me that itemized bills take weeks or months to arrive or never even show up. But the very act of asking to receive an itemized bill serves to protect your financial health. If a biller threatens to send you to collection or has already done so, tell the company that you're waiting to receive the itemized bill and disputing charges. In this way you can short-circuit the process and can protect your credit record.

4. Protest bills in writing to create a record. Protests via e-mail or letter are harder to outsource than phoned complaints, which can be easily referred to an operator in a distant call center. Send a copy of your letter to a reporter at your local newspaper and the state insurance commissioner or consumer protection bureau. If your protest is about a doctor's charge, send a copy to his national specialty society (for example, the American Society of Plastic Surgeons or the American Academy of Orthopaedic Surgeons). These societies care about professional reputation and can sanction doctors for outrageous charges. That $50,000 charge for stitches needed by Dr. Ann Winters's toddler was reduced to $5,000 after a specialty society intervened and threatened the doctor's accreditation.

Arm yourself with embarrassing statistics. Look up the Medicare payment rate for your procedure to determine a reasonable offer. Medicare pays out according to each hospital's own calculated cost for delivering care, plus a small profit. The hospital's IRS Form 990 will give you its operating profit ("surplus"), as well as what it claims are its payment policies and rates for patients who are uninsured or underinsured. Depending on the hospital, it may be worth applying for a bill reduction under those policies. The system is so arbitrary, you never know. When one patient found himself billed for $1,800 of a $2,700 ER bill (after insurance, and not including the doctors' fees), he sent in his pay stubs, as instructed. "Usually I think I am too rich to be poor and too poor to be rich with my average income and don't bother," he said. "But this time I asked for an application and sent them my pay stubs. And lo and behold I qualified for fifty percent off my bill."

For patients who pay cash, a growing number of online pricing tools, such as Healthcare Bluebook, Pratter, ClearHealthCosts, and FAIR Health, are available to determine and compare costs for outpatient hospital procedures in your zip code (see appendix A). They will help substantiate the good faith nature of your offer. Be cognizant that these tools employ local "reasonable and customary" charges or locally reported charges as their metric—remember that in some high-priced areas that benchmark is extortionate. For an expensive procedure, it might behoove you to look at prices in another nearby city or state. They may be much lower and a better barometer of what's reasonable.

Finally, if you are lucky and live in one of the few states that have managed to create a functional claims database ("All Payer Claims Database"—APCD), you can check online to see what medical providers in your state charged for your needed encounter. Unfortunately, the creation and quality of such programs have been hampered by lawsuits from insurers and health plans as well as by reluctance on the part of companies to turn claims data in.

5. Argue against surprise out-of-network bills. Sometimes, in spite of your best efforts to choose providers and facilities in your insurance network, one or more of the doctors involved in your hospital care, perhaps the pathologist or the surgical assistant or the anesthesiologist, ends up outside your network: "We regret to inform you that this provider does not participate in your insurance plan," the bill reads. Until the laws and regulators in your state better address this problem, you have to push back yourself. You have grounds not to pay.

Informed consent is a bedrock legal and medical principle. This is the essence of your argument: You went to an in-network hospital so that your care would be covered. You were not informed of the out-of-network status of these providers and did not consent to them participating in your care. The doctor and the insurer will have to work out a fair price themselves. You will pay only the co-pay you would have had to pay for an in-network provider. The same argument can be made for serious emergency care, because you had no say about where to go after a car accident or woke up paralyzed. (See appendix E for some templates for protest letters that you may adjust to suit your situation. They work. I've used them myself.)

Hospitals and doctors get away with unconscionable prices and practices because they think patients will be too timid to call them out on their greed, but they are very sensitive to bad publicity, to being exposed, or to the prospect of losing the confidence and support of a big local employer.

Part 2. System Change: What We Want from Hospitals and Hospital Regulators

Many states make a big deal of requiring all hospitals to post a long, elaborate "Patients' Bill of Rights," which is usually a mix of the absurd, the meaningful, and everything in between. In New York, for example, the bill includes perplexing features like the right to "a no smoking room" (smoking has long been illegal in hospitals), as well as the right to "receive complete information about your diagnosis, treatment and prognosis" and the right to "receive an itemized bill and explanation of all charges." But the right to a basic up-front estimate of your charges is not included. Nor is the right to not be charged excessive rates.

Patient-Friendly Price Disclosure

It's easy for hospitals to give us good binding estimates or even precise charges. Voters should lobby state regulators to require it or at least press hospitals for more complete disclosure of costs.

Every hospital has a master price list—the infamous and generally hidden chargemaster—often developed with input from business consultants. Since 2004 California law has required most hospitals in that state to post their chargemasters on a regulatory Web site. The law was intended to shed light on how hospitals calculate their prices. It also requires the state regulators to determine the twenty-five most common inpatient stays, and in each case to list each hospital's average charge. In 2006 an addendum to the law required hospitals to provide uninsured patients with a written estimate for services they "reasonably expected to provide" during a hospital stay—if a patient requests it.

In practical terms, the law is of little benefit to patients. The estimate service only applies to the uninsured and only if they ask. State regulators were given no authority to "set or limit" the chargemaster prices, no matter how outrageous. Chargemasters do not have to be presented in any standardized format, making prices nearly impossible to compare from one hospital to the next.

In fact, hospital chargemasters are tailored to obfuscate, consisting of tens of thousands of entries with little logical order, using codes and idiosyncratic medical abbreviations. Here's my attempt to translate some typical items from the chargemaster of Mills-Peninsula Medical Center, the hospital where Susan Foley had her knee surgery:

SURG LVL 4 ADD 15M.. . . .$2190.43 [each additional fifteen
    minutes of operating time after the first thirty minutes in a
    "level 4" case—whatever that is]
PT MMT BODY WO HAND 45.. . . .$688 [some kind of
    physical therapy session]
XR FB IN EYE for $407.95 [X-ray of foreign body in the eye]
KAO PLAS DOUB FREE KNEE MOL J.. . . .$4284.02
    [a piece of an implant for a joint replacement]

The California chargemasters provide so much disorganized information that essentially none of it is useful for the consumer-patient. The other forty-nine states do not require hospitals to disclose their chargemasters at all. In fact, hospitals fiercely guard these price lists. Even in billing lawsuits, judges often require hospitals to merely provide screen-shots of the subpoenaed chargemaster's relevant pages.

But the California law plants seeds of change. Hospitals should publish their chargemasters in a standard, easy-to-understand format. State regulators could force disclosure, as they've done in California. Doctors and patients could also apply pressure for voluntary release with ballot initiatives and petitions to their local hospitals. If hospitals, medical offices, and testing centers knew they'd have to publish prices for everyone to see, an outrage like $50,000 for three stitches would become a thing of the past. "No Surprise Charges" could become the industry mantra. Hospitals making that promise would have my business.

Hospitals in your network should also be required to guarantee that all doctors who treat you are in your insurance network. State regulators should insist that this be written into insurance contracts, and your company HR representatives should insist on this during annual policy negotiations. The hospital has contracts with emergency room doctors, anesthesiologists, pathologists, and radiologists. It has up-front bargaining power to ensure they join networks if they want to work under the hospital's roof. Of course, not every single doctor has to participate in the many insurance plans with which the hospital has contracts. But if you have Aetna insurance, and the hospital takes your plan, the ancillary doctors who treat you should take Aetna too.

A few states have recently passed laws offering patients some protection from surprise out-of-network charges. New York is considered a national model. Its laws are a start, but still inadequate. They stipulate, generally, that if you visit an out-of-network hospital in an emergency or get treatment from an out-of-network doctor at your in-network hospital, you are only responsible for an amount equal to your plan's in-network charges. The insurer and the hospital have to work out the rest of the payment.

Unfortunately, this still places the onus on the patient. First, you have to know such a law exists. Then, you exercise that right by sending the errant bill back to your insurer and to the hospital, along with a new surprise billing form that can be downloaded from the Internet, all in duplicate and on paper. I have tried to do it after receiving a surprise out-of-network charge, but six months later—after filling out the form twice—I was still receiving monthly bills and demands for payment from a collection agency in a distant state that appeared not to know of the law's existence.

"Care Packages" with All-Inclusive Rates

Some hospitals and surgery centers have created packages with all-inclusive rates that cater to self-paying patients, people with very-high-deductible plans, or libertarians who choose not be insured. Ralph Weber's MediBid, an online service based in Tennessee, matches paying customers with vetted doctors who are willing to offer a good package price. Colonoscopies and MRIs are the most requested procedures. Colonoscopies range from $535 to $1,200 all-inclusive; prices for hip replacement packages run from a low of $7,500 (overseas) or $12,000 (in the United States) to a high of $21,000. When Mr. Weber's wife needed arthroscopic knee surgery that he anticipated would cost $20,000 or more at their local hospital, he put the procedure out for bids on his Web site. A surgeon at a major university medical center in Virginia offered to do it for a total cost of $3,700. The couple accepted. The Surgery Center of Oklahoma likewise offers all-inclusive pricing if up-front payment is made. On its Web site, a total knee or hip replacement is listed for $25,000 and a knee ligament repair for $6,790.

There are even a few financially strapped public hospitals that now offer all-inclusive prices and packages, although for very different reasons. A few years ago, Maricopa Integrated Health System in Arizona, whose population includes many uninsured and undocumented patients, began offering fixed-price maternity care for $5,460 for county residents and

$6,500 for other Arizonans, but the package is only available to women without insurance. It includes a normal vaginal delivery (with or without epidural) as well as all prenatal visits, doctor's appointments, scans, lab tests, and initial follow-up care for baby and mother. There is an extra $1,750 ($1,850 for noncounty residents) charge if a woman needs an emergency C-section, and $200 extra for twins. These types of packages, called "bundled" or "episode" pricing, shouldn't be a choice only for cash-paying patients. Why aren't they routinely offered to people who use health insurance? One likely reason is that this type of pricing cuts into the profit margins of hospitals whose patients have good coverage.

Pursue Your Charitable Mission . . . or Pay Your Taxes

States and municipalities should more aggressively challenge hospitals' tax-exempt status. In 2015 Judge Vito Bianco of the Tax Court of New Jersey revoked the tax-exempt status of Morristown Medical Center, part of the Atlantic Health System, sending shock waves through the industry. The mayor of Morristown had sued to collect property taxes. In his bluntly worded decision, the judge wrote that "modern nonprofit hospitals are essentially legal fictions," which have for-profit affiliates, like doctors' practices, and CEOs paid as much as those of banks. These hospitals advertise on TV alongside luxury automakers.

The looming threat of losing tax-exempt status would motivate hospitals to limit their more egregious business practices—such as turning inflated patient bills over to debt collectors—and to think more about providing affordable community-minded care. If not, these highly profitable conglomerates should be treated the same way as Microsoft or Walmart by the Internal Revenue Service. Instead of giving them tax-exempt status, tax them, and allow them to take credits or deductions when they perform charity. Few local politicians have dared to challenge hospitals on their tax status. Make this an issue in your next mayoral election. Your local hospital is likely one of the candidates' biggest campaign contributors. Patient-voter voices can counteract that influence.

Use Antitrust Law to Break Up Oversize Hospital Conglomerates

Antitrust regulators and attorneys general who prosecute wrongdoing on behalf of the people should also be more aggressive in blocking the kind of extreme consolidation in healthcare that is leading to today's high prices. Many legal scholars believe that existing antitrust legislation could be applied far more forcefully. The Sherman Antitrust Act of 1890 prohibited cartels, monopolies, and trusts to prevent price gouging and protect consumers. The Clayton Antitrust Act, passed two decades later, forbids specific anticompetitive behaviors, such as agreements between parties that restrain trade, mergers that create monopolies, and acquisitions where the effect "may be substantially to lessen competition, or to tend to create a monopoly."

Many expanding hospital systems would seem to be in clear violation of these acts. When a hospital doesn't let outside radiologists feed results into its electronic medical record system, is that a restraint of trade? When the neurosurgeon enters into a secret deal with the hospital to get exclusive access to patients in its emergency room, is that anticompetitive behavior?

"I do think there's a legal means for interrupting this march," Jaime King, a professor of health law at the University of California, Hastings College of the Law, told me. "I would like to see the FTC and the DOJ take a more global perspective." While both the Federal Trade Commission and the Department of Justice have jurisdiction over healthcare-related mergers, they tend to divide oversight, with the former overseeing hospitals and doctors' groups and the latter taking care of insurers. They judge whether the gains in efficiency achieved by a merger outweigh the loss of competition. If a merger is regarded as problematic, the agencies can sue to block it, or challenge it with an injunction. In recent decades they have been business-friendly and somewhat lily-livered in using their power.

Twenty years ago, the FTC lost a number of high-profile antitrust cases in healthcare, tempering its appetite for such expensive litigation— especially since hospital legal departments are now very well-funded adversaries. Also, in that earlier era, more cooperation between hospitals in an area was seen as a good thing, so mergers were allowed. But healthcare has now reached the point where consolidation is leading to price inflation, with little benefit for patients. In many regional and local markets, one or two health systems exert extraordinary control. The legal pendulum needs to swing back, with renewed FTC leadership and action. Happily, it may be doing so: there's been a spate of enforcement activity since mid-2015, including a few victories.

State attorneys general frequently initiate the cases that the FTC joins. They are elected officials, many with a populist bent. Patients are a huge voting block and should let AGs know that this matters. A high-profile win in court against a health system that has been throwing its weight around with predatory pricing would work wonders for a young AG's reputation. Many judges are also elected officials, and an evenhanded decision in this regard will win the public's trust.

Unfortunately, the current interpretation of the antitrust law often leaves out practical patient considerations. If one health system has acquired all the radiation oncology centers in an area and raises prices with its monopoly, currently the FTC may be inclined to accept the arrangement because it is economically possible for radiation oncologists from elsewhere to move into the market and set up shop. Similarly, the FTC does not intervene in pharmaceutical cases where only one company ends up owning the market for a particular medicine and uses that power to raise prices, as notoriously occurred in 2016 with the EpiPen. With prices high, new competitors will enter the market, leading to a price correction, or so the theory goes. "In this country, it's not illegal to have a monopoly and to use it to raise your price," an agency official told me, explaining the inaction. "We believe in the market to solve the issue."

But this logic fails to take into account the many barriers that a new doctor or drugmaker faces before selling services or products. What happens to the cancer patient who needs radiation before a new physician is recruited, sets up practice, gains local insurance contracts, and secures hospital admitting privileges, which can take years if it is possible? What happens to the elderly person who needs heart medicine every day, while a new drug manufacturer decides to enter the market, gains FDA approval, and sets up a production plant?

To protect consumers, its original mission, the FTC will need to be more proactive in reviewing and halting creeping consolidation, rather than waiting for mandatory reviews to be triggered by large mergers. Under the 1976 Hart-Scott-Rodino Antitrust Improvements Act, mergers valued under $76 million do not need to be reported to the commission for review. But many healthcare systems consolidate by a gradual series of lesser acquisitions: a few surgery centers here, a cancer treatment center there, a bunch of doctors' practices a year later. In this way, a near monopoly can accumulate under the radar.

When Health First bought the Space Coast Cancer Center for just under $20 million, the deal didn't have to be reviewed, even though it meant Health First controlled oncology for a wide swath of Florida. Health First is both an insurer and an owner of hospitals in the region. The merger meant cancer patients had to travel more than thirty-five miles to find another provider if they did not sign on for Health First's insurance, a huge burden for those undergoing regular chemotherapy or radiation treatment. This stranglehold on the market is now the subject of several lawsuits brought by other local hospitals and oncology practices, who say that Health First has used its monopoly power to destroy their ability to offer cancer therapy.

The FTC and state AGs may even need to break up some larger health systems to ensure that healthcare markets function.

Some state AGs armed with FTC backing seem inclined to jump into the fray. In January 2015 a case brought by the Massachusetts AG essentially blocked the Harvard-affiliated Partners HealthCare from acquiring three community hospitals and a large number of doctors' practices in eastern Massachusetts. The arrangement would have dangerously given Partners "market muscle, to exact higher prices from insurers for the services its providers render," the judge wrote. Around the same time, an Idaho federal court of appeals overrode Saint Luke's Health System's 2012 acquisition of the Saltzer Medical Group, a large network of doctors, on the grounds that whatever efficiencies resulted paled when compared with the threat of hospitals and doctors driving up prices. Such cases have been a "wake up call to hospitals" said Matthew Cantor, an antitrust lawyer with the firm Constantine Cannon in New York. They are hopeful signs that state and federal regulators are ready to adopt a more consumer-oriented interpretation of the hundred-year-old statutes meant to protect us.

Standards for Hospital Billing and Collection

There is no industrywide or legal standard about when medical accounts should be considered seriously delinquent—one hospital might send a bill to collections after 30 days, another after 120, and another not at all, said Mark Rukavina, the CEO of Community Health Advisors, a policy and consulting firm in Boston, and a healthcare executive with more than two decades' experience. There is likewise no good way to predict which hospitals will go even further, such as putting liens on property.

For these reasons the U.S. Consumer Financial Protection Bureau has recommended reforming medical billing by including more fair and predictable timetables. But even modest congressional bills such as the Medical Debt Responsibility Act (2014), which would require all credit bureaus to delete reports of delinquent medical debt once settled or resolved, have never even made it out of committee because of opposition from credit agencies.

Patients should insist on a clear commitment from hospitals on the terms of our financial engagement. After what time period of delinquency will bills be sent to collection? Six months would seem a minimum, given how long it takes for insurers to process their portion of the payment. There should also be a promise that no bill will be sent to collection while the patient is disputing its legitimacy. If hospitals do not voluntarily define acceptable practices—locally and nationally—state or federal legislation should create and enforce them, just as they have done for mortgage lenders.

15

INSURANCE COSTS
(NOT EVEN CALCULATED INTO OUR $3 TRILLION BILL)

Part 1. What You Can Start Doing Now

Selecting a Plan

Shopping for health insurance is perhaps the hardest task facing any consumer. Think about choosing among the four or five cell phone providers in your area, and imagine your life or the life of your child depends on the choice. It's much harder to predict your health needs than your cell phone use in the coming year. Will someone have a heart attack, break an arm, or get cancer?

One depressing fact about the Affordable Care Act is that the final version had the government allocate $67 million to pay "navigators" to help patients choose from its offerings, even though the plans are more standardized than those on the commercial market.

Navigators can help you work through your choices and questions—they are free at the point of service, but of course you're paying them with your taxes. They have diverse credentials: some are brokers who may have a long-standing relationship with a particular insurer (though they are not permitted to take money for referrals), and others are employees of community organizations who've received a bit of training. Lean on them for advice, but they may be only marginally more informed than you, so understand your options and have a strategy for shopping policies.

Many patients only look at premiums when they purchase health insurance. That made sense in the old days, when insurance covered almost everything with little extra payment, but today you must consider the entire dizzying package. The premium: the amount you pay each month to be insured. The deductibles: the amount you must pay out of your pocket before insurance kicks in. The co-payments and coinsurance: the patient's contribution for each medical purchase or encounter. The out-of-pocket maximum: the limit on how much you will be expected to pay in a given year, *if* you've played by the plan's rules. The network: the collection of contracted doctors and hospitals you must use in order to have the plan cover your care or, at least, to reap the plan's full financial benefits and promises.

1. Premiums. For those lucky enough to have employer-sponsored healthcare, find out what percentage of your premium you are paying, and just how much is being paid in total for your healthcare. When it's just a number deducted from a weekly paycheck, we don't feel the appropriate outrage. When I went on leave to write this book and had to write checks for my entire insurance premium myself, I discovered that my family policy costs over $2,200 a month.

2. Deductibles. Most health policies don't kick in anything until you've paid a certain amount out of your own pocket. So-called high-deductible plans are increasingly common and may not kick in at all until you've paid out thousands of dollars. This type of insurance, which requires lower premium payments, used to be called "catastrophic" coverage. You just pay as you go for regular doctor's visits and tests, until you require a procedure or have a serious medical need that pushes you beyond, say, your $5,000 or $10,000 deductible bar. You need to be crystal clear about your deductible and how it's calculated. Is the $3,000 deductible calculated per person or for your whole family? Are there separate deductibles for in-network and out-of-network care? Many plans only count care that is in-network or care that would be covered by your policy toward your deductible. So the $250 per week you've elected to spend on private psychoanalysis or the $350 you've spent for a new asthma inhaler that isn't in your plan's formulary doesn't help you reach that magic number when your insurance kicks in.

3. Co-payments and coinsurance. Not very long ago, co-payments were likely to be fixed and low—say, $20 for an office visit or a prescription. Today, the portion of a medical bill the patient is expected to pay varies widely, and is often a percentage of the physician or pharmacy bill. The devil is in the details. Your co-payment may depend on whether care is rendered by a generalist or a specialist. For drugs, it will depend on whether the medication is included in your plan's approved formulary (meaning the plan has a contract with the drugmaker) and whether your insurer regards it as a basic drug to be widely dispensed or a specialty drug to be sparingly used. Profit is often the primary metric, so the tiers are based not on medical need but on the contracted price. Insurers put generic or cheaper drugs in the lower tiers and more expensive ones higher. The lower-tier drugs may require only a $5 co-payment while the higher-tier "specialty drugs" may require a 30 percent patient contribution amounting to thousands of dollars, even though those drugs are sometimes medicines for which there are no substitutes and which some patients can't do without.

Pay close attention to how a plan structures its co-payments and keep in mind what medical attention you typically need. If you visit doctors often, avoid a plan that requires a percentage co-payment for office appointments. If you need to have your blood checked frequently, look for one that requires no patient cost sharing for in-network lab tests. If you're in the ER once a month—say you have an accident-prone toddler—avoid a plan with a co-payment of $500 per ER visit. You should know if a trip to urgent care is covered as a doctor's visit (with a $20 co-pay) or requires a 30 percent patient coinsurance—leaving you with hundreds, if not thousands, of dollars to pay. Finally, and perhaps most important, check to make sure the drugs you take on a regular basis are included in the insurer's formulary and to what extent their cost is covered. Is there a clause that will require you to try what the plan considers to be a more "cost-effective" drug? Just because you and your physician consider a particular medicine to be essential for maintaining your health does not mean your insurer will bear the cost.

4. Annual out-of-pocket maximum. The idea of a yearly out-of-pocket limit on patient payouts was a noble improvement imposed by the ACA that protects people with major illnesses from losing their homes or their entire retirement savings. In 2016 the legal maximums were $6,850 for an individual and $13,700 for a family (some plans offered out-of-pocket maximums that were less than the legal limit). But, as with deductibles, you must have a very clear understanding of how your insurer defines these limits and what will count toward them. For example, some insurers do not count drug costs or may continue to ask for co-payments for office visits even after you've reached the magic number. Treatment you considered necessary but was never approved by your insurer is unlikely to be counted. This means that you must be vigilant about securing preapproval and sending in claims forms, even before you've reached your deductible, so that you get proper credit toward the magic number when insurance is obliged to take over the cost. It also means that if you choose to visit a world-renowned specialist rather than one in your network, you may well be paying on your own.

5. The network. Choosing a network is perhaps the most important and the hardest part of shopping for health insurance. The information provided by insurers is notoriously outdated and unreliable. Remember that all plans from the same insurance brand are not created equal: for example, a dermatologist considered in network for one Aetna plan may be out of network for another. You need to get very specific. Likewise, don't be hoodwinked by terms like "Freedom" or "Liberty" in network names. These attempts at sales and branding do not indicate more choice or a broader array of options. In an era of narrow networks, it is extremely important to understand how you are covered outside of your immediate geographic area. The Affordable Care Act allows children to stay on their parents' plans until they turn twenty-six, but many families discover that their new plan offers no in-network coverage for a young adult child who goes to college or gets a first job in another state. While Medicare is accepted across the nation, snowbirds under sixty-five, who spend half the year in Florida or Arizona and the other up North, will belatedly discover that their commercial insurance covers their healthcare in one place or the other, but not both.

It is often simplest to work backward as a strategy to choose the best option. If you want to stick with your current doctor or your current pediatrician, start by calling the office and asking for a list of plans in which he or she participates. If you or someone covered by your policy has a serious medical condition for which you need to retain a particular hospital or doctor, start there. One of my children had complicated neurosurgery as a teenager, so the single most important factor in choosing insurance plans subsequently was whether that doctor (and the hospital where he operates) was in my network. Check to see that the plan offers a reasonable local selection of the types of doctors people are likely to need (orthopedists and gynecologists, for example). Many plans are lacking in these specialties. On lists of providers, be wary of dozens of doctors at a single address. These are often clinics in or affiliated with a hospital; they may even be run by doctors in training, or residents. They may be a fine place to get healthcare, but you should call and inquire about the nature of the practice; you may not be able to see the same doctor at each visit, and residents will leave after a few years, compromising continuity of care. You should decide in advance if you're comfortable with that. Also be prepared to think outside the box. Many women prefer a female gynecologist, but you have a better chance of finding an experienced OB/GYN in network if you're willing to go with a male as I have done. (There were essentially *no* fully trained women gynecologists affiliated with my preferred hospitals anywhere near my Manhattan home in my network.)

When considering a plan, carefully review the hospital offerings in the network. Pay particular attention to specialty hospital offerings. Any hospital can take out an appendix, treat an asthma attack, or deliver a baby, but some conditions require higher levels of expertise. Does the network include a nearby hospital with a good neonatal intensive care unit, or a designated national cancer treatment center? In New York City, for example, if I have a rare cancer, I want to retain the option of going to Memorial Sloan Kettering Cancer Center in network, if only for a second opinion. Even a biopsy review and some tests out of network could run you many thousands of dollars if you're paying on your own.

6. HMO options. Surveys show that Americans strongly value having the "freedom to choose any doctor." Many HMOs got a deservedly bad reputation in the early 1990s, when they were far more concerned with saving money than delivering quality care. But some have survived and now provide excellent care within their closed networks. In healthcare the ability to choose may not be as important as your emotions tell you, especially when there is so little transparent information about price or quality, and we are bombarded with misleading advertising.

Jane Moyer, a Penn State professor who has designed healthcare benefits for major corporations in both the United States and Europe, is surprised that freedom is such an American priority. "My students say they want choice and control," she told me. "Even if they know that other ways will lead to better outcomes and lower cost. But when I ask them, 'So how do you choose a doctor or a specialist?' they say things like 'I ask my neighbor.' It makes no sense at all."

In theory, many policy makers and primary care physicians are great fans of closed medical systems like HMOs because doctors from many disciplines work together—rather than in silos—to provide highly coordinated care. In fact, many doctors and health researchers point to the U.S. Department of Veterans Affairs (VA) system as a model for all-inclusive care. It has many enviable features.

In recent years, some VA hospitals have come under fire for long wait times and delays in certain areas of service, particularly mental health; administrators falsified data on wait times, to make them more acceptable. But part of the reason that we even know about those failures is that the VA operates as a *system,* with standards and transparency. It publishes prices for drugs and uses its buying power to negotiate good discounts. It has clear standards for how often patients should get a particular test, like a colonoscopy or a pap smear, and follows them. It has stated maximum wait times for different types of appointments, generally thirty days for nonemergency care. It tracks when they are not met.

The VA has centralized record keeping so patients' doctors know what all their other doctors have done. Because all treatment comes from one fixed budget and there is no payment per procedure, there is no incentive to order tests on people who will not benefit from them. There are no facility fees, which means there is no motivation to do procedures in an operating room that could be performed in an office. There is little spent on marketing.

One physician who had recently started working at a VA hospital told me how elated he was to join a system where it is so easy to deliver preventive care. He mentioned the VA's ten-year-old MOVE! Weight Management Program, which provides counseling and exercise programs for patients with obesity and type 2 diabetes; it is by far the largest medical program of its kind in the United States. Every veteran is screened annually for weight and referred if needed. "I have not seen such a comprehensive weight management program in the private sector," the doctor said, where "care for the same condition seems oriented toward profitable expensive medications and lucrative weight-loss surgery."

Long-term financial incentives support good HMO care. Because patients typically remain in such systems for a decade or longer, HMOs benefit from offering preventive care that will stave off diseases much later. In the commercial sector, patients and employers shop annually for better insurance deals, so customers are here today, gone tomorrow. "Overall, the available literature suggests that the care provided in the VA compares favorably to non-VA care systems" in the private sector, a large comparative review of the literature found. Of course, only military veterans can use the VA's system.

In the private sector, some HMOs offer a similar, all-inclusive approach to patient care—complete with better amenities and fancier patient-friendly features than in the somewhat bare-bones VA system—and have excellent reputations. Intermountain Healthcare in Utah and Idaho and Geisinger Health System in northeastern Pennsylvania are two notable offerings. The well-established HMO leader is Kaiser Permanente, which has a wide coverage area in California (and a smaller footprint in the Northwest and Washington, DC); it operates hundreds of clinics and dozens of hospitals. (The organization evolved from company industrial healthcare programs started in the late 1930s and 1940s for workers at the Kaiser family's network of shipping yards.)

Protocols govern care and treatment at Kaiser, including preventive visits. All of the doctors work on a salary with small bonuses for achievements like having patients' blood pressure under control rather than "productivity." Specialists make more money than primary care doctors, but there is much less of a salary gulf than in the fee-for-service market. Kaiser invests heavily in information technology to allow better communication between its members and the vast array of doctors, nurses, and ancillary personnel on their team. If you see a general practitioner for a rash, he or she can send a picture to a dermatologist for an instant opinion. If a member is worried about symptoms that may represent a stroke, a neurologist and a cardiologist are on call 24/7 to take video-enabled calls; the specialists are able to watch the patient's mouth move when he or she talks, for example, gathering important clinical evidence for a diagnosis. There are no extra charges for these types of services.

Kaiser enjoys a devoted patient clientele and physician loyalty, including among medical specialists who could earn more if they were in private practice. The HMO generally performs well in J.D. Power's annual health plan quality ratings, ranking first in California, Colorado, the Mid-Atlantic region, the Pacific Northwest, and the Southeast. Kaiser Permanente of the Mid-Atlantic States, an East Coast outpost, scored first among hundreds of health systems in ten out of fifty-five categories, including breast cancer treatment.

There is strong pressure in systems such as Kaiser to keep patients at proprietary facilities. An ambulance might be instructed to drive a patient with chest pain a short distance past other medical centers to a Kaiser-affiliated hospital. But, as we've seen, where an ambulance takes you in the fee-for-service world is also governed by many forces, some of them financial.

During the 1990s, HMOs catered to the low-end market, mostly unions and people who couldn't afford the more expensive fee-for-service options. But today, in some parts of the country, they are the choice of many patients who could go anywhere. "Kaiser focuses on what matters to me," said Professor James Robinson, a health economist at Berkeley and a Kaiser member. "The hospitals are new and the care is great, but they use generic drugs and they don't give you free champagne when you have a baby."

Here's what to look for if you're thinking about joining an HMO (unfortunately, there are no plans that meet these standards in some states):

- Genuine systemwide integration of services; avoid brands that feature individual physicians operating independently (for example, can an orthopedist get immediate advice from an infectious disease specialist, or do you have to schedule two appointments so both can bill?)
- Salaried physicians; no productivity bonuses
- A physician-managed system—or at least one that bestows significant decision-making power on physicians
- A meaningful use of technology: connecting patients and caregivers after hours; free access to all medical records within the HMO
- A clear process for, and a history of, referring patients who have rare conditions that require expertise or treatment not available within the HMO to outside providers

7. Is a nonprofit right for you? Finally, always take a special look at any *nonprofit* options. There are the few cooperatives still standing that were created by the Affordable Care Act and a smattering of nonprofit insurers in the commercial market. Nonprofit plans are few and far between at the moment, but the very fact that nonprofit insurers have no shareholders means that none of the money they take in goes to investors. Their primary customer is you and your health. Of course, in an industry rife with gamesmanship, the choice to go with an insurer that labels itself nonprofit requires due diligence: California stripped Blue Shield of California of its nonprofit status in 2015, after noting that its behavior didn't qualify for the moniker. I hope to see a renaissance of plans that hark back to the days when the nonprofit Blue Cross Blue Shield plans evoked a trusted brand instead of a lucrative conglomerate.

Part 2. System Change:
What We Want from Insurance

We deserve a simpler, more transparent system for choosing insurance. There are reforms that could make this possible. Employers and insurance regulators could do a lot to curb system excesses today by exercising powers they have right now and applying laws that are already on the books. But they have interpreted their mandates narrowly, ceding to the business of medicine a wide swath of dubious territory. Employers outsource the byzantine task of plan design to consultants—some good, some incompetent—for whom the only metric of success is to control spiraling expenses. It's time for consumers to urge both regulators and employers to marshal their enormous clout to demand better for patients.

State Insurance Regulators

In January 2015 California's state insurance commissioner, Dave Jones, dropped a bombshell as he was being sworn in. He was enacting a new Emergency Medical Provider Network Adequacy Regulation because many health insurers offered such limited numbers of doctors and hospitals that it was essentially impossible for patients to find care in the narrow networks. As a result, "consumers have been forced to pay huge out-of-network charges," he said.

The new regulation addressed the problem in several ways. It required insurers to maintain adequate rosters of primary care doctors, specialists, and hospitals to fulfill the medical needs of their policyholders, as well as to maintain up-to-date and accurate directories. The provisions might seem obvious, but at the time they were revolutionary. Mr. Jones, a Harvard-trained legal aid lawyer, is an anomaly in his field: in most other states the insurance commissioner is a veteran executive from the insurance industry and finely attuned to its needs.

Most state insurance commissioners have been far too passive thus far in regulating and policing policies, in part because their backgrounds make them disinclined to do so and also because there is little organized public pressure. Instead of being proactive in setting rules and clear standards for policies, they wait for complaints from patients. After navigating mountains of medical bills, how many patients have the knowledge or energy to complain to state officials?

With little up-front policing, health insurance provider directories are almost laughably inaccurate, and formularies are no better: from one month to the next, a low-tier drug covered with a $20 co-payment suddenly vaults to a tier that demands 20 percent of its $1,500 cost.

Consumers should be able to expect some fair standards from their health insurance policies—standards that states should mandate and enforce. If yours does not live up to these standards, complain in a loud voice to your company and your insurance commissioner.

1. The network provider contract must be in force for the same period of time as the health insurance policy. Consumers buy health insurance based on provider lists, so they should not change during the term of the policy.

2. If a procedure is listed as covered under a plan, then all tests and ancillary services normally associated with the procedure should also be covered. It's time to put an end to surprise out-of-network bills for anesthesia or pathology or intraoperative monitoring.

3. Provider directories must be kept up to date. (That's easy with computers.)

4. A patient should pay only in-network fees if there is no other choice but to use a facility or a provider outside the network for treatment (as in an emergency or if a patient's hospital doesn't provide an in-network referral).

5. Directories should not be able to list meaningless categories to describe doctors and hospitals, such as "in-network but not available" or "not in-network for that procedure" or "not taking new patients." Such terms artificially pad the insurer's list to make its network seem larger. They are not useful for a patient. A provider who wants to serve my lucrative medical needs should be there for my less lucrative ones too.

6. Streamline statements that define annual "out-of-pocket" maximum payments. Impose the same clarity that regulators demanded banks adopt to describe the terms of loans after the housing crisis. As it stands, this maximum payment may or may not include drug costs or out-of-network care. As Marisa Maupin of Lancaster, California, discovered, it can even go up 50 percent from one year to the next without your being informed, or with that huge change buried in a thirty-page legal document.

THE AFFORDABLE CARE ACT has taken baby steps in the right direction to address consumer concerns. For example, it requires insurers to disclose and justify in advance proposed premium increases greater than 10 percent, and gives state or federal regulators the power to review them. That authority, in theory, gives experts a chance to "evaluate whether the proposed rate increases are based on reasonable cost assumptions and solid evidence and gives consumers the chance to comment on proposed increases." But in most states, the regulators do not then have the concomitant power to deny the increases, making the exercise moot. Even in states where insurance commissioners possess that authority, called "prior approval," they overwhelmingly do not use it.

"Generally, the rate review looks at whether the calculation is actuarially accurate: Did they do the math right and did they make reasonable assumptions?," Larry Levitt of the Henry J. Kaiser Family Foundation told me. "That includes notoriously unpredictable assumptions about whether healthcare costs will rise or fall. Depending on what assumptions you make, you can produce premiums that are whatever you want."

Premium hikes of 9.9 percent can pass through without being scrutinized or justified at all under the ACA, even though many patients find such increases financially challenging. Some states have tried to use even higher bars for health insurance reviews. In 2012 Alaska proposed moving its threshold for reporting and review to premium increases of 17 percent, for example.

Regulators should also exercise their authority to judge whether an insurer's network is adequate. Does the plan have enough specialists in a fifteen-mile range? Can subscribers get in to see a doctor within a couple of days for urgent matters and two weeks for less pressing health needs? Does the network offer cancer care, maternity care, and emergency care by fully trained doctors within a reasonable geographic radius—not just at resident teaching clinics? What might that radius be in a city or a rural area? Standards are needed.

Most important, we need to hire consumer advocates—not industry gadflies—as state insurance overseers. If we pay attention we can influ-

294 AN AMERICAN SICKNESS

ence who gets these jobs. Look up your state insurance commissioner. In thirty-seven states, governors appoint insurance commissioners quietly with little public scrutiny; in Virginia and New Mexico they are appointed by "a multi-member commission." This is an extremely important position for your healthcare, which deserves a public vetting. If you do happen to live in a state where the insurance commissioner is an elective official, pay attention to this down-ballot issue.

More Creative Plan Designs

Our employers and unions, through which most of us buy insurance, should demand new types of patient-centered products from the health insurers with whom they negotiate. Some interesting models that are in use on a small scale deserve far broader adoption. Look for the features that follow when you select a plan or ask your company to use its muscle to request these kinds of innovations when it selects insurance plan options for its employees; large employers and unions can have clout, if they choose to use it. A few of the new, hungry-for-customers insurance start-ups should be eager to play ball, if they stand true to their promise of aiming to be disruptive innovators in a pretty ossified field.

1. Reference pricing. CalPERS (the California agency that manages health benefits for public employees and retirees) and some large West Coast companies are experimenting with an innovation called "reference pricing" that essentially leverages contracted insurance plans to prod hospitals or doctors to create well-priced all-inclusive packages for common procedures like joint replacement, cataract surgery, and colonoscopy.

Having discovered that it was paying anywhere between $10,000 and $125,000 to hospitals for joint replacements, CalPERS enlisted health researchers to determine how much it should cost to buy a high-quality procedure in California. They came up with $30,000 as the "reference price." CalPERS then told its insurance vendors and covered patients that it would contribute that amount for a hospitalization for joint replacement. If the patient kept to that price or chose a lower-priced option, he or she paid the usual co-payment. If the patient chose a center that charged more, he or she paid the co-payment plus the entire difference. Because CalPERS represents nearly two million members (and, for health insurance, some family members as well), California hospitals turned somersaults to meet the reference price rather than lose that potential customer base. The number of California hospitals charging prices below the CalPERS reference price rose from forty-six in 2011 to seventy-two in 2013.

The reference price plan likewise gave patients a powerful new incentive to seek out a hospital that came in under the bar. One big problem with typical high-deductible health insurance policies is that while they make patients far more cost-conscious and (perhaps) judicious about outpatient tests that cost under $5,000 or $10,000, they do little to influence decision making about $100,000+ bills for hospital stays. For cancer chemotherapy, heart surgery, or even a hip replacement at an American hospital, the yearly out-of-pocket maximum barely gets you through the door. After that, the insurer is paying, and patients put the costs out of their minds. Reference pricing changes that.

In the first two years after implementation, reference pricing saved CalPERS—and California taxpayers—$2.8 million for joint replacement surgery, $1.3 million for cataract surgery, $7 million for colonoscopy, and $2.3 million for arthroscopy, with no change in success rates or patient satisfaction.

2. Bundling. The progressive unbundling of every medical encounter has inflated medical bills. To fight back, Medicare has been experimenting with new types of all-inclusive or bundled payments, and more insurers should be doing so. Overall, bundling has much the same effect as reference pricing, though it leaves the patient's willingness to save or spend on their healthcare out of the equation.

Medicare has long bundled the portion of payments that went directly to the *hospital* for inpatient stays (essentially room, board, nursing, and tests) via its DRG (diagnosis related group) system. Hospitals receive a set payment for Medicare patients with simple pneumonia, for example, no matter how many tests are done or how many days the patient is hospitalized. But Medicare has lately concluded that it may well be wiser to wrap *all* aspects of treatment into bundles and not just for patients in the hospital.

When kidney dialysis centers were allowed to bill separately for dialysis and for giving injections of Epogen, a drug that can fight anemia, clinics were using huge amounts of the drug. Anemia is common in people with kidney failure. By 2005 Epogen had become the single largest drug expenditure for the Medicare program. That was true, even though studies showed Epogen was not particularly useful for most patients whose anemia was caused by kidney failure, and could even be harmful. Then, in 2011, Medicare announced a bundled payment scheme in which providers would, on average, receive $230 per treatment to cover dialysis, including the cost of all injectable medications or their oral equivalents and typical laboratory tests. The use of Epogen plummeted.

In July 2016, Medicare proposed that it pay an all-inclusive bundled price for hip and knee replacements in many parts of the country, building on a voluntary program it has been testing for several years. The bundle will cover all care from the day surgery is recommended until ninety days after it has been performed. The level of payment will cover the hospital, all the doctors, physical therapy, and any rehabilitation. Each party will bill separately and if the charges come in below the bundled price the hospital gets to keep some of the difference. It is penalized if they come in above it.

In pilot programs, the scheme produced great savings, with equivalent results. At NYU Langone Medical Center, for example, the cost and standard practices involved in hip replacement surgery radically changed with the financial incentives. When not paid for each service, the hospital decided that patients required only $742 of inpatient rehabilitation compared with $6,228 before the program; it also decided that if patients were extremely obese they should not be offered the surgery unless they lost weight, because surgery was unlikely to help or be much more complicated otherwise. Other centers concluded that extended formal physical therapy after hip replacement (which typically today costs thousands of dollars in the United States) doesn't yield benefits over exercises patients can do at home, which is how patients recover in much of Europe.

Medicare is also looking at how bundling can be applied to more chronic conditions. In theory, for example, a primary doctor might be paid, say, $50 a month as a management fee to take care of each patient with asthma or high blood pressure. There would no longer be an incentive to call the patient into the office for a visit or to order another test to capture revenue. This makes sense given that home monitoring has vastly improved and advice about issues like medicine dose adjustment can be easily dispensed via text.

Taken to its extreme, bundling could even lead to a payment system called "capitation": a yearly fee for health systems to meet all of a patient's needs. On January 1, 2015, the Boeing Company contracted with two Washington State hospital systems to care for its twenty-seven thousand employees. It pays the systems a set yearly per capita fee for all of the care. The deal has much in common with HMO care and with that historic first insurance arrangement that the Texas teachers' union struck with Baylor in Dallas a century ago.

States have wide-ranging powers to impose such creative insurance schemes if they dare to use them. Healthcare is, at heart, a local service. In the past few years, Vermont and Colorado have debated implementing some sort of statewide single payer system, though these initiatives have ultimately failed.

Most notably, Maryland has long been a creative outlier in the way it pays hospitals. For more than thirty-five years, its independent Health Services Cost Review Commission has set bundled rates for hospitalization; all insurers, including Medicare, pay the same rate for the same procedure on every patient. (To undertake such experiments, states need only to get a waiver from the Centers for Medicare and Medicaid Services.)

In 2014 Maryland's experimentation got still bolder: the state assigned hospitals a "global payment" based on the number of patients in their system—similar to the capitated payments Boeing negotiated for its employees. They will have to use the money wisely and well to benefit patient health rather than profit by doing more visits and procedures. Patients and insurers will still see bills on the basis of the services provided to them, which will be used to determine co-pays. If the volume of procedures decreases, leading to less calculated revenue than the global payment benchmark, the hospital will get to keep a portion of the savings.

Bundled payments will succeed in controlling costs only if insurers draw a clear wall around what's included in the bundle and take the trouble to defend it ferociously. If a bundle for childbirth doesn't explicitly include epidural anesthesia, then a hospital will be tempted to make money by jacking up charges for that. (How many new mothers have been charged a "rooming in fee" when they tried to avoid nursery charges by having the baby stay in their room?) If the bundle for back surgery doesn't include neurological monitoring, it leaves patients at high risk for receiving huge bills for this essential service. And if there's an extra "management fee" for each patient with diabetes or high blood pressure, there is a temptation to try to place more borderline patients in those categories rather than pursue the hard work of encouraging them to change their lifestyles.

Better measures are needed to ensure that preventive care is increased and the quality is maintained as the amount of care, particularly expensive highly specialized care, is decreased. National studies have found that an estimated one-third of procedures are unnecessary. How do physicians decide which patients will benefit from an expensive Toric lens or Mohs surgery? In a system where everyone was paid more for doing more, no one really wanted to know those answers. Bundled payments give the medical world new incentives to find out what treatments actually work best.

Commercial insurers are ambivalent about bundled pricing. It means they will have to work much harder to fight hospitals' attempts to add on charges of $5,000 or $10,000, rather than just pass on costs to you. Hospitals, physicians' groups, and drug and device manufacturers, used to charging whatever they want to for their services, are opposed to the concept. If our complicated healthcare system were to switch to bundled pricing, then all the players would have to fight with one another to get their share of the spoils—instead of just robbing us.

3. Insurance policies designed to meet patient needs. Though new insurance products have been effective at protecting the industry's revenues, we (and our employers) should demand new types of plans that promote better health and more affordable healthcare for us instead.

For example, I have not seen health insurance plans in the United States that link the size of patient co-payments to a procedure's medical worth. Insurers could design plans that pay 100 percent for emergency or urgent surgeries and essential medicines, but only 80 percent for interventions that are semielective or entirely avoidable. Such a plan would not cover bypass surgery and appendectomies in the same way as elective sinus surgery and knee replacement. Full coverage for sinus surgery could be delayed until the patient had first enrolled in a six-month trial of nasal steroids to better control allergies; the patient with an aching knee would attempt a serious six-month weight-loss program before going under the knife. In both cases, the alternative temporizing interventions would be covered by insurance. In many European countries, medicines like asthma inhalers and insulin are free because their use prevents serious diseases that lead to expensive hospitalizations and long-term complications. For-profit insurers may not care about cost considerations down the road, be-cause people can change their plans from year to year, but companies and unions want to retain their workers for far longer than that, so they should carefully weigh the long-term pros and cons of the health plans they design.

Reward patients for working to improve their health or keeping up with recommended preventive care—that's what some German sickness funds do. A patient who gets routine dental checkups should be eligible for a discount if he or she needs a filling. Subsidize gym membership, or offer it for free, as long as the member uses it at least twice a week. Compass Professional Health Services designs wellness programs in which enrollees who participate and meet goals are rewarded with reduced pre-miums the following year. Plans could cover lung cancer treatment with $0 co-payment for those who had never smoked or who had quit.

Insurance plans should refuse to pay those dishonest "facility fees." A 2013 Medicare study found that the number of echocardiograms per-formed in a hospital, with a 50 percent markup attributable to a facility fee, was rising 7 percent annually, even though echocardiogram machines are now so small and portable that this test could be performed on a sub-way or a park bench.

Insurers could have been saying "no more" to those fees for years, but as long as the costs could be passed on to the consumer in the form of higher premiums and co-payments, they keep paying. In 2013 the Medi-care Payment Advisory Commission (MedPAC) recommended "site neu-tral payments"—fixed fees for studies, surgeries, and tests, regardless of where they are performed. No more minor hand surgeries costing tens of thousands of dollars thanks to added-on hospital fees. No more doctors' offices rebranded as hospitals for profit. Site-neutral payments could save Medicare an estimated half a billion dollars a year.

President Obama supported the idea in his 2016 budget, prompting a firestorm of protest from groups like the American Hospital Association, of course. The resulting congressional Bipartisan Budget Act of 2015 included a pale compromise, prohibiting hospitals from billing facility fees for services performed in a doctor's office that had not been considered part of a hospital before that date. This was a tiny step toward solving a much bigger problem. All the doctors' offices that had already been rebranded as hospitals were allowed to continue charging facility fees; also, the law applies only to Medicare patients, and it doesn't go into effect until 2017. What's more, it is still perfectly legal for simple tests and procedures, such as echocardiograms or the insertion of an IUD, to be performed at hospitals, just to pad a patient's medical bill with hefty facility fees.

16

DRUG AND MEDICAL
DEVICE COSTS

(ABOUT 15 PERCENT OF OUR $3 TRILLION BILL)

Americans comparison shop for cars, bread, electronics, and just about everything else—except prescription drugs. More than half of us regularly take prescription medications, and the contents of these pills, potions, and creams are highly regulated. We should be able to—simply and easily—buy from the cheapest vendor and at the lowest personal cost, but we can't. From month to month, the price of medicines can change, along with our co-pays, and we don't find out until we're picking up our filled prescriptions at the pharmacy counter. How much we pay depends on our insurance plans and their formularies.

In 2015, 72 percent of Americans said they considered drug costs unreasonable and about a quarter said they have a difficult time paying for their drugs, a proportion that rises dramatically for people who are poor or in poor health. Surveys show that millions of Americans don't fill a prescription because of cost. The government will eventually take action to address burdensome drug expense and inequities, since virtually every politician has recognized this as a major problem. But many of us simply can't afford to wait for our frustration to overcome DC gridlock, so in the meantime it's best to adopt some personal strategies to dampen the impact.

Part 1. What You Can Start Doing Right Now

Learn more about the contents and cost of the medications you are taking. Many expensive prescription medicines are just reformulations of older versions of the same drugs creatively repatented, not improved. Pills that combine two medicines, extended release tablets, and creams and ointments are often available in older, less expensive forms that are equally effective. For example, you can save a lot of money if you're willing to take two pills instead of one. (Sometimes those two pills may even be sold over the counter for a fraction of the cost of the combined medication, as in the case of Duexis.) Don't equate sudden price hikes with an increase in value; research alternatives. Ask your pharmacist or doctor if there are more cost-effective ways to take your prescribed medications.

My favorite antibiotic for smearing on infected cuts is a prescription preparation called mupirocin (brand name Bactroban), which is available in ointment or cream form. The clear ointment, which is older and off patent, costs $10 a tube. The white cream, which the drug company created when the ointment's patent was about to expire, is no better or worse in my experience and costs $115. A doctor writing the prescription likely doesn't know there's a huge price difference. Many steroid creams, whose actual contents are little more than a modified version of hydrocortisone, are absurdly expensive. Some acne preparations that cost $100 to $300 a month, such as Epiduo, are no more than a far cheaper generic topical antibiotic or a vitamin A derivative combined with peroxide.

Check your insurer's formulary to find out if different strengths of the medication are covered. One patient saw her co-payments for her usual dose of a thyroid drug quadruple overnight to nearly $300 a month, because that strength was removed from her insurer's preferred formulary. But she discovered that she could negate the increase if she bought a higher dose (still on formulary) and cut the pills in half.

Shop Around

GoodRx.com, a Web site and mobile app, will give you the *cash* price of every medicine at pharmacies in your area and provides coupons for discounts (the price you will pay if you forgo using insurance). A prescription's price at the pharmacy depends largely on the wholesale prices agreed to by your pharmacy, the drugmaker, the pharmacy benefit manager, and your insurer, plus the markup at the store. In some cases, the full cash price will be less than your insurance co-payment, in part because many chain stores offer rock-bottom cash prices on common pharmaceuticals to get shoppers in the door. If that's the case, tell the pharmacist you want to pay cash instead. (Pharmacy pricing resources are given in appendix A.)

The pharmacist may tell you (as I've been told when trying to pay cash for a prescription) that if you have insurance you "have to use it." But that is not the case: no law, no regulation, no waiver you've signed stipulates that you cannot pay cash for a prescription. What the pharmacy wants is the higher price and profit margin it obtains by forcing you to buy medicine through your insurance policy. Exercise your power as a consumer and either complain or have your prescription transferred to another pharmacy.

As of 2016, GoodRx.com began offering an online platform for Medicare patients that allows them to view their drug prices in advance as well as what their actual co-payment will be at different stores. It's a great tool for consumers to use to ensure that they're getting the medications they need at the lowest possible price. Unfortunately, GoodRx.com cannot offer the same platform to the rest of us, because commercial insurers consider pricing data to be proprietary information that is only revealed once a prescription is filled.

Consider Imports

If you need to take a drug but really can't afford it, you may want to consider buying it from a source outside of the United States. The cost is likely to be one-third to one-half of the U.S. price. Experts estimate that each year five million people order medicines abroad, though the real number is almost certainly greater because many people are reluctant to admit to doing something that's technically against the law (but rarely prosecuted). I've heard from a number of physicians who do so for themselves. If you decide to go this route, here are a few shopping guidelines:

1. If you're traveling to a country whose health system you trust, buy refills of medicines there. Pharmacists worldwide can often honor such requests because they have independent prescribing power. (Carrying a prescription helps. A foreign pharmacist may want to confirm that you're taking the medicine at the advice of a doctor.)

A few years ago, the manufacturer's recommended wholesale price of Advair, a popular asthma inhaler, was $250 in the United States, but $45 (for cash) in Paris. The money you save pays for your airfare to Europe, as one young man who used the strategy pointed out to me. You may even find that your medicine is sold over the counter in other countries. Steven Francesco, a drug company consultant, asks friends who are traveling in Europe to buy him Voltaren Gel, a nonsteroidal anti-inflammatory, for his tennis elbow and other musculoskeletal aches. In the United States, it requires a prescription and costs over $50 (with a coupon), but in Europe it is sold over the counter for under $10.

2. Rely on overseas mail-order pharmacies to order long-term medicines whose efficacy can be clearly measured, such as those that control cholesterol or an expensive medicine for low-grade type 2 diabetes; neither requires precise results and you can check these parameters to ensure that the medicine you received is working well. Starting a regimen with a foreign substitute might be less well advised for a drug used to prevent organ transplant rejection or seizures (since blood levels of these medicines are notoriously finicky).

Companies like PharmacyChecker.com will help you to ensure that the medicines you are ordering are not fakes. These online clearinghouses vet the pharmacies that sell drugs on their Web sites and source from English-speaking countries, so packaging instructions and warnings labels are understandable.

Importing drugs for personal use is technically illegal, but intercepting small packages of medicine is impossible from a practical standpoint—and the U.S. government has for a long time intentionally turned a blind eye to the practice so long as the supply is for three months or less.

Be Skeptical of Advertising and Marketing

The healthcare industry spends $15 billion a year on advertising, about the same as auto manufacturers. These are not public service ads: their purpose is to get you to spend money.

In the 1990s, when the United States became one of only two countries to allow television drug advertising, regulators attempted to balance promotion with a dose of reality by requiring manufacturers to list all side effects and adverse reactions. Manufacturers bury important information in these lists by including common, minor annoyances alongside serious and exceedingly rare reactions. Invokana, for example, an expensive and widely advertised new drugs for type 2 diabetes, can cause serious bone density loss and predispose to fracture—but you could easily overlook that amid the other cautions.

The FDA doesn't require the manufacturers' ads to compare a drug's efficacy with that of other drugs or treatments—prescription or over-the-counter—or to list a price. Jublia, a topical drug for toenail fungus approved in 2014, was advertised during the 2016 Super Bowl. A little bottle of the solution sells for between $550 and $650 and the full forty-eight-week course of treatment for all your toes costs over $20,000. But Jublia's cure rates are under 20 percent. Lamisil (terbinafine), a pill that does the same with a higher cure rate, costs under $20. Of course, that isn't mentioned in the ad.

So if you are tempted by a product in an advertisement, perform a bit of due diligence before "asking your doctor if it's right for you." Check the price on GoodRx.com, which will also inform you of cheaper and potentially equivalent options. Visit the Centers for Medicare and Medicaid Services Web site to see if Medicare covers the drug or machine, since the agency is reluctant to pay for useless treatment. Even the AMA, with its free market bent, seems to have gotten fed up with industry's dubious marketing, calling for a ban on pharmaceutical advertising in late 2015.

Part 2. System Change: What We Want from Manufacturers and Regulators

The U.S. system for approving, distributing, regulating, and (especially) pricing prescription drugs is different from that of any other developed country. Doctors abroad are dumbstruck when they hear the prices we pay for pharmaceuticals. And the sense of disbelief is just as palpable on our own shores: a high-level U.S. government official called me to complain about the exorbitant prices charged for some of the children's vaccines the government distributes for free. Though the federal Vaccines for Children Program does negotiate for discounts compared with the private market, it still pays prices that are higher than in much of the world because it can buy only versions that have gone through the FDA approval process.

For years, we have witnessed the occasional high-profile hand-wringing about drug prices performed by lawmakers on both sides of the aisle; true to form, no action follows. Do you even know where your representatives stand on this all-important issue? Here are some ideas that deserve serious consideration:

1. Import drugs. The idea of officially allowing the importation of drugs—by pharmacies or individuals—has long been supported by some lawmakers in both parties. It has been stymied by the pharmaceutical industry and its congressional proxies. The late senator Edward Kennedy championed the cause, but the only legislation he could pass before his death was an agreement that the FDA would not prosecute individuals who ordered drugs for personal use for less than ninety days. During the 2008 presidential campaign the then senator Barack Obama promised to "allow Americans to buy their medicines from other developed countries if the drugs are safe and prices are lower." In 2014 and 2015 Republican senator John McCain and Democratic senator Amy Klobuchar cosponsored a bill to allow drug importation, making it one of the few issues at least some members of both parties can agree on. It went nowhere.

These proposals generally aim to give Americans the right to buy their medicines from licensed Canadian, British, Australian, and Japanese pharmacies that are thoroughly regulated and vetted. These pharmacies would require a doctor's prescription from American purchasers, just as they do from their native customers. Only medicines tested and approved by their countries' versions of the FDA would be sold. If the right to import medicines in this controlled way was enshrined in law and supported by regulation, shopping for pills from overseas pharmacies would certainly be a lot safer.

By 2015 the Obama administration seemed to be moving in the opposite direction. President Obama's FDA commissioner, Dr. Margaret Hamburg, said the administration opposed importation out of concern that medicines could be counterfeit or unsafe and that guaranteeing their provenance was too complicated. (This is PhRMA's refrain.) In July 2015 President Obama signed into law a new FDA rule, officially implementing "its authority to destroy a drug valued at $2,500 or less . . . that has been refused admission into the United States." The Department of Treasury deals with higher-value packages, so this rule clearly targets personal prescription drug imports.

As more Americans are becoming comfortable with the practice of sourcing drugs from overseas (or perhaps because of it) the pharmaceutical industry is redoubling its efforts to stop importation, at both national and state levels.

Maine residents had long crossed the Canadian border to buy cheaper medicine, and city employees in Portland and some state employees had for years even been allowed to use their insurance to mail-order from up north. But a new Republican state administration forbade the practice in 2012, even though there had never been "one single problem," Troy Jackson, a Democratic state legislator and former logger, told me.

In 2013 Senator Jackson spearheaded the passage of a clever new law meant to allow Mainers to continue mail-ordering drugs from a few English-speaking countries, essentially by declaring that select licensed pharmacies in these nations were officially licensed in Maine. The Pharmaceutical Research and Manufacturers of America and groups representing Maine pharmacists quickly sued to block Mr. Jackson's legislation. While a judge ruled that PhRMA had no standing and could not be party to the suit, the pharmacists continued the quest, with generous industry backing. The brunt of the arguments to block the law seemed not to focus on whether the new scheme would benefit patients but that it would "cause Maine pharmacists to lose market share to these revitalized competitors." Ultimately, Mr. Jackson's law was overturned in 2015 (after he had left the state senate), when a judge ruled that it overstepped states' purview to contravene federal policy. Despite the defeat in Maine, drug importation might well be the next frontier for independent state action, if voters demand it. Many states have passed laws at odds with federal statutes, such as those governing gay marriage and marijuana sales. Once one state allows drug importation the rest will more easily follow. Blocking such laws should cost state legislators their seats in the next election.

2. Give pharmacists more prescribing power. In 2015 and 2016 California and Oregon enacted new laws allowing pharmacists to prescribe birth control pills, a cost-saving innovation. Since pap smears are only recommended once every three years, many women had to pay for a visit to the gynecologist merely to renew their regular contraceptive prescription. States could allow pharmacists far more leeway to dispense long-term medicines, such as asthma inhalers or thyroid pills. Medical society–backed "scope of practice" laws have long relegated these highly trained health professionals with Ph.D.s to counting out pills. States should allow us to take advantage of their knowledge and have three classes of medicines, as exist in much of Europe: over-the-counter, prescription, and pharmacist dispensed.

3. The FDA should reform the patent process and revamp drug and device approval. During the 2015 confirmation hearing of Dr. Robert Califf to run the FDA, Thomas Marciniak, a former drug reviewer at the agency, said that the FDA has allowed U.S. drugmakers to pervert the approval process. Dr. Califf, a Duke professor with long and deep ties to the pharmaceutical industry, was nonetheless handily confirmed by Congress. But many experts agree that the drug and device approval process could use some serious revision.

The lure of easy patents and big profits has induced drugmakers and device manufacturers to invest heavily in research and development to tease out new cures. For better or worse, this is how we reward innovation. (A Nobel Prize or a tenured professorship is seemingly no longer sufficient.) For many years, when vaccines sold for pennies, pharmaceutical companies weren't developing any new ones. Now that the price point has passed $150 there is a renaissance of research interest. In a similar vein, we count on big profits from one drug to finance a company's future research: so when a company gets quick approval for a drug to treat a rare disease and prices it at $30,000, profits can be used to study whether that drug will be a useful remedy for more common conditions. The process has benefits in some situations.

But it has also enabled aberrations like Hetlioz, an $8,000-a-month sleeping pill, and basic albuterol asthma inhalers that cost ten times as much today as they did two decades ago. Some pharmaceutical manufacturers and device makers have certainly been more restrained and accountable than others. But our system has no mechanism whatsoever to control the price of new wonder drugs, or independently estimate their true value for pricing. So they come onto the U.S. market costing two times more than anywhere else in the world, and then rise in price, rather than fall, as they age. Here are a few regulatory fixes that would start to address such outcomes:

The FDA maintains the so-called Orange Book, a list of all the patents that protect approved drugs, currently compiled regardless of the clinical importance of the innovation. It includes not just active chemical ingredients but also "peripherals," such as an inhaler case or the technology that makes a tablet chewable. All patents in the Orange Book must be expired or litigated before a competitor can start production of a generic. The agency could be more discerning about which patents it chooses to honor with a listing in the Orange Book, says Lisa Larrimore Ouellette, a patent law scholar, but it has "washed its hands of the matter."

The U.S. Patent and Trademark Office could restrict the patents available to drugs that do not offer true novelty or benefits, a proposal supported by Mark Lemley, director of the Stanford Program in Law, Science and Technology. The FDA could distinguish between patented products of high and low value to patients. For example, a drug that represents a genuine medical breakthrough could be rewarded with a prolonged period of market exclusivity, while a replica drug or a modification that merely offers greater convenience, such as a once-a-day formulation, could be granted shorter periods. Drugs judged to offer no significant benefit to patients (a chewable birth control pill?) could receive no market protection at all.

A grand jury–like panel should decide if there is a legitimate patent question on the table before a lawsuit can be initiated. In the opinion of many experts, drugmakers frequently file frivolous lawsuits that claim patent infringement solely to be rewarded with that automatic extension of patent protection for thirty months, while the case is adjudicated or settled.

The FDA should revamp its policies about the types of studies it requires drugmakers to perform before a drug is approved for use. For example, according to agency regulations, drugmakers' efficacy studies have only to compare new drugs with a placebo or nothing, instead of similar products already on the market. Crowded markets create a lose-lose situation for doctors and patients, who are forced to choose among half a dozen pricey drugs that have never been properly compared with one another to see which one is most effective.

The FDA could be more willing to accept the results of scientific studies from other countries and be more collaborative in deliberating with foreign counterparts like the European Medicines Agency, which approves drugs for use throughout the European Union. The enhanced cooperation would result in faster approvals and greater availability of some useful but not terribly profitable drugs: for example, the meningitis B vaccine called Bexsero that was unavailable in the United States when college campuses were fighting outbreaks. "All the data was that it is safe and effective," Dr. Andrin Oswald, a Novartis executive at the time, told me, "for which reason it was licensed in Europe, Australia, and Canada already."

Just as drug companies need approval to start producing a medicine, perhaps they should also need approval to cease production, especially if the event is likely to have a negative effect on the drug market. If a company's withdrawal would create a monopoly or a near-monopoly, the government could activate its "march-in rights," which allow it to assign certain patent licenses to a new company to make the drug because of a threat to public safety. Tripling the price of a lifesaving drug should be considered such a threat. Though the National Institutes of Health has never before used its march-in rights, in early 2016 fifty-one lawmakers wrote a letter to the secretary of health and human services urging the agency to determine if it could do so, to address soaring drug prices.

4. Negotiate national prices. National price negotiations are an extremely effective tool in setting and curbing prices for drugs and devices, which is why the strategy is used by every other developed country. In the United States, the VA and the Medicaid program bargain for considerable discounts or rebates across the country. But Medicare, the largest U.S. health program, which covers a wide swath of Americans, is legally forbidden from doing so.

In 2006, when prescription drug coverage was added to Medicare, drugmakers got the prohibition written into the legislation by claiming that the government's huge negotiating power would whittle down their profits and thus end groundbreaking research. The pharmaceutical companies' predatory pricing of essential drugs and corporate relocation overseas to avoid U.S. taxes have betrayed our trust. We should negotiate.

Countries use various strategies when negotiating drug prices. The British National Health Service tells pharmacists how much they will be reimbursed for dispensing a certain medicine, based in part on government researchers' estimate of the drug's worth. The pharmacists can then source that particular drug from any corner of the European Union. If a cheaper generic is for sale in Greece, then they will make more profit. Every four to five years, as drugs age, there are across-the-board price cuts. In France, the Ministry of Health negotiates the prices it will pay for manufacturers' drugs by comparing their prices with those of medicines in other European countries. If Medicare was able to negotiate reasonable prices on behalf of Americans in a similar way, commercial insurers could simply follow their payment guidance, getting rid of the many layers of middlemen and inefficient one-on-one corporate wrangling that drive up prices for American patients.

Just in the last couple of years, AbbVie charged $86,000 for a new hepatitis C drug in the United States, 50 percent more than the price in Great Britain; Martin Shkreli, a brash entrepreneur, charged close to $1,000 for an antiparasitic tablet that had once cost under $10; and Pfizer attempted to move its tax base to Ireland. It's time to fight back at a national level.

There are simple solutions. Congress could declare to the pharmaceutical industry that the United States will pay for its drugs no more than Canada is paying, for example. It could vote to allow Medicare to negotiate with the drugmakers, achieving prices one-third of those Americans get now, by some estimates. It could require the drugmakers to justify yearly price increases for long-used drugs and get preapproval. List prices for drugs increased more than 12 percent in 2015 alone.

In 2016 Jason Chaffetz, the Republican chairman of the U.S. House Committee on Oversight and Government Reform, held hearings on the high cost of prescription drugs. But political finance makes effective actions unlikely, unless patients speak up. During the first seven months of 2016 alone, Mr. Chaffetz had received over $95,000 from the health and pharmaceutical industry.

5. Promote pharmaceutical transparency, cost-effectiveness at all stages of the approval process. A business-friendly peculiarity of U.S. law means that the government bodies charged with the responsibility to ensure patient-centered healthcare cannot directly consider the pricing of treatments, medicines, or devices in their recommendations and deliberations. Even the Patient-Centered Outcomes Research Institute (PCORI), which was established in 2010 as an offshoot of the Affordable Care Act, is forbidden to do so. "Our founding legislation prohibits us from doing cost-effectiveness analysis," it notes on its Web site. "We don't consider cost effectiveness to be an outcome of direct importance to patients."

The theory behind the provision is that valuable treatments should not be rejected just because they are costly. But it has also meant that we don't know the prices or have cost-effectiveness data on *any* treatment, even those that have little or no medical worth at all. Here are two modest policy proposals in this sphere that patients should request:

Insist that makers of drugs and medical devices estimate a price point from the very start of the FDA application process. According to the FDA's mandate, it approves drugs based solely on whether they are "safe and effective," but the agency has the right to ask about cost. Include price as part of the debates at the FDA and in the broader medical community from the very beginning, even if it can't be considered as a factor for approval. The publicity alone could shame some drugmakers and device manufacturers from attempting to impose ex post facto exorbitant charges after approval has been gained—at least those that cared about their public image. It would also give doctors an opportunity to pressure drug companies to curb costs in advance, instead of being blindsided by sticker shock once a new pill is already on the market.

Create a national body like the United Kingdom's National Institute for Health and Care Excellence (NICE) that is tasked with assessing the value of new drugs and treatments. Are they cost-effective compared with other options already available and at what cost are they worth buying? The British National Health Service uses those judgments to negotiate for lower prices. Britain pays about 60 percent of the U.S. price for Sovaldi, a hepatitis C drug, and a third of the U.S. price for the asthma inhaler Advair.

Many countries perform similar cost-benefit analyses, whether or not they run a national health system. Switzerland's market-based system permits the sale of only drugs that have been judged to be cost-effective and sets a maximum allowable price; pharmacists can charge whatever they want to beneath that ceiling. France's national health plan ranks drugs on a scale of 1 to 5 in deciding which should be offered for free. (A once-a-day version of a drug that quadruples the price scores lower than twice-a-day pills.)

In the United States, such crucial impartial cost-benefit analysis is scattershot, usually left to academic journals and performed only after a new drug is already on the market. By then, it may be too late to have as much impact. In 2015 a respected Boston nonprofit research group called the Institute for Clinical and Economic Review initiated a new "Emerging Therapy and Pricing" program to compare the effectiveness of drugs and set a value-based benchmark for their price tag in the United States. In one of its first reports, it said that a new class of cholesterol-lowering agents, the PCSK9 drugs, which manufacturers had priced at about $14,000 a year, was worth only "$5,404–$7,735 linked to long-term value to patients, and as low as $2,177 when potential short-term budget impact is considered" in terms of benefit. But the horse was already out of the barn.

Doctors and Professional Organizations: Ally with Patients, not Pharma

In 2012 three highly respected physicians at Memorial Sloan Kettering Cancer Center, Leonard Saltz, Peter Bach, and Robert Wittes, convinced their hospital not to offer Zaltrap, a newly approved cancer treatment. Studies had shown that Zaltrap was no more effective than a drug that was already available and cost half as much.

Memorial Sloan Kettering could have made a pretty penny dispensing Zaltrap, adding on a markup and an infusion fee. A less reputable hospital might even have promoted the fact that it was offering "the newest FDA-approved treatment." "Ignoring the cost of care . . . is no longer tenable," the doctors wrote in an editorial explaining their decision. "When choosing treatments for a patient, we have to consider the financial strains they may cause alongside the benefits they might deliver."

It was an isolated but exemplary action that should be emulated by doctors, hospitals, medical societies, and disease research charities. The leadership of these organizations can pressure drug companies to deliver value and reduce prices; after all, if doctors don't prescribe treatments they consider overpriced, there is no market.

Unfortunately, the medical profession often allies itself with the pharmaceutical industry. Instead of publicly shaming pharmaceutical firms for the price tags on MS drugs the American Academy of Neurology and the National Multiple Sclerosis Society "have been standoffish because they all have pharmaceutical dollars flowing in," said Dr. Daniel Hartung, a professor of pharmacy at Oregon State University, who has tracked the manifold increases in the price of even long-used MS drugs.

But much of the National MS Society's annual income of about $100 million comes from the companies—"corporate sponsors"—that make MS drugs. In 2012 it raised only about $200,000 from events like Walk MS and Bike MS, and about $16 million in direct mail solicitations.

The American Academy of Neurology offers pharmaceutical companies membership in its "Industry Roundtable"; they pay $20,000 to $40,000 annually depending on the opportunities desired. Drug companies underwrite medical conferences. The leaders of many medical societies—the American Academy of Neurology, the American Lung Association, and the American Heart Association, to name a few—are paid as industry consultants and speakers.

You can help end this behavior. Medical charities, hospitals, and professional societies rely on donations from foundations and their members—from you. Make them earn your support. If you're asked to send money, participate in a disease walk, or add $1 at the pharmacy checkout counter to help a foundation combat a particular disease, find out about the group's finances before you agree. Use Charity Navigator to check how it spends donations. Review its IRS Form 990 to see how much it pays its officers.

Let's ask all medical organizations to take a pledge: Don't allow industry to underwrite events, dinners, or conferences or pay for access to members. Most important, no one in a leadership position should take industry money. It may take some time, but they must wean themselves from this lucrative cash flow to maintain our trust in their scientific independence. If an officer of one of these influential groups believes that a new drug will produce huge benefits for patients, he or she can speak for free.

17

BILLS FOR TESTS AND ANCILLARY SERVICES

(20 TO 30 PERCENT OF OUR $3 TRILLION BILL, BY SOME ESTIMATES)

In the past, the costs of tests and ancillary services used to be covered by insurance with little or no patient contribution; today patients are often expected to foot at least part of the bill. Because these services are almost always ordered with no patient input about where they are to be performed, hospitals and doctors can manipulate that choice as a means to increase revenue. In chapter 13 you've already learned some strategies for avoiding expensive tests ordered by physicians. Here are a few extra pointers:

1. Protect your wallet: do not have any test or service performed by a provider outside your network.

2. As a general rule, avoid having your ordinary blood and fluid specimens sent to a hospital lab. Ask your doctor to direct them to a commercial lab that's in your network. Labs based in hospitals and in doctors' offices tend to be much more expensive than commercial labs. Most blood testing is totally automated and any licensed lab will do a fine job.

3. Ask the commercial lab for a printout of your results as backup just in case it is unable to transmit them electronically to your doctor. Do the same if you have a scan performed at a center that is not affiliated with your hospital. Make sure to get a copy of the actual X-ray or scan; a "report of findings" is of much less value to your doctor.

4. Some situations demand top-dollar testing. If you have a biopsy of a suspicious lesion, where cancer or an unusual infection is suspected, a pathology reading by a top-flight pathologist—my preference would be at a teaching hospital—is essential. Accurate diagnosis will have a huge impact on the course of your treatment, so stay with the experts. Don't get cheap when the interpretation of a pathology biopsy or a sophisticated sonogram or an unusual blood test will decide whether or not you need surgery.

18

BETTER HEALTHCARE
IN A DIGITAL AGE

n the last twenty-five years, nearly every aspect of our day-to-day lives
has been made easier by digital technology: banking, watching films,
traveling, communicating with loved ones near and far away, purchasing a new home. But healthcare is an exception to the rule.

That's not because of a lack of investment. Silicon Valley is hot on
healthcare. Even though tech funding in general has fallen off lately, digital health funding went up 13 percent in the first quarter of 2016, with
investment for the quarter reaching nearly $1 billion. Every week I get
more than a half-dozen pitches from start-ups touting new machines or
claiming that their algorithms and apps will empower consumers and
solve the healthcare cost crisis.

The problem is that these huge investments and the products they
spawn are of highly variable benefit to patients. Health technology can be
deployed for enormous patient good, but often all it offers up are useless, but profitable, services. If a company exists to untangle or parse the
data in our convoluted system, the real answer is not to add another layer

designed by entrepreneurs looking for profit, but to make the system simpler.

Consider the five largest healthcare start-up deals in that first boom quarter of 2016: $175 million for a start-up that describes itself as a "clinical intelligence platform for cancer care providers" (funded largely by drug companies that want to mine the data for faster approvals); $165 million for a company that develops and sells wearable wrist monitors that provide "personalized insights into how [users] sleep, move and eat; $95 million for an (or "another") online platform that offers "intelligent health information" to patients; $70 million for a company that promises to "warehouse" healthcare data; $40 million for an outfit that developed a kiosk to deploy in drugstores and malls that can screen for blood pressure, weight, pulse, and body mass index. (Automated measurements are notoriously inaccurate; there are simpler ways to measure these parameters and no medical reason to regularly monitor some of them anyway.)

With our purchases and our votes, we should make sure that new technology serves patients before investors' profits.

Part 1. How You Can (and Can't) Benefit from New Technologies Now

1. Wearables. These wristbands or patches are affixed to your body to gather health data in real time: heart rate and rhythm, the number of steps you take, sleep quality, glucose levels. You may buy one, your doctor may prescribe one, or your insurer may provide one for free. There are dozens of different options, by a number of manufacturers. Whether they are a cool gizmo or life-altering medicine depends on your illness, your health, and your state of mind.

Like many Americans, I have a Jawbone fitness tracker sitting in a drawer, which I abandoned after several months of learning how many steps I take a day (plenty) and how many hours I sleep (not enough). I did not trust it to measure my sleep quality and there seemed to be little science behind such determinations. It was kind of fun, but definitely (for me) not medicine. Some people like constant data. Some people find such data motivating to exercise more. You decide if you want to buy one. But don't accept it from an insurer or a company in lieu of a well-thought-out wellness or weight-loss program. In 2016 Fitbit, another popular fitness tracker, announced it was moving into the medical-grade tracking device market, which means the company will be seeking to bill insurance for its products.

For some people with certain chronic conditions wearable monitors can be transforming. If you're prone to abnormal heart rhythms, a wrist monitor may provide an early warning system and even transmit potentially lifesaving information to your doctor. If you are a diabetic on insulin who is prone to wild swings in blood sugar, a continuous glucose monitor gives you frequent readings and alarms for dangerous levels. But very few patients fall into these categories and, at this time, many of the devices promise greater accuracy than they deliver and less than human health requires. Like an airbag that deploys at random stop signs, an inaccurate glucose monitor will set off alarms for no reason. The pros and cons are very specific to your health needs. Rely on advice from your doctor.

2. Technology-enhanced screening. Screening has become a marketing buzzword in American medicine. Early detection can be lifesaving for some conditions: pap smears have long prevented cervical cancer; cholesterol screening can prevent heart disease (although if it's normal, it needs to be done only once every five years or so). But the scientific consensus is that many of the new high-tech screening techniques being promoted to healthy patients, such as checking for "low T" or getting an ultrasound of your neck to see if you have some narrowing of arteries, are not much more useful than snake oil. There is no "normal" for such tests and treatment brings new risks and dangers. Neither the U.S. Preventive Services Task Force nor Choosing Wisely, the campaign led by doctors' groups to do away with unneeded tests, recommends either of these offerings. Look at the published guidelines from these two organizations for screening and refuse everything else, unless your primary care doctor gives you a convincing reason.

3. Telehealth. One of my friends called to sing the praises of telehealth. For $100 charged to his credit card, a nameless doctor he'd never met prescribed antibiotics via video chat for a sinus infection. A number of companies have sprouted up to offer phone or video consultations for a price—employing doctors who work from home getting "paid to treat patients wherever and whenever" they choose. This service may be helpful under certain circumstances and conditions; for example, as a weekend stopgap if you can't reach your doctor. But the quality of the care is hard to assess, and this is advice and treatment that your doctor or your health system should be providing for free. Telephone advice is part of what doctors have always dispensed, and they should not abdicate that responsibility now. After my friend got telehealth treatment, he needed to see a doctor anyway since the symptoms persisted; what he really had was a tooth infection.

Part 2. System Change: What We Want from Technology

In recent years, the government has invested more than $30 billion of taxpayer money to help hospitals and doctors go digital. While we now routinely see doctors behind their computers, the payoff for patients has been limited.

We could be deriving enormous benefits from new technology, if only it was deployed with more forethought about how it might contribute to high-quality affordable healthcare rather than just bureaucratic record keeping and industry profit.

The following are a few simple features that patients and their employers should be demanding of their insurers, health systems, and doctors. Government supervision should help ensure that the products that resulted from our $35 billion investment are used to our benefit.

The Means to Possess Your Medical Data

Right now our medical information is held captive in disparate doctors' offices and hospitals. That isolation translates into pointless expense, because patients frequently have tests repeated. It means worse care, because doctors don't have previous test results for comparison.

Start-ups like PicnicHealth offer to collate and store all your medical information and chart material online for a monthly fee, kind of like a Dropbox for medical records. But their full utility is limited at this time by the fact that many hospitals and doctors are not capable of transmitting your full chart electronically in a standardized format.

A universal, national program supported by taxpayer money might make more sense.

All that information could be placed on a chip card to carry in a wallet, which could be scanned by each new provider. Or, as Jim McGroddy, a former IBM executive who has served on many healthcare boards, suggests, it could be stored in a national data collection system akin to a credit agency like Equifax. If a public agency kept records of all your medical encounters in a secure and searchable form, they could be made available to providers of your choosing. Either private or public players could create such a system, the likes of which exists in many other countries. Researchers point out that such a database would also act as a national early warning system if people using a new drug or device were having unexpected serious side effects or benefits. Problems like those with the mesh pelvic sling would be detected much faster.

Connected Programs for Pricing and Scheduling

The latest stage of the HITECH Act required doctors to electronically generate 50 percent of prescriptions by 2015, which the government describes as "meaningful use." But real meaningful use would allow physicians and patients to know prices, co-payments, and alternatives in real time in the office, before the prescription is written for a particular medicine, or before the test is scheduled at a particular facility.

Technology should allow for one-stop shopping and payment in healthcare, as it has in most other industries. If I have a sore knee and want to see an in-network orthopedist next Tuesday between 1 and 5 p.m., I should be able to go to my plan's online directory, which would show me which in-network orthopedists within a five-mile radius were available, because it would be connected to its providers' scheduling books. I could schedule my appointment, know how much I had to pay, and even prepay the co-payment, rather than calling three receptionists to see which doctor is available, checking coverage with insurers, filling out the same form every time I visit a new provider, and having a mailbox filled with paper statements for months afterward.

These sorts of interlocking online arrangements could become standard features of every contract between insurers and drugmakers or medical providers. The government could mandate adoption or offer financial incentives to develop such patient-friendly features, such as Medicare bonus payments to doctors and hospitals that participate. That would be "meaningful use" of digital technology.

Thanks to digital technology you can price, book, and pay for a hotel in Tbilisi, Georgia, on your computer. Why can't you do the same for an X-ray down the block or a doctor's appointment?

EPILOGUE

The *Fate of Empires* describes an age of decadence into which all great societies—Rome, Greece, Persia, Great Britain—descend before they finally fall for good. The decadence, according to the author, Sir John Glubb, is due to a period of wealth and power, selfishness, love of money, and loss of a sense of duty. Does this sound familiar? Societies, it says, typically take over two hundred years to get to the age of decadence. American healthcare has arrived far faster.

The fathers of modern medicine—doctors and scientists like Frederick Banting, who pioneered insulin treatment; Jonas Salk, who discovered the polio vaccine; Albert Starr, who invented a lifesaving artificial heart valve; and Thomas Starzl, who fathered modern organ transplant—helped usher in a new era of scientific healing. They are the reason for medicine's lofty reputation. But the respect they earned through their noble efforts has been squandered in the past quarter century. The treatments we get and the prices we pay are governed as much by commerce as by humanism or science. The mission of this book is to advocate for a return to a system of affordable, evidence-based, patient-centered care.

No one player created the mess that is the $3 trillion American medical system in 2017. People in every sector of medicine are feeding at the trough: insurers, hospitals, doctors, manufacturers, politicians, regulators, charities, and more. People in sectors that have nothing to do with health—banking, real estate, and tech—have also somehow found a way to extort cash from patients. They all need to change their money-chasing ways.

To make that happen, however, we patients will need to change our ways too. We must become bolder, more active and thoughtful about what we demand of our healthcare and the people who deliver it. We must be more engaged in finding and pressing the political levers to promote the evolution of the medical care we deserve.

I hope the book you have just finished has made you not just outraged but also better prepared for these tasks. Now you understand that the free coffee and artwork display in a hospital's marble atrium aren't free at all. That what's sold to you as the newest drug or device to treat your illness may not be, in fact, the best. That the anesthesiologist who comes in to say "hi" before a procedure is perhaps not being kind, but making an appearance so that he and/or his extender can bill for a consult. You're wise to the heist and emboldened with new tools and ideas about how to take back your health and our medical system.

Medicine is still a noble profession. There are many great doctors, nurses, pharmacists, and others working their hearts out, even in these troubled and troubling times. Even as the healthcare sector faces a future of great financial uncertainty and humiliating bureaucracy, many of the best and brightest students are flocking to medical school. They're doing it because they want to take care of patients, to heal using some of the time-honored tools in the doctor's black bag as well as the miraculous scientific innovations of the last twenty-five years. That is, after all, the only really compelling reason to go into medicine.

They *want* to deliver patient-centered, evidence-based care at a reasonable price. We, the patients, need to help, to rise up and make that possible. We have to remind everyone who has entered our healthcare system in the past quarter century for profit rather than patients that "affordable, patient-centered, evidence-based care" is more than a marketing pitch or a campaign slogan.

It is our health, the future of our children and our nation. High-priced healthcare is America's sickness and we are all paying, being robbed. When the medical industry presents us with the false choice of your money or your life, it's time for us all to take a stand for the latter.

AFTERWORD

I n the time since the manuscript was completed and the first edition of this book was published, America's healthcare system has—once again—been the focus of a series of dramatic political crises.

Trump squeaked into office with a vague pledge to "repeal and replace" Obamacare with "something better." But the new president, along with the GOP-controlled Congress, had neither the knowledge nor ability to accomplish that, in spite of years of campaign promises. During their first eight months in power, they stumbled over and over, failing to attract support for a series of bills with appealing monikers, such as the "Better Care Reconciliation Act." Each and every one was skewered by the Congressional Budget Office, which revealed that the GOP's proposals would send premiums skyrocketing for many Americans and leave tens of millions more uninsured. The numbers just didn't add up.

Ironically, these GOP plans failed for the same underlying reason that the ACA has in some states ended up in rough waters: They didn't do anything much to tackle healthcare's spiraling price inflation or the business interests driving our highly dysfunctional $3 trillion health market.

In 2003, a group of health economists published a scholarly article in *Health Affairs*, which today reads like a Cassandra-call for why healthcare in the United States is so different from the rest of the world. Its title began: "It's the Prices, Stupid . . ." In passing Obamacare, the Democrats tried to ignore the math in order to promise decent health insurance to every American, which ultimately necessitated some skyrocketing premiums and higher deductibles. First-time insurance for many, to be sure. But unsupportable costs for others.

Instead, the Republicans' efforts in the new administration sought to make the math work out by placing trust in the "invisible hand" of the marketplace, providing less guaranteed care.

Business friendly, anti-regulation, and with a strong libertarian bent, each of the GOP proposals sought to save money by leaving patients on their own to shop in the cutthroat market filled with whatever kinds of products the insurance and hospital and pharma industry wanted to sell. If you've read this far, you can likely guess how that would have worked out. The GOP wanted to "streamline" drug approvals to make it easier for new drugs to get to market. It sought to allow insurers to offer the kinds of bare-bones plans that Obamacare had outlawed, such as those that didn't cover maternity care or prescription drugs as well as those that permitted insurers to reject applicants with pre-existing conditions. Under some of the proposals, insurers could end up with the ability to reject applicants with even minimal medical history, like depression or mild asthma. Many of us, including myself, could have been vulnerable to being thrown into high risk pools, with premiums trending ever skyward, according to the predictions of the CBO.

The Republicans claimed that medicine would be improved by less regulation and that Americans wanted the freedom to choose whether to be insured or roll the dice. Feeling healthy and invulnerable? Buy cheap insurance that doesn't include cancer coverage. (From Chapter 2, The Age of Insurance, you can predict what kinds of plans might be on offer.)

But by early 2017, Americans—fed up with bankrupting bills, worried about losing their insurance, and alarmed by the Draconian cuts to Medicaid proposed by Republicans—were feeling played by the business and politics of healthcare. They weren't buying it. Obamacare, which had lackluster approval ratings before Trump took office, was suddenly popular, flaws and all. Better the devil you knew. More than 20 million people—many in red states—had gained access to health insurance and healthcare through the Affordable Care Act. They got help paying premiums through subsidies. There were undeniable problems with the policies' prices, but it was still preferable to hollow promises based on magic math.

By April, 2017, for the first time, more than half of Americans approved of the health law—in fact, nearly 60 percent. That was compared to less than 20 percent approval for the GOP proposal. By August, a Kaiser Family Foundation poll found that 78 percent of Americans felt that the Trump administration "should do what it can to make the current health law work."

Shortly after Trump took office, one poll showed that the cost of healthcare had become Americans' top concern "across all income levels and political affiliations," leapfrogging unemployment. Another poll found that "lowering the amount individuals pay for health care" should be a "top priority" for President Trump and Congress. Nearly a third of Americans said they had problems paying medical bills, many among those forced to cut back on food, clothing, or basic household items.

But will Congress head their distress call? Or will the powerful business of medicine hold sway, as it has for the past thirty years? Time will tell, but there's a glimmer of hope on the horizon. But that glimmer comes from you, not from Washington.

BEFORE HE TOOK OFFICE President Trump, who billed himself as the consummate deal maker, said that drug manufacturers were "getting away with murder" and vowed to bring prices down. At times he's even pro-posed letting Medicare negotiate. But by the end of January 2017, he was meeting with pharma heads and had appointed an industry-friendly advisory panel, whose cost-saving advice involved increasing the length of patent protection and further speeding-up approvals. (From Chapter 4, The Age of Pharmaceuticals, you know why that likely won't work).

Drug makers spent more on lobbying in the first six months of 2017 than in any year since at least 1999. Campaign donations to members of Congress nearly doubled from the year before—directed heavily toward Republicans and Democrats on key committees that served as gatekeepers for any legislation that might affect the industry. On March 22, the day after Trump delivered a stump speech in which he reiterated his populist promise to go after pharma, a flood of big pharma campaign contributions poured in to key members of Congress to the tune of nearly $300,000.

With Tom Price, a conservative private practice orthopedist from the suburbs of Atlanta, as the newly appointed Secretary of Health and Human Services, the Trump administration pushed a free-market agenda for medical practice. Historically, health and human services secretaries devoted themselves to protecting the public's health. Dr. Price often seemed more interested in protecting his surgical colleagues and their right to practice as they wanted, as well as their varied businesses.

Dr. Price, who has cut his political teeth in the 1990s opposing Hillary Care and later became a Tea Party Congressman, quickly put on hold expansion plans for one of the demonstrated cost-saving, quality enhancing innovations that came out of Obamacare: that Medicare scheme you've read about (p. 295) to mandate all-inclusive package payments for hip and knee replacements, called bundled payments. He said he wanted the government out of healthcare, railing against federal waste and spending. In one of the supreme ironies of healthcare politics, Dr. Price resigned less than 8 months into the job after a Politico investigation revealed he has spent nearly half a million dollars of taxpayer money on private jets during his brief time as secretary.

Pity the patients.

Like most Americans, the courageous patients you've met in this book have continued to muddle through disease, finding needed treatments—though not without hardships and, literally, pain.

After a new hospital jacked up the charges for his monthly drug infusions to treat autoimmune arthritis from about $20,000 to more than $110,000 a session (thanks, in part, to it taking place in a fancy room), an outraged **Jeffrey Kivi (Chapter 1)** decided to switch to a related drug, which was sold in a form he could inject at home to avoid an outrageous "facility fee"; he made the switch even though his insurer was picking up the tab. Unfortunately, the new medicine didn't work nearly as well. A teacher who's on his feet most of the day, he could barely get out of bed. "I had to put two chairs next to my bed so that, in the morning, I could use those chairs to help pull myself up out of bed onto my feet." He was worried about having to go on disability.

But when his rheumatologist tried to restart the old drug, Remicade, the insurer that had previous paid suddenly balked, noting that there were cheaper alternatives. Dr. Kivi reflected: "I suspect that, if I ever want to get back on Remicade again, I may have to hire a lawyer."

Mary Chapman (Chapter 4), who has spent years trying to pay for ever more expensive drugs to treat her complex case of multiple sclerosis, decided to leave California and moved to South Carolina. "I had no choice but to leave the Bay Area due to costs and, as you know, draining my funds," she wrote me. After two disastrous appointments at a hospital near her new home—one in which she was prescribed the wrong dose of a medicine and another in which doctors failed to call back for two days after some serious postoperative problems—she now flies to Johns Hopkins every month or two for care and stays in a cheap hotel during treatment.

Wanda Wickizer (Chapter 7), the uninsured patient who was sued by the University of Virginia Medical Center to pay up on a $356,000 bill for emergency neurosurgery, never faced off in court with the hospital. It was on the docket for April 29, 2016. Her lawyers had made arrangements to attend. In the two years since her lifesaving surgery, the hospital had rejected Ms. Wickizer's repeated offers to pay the hospital and doctors all the money in her retirement account, a sum—about $100,000—that was more than Medicare and some other insurers would have paid for the services she received. They suggested putting a lien on her house.

A few days before the trial, I called the hospital to make arrangements for an interview. Shortly thereafter the suit was dropped and settled for an undisclosed sum and covered by a non-disclosure agreement. She is now remarried to a veteran and covered by Tricare.

Hope Marcus (Chapter 4), who had been buying medicines from India to manage her longstanding ulcerative colitis, thought she had solved her price problems when she found a Medicare advantage plan that covered generics at no patient copay. But in January she was shocked to see her old generic drug, mesalamine, was selling for $1,100 a month through the plan, compared to $75 overseas. Even more surprising was the fact that by April, the insurer no longer had the generic on its formulary so she was forced to go on a new branded pill (that she wasn't sure would work) at an even higher price, for which she has to contribute thousands a year. She is appealing the decision.

But patients, physicians, and (some) policy makers seem to be waking up to the heist of America's healthcare. With Washington in a state of paralysis and so many of our representatives beholden to the industry, now more than ever, every patient needs to take action. Remember, most of the solutions in Part 2 of this book don't require (at least initially) an act of Congress.

They start with an informed, engaged, and active patients, who feel entitled to make their needs known to their doctors and hospitals, and to vote accordingly. If we do that, government will follow. Even in this era of government turmoil, we now have some proof that the wheel can turn.

A growing number of states—both red and blue—have enacted some form of Surprise Bill legislation, protecting consumers for unexpected (and exorbitant) out-of-network charges. This year both Texas and California passed new laws in the face of objections from some medical groups. In October 2017, Maryland enacted the first law that would allow a state to reject some pharmaceutical price hikes, and a number of other states had bills to curb prescription drug costs in process.

At a national level, the Republican efforts to repeal and replace the ACA have served as a wake-up call to many patients and they have made their voices heard. In angry town hall meetings this spring, Americans hurled questions at GOP senators and congresspeople about plans to remove protections for those with pre-existing conditions and to shrink the Obamacare insurance expansions, which had given health insurance for the first time to many low-income Americans. Many of those voters were in red states. The budget-cutting Congress couldn't come up with a plan that accommodated these constituent demands and so the political promise to "repeal and replace" Obamacare went down in flames and amid massive GOP discord. "I did not come to Washington to hurt people," said Shelley Moore-Capito (R-WVa.) during the drama—although she ultimately voted for her party's bills.

It was epic: For the first time, Americans—patients-consumers-*voters*—successfully stood up for their healthcare. Against business. Against politics. That's a first win in the crusade to take back our health system. But it's going to be a long war.

Acknowledgments

Writing a book is an intensely lonely experience. I have new admiration for anyone who embarks on this thrilling and terrifying journey. But this book is built on a foundation laid by others and took a small village to find its final shape. So here is a pageful of thanks:

I want to thank the many scholars, doctors, patients, and businesspeople quoted and cited by name in the text and notes who shared generously their years of wisdom, experience, and insight. They provided the points of light that allowed me to draw this portrait of the troubled American healthcare system and to arrive at some ideas for how to fix it. At a deeper level, no one can write about the history of modern American medicine without a bow to Paul Starr, whose classic *The Social Transformation of American Medicine,* published in 1982, in many ways is the starting point where this book takes off. Likewise, I'm deeply indebted to the decades of writings of Dr. Arnold Relman, the longtime editor of the *New England Journal of Medicine,* who first warned on the emergence of a "new medical-industrial complex" in 1980 and continued to issue Cassandra calls about the commercialization of medicine until his death, at ninety-one, in 2014. Also to Professor Uwe Reinhardt, of

Princeton University, whom I first interviewed on this topic as a naïve young reporter more than twenty years ago. He raised my antennae to the business of healthcare and they've never gone down.

To my editors and colleagues at the *New York Times* who started me on this exploration of medical costs by supporting my two-year-long "Paying Till It Hurts" series, I offer my endless gratitude. At a time of shrinking journalistic resources, I had extraordinary time and space to pursue the topic. Dean Baquet green-lighted a project that many were skeptical would shed new light. He assigned me to work with Rebecca Corbett, the editor of a lifetime and also a very wonderful person. Rebecca helped me think the biggest thoughts possible while paying attention to every small detail. That work was made better at every turn by Catrin Einhorn, my multimedia co-conspirator, and Beth Flynn, my photo editor. Many thanks also to Nick Kulish, Jodi Kantor, and Sheri Fink, the other New York–based reporters in the small but mighty New York Times Enterprise Group. Their prior expertise gained in writing their books made writing my first book so much easier.

Deepest thanks go, too, to the people who helped turn a somewhat barebones proposal by a rookie book author into what I hope is a lively, informative, game-changing book. I had thought knowing how to write a good three-thousand-word newspaper article for the *New York Times* would readily translate into writing a three-hundred-page work of nonfiction. It doesn't. To my best-ever agent, Elyse Cheney, who immediately saw the potential in my idea for a book about our dysfunctional medical system. Sharing my excitement, she helped me and pushed me to hone that into a smart, enticing proposal. To Ann Godoff, my brilliant editor, who taught me how to turn a series of story ideas into a coherent and useful narrative for readers, as she patiently (and, thankfully, sometimes not so patiently) shepherded this project along. Her advice, though blunt ("I have done away with Part 1"—twenty-five thousand words) was spot-on. The teams at Cheney Literary and Penguin Press have been fantastic, particularly Adam Eaglin, Will Heyward, and Karen Mayer, whose input and enthusiasm for this project at each step have made it smarter and propelled it forward. My special gratitude to Julie Tate, who came to the rescue with expert fact-checking with little advance notice.

Jeremy Heimans, Dan Shannon, and their colleagues at Purpose.com are helping me build an interactive "We the Patients" Web site so that every American can have a voice in healthcare and healthcare reform from now on; their creativity is revolutionary. Thanks to Penguin Press for helping to support this, my vision of a patient movement, and to Drew Kitchen, who volunteered his legal advice to create a plan.

My thanks are boundless for Drew Altman and David Rousseau of the Kaiser Family Foundation. I had so many insightful, inspiring conversations with the pair while writing this book that, by the end, I realized I had to leave the *New York Times* and go work for them. Tomorrow is my first day as editor in chief of the foundation's young and fast-growing nonprofit health journalism service, Kaiser Health News.

On a more personal note, deep gratitude goes to my amazing circle of friends, which fortunately includes a collection of fine authors and journalists. To Esther Fein, my long-ago reporting partner at the *New York Times* and longtime dearest friend, who read much of this book as an ugly first draft and offered suggestions to make it better. To David Remnick, her husband, for sage advice on book writing and for reminding me that I had something worthwhile to say. To my running group—Esther, Lisa Green, and Laurie Hays—who pep talked me into taking on this project and talked me down when I was panicked I couldn't complete it. To Clare McHugh and Leslie Kaufman, who were there at short notice with encouragement and smart ideas. Now it's their turn to write books so I can return the favor. To Mark Philips and Sylvia Stein, who allowed me to decamp to their home by the water as a writing haven when I couldn't stand one more day at my desk.

I owe my greatest thanks—and apologies—to my family, who were endlessly supportive and tolerant during this project, each individual offering whatever kind of help he or she could give. To my mom and brothers for loving me despite all the family gatherings I missed or was only half there for. To my husband, Andrej, who lived with this extremely intrusive third presence in our lives and our home for nearly two years. He stayed by my side through all the ups and downs, always believing. To my children, Andrew and Cara, who read chapters, offered wise opinions, and even provided fact-checking services during what was supposed to have been a rare beach vacation together. It's a great joy to watch two beloved children grow to be such smart, thoughtful adults.

All of these people shared my passion for the need to create a system of affordable patient-centered, evidence-based medical care. With them in my corner, how can we go wrong?

Appendix A:
Pricing/Shopping Tools

Price Calculators for Procedures

(Note: These calculators all reflect prices when the patient pays. Many offices quote higher prices if you are using insurance. These sites will not tell you what your insurer will actually pay—its negotiated rate; there are occasions when your insurer may have negotiated a particularly low price from a high-priced provider or agreed to one that is needlessly high. This is a list of some of the options I find most useful, though it is by no means complete.)

HEALTHCARE BLUEBOOK
(www.healthcarebluebook.com)

This is one of the oldest and most extensive of the medical pricing sites. Based on the data it collects from patients, insurers, and companies, it calculates a "fair price" for a large number of procedures, in different geographic locations. It is clear about what aspects of the care its "fair price" covers, such as whether or not it includes anesthesiologist fees. Many doctors and hospitals charge several times the Healthcare Bluebook "fair price." If you enter your zip code it will identify which options in your area are at or below the "fair price," and which are far above. It offers cost-saving tips, such as whether your procedure could be performed as an outpatient for less money. Healthcare Bluebook's "fair price" may also be useful in bargaining with your hospital or insurer over whether charges are reasonable.

CLEARHEALTHCOSTS
(www.clearhealthcosts.com)

ClearHealthCosts uses crowdsourcing to uncover the prices of medical encounters in the dozen or so cities where it now operates. It is still young, but the more data it takes in, the more useful it will come to be. It also tells you how much Medicare would pay for the encounter you're seeking, which is a useful reference point, though it will nearly always be lower than anything available with commercial insurance. That said, the information it provides is often piecemeal, in part because it relies on self-reporting. Its Medicare charge for a colonoscopy, for example, is only the doctor's fee. One person may report what the doctor charged, but omit to add in the facility fee—especially if that bill arrived much later.

FAIR HEALTH
(www.fairhealthconsumer.org)

FAIR Health uses a huge national database of insurance claims to provide a picture of the range of physician charges for a particular type of medical encounter in your zip code. It includes facility fees for outpatient procedures. But remember, if all the doctors and facilities in your area charge a lot, the FAIR Health price will be high too.

PRATTER
(https://pratter.us)

The name Pratter stands for "prices matter," and this is a Web site where you may find the range of cash prices for procedures where you live, and where you can be directed to the facility associated with each. For entries that have an orange tag, the price has been provided by the facility and is guaranteed. Since the company is young, few entries currently boast an orange price guarantee. Unless the orange tag is displayed, the prices here are not all-inclusive, so you may find they do not include anesthesia, for example.

MEDIBID
(www.medibid.com)

MediBid is a Web site to consider if you have a high-deductible plan, meaning you're likely to have to pay for a procedure entirely out of pocket. It is a true marketplace. You post the procedure you're looking for (say a colonoscopy) and doctors offer you a competitive price. Don't assume that doctors who work this way are substandard. Sometimes they may just have a little extra space in their procedure schedule or may like the idea of working independently of insurance bureaucracies.

Price Calculators for Prescription Drugs

GOODRX
(www.goodrx.com)

GoodRx asks you to plug in the name of your drug and your zip code and then gives you all the cash prices available in your neighborhood and lets you know about any deals to be had. A special feature for patients on Medicare will calculate your actual co-payment in advance, which allows you and your doctor to choose a different medicine or pharmacy if the price is too high.

PHARMACYCHECKER.COM
(www.pharmacychecker.com)

This was started by a physician and connects patients to overseas mail-order pharmacies, which it vets for quality. It's a good resource for patients who want to import medicines as a way to reduce their drug costs.

Appendix B:
Tools for Vetting Hospitals

NEW YORK TIMES HOSPITAL PRICING CALCULATOR
(www.nytimes.com/interactive/2013/05/08/business/how-much-hospitals-charge.html)

Using the data on hospital bills released by Medicare, the *New York Times* created a lookup tool that allows you to vet pricing at hospitals in your area—overall and for various procedures. Here you can find the Medicare hospital payment for different types of hospitalizations (treating pneumonia or placing a stent in the heart, for example). You can see how much more than the Medicare rate your hospital typically bills patients.

THE LEAPFROG GROUP
(www.leapfroggroup.org/ratings-reports)

This respected nonprofit rates hospitals on a wide variety of quality issues. See how yours stacks up. The Leapfrog program is voluntary, but most hospitals participate.

HOSPITAL COMPARE
(www.medicare.gov/hospitalcompare/compare.html)

This recently launched Web site run by Medicare allows patient-consumers to look at various measures of hospital quality, in general and in relation to particular procedures. You can choose three hospitals at a time and see how they stack up on a wide variety of metrics—such as infection rates after surgery, the presence of resistant microbes, and their use of scans (with guidance about how to figure out if they're doing too many or too few). It offers a fascinating warts-and-all profile of your local hospital.

PROPUBLICA NONPROFIT EXPLORER
(https://projects.propublica.org/nonprofits) and
GUIDESTAR (www.guidestar.org)

These Web sites allow you to download an IRS Form 990 for most hospitals. The tax form is generally a couple of hundred pages long, but you need not read it all. In the first section you'll find the hospital's mission statement and the compensation of its highest-paid executives and doctors. In Schedule H, you'll find what it claims as "charitable" work.

Appendix C:
Glossary for Medical Bills
and Explanations of Benefits

Adjustment/plan discount—The difference between the provider's billed amount and the price your insurer has negotiated for the service. (In other words, the amount subtracted from the billed amount to determine what your insurer pays.)

Allowance/payment/credits—The amount your insurer has negotiated to pay, or has paid, for a particular service.

Charges/price—The amount the provider has billed for that line item, based on its price list (chargemaster).

Co-payment or coinsurance—The portion of the allowed amount that you are required to pay under the terms of your insurance contract.

Deductible—Most insurance policies do not begin paying until you have laid out a cetain amount out of your pocket: your deductible. On bills, this heading indicates what you must pay because you have not reached this yearly bar.

Patient balance/responsibility—What the hospital says you owe.

Plan covers—The percent of the charge that your insurance will pay under the terms of your contract for that particular service.

Procedure code—The numerical billing code(s) that explains what you're being billed for. If you Google "code" and the five- or six-digit number you see on your bill, you will learn what it stands for.

Procedure description—A description of what was done in words, though often filled with abbreviations. Each provider uses its own terminology, so there is no standard translation.

Prompt payment discount—An attempt to get you to pay your bill before you've scrutinized it to understand what you've been charged for!

Provider—The name and (often) professional title of the person in whose name the service is being billed. If the treatment was rendered at a clinic or by a physician extender, you will usually see the name of the supervising doctor, even if he or she didn't directly treat you. Common titles include MD, CRNA (nurse-anesthetist), CNM (certified nurse-midwife), PA (physician assistant), LPN (licensed practical nurse), PT (physical therapist), and OT (occupational therapist).

Type of service—This heading often appears on bills to indicate a broad category of medical services on bills that are not really itemized. (If you see it and are not satisfied, remember to request a fully itemized accounting.) This category may include the following:

> **Accommodation or room charge**
> **Ambulance.** Labeled BLS for basic life support (putting on an oxygen mask) or ALS for advanced life support (a team skilled enough to treat a serious car crash or a heart attack). The charge depends on the training level of the team dispatched, *not* on what you needed.
> **Anesthesia.** Putting a patient to sleep for surgery, pain consultations, and giving a patient an IV sedative before a procedure are examples of services billed in this category.

Critical care. A charge for time spent in an intensive care unit.

Emergency department (ED). A charge for time spent in the ER, independent of any procedure performed there. A "trauma activation fee" is sometimes billed, meaning that the hospital's surgical trauma team was summoned—it doesn't matter if they actually did anything.

IV therapy. A charge for the administration of standard intravenous fluids and sometimes intravenous medicines.

Laboratory services. Routine blood work, sophisticated biomarker tests, and urinalysis are examples of services billed in this category.

Occupational or physical therapy. This could be anything from an actual physical or occupational therapy session in a gymlike setting to a quick visit from a therapist after surgery to teach you how to use crutches.

Pathology. During most surgical procedures, some of the material removed from the body is sent to pathology for analysis. A charge for a pap smear also falls into this category.

Pharmacy. Charges for all the medicines dispensed while you were in the hospital; includes intravenous and shots as well.

Professional fee. A specific charge for the work done by a physician or another healthcare provider. For example, an X-ray will generate two charges: one from the facility where the X-ray was taken and a second from the physician who interprets the X-ray.

Radiology. X-rays, scans, sonograms, tests that involve injecting dye into the blood vessels of the heart or brain, and even ultrasound guidance when a doctor is doing a needle biopsy are examples of procedures billed in this category.

Recovery room. This charge for the time after surgery but before you've been moved to a hospital bed or been discharged after same-day surgery is often billed in fifteen-minute intervals. After a procedure, all patients spend some time here, and that time is generally billed.

Sterile supplies. Bandages and hardware used in surgery are two
examples of sterile supplies you will be charged for.

Supplies. This catchall category includes charges for a wheelchair or
crutches or a breast milk pump or other equipment.

Surgery/OR. A charge for the operating room and the services of OR
personnel, such as technicians and nurses.

Appendix D:
Tools to Help You Figure Out
Whether a Test or a Procedure
Is Really Necessary

U.S. PREVENTIVE SERVICES TASK FORCE
(www.uspreventiveservicestaskforce.org)

According to its Web site, the task force "works to improve the health of all Americans by making evidence-based recommendations about clinical preventive services." Compiled and revised by an expert panel, these government guidelines address issues such as what screening tests are useful at different ages, and at what intervals.

CHOOSING WISELY
(www.choosingwisely.org/patient-resources)

This initiative of doctors' groups identifies tests and procedures that are overused and should not be done. Each specialty was asked to identify five tests or practices that are frequently ordered on patients but have little or no utility. The results can be viewed in a searchable, consumer-friendly format codeveloped by *Consumer Reports* on the Choosing Wisely Web site and app. You can check out your ailment or any procedure you're contemplating.

COCHRANE
(www.cochrane.org)

This international network of scientists and doctors evaluates the strength of the research and studies that support medical practices. It accepts no commercial funding. It issues periodic reports and publishes them on a searchable Web site in a patient-friendly format. Before you decide to undergo any treatment, take a look at what the relevant Cochrane report has to say.

Appendix E: Templates for Protest Letters

1. TO TACKLE A SURPRISE OUT-OF-NETWORK BILL

Dear Sir or Madam:

The bills enclosed were for out-of-network services performed on _____ during my admission to _____ Medical Center, a hospital that is in my insurance network. I went to _____ Medical Center precisely because it was in my network. I was not informed of these providers' out-of-network status and did not consent to being treated by any out-of-network providers. Since I did not give informed consent for treatment beyond the terms and network of my insurance policy, I suggest you contact my insurer to work out payment; I will pay only that portion of the bill that I would have paid for in-network services.

Please stop this effort to collect a bill I do not owe for a service I was never informed would be out-of-network. If I get another notice, I will report this collection effort to the _____ State Department of Insurance and _____ State Department of Consumer Affairs.

Sincerely,

2. TO OBTAIN MEDICAL RECORDS AND ITEMIZED BILLS

Dear Sirs or Madam:

I have now requested my medical records/itemized bill _____ times and have yet to receive the material. It is my right to receive these records in any form I request under the Health Insurance Portability and Accountability Act within thirty days and for a reasonable handling and processing fee. If this material is not quickly forthcoming, I will file a complaint with the federal Health and Human Services' Office for Civil Rights, which prosecutes HIPPA violations.

Sincerely,

3. TO CHALLENGE OUTRAGEOUS CHARGES/BILLING ERRORS

Dear Sirs or Madam:

I'm writing to protest what I regard as excessive charges for my operation/hospitalization/procedure at your medical facility. The operation/hospitalization/procedure was billed to my insurer/me at $_____,_____. This total included several itemized charges that were well above norms for our nation and our region, such as a $_____,_____ charge for _____ and a $_____, _____ charge for _____. The Healthcare Bluebook says a "fair price" is $_____,_____ and $_____,_____. Likewise, my bill includes entries for treatments I simply did not receive, such as $_____ for _____ and $_____ for

_____. Before sending in any payment, I'm requesting that your billing and coding department review my chart to revise the charges, or explain to me the size and the nature of such entries.

I have been a loyal customer of your hospital for many years and have been happy with my excellent medical care. But if these billing issues are not resolved, I feel compelled to report them to the state attorney general/consumer protection agency, to investigate fraudulent or abusive billing practices.

Sincerely,

Notes

Unless otherwise indicated, quotations and stories in this book are based on personal interviews and written communications. The subjects agreed to have their real names appear in print. They have provided copies of their bills, insurance statements, correspondence, and other documents to provide verification.

INTRODUCTION

2 **spends nearly 20 percent:** Commonwealth Fund, "Mirror, Mirror on the Wall, 2014 Update: How the U.S. Health Care System Compares Internationally," www .commonwealthfund.org/publications/fund-reports/2014/jun/mirror-mirror.

4 **a test that costs $1,000:** These are prices for an echocardiogram, culled from patient bills (United States) and national price lists (Germany and Japan).

CHAPTER 1: THE AGE OF INSURANCE

13 **Dr. Jan Vilcek:** The two sources that follow tell how Dr. Vilcek gave royalties to NYU in 2005 and how NYU sold most of the rights in 2007: www.medscape.com /viewarticle/538314; "Royalty Pharma Acquires a Portion of New York University's Royalty Interest in Remicade® for $650 Million," press release, May 4, 2007, www .royaltypharma.com/press-releases/royalty-pharma-acquires-a-portion-of-new-york -university-s-royalty-interest-in-remicade-for-650-million.

15 **In the 1890s:** www.bls.gov/OPUB/MLR/1994/03/art1full.pdf.

15 **$50,000 in funding:** $1.3 million in 2016 dollars (www.intodaysdollars.com).

15 **Within a decade:** www.bcbs.com/blog/health-insurance.html.

16 **The original purpose of health insurance:** Jane Moyer, a benefits specialist who has worked for many companies in diverse countries and who teaches about the field at Penn State. Personal interview/communication.

18 **CEO Angela Braly:** www.yahoo.com/news/outgoing-wellpoint-ceo-made -over-224206129.html.

19　**before raising premiums:** Dave Jones, California's vocal insurance commissioner, accused Anthem of "once again imposing an unjustified and unreasonable rate increase on its individual members." Using his bully pulpit to publicly voice his objections was Jones's only recourse: while state insurance commissioners usually have the legal authority to reject home and auto premium increases, they cannot do the same for health insurance.

19　**The medical loss ratio at the Texas Blues:** www.prwatch.org/news/2011/05/10696/blue -cross-blue-shield-getting-richer-corporate-insurers.

20　**to rise by double digits:** http://khn.org/news/study-projects-sharper-increases-in -obamacare-premiums-for-2017/.

CHAPTER 2: THE AGE OF HOSPITALS

23　**about ten times the cost:** International Federation of Health Plans Price Report 2013, www.ifhp.com/1404121/.

24　**building Zen gardens:** According to Glenn Melnick, a distinguished economist and a professor of health economics and finance at the University of Southern California, "They raise price as much as they can all the time, and they price to maximize revenue. Research supports that. The nonprofit sector is wildly underregulated. And I say that as an economist and I don't like regulation." Personal interview/communication.

25　**have religious affiliations and names:** "20 Largest Nonprofit Hospital Systems 2015," *Becker's Hospital Review,* December 21, 2015, www.beckershospitalreview.com/lists /20-largest-nonprofit-hospital-systems-2015.html.

25　**to establish an outpost:** The history of the founding of Providence Health is taken from its Web site: http://oregon.providence.org/~/media/Files/Providence%20OR%20PDF /About%20us/OurProvidenceTradition.pdf.

25　**Dr. Starr then opened:** See www.ohsu.edu/xd/health/services/heart-vascular/about/starr /profile.cfm for a brief bio of Dr. Albert Starr, from Oregon Health & Science University, with which he is currently affiliated.

26　**at its peak:** Robin A. Cohen, Diane M. Makuc, Amy B. Bernstein, Linda T. Bilheimer, and Eve Powell-Griner, "Health Insurance Coverage Trends, 1959–2007: Estimates from the National Health Interview Survey," www.cdc.gov/nchs/data/nhsr/nhsr017.pdf.

26　**modified Providence's "core values":** Providence Health & Services, "Our Mission, Vision and Values," www2.providence.org/phs/Pages/our-mission.aspx.

27　**"but they didn't, and that's more expensive":** When Paul Levy, a former CEO of Harvard's Beth Israel Deaconess Medical Center, first suggested the hospital track and publish infection rates when he arrived in 2002, the board was horrified: "Why would you want to highlight that—it will make us look bad." It later relented, and the hospital earned great kudos for its transparency. From personal interview/communication, 2016.

27　**third-largest nonprofit hospital system:** www.bizjournals.com/seattle/print -edition/2016/03/04/merger-will-make-providence-third-largest.html.

27　**paid about $3.5 million a year:** From 2014 IRS Form 990, Return of Organization Exempt from Income Tax.

28　**nuns from Providence Ministries:** Some of the nuns have long-standing ties to the Vatican; see www2.providence.org/phs/Pages/Sponsors.aspx.

28　**the Cross Pro Ecclesia et Pontifice:** Jon Reddy, "Retired Providence Head to Receive Papal Medal," *Catholic Sentinel,* March 15, 2002, www.catholicsentinel.org/main.asp?Sec tionID=2&SubSectionID=35&ArticleID=1938.

28 **one day it is donating $250,000:** "Providence Helps Build in Haiti," n.d.,
    www2.providence.org/phs/news/Pages/Providence-helps-build-in-Haiti.aspx.

28 **$150 million venture capital fund:** "Providence Launches $150 Million Venture Capital
    Fund," news release, September 16, 2014, www2.providence.org/phs/news/Pages
    /Providence-Launches-150-Million-Venture-Capital-Fund.aspx.

28 **Planned Parenthood center:** Carole M. Ostrum, "Under Pressure on Abortion, Swedish
    Backs New Planned Parenthood Clinic," October 15, 2011, www.seattletimes.com/seattle
    -news/under-pressure-on-abortion-swedish-backs-new-planned-parenthood-clinic/.

28 **"will provide all emergency services":** Harris Meyer, "Will Swedish Limit Choices for
    Women and the Dying Under Providence Deal?," October 12, 2011, http://crosscut
    .com/2011/10/will-swedish-limit-choices-for-women-dying-under-p/.

29 **"The financial structure":** Howard J. Berman and Lewis E. Weeks, *The Financial
    Management of Hospitals,* 5th ed. (Ann Arbor, MI: Health Administration Press,
    1982), 54.

30 **$37 billion nationwide:** Office of the Inspector General Medicare, "Hospital Prospective
    Payment System: How DRG Rates Are Calculated and Updated," August 2001, http://oig
    .hhs.gov/oei/reports/oei-09-00-00200.pdf.

31 **it began paying according to:** MedPAC, "Payment Basics: Hospital Acute Inpatient
    Services Payment System," revised October 2007, www.patientcareanalyst.com/common
    /MedPAC_Payment_Basics_07_hospital.pdf. Medicare's level of payment is "intended to
    cover the costs that reasonably efficient providers would incur in furnishing high quality
    care, thereby rewarding providers whose costs fall below the payment rates and penalizing
    those with costs above the payment rates." The target is to pay 1 percent above costs,
    although government studies have repeatedly found providers get more.

31 **move patients into health maintenance organizations:** J. Gabel, "Ten Ways HMOs
    Have Changed During the 1990s," *Health Affairs* 16, no. 3 (1997): 134–45, http://content
    .healthaffairs.org/content/16/3/134.full.pdf.

32 **U.S. health spending did not increase:** Ibid. "For the past two years, overall health
    insurance premiums have increased at a lower rate than the overall rate of inflation, the
    medical care component of the consumer price index, and workers' earnings."

32 **creating quality cost-effective care:** J. Gabel, "HMOs and Managed Care," *Health Affairs*
    10, no. 4 (1991): 189–206, http://content.healthaffairs.org/content/10/4/189.full.pdf.

32 **failing to reimburse hospitals:** Esther B. Fein and Elisabeth Rosenthal, "Past Due:
    Delays by HMO Leaving Patients Haunted by Bills," *New York Times,* April 1, 1996,
    www.nytimes.com/1996/04/01/nyregion/past-due-a-special-report-delays-by-hmo-leaving
    -patients-haunted-by-bills.html.

32 **"The chief medical officer":** "Hospitals' New Physician Leaders: Doctors Wear Multiple
    Medical Hats," amednews.com, April 4, 2011, www.amednews.com/article/20110404
    /business/304049965/4/.

33 **Medical purchases became an "investment":** National Conference of State Legislatures,
    "CON—Certificate of Need State Laws," July 12, 2016, www.ncsl.org/research/health
    /con-certificate-of-need-state-laws.aspx.

35 **Deloitte is ranked number one:** "Kennedy Ranks Deloitte as the Top Global Health
    Care Consulting Practice," High Beam Research newsletter, April 22, 2011, www
    .highbeam.com/doc/1G1-254526365.

35 **fueled by more than 17 percent:** Reed Abelson, "Health Insurance Deductibles
    Outpacing Wage Increases, Study Finds," *New York Times,* September 23, 2015, www

.nytimes.com/2015/09/23/business/health-insurance-deductibles-outpacing-wage
-increases-study-finds.html. Most patients have become accustomed to bills conceived
through "strategic pricing," even as these charges have become less connected to value.
As bills were rising, co-payments stayed low, so it was easy not to pay attention to these
numbers. But that is no longer true. Since 2010 deductibles have risen six times faster
than family earnings.

35 **Dr. Randy Richards:** Personal interview/communication, 2014.

36 **an internist named Dr. W.:** When Dr. W. first contacted me in 2014, he was considering
allowing his name to be used. It's a discussion I have with everyone I interview. When
his wife, who is on his insurance, fell seriously ill, the calculation changed for him for
fear he would lose his job and their all-important coverage. It is a sign of how much
Americans are over a barrel when it comes to expressing misgivings about the healthcare
system.

37 **tie those salaries to physicians' RVUs:** Some documents showing how different
hospitals mentioned use productivity bonuses: for Partners HealthCare, see https://
bobkocher.files.wordpress.com/2015/01/table-1.png; for the Henry Ford Health System,
see http://healthaffairs.org/blog/2010/12/20/productivity-still-drives-compensation-in-
high-performing-group-practices/; for Duke Health, see www.linkedin.com/jobs
/view/153824585; for Baylor Scott & White Health, see http://jobs.baylorscottandwhite
.com/job/5998724/dermatologist-waco-tx/.

37 **71 percent of physician practices:** PowerPoint presentation by Merritt Hawkins, a
physician staffing firm, "Doctors, Dollars and Health Reform," www.sdhfma.org/site
/files/1071/157586/517859/756953/Doctors_Dollars_and_Health_Reform_Physician
_Reimbu.

38 **two most expensive codes:** Joe Eaton and David Donald, "Hospitals Grab at Least $1
Billion in Extra Fees for Emergency Room Visits," Center for Public Integrity,
September 20, 2012, www.publicintegrity.org/2012/09/20/10811/hospitals-grab-least-1
-billion-extra-fees-emergency-room-visits. The foundation of this investigation is the
Center for Public Integrity's access to about two terabytes of Medicare claims data that
was obtained by the center in 2010 as the result of a settlement from litigation against
the CMS.

38 **charging facility fees:** Fred Schulte, "Hospital 'Facility Fees' Boosting Medical Bills, and
Not Just for Hospital Care," Center for Public Integrity, December 20, 2012, www
.publicintegrity.org/2012/12/20/11978/hospital-facility-fees-boosting-medical-bills-and
-not-just-hospital-care.

38 **the bill was almost $5,000:** Ronald Anderson, MD, personal interview/communication.

39 **"When you buy anything":** Yevgeniy Feyman, "Payment Reform: Flat Facility Fees &
ACOs Aren't Enough," *Health Affairs Blog*, October 23, 2013, http://healthaffairs.org
/blog/2013/10/23/payment-reform-flat-facility-fees-acos-arent-enough/.

40 **bariatric surgery was a boom field:** "Healthgrades Bariatric Surgery Report 2013
Evaluates Hospitals Performing Obesity Surgery in the U.S.," PR Newswire, July 16,
2013, www.prnewswire.com/news-releases/healthgrades-bariatric-surgery-report-2013
-evaluates-hospitals-performing-obesity-surgery-in-the-us-215651741.html.

40 **Being overweight was rebranded:** Andrew Pollack, "AMA Recognizes Obesity as a
Disease," *New York Times*, June 18, 2013, www.nytimes.com/2013/06/19/business
/ama-recognizes-obesity-as-a-disease.html.

40 **The returns were exceptional:** According to its 2013 IRS Form 990, NewYork-

Presbyterian / Weill Cornell Medical Center had more than $3 billion in revenue and $300 million in overseas investments on its tax return, and paid thirty administrators more than $500,000 a year.

41 **"proton beam therapy":** "New Finding Likely to Fuel Cost-Benefit Debate over Cancer Care," *KHN Morning Briefing,* December 14, 2012, http://khn.org/morning-breakout /costly-cancer-care/. The study itself: James B. Yu et al., *Journal of the National Cancer Institute,* December 13, 2012, http://jnci.oxfordjournals.org/content/early/2012/12/13 /jnci.djs463.full.pdf+html.

41 **more than $100 million:** On the first two rounds of equity funding, $35 million each, see www.procure.com/ProCure-Secures-35-Million-from-McClendon-Venture. On the final round, $40 million, see www.procure.com/About-Procure.

41 **The British National Health Service:** http://scienceblog.cancerresearchuk.org/2015 /07/16/proton-beam-therapy-where-are-we-now/. For the National Health Service policy, see www.england.nhs.uk/commissioning/spec-services/highly-spec-services/pbt/.

41 **there should be three:** For more information on the proton beam therapy boom in the United States, see M. Beck, "Big Bets on Proton Therapy Face Uncertain Future," *Wall Street Journal,* May 26, 2015, www.wsj.com/articles/big-bets-on-proton-therapy-face -uncertain-future-1432667393.

41 **According to a 2006 survey:** Waller Lansden, Dortch & Davis, "2006 Hospital Outsourcing Trends in Clinical Services Commentary," www.wallerlaw.com /portalresource/2006-Outsourcing-Survey. Patient care outsourcing decisions continue to be driven by reimbursement considerations. For instance, it is not surprising that dialysis services were the number one outsourced patient care services. Despite the fact that Medicare pays hospital-based end-stage renal disease (ESRD) facilities slightly more than freestanding ESRD facilities, hospitals typically lose money on the provision of dialysis services to inpatients. Therefore, many hospitals have chosen to cease providing dialysis services completely.

41 **Innovative Health Strategies:** For the private dialysis industry, see www.law360.com /articles/416469/dialysis-industry-continues-to-see-robust-pe-activity.

41 **"Today's challenges require":** Innovative Health Strategies, Fact Sheet on Dialysis Outsourcing, www.ihsconsult.com/pdf/IHSDialysisOut.pdf.

42 **plans to close its transitional care unit:** See Gene Dorio, "No TLC for the Transitional Care Unit," *Henry Mayo Newhall Memorial Hospital Rant/Rave* (blog), September 12, 2011, http://hospitalrantandrave.blogspot.com/2011/09/no-tlc-for-the-transitional-care-unit .html; and www.hometownstation.com/santa-clarita-news/transitional-care-at-hmnmh-to -disappear-june-5-12850.

43 **paid trainee stipends:** For a review of how medical training came to be funded by Medicare, see Jared Harwood and Andrew Pugely, "The Evolution of GME Funding," American Academy of Orthopaedic Surgeons, www.aaos.org/AAOSNow/2014/Sep /advocacy/advocacy3/: "Until the community undertakes to bear such educational costs in some other way, that part of the net cost of such activities (including stipends of trainees, as well as compensation of teachers and other costs) should be borne to an appropriate extent by the hospital insurance program."

44 **sufficient numbers of doctors:** Gail R. Wilensky and Donald M. Berwick, "Reforming the Financing and Governance of GME," *New England Journal of Medicine* 371 (August 28, 2014): 792, www.nejm.org/doi/pdf/10.1056/NEJMp1406174. Pathologist Oversupply is a Web site run by pathologists who are concerned about the surfeit of practitioners

compared with the number of jobs in their field; see http://pathologistoversupply.weebly
.com/about.html.

44 **"directly threaten the financial stability"**: American Hospital Association Fact Sheet
on graduate medical education, www.aha.org/content/13/fs-gme.pdf.

46 **"There are an infinite number"**: James Robinson, personal interview/communication.

46 **Three years after Nancy Schlicting**: "Schlichting to Retire from Henry Ford Health,
Lassiter Taking the Reins," *Modern Healthcare,* September 29, 2014, www
.modernhealthcare.com/article/20140929/NEWS/309299938.

46 **"We focused on people"**: Nancy Schlichting, personal interview/communication.

47 **"to lead the patient experience industry"**: Press Ganey Web site, "Our History," https://
helpandtraining.pressganey.com/aboutUs/ourHistory.aspx. The 50 percent figure can also
be found on the Press Ganey Web site, "Hospital Patient Satisfaction": https://
helpandtraining.pressganey.com/resources/hospital-patient-satisfaction.

47 **surveys have only a "tenuous" link**: Joshua J. Fenton et al., "The Cost of Satisfaction:
A National Study of Patient Satisfaction, Health Care Utilization, Expenditures, and
Mortality," *Archives of Internal Medicine,* March 12, 2012, http://archinte.jamanetwork
.com/article.aspx?articleid=1108766.

47 **"So if a patient asks"**: Dr. Richard Duszak, professor of radiology at Emory University,
personal interview/communication, 2015.

47 **the CEO typically picks**: James McGroddy, a former IBM executive who has served on
multiple hospital boards, personal interview/communication, 2015.

47 **highest-paid nonprofit executive**: "Since the 1990s there has been a huge increase in the
number of executives and executive salaries," Cathy Schoen of the Commonwealth Fund
told me in an interview. "We have a lot more senior VPs and VPs of this and that. You
need someone who specialized in negotiating with the Blues and someone who deals with
the Joint Commission on Hospital Accreditation."

47 **In 2012 Jeffrey Romoff**: www.beckershospitalreview.com/compensation-issues
/ceo-compensation-of-the-25-top-grossing-nonprofit-hospitals-2014.html.

47 **the CEO of one small nonprofit suburban hospital**: For compensation stats for New
Jersey hospital heads, see www.njbiz.com/article/20140305/NJBIZ01/140309913/medical
-millionaires-the-compensation-packages-of-hospital-heads-are-drawing-attention.

48 **assets valued at about $12 billion**: For the Ford Foundation's IRS Form 990, see www
.guidestar.org/FinDocuments/2013/131/684/2013-131684331-0b088a10-F.pdf. The
foundation's tax return doesn't list Mr. Walker's salary because he's not one of the five
top-paid employees—they are finance people. But even they get only about $1 million,
so he earns less.

48 **compensation for hospital CEOs**: Rachel Landen, "Another Year of Pay Hikes for Nonprofit Hospital CEOs," *Modern Healthcare,* August 9, 2014, www.modernhealthcare.com
/article/20140809/MAGAZINE/308099987. Of the 147 chief executives included in
Modern Healthcare's analysis of the most recent public information available for not-for-
profit compensation, twenty-one, or 14.3 percent, saw their total cash compensation rise
by more than 50 percent. Another fifty-one, or 35.7 percent, received total cash
compensation increases of 10 percent or higher. The average 2012 cash compensation for
the CEOs was $2.2 million, but that masks wide disparities. "It is somewhat unique
in the nonprofit sector that you have a class of CEOs that are working for public charities
that are becoming millionaires," said Ken Berger, president and CEO of Charity

Navigator. "An average CEO salary for a mid- to large-size public charity is around $125,000. When it comes to not-profit hospitals, it's off the scale."

48 **Those bonuses are typically linked:** "Hospital CEO Pay and Incentives," chart, Kaiser Health News, June 16, 2013, http://khn.org/news/hospital-ceo-compensation-chart/.

48 **the largest nongovernmental employer:** University of Pittsburgh Medical Center Fact Sheet, www.upmc.com/about/facts/pages/default.aspx.

49 **at $12.6 billion in 2002:** Sara Rosenbaum et al., "The Value of the Nonprofit Hospital Tax Exemption Was $24.6 Billion in 2011," *Health Affairs,* June 2015, http://content .healthaffairs.org/content/early/2015/06/12/hlthaff.2014.1424.

49 **"the David versus the Goliath":** Moriah Balingit, "Pittsburgh Lawsuit Challenges UPMC's Tax Status," *Pittsburgh Post-Gazette,* March 21, 2013, www.post-gazette.com /local/city/2013/03/21/Pittsburgh-lawsuit-challenges-UPMC-s-tax-status/stories /201303210210.

50 **three of the twenty hospitals:** "List of Inpatient Hospitals Qualifying for Medical Assistance Disproportionate Share Payments," *Pennsylvania Bulletin,* September 27, 2014, www.pabulletin.com/secure/data/vol44/44-39/2022.html.

50 **that would justify the value:** "They are classified as charitable organizations by the IRS—they are supposed to provide 'community benefit' in return," said Paula Song, formerly at Ohio State University and now an associate professor of health policy and management at the University of North Carolina at Chapel Hill, in a 2013 interview. "But there's no consensus on what that means, or what is the required amount of charity care. Policy makers and researchers say you should get close to the value of the tax exemption and I think you'll find hospitals aren't providing that much, but it depends how it's defined."

50 **got more dollars in tax breaks:** *The Labor Blog* of *In These Times Magazine* provides a summary of the findings; see www.alternet.org/labor/not-profit-hospitals-make-billions -and-provide-little-charity-care. For a broader look at the issue, see Robert J. Rubin, "For-Profit/Not-for-Profit Healthcare: What's the Difference?," MedPageToday, May 1, 2015, www.medpagetoday.com/HospitalBasedMedicine/GeneralHospitalPractice/51317. Half of nonprofits spent less than 2.46 percent of their operating expenses on charity care.

51 **"building a global health care brand":** University of Pittsburgh Medical Center Facts, www.upmc.com/ABOUT/FACTS/NUMBERS/Pages/default.aspx.

51 **"best-known health care institutions to China":** Alexandra Stevenson, "The Chinese Billionaire Zhang Lei Spins Research into Investment Gold," *New York Times,* April 2, 2015, www.nytimes.com/2015/04/03/business/the-chinese-billionaire-zhang-lei-spins -research-into-investment-gold.html.

51 **"UPMC would owe the city $20 million":** Robert Zullo, "UPMC, City Drop Legal Fight Over Taxes," *Pittsburgh Post-Gazette,* July 29, 2014, www.post-gazette.com/local /city/2014/07/29/UPMC-city-drop-legal-fight-over-taxes/stories/201407290183.

52 **was not providing care commensurate:** I was told this by a longtime member of the San Francisco Department of Public Health during a 2014 interview.

52 **a stick the city uses to demand:** A unique tool, the Charity Care Ordinance "was meant to shine a light on what hospitals provide in exchange for the benefits that result from their tax-exempt status"; see www.sfdph.org/dph/files/reports/PolicyProcOfc/SFCC -Report-FY12.pdf.

52 **covered city employees:** Agreement between Sutter Health/UPMC and the city of

San Francisco; see http://default.sfplanning.org/publications_reports/cpmc/cpmc
_DevAgrmtFinal_exhibits.pdf.

53 **8 percent of people:** Medicare noted that the rate of long-stay observation cases lasting
more than two days had increased from 3 percent of all observation cases in 2006 to
8 percent in 2011; see "Health Policy Brief: The Two-Midnight Rule," *Health Affairs,*
January 22, 2015, www.healthaffairs.org/healthpolicybriefs/brief.php?brief_id=133.

53 **persist for more than "two midnights":** Ibid.

53 **That ruling prompted articles:** "Members Ask: How Can Our Hospital Succeed Under
the Two-Midnight Rule?," Advisory Board, the Daily Briefing, October 25, 2013,
www.advisory.com/Daily-Briefing/2013/10/25/Members-ask.

54 **a bill requiring hospitals:** "Obama Signs Medicare Observations Stays Bill," *Modern
Healthcare,* August 7, 2015, www.modernhealthcare.com/article/20150807/NEWS
/150809895.

CHAPTER 3: THE AGE OF PHYSICIANS

55 **"I promise to deal":** American College of Surgeons, Statements on Principles, revised
March 2004, www.facs.org/about-acs/statements/stonprin#fp.

56 **did not survive into the 1980s:** For the current AMA Code of Medical Ethics, see
www.ama-assn.org/ama/pub/physician-resources/medical-ethics/code-medical-ethics
.page.

57 **American orthopedic surgeons:** M. J. Laugesen and S. A. Glied, "Higher Fees Paid to
U.S. Physicians Drive Higher Spending for Physician Services Compared to Other
Countries," *Health Affairs* 30, no. 9 (September 2011): 1647–56.

57 **27.2 percent fall into that category:** "Top One Percent: What Jobs Do They Have?,"
New York Times, January 15, 2012, www.nytimes.com/packages/html/newsgraphics
/2012/0115-one-percent-occupations/.

57 **not even hedge fund managers:** www.nejmcareercenter.org/article/compensation-in-the
-physician-specialties-mostly-stable/.

57 **between $120,000 at a state school:** The Association of American Medical Colleges
provides a list of estimated expenses at U.S. medical schools; see https://services.aamc.org
/tsfreports/report.cfm?select_control=PRI&year_of_study=2016.

57 **mean debt of about $170,000:** "How Much Does Medical School Cost?,"
http://gradschool.about.com/od/medicalschool/f/MedSchoolCost.htm.

58 **"they pay that off quite readily":** Miriam Laugesen, personal interview/communication,
2014.

58 **In a recent survey:** Medscape Residents Salary & Debt Report, July 2016,
www.medscape.com/features/slideshow/public/residents-salary-and-debt-report-2016.

58 **"I have $240,000 in debt":** Dr. Logan Dance, personal interview/communication, 2015.

58 **"I'm not terribly sympathetic":** Dr. Joanne Roberts, personal interview/communication,
2016.

59 **"no fee, not even a large one":** David Schiedermayer, "Wages Through the Ages: The
Ethics of Physician Income," http://religion.llu.edu/bioethics/resources/bioethics-library
/wages-through-ages-ethics-of-physician-income.

60 **"Employer provided insurance plans":** Richard Patterson, "Money Isn't Everything, but
It Does Matter," www.generalsurgerynews.com/Article/PrintArticle?article ID=21693.

60 **hardwiring high payments into our bills:** "How did we adopt 'usual and customary' as
a reasonable standard?" asked Steven Schroeder, a professor of medicine at the University

of California and the chairman of the National Commission on Physician Payment Reform, during an interview with me. "The medical profession was opposed to Medicare, so when the regulations were written it said the 'government will not interfere with the practice of medicine.' It was a handshake with organized medicine to get them on board."

61   **where more doctors are:** Dr. Scott Breidbart, then a medical director at Empire BlueCross BlueShield (now chief clinical officer at EmblemHealth), personal interview/communication, 2013.

62   **While the RBRVS:** Gregory Przybylski, "Understanding and Applying a Resource Based Value Scale to Your Neurosurgical Practice," *Neurosurgical Focus,* 2012, www.medscape.com/viewarticle/4332883.

62   **According to the Medical Group Management Association:** Thomas Bodenheimer et al., "The Primary Care–Specialty Income Gap: Why It Matters," *Annals of Internal Medicine,* February 20, 2007, http://annals.org/article.aspx?articleid=733345.

62   **Average real income:** On income stagnation, see David Cay Johnston, "'04 Income in U.S. Was Below 2000 Level," *New York Times,* November 28, 2006.

63   **"26 sharks in a tank":** Elisabeth Rosenthal, "Patients' Costs Skyrocket; Specialists' Incomes Soar," *New York Times,* January 19, 2014, www.nytimes.com/2014/01/19/health/patients-costs-skyrocket-specialists-incomes-soar.html.

63   **in recent years a few extra generalists:** The RVS Update Committee, the American Medical Association, www.ama-assn.org/ama/pub/physician-resources/solutions-managing-your-practice/coding-billing-insurance/medicare/the-resource-based-relative-value-scale/the-rvs-update-committee.page?.

64   **"It's not about science":** Dr. Christine Sinsky, personal interview/communication, 2014.

64   **wildly inaccurate:** Laugesen and Glied, "Higher Fees Paid to U.S. Physicians," 1647.

64   **estimates were longer than actual times:** Miriam J. Laugesen, "Valuing Physician Work in Medicare: Time for a Change," October 2014 Expert Voices in Health Care Policy series sponsored by the National Institute for Health Care Management, www.nihcm.org/pdf/Valuing_Physician_Work_in_Medicare_Laugesen_EV_2014.pdf.

65   **The RUC does not always give:** For the April 2013 RUC minutes, see www.ama-assn.org/ama/no-index/physician-resources/ruc-recommendations.page.

65   **defeated once and for all in 2015:** "Congress Tries to Fix Medicare 'Doc Fix' Before It Fixes to Leave Town," McClatchyDC, March 24, 2015, www.mcclatchydc.com/news/politics-government/congress/article24782179.html#storylink=cpy.

65   **Ambulatory surgery centers:** For a brief history of ambulatory surgery centers from their professional organization, see www.asge.org/uploadedFiles/Members_Only/Practice_Management/Ambulatory%20Surgery%20Centers%20%E2%80%93%20A%20Positive%20Trend%20in%20Health%20Care.pdf.

66   **"They guarantee a return on investment":** Dr. Michael Zapf, personal interview/communication, 2015.

68   **according to Merritt Hawkins:** "Of those, thirty-one percent used local self-organized groups and thirty-four percent used one of several national players," said Phil Miller, vice president, communications, of Merritt Hawkins, in a 2015 interview with the author.

68   **"The game with the PARE":** Personal interview/communication, 2014–2015.

71   **In 2014, Robert Jordan":** Robert Jordan, personal interview/communication, 2016

72   **physician assistant training programs:** For a history of the development of the physician assistant profession in the United States, see J. F. Cawley, E. Cawthon, and R. S. Hooker, "Origins of the Physician Assistant Movement in the United States,"

Journal of the American Academy of Physician Assistants, December 2012. The full article can be found at https://medicine.utah.edu/dfpm/physician-assistant-studies/files/pa_history_2011.pdf.

One of the leaders was Duke University, where Dr. Eugene Stead sought to replicate the relationship between a rural doctor he knew, Dr. Amos Johnson, and Johnson's personally trained assistant, Henry Lee "Buddy" Treadwell. The article quotes many discussions in the medical community about the PA concept in the 1960s. For example: "By having someone [Johnson] can trust to coordinate patient care when he is away, he feels free to spend more time at medical meetings or participating in activities of organized medicine." Another quotes Johnson as saying, "I don't know any other way a doctor is going to get significant amounts of time for himself."

73 **In 2014, when Peter Drier:** Peter Drier, personal interview/communication. Other aspects of Mr. Drier's shocking story of being bilked after spine surgery are covered in Elisabeth Rosenthal, "After Surgery, Surprise $117,000 Medical Bill from Doctor He Didn't Know," *New York Times,* October 7, 2014, www.nytimes.com/2014/09/21/us/drive-by-doctoring-surprise-medical-bills.html.

73 **"WORK FROM HOME":** The position was filled, so the ad has been taken down, but here's how it read: "Home Based Staff Neurologist— Intraoperative Monitoring Job www.theladders.com/Staff-Neurologist%7CSaint-Louis-MO%7C156 . . . WORK FROM HOME POSITION. CAN BE LOCATED ANYWHERE IN THE US. NO TRAVEL. . . . This position will supervise certified NIOM technologists in the operating room to help in the prevention of neurological problems during surgeries. . . . Procedures commonly monitored include but are not limited to: Spine surgery . . ."

74 **"split 50-50 between the two parties":** This advisory document for certified registered nurse-anesthetists, from the American Association of Nurse Anesthetists, lays out what's kosher for billing: Reimbursement of CRNA Services, www.aana.com/aboutus/Documents/reimbursement_crnaservices.pdf.

75 **In 2000 a press release:** Debra P. Malina, "Education and Practice Barriers for Certified Registered Nurse Anesthetists," *Online Journal of Issues in Nursing,* May 2014. http://www.medscape.com/viewarticle/833517_2.

75 **when the patient is on cardiac bypass:** Their trade association is constantly expanding their territory, claiming in a 2010 article that "anesthesiologists and CRNAs [certified registered nurse-anesthetists] can perform the same set of anesthesia services, including relatively rare and difficult procedures such as open-heart surgeries and organ transplantations, pediatric procedures, and others." See Paul F. Hogan et al., "Cost Effectiveness Analysis of Anesthesia Providers," *Nursing Economics* 28, no. 3 (May–June 2010): 159.

75 **"Maximizing Reimbursement for Physician Assistant Services":** *Clinical Advisor,* May 26, 2013, www.clinicaladvisor.com/aapa-2013/maximizing-reimbursement-for-physician-assistant-services/article/295002/.

76 **they had to be present:** See "The Role of CMS" section at www.patientsafetysolutions.com/docs/November_10_2015_Weighing_in_on_Double_Booked_Surgery.htm.

76 **Dr. Kenan W. Yount:** For Dr. Yount's study, see http://aats.org/annualmeeting/Program-Books/2014/2.cgi.

76 **Dr. Gerald Weisberg:** Dr. Weisberg relayed the Lupron story to me in an interview; he provided requested documents.

77 **make money by charging:** According to Dr. Gerald Weisman, the United States is one

of only a few countries in the world where the approved route of administration for Lupron is an injection deep into the muscle, rather than by a subcutaneous injection that can be self-administered at home.

78 **"afoul of the law"**: Andrew Zajac and Laurie Cohen, "Tapping Medicare Bonanza," *Chicago Tribune,* May 23, 1999, http://articles.chicagotribune.com/1999-05-23/news /9905230398.

78 **$885 million in restitution**: Bruce Japson, "Ex-TAP Manager Found Guilty," *Chicago Tribune,* January 27, 2004, http://articles.chicagotribune.com/2004-01-27/business /0401270256_1_astrazeneca-plc-lupron-lahey-clinic.

79 **"Drugs and biologicals make up"**: For a further discussion of the income doctors derive from selling drugs, see one of Mr. Holland's publications: R. P. Langdale and B. F. Holland, "Practice Benchmarking in the Age of Targeted Auditing," *Journal of Oncology Practice* 8, no. 6S (2012): 71–74, doi:10.1200/JOP.2012.000633.

79 **lots of infusions**: By 2012 Medicare instructed its inspector general to examine outpatient billing for office-based chemotherapy. "Poor timekeeping and manipulation of timing thresholds has created a predictable level of coding abuse, and Medicare intends to crack down on the practice," said Ben Holland, an executive at Oncology Solutions. See Langdale and Holland, "Practice Benchmarking."

79 **Betsy Glassman's insurers**: From personal interview/communication, 2014–2015 and communication of documents.

80 **£500 per infusion**: People with Medicare and commercial insurance were somewhat protected from large out-of-pocket bills, but uninsured patients faced prices for chemotherapy that were two to forty-three times as much as the total Medicare-allowed amount and two to five times as much as that paid by private insurance. See Stacie B. Dusetzina, Ethan Basch, and Nancy L. Keating, "For Uninsured Cancer Patients, Outpatient Charges Can Be Costly, Putting Treatments Out of Reach," *Health Affairs* 34, no. 4 (April 2015): 584–91.

80 **The average price paid**: Corcoran Consulting Group guidelines for doctors selling the Toric lens, www.corcoranccg.com/digital_files/monographs/Toric%20IOL%20 STAAR_100713.pdf.

81 **cataract surgeries were cut**: See the 2014 complaint letter to CMS from the American Society of Cataract and Refractive Surgery at http://policymed.typepad.com/files /american-society-of-cataract-and-refractive-surgery.pdf. For example, in 2013 the cataract removal (66984) and complex cataract (66982) codes were revalued by the RUC.

82 **In one study in St. Louis**: W. Shrank, "Effect of Physician Reimbursement Methodology on the Rate and Cost of Cataract Surgery," *Archives of Ophthalmology* 123, no. 12 (December 2005): 1733–38, www.ncbi.nlm.nih.gov/pubmed/16344447.

82 **Glasses, though perhaps with a weaker prescription**: H. Lee et al., "Corneal Astigmatism Analysis for Toric Intraocular Lens Implantation: Precise Measurements for Perfect Correction," *Current Opinions in Ophthalmology* 26, no. 1 (January 2015): 34–38, www.ncbi.nlm.nih.gov/pubmed/25415298.

83 **on the right side of the Medicare law**: Corcoran Consulting Group guidelines for doctors selling the Toric lens.

83 **"You would lose money on every procedure"**: James Brice, "Femtosecond Laser Cataract Surgery: Advantages Await Clinical Trial Results," Medscape Ophthalmology, November 26, 2012, www.medscape.com/viewarticle/774568_2.

83 **little if any evidence**: When Dr. Ming Chen at the University of Hawaii pulled together

the limited evidence available to decide if he should use the femtosecond laser in his practice, he found studies with "small sample size and short-term follow-up." He wrote: "Long-term studies to compare the complication rate and visual outcome between the laser and conventional cataract surgery are warranted"; see www.ncbi.nlm.nih.gov/pmc /articles/PMC3689514/.

83 **"few products have captured the imagination":** Riva Lee Aspell, "Femto Reimbursement," *Review of Ophthalmology,* April 5, 2012, www.reviewofophthalmology .com/content/t/finances/c/33271/.

83 **2011 International Conference on Femtosecond Lasers:** See the discussion in *EyeNet Magazine,* an academic ophthalmology online newsletter, www.aao.org/eyenet/article /femtosecond-cataract-are-lasers-good-business.

84 **"Are Lasers Good for Business?":** Ibid.

84 **"Sure, in several years":** Ibid.

86 **the idea that nephrologists:** Kristina Fiore, "Nephrologists Take Fistulas into Their Own Hands," MedPageToday, May 9, 2014, www.medpagetoday.com/nephrology /generalnephrology/45696.

86 **"Medicine is a business":** Dr. William Sage, personal interview/communication, 2015.

86 **which paid him $82:** Dr. Robert Morrow, personal interview/communication, 2014.

CHAPTER 4: THE AGE OF PHARMACEUTICALS

87 **Hope Marcus has spent much:** Hope Marcus, personal interviews/communications, 2014–2015.

87 **better because it had fewer:** personal interview/communication, 2015, with John Mayberry, professor of gastroenterology at the University of Leicester, who has studied the history of mesalamine: "Mesalamine had been used to treat inflammatory bowel disease since the 1930s. Its discovery was important because its predecessor, sulfasalazine, at high doses came with unpleasant side effects for many patients—headache and fevers, for example—that mesalamine alone did not produce." By 1990 it was hailed by doctors who now had a drug that offered "the efficacy of sulfasalazine without the risk of adverse events."

88 **"offset the generic threat":** www.istockanalyst.com/finance/story/6300463/warner -chilcott-plc-numerous-sources-of-potential-upside.

89 **"It is very hard for me:** Mayberry, personal interview/communication.

89 **people with private prescriptions:** Pricing statistics on medicines in Great Britain provided by Thomas Wilkinson, a British health economist and an adviser to NICE International, which assesses the cost benefit of prescription drugs; see www.linkedin .com/in/thomas-wilkinson-185a0140.

90 **"They can enjoy the holidays":** www.fda.gov/downloads/Drugs/Guidance ComplianceRegulatoryInformation/EnforcementActivitiesbyFDA/Warning LettersandNoticeofViolationLetterstoPharmaceuticalCompanies/UCM173187.pdf.

90 **Rowasa, previously owned by Solvay:** That left only one generic maker, Perrigo, and, weirdly, two companies that made the brand form of the drug: Meda, which acquired the drug when it bought Alaven Pharmaceutical in 2010, and AbbVie, formerly Solvay Pharmaceuticals.

90 **One of the last to move:** "Perrigo to Buy Elan for 8.6 Billion, Get Irish Domicile," Bloomberg News, July 29, 2013, www.bloomberg.com/news/articles/2013-07-29/perrigo -to-buy-elan-for-86-billion-get-irish-domicile.

91 **to make the deal somewhat less rewarding:** Brett LoGiurato, "Obama May Have Just Scored His First Huge Victory in His Battle Against Inversions," *Business Insider,* October 15, 2014, www.businessinsider.com/abbvie-shire-inversion-obama-2014-10.

91 **inventing a sugar coating for pills:** *Encyclopedia.com,* s.v. "Warner-Lambert Co.," www.encyclopedia.com/topic/Warner-Lambert_Co.aspx.

91 **Perrigo was started in 1887:** www.perrigo.com/about/perrigo-history.aspx.

91 **a mysterious "liver pill":** www.wallacepharmaceuticals.com/aboutus.html.

92 **who took Elixir Sulfanilamide died:** For the sulfanilamide story, see www.fda.gov /aboutfda/whatwedo/history/productregulation/sulfanilamidedisaster/default.htm.

93 **The FDA promulgated guidelines:** "Social Reassessment, Regulation, and Growth: 1960–80," *Chemical and Engineering News,* pubs.acs.org/cen/coverstory/83/8325 /8325social.html.

94 **process to merit intellectual protection:** Michael Hiltzik, "On Jonas Salk's 100th Birthday, a Celebration of His Polio Vaccine," *Los Angeles Times,* October 28, 2014, www.latimes.com/business/hiltzik/la-fi-mh-polio-vaccine-20141028-column.html.

94 **a number that has only increased since:** Thanks to Stanford law professor Lisa Larrimore Ouellette for the figures, which may include many older medicines covered by just one patent. For her review of the high number of patents that today cover many drugs, see Lisa Larrimore Ouellette, "How Many Patents Does It Take to Make a Drug? Follow-On Pharmaceutical Patents and University Licensing," *Michigan Telecommunications and Technology Law Review* 17, no. 1 (2010): 299–336, http:// repository.law.umich.edu/cgi/viewcontent.cgi?article=1044&context=mttlr.

94 **known as Hatch-Waxman:** For a free summary of all the provisions of Hatch-Waxman, from a law firm, see www.finnegan.com/resources/articles/articlesdetail .aspx?news=dfef53ed-54e4-491a-802a-01becb1f47bb.

95 **bring cheaper versions onto the market:** Hatch-Waxman was a compromise that "allowed for the extension of a patent's life for the New Drug Application holder, while providing a streamlined system for the approval of generic copies of the innovator's product." See Dennis B. Worthen, "American Pharmaceutical Patents from a Historical Perspective," *International Journal of Pharmaceutical Compounding,* November/December 2003, www.lloydlibrary.org/scholar/Patents%20-%20V8%20-%20I1.pdf.

95 **"medicines with a single indication":** Ibid.

96 **The Generic Drug Enforcement Act:** John R. Fleder, "The History, Provisions and Implementation of the Generic Drug Enforcement Act of 1992," *Food and Drug Law Journal* 49 (1994): 89–107, www.hpm.com/pdf/0001000JRF.pdf.

96 **where government price setting was increasingly common:** Bruce Lehman, "The Pharmaceutical Industry and the Patent System," 2003, http://users.wfu.edu/mcfallta/ DIR0/pharma_patents.pdf.

96 **grown twice as fast as the economy:** Ibid.

96 **"In the 1980s people":** Dr. Marcus Reidenberg, personal interview/communication.

98 **lasted just nineteen weeks:** Irving Molotsky, "US Approves Drug to Prolong Lives of AIDS Patients," *New York Times,* March 21, 1987, www.nytimes.com/1987/03/21/us /us-approves-drug-to-prolong-lives-of-aids-patients.html.

98 **"most expensive prescription drug in history":** "AZT's Inhuman Cost," *New York Times,* August 28, 1989, www.nytimes.com/1989/08/28/opinion/azt-s-inhuman -cost.html.

99 **"Often, sponsors of drugs":** Thomas Fleming, "Surrogate Endpoints and the FDA

Approval Process," *Health Affairs* 24, no. 1 (January 2005): 67–78, http://content
.healthaffairs.org/content/24/1/67.full.

99 **An in-depth data investigation:** John Fauber and Elbert Chu, "The Slippery Slope: Is a
Surrogate Endpoint Evidence of Efficacy?," October 24, 2014, http://www.medpagetoday
.com/special-reports/slipperyslope/48244.

100 **wasn't the only novel practice:** Julie Donahue, "A History of Drug Advertising: The
Evolving Roles of Consumers and Consumer Protection," *Millbank Quarterly* 84, no. 4
(December 2006): 659–99, www.ncbi.nlm.nih.gov/pmc/articles/PMC2690298/#b61.

100 **"a brief summary of all":** Ibid.

100 **40 percent of total pharmaceutical promotional spending:** Ibid.

100 **promotional spending was for direct-to-consumer advertising:** J. Ma et al., "A
Statistical Analysis of the Magnitude and Composition of Drug Promotion in the United
States in 1998," *Clinical Therapeutics* 25, no. 5 (May 2003):1503–17, www.ncbi.nlm.nih
.gov/pubmed/12867225.

100 **That year drug sales for Vioxx:** Ismael Bradley, "DTC Advertising, and Its History with
the FDA," *KevinMD.com* (a popular physician blog), September 18, 2010, www.kevinmd
.com/blog/2010/09/dtc-advertising-history-fda.html.

100 **The company ultimately paid:** Snigdha Prakash and Vikki Valentine, "Timeline: The
Rise and Fall of Vioxx," NPR, November 10, 2007, www.npr.org/templates/story/story
.php?storyId=5470430.

101 **$43.4 million and $125 million:** Scott Gavura, "What Does a New Drug Cost?,"
Science-Based Medicine, April 14, 2011, www.sciencebasedmedicine.org/what-does-a
-new-drug-cost/.

101 **Dr. Robert Sack's late-night gardening show:** Dr. Robert Sack, personal interviews/
communication, 2015.

103 **according to a 2009 study:** Shantha Rajaratnam et al., "Melatonin Agonist Tasimelteon
(VEC-162) for Transient Insomnia After Sleep-Time Shift: Two Randomised Controlled
Multicentre Trials," *Lancet* 373, no. 9662 (February 7, 2009): 482–91, www.thelancet
.com/journals/lancet/article/PIIS0140-6736(08)61812-7/abstract.

103 **"Vanda's Sleep Disorder Drug":** Adam Feuerstein, "Vanda's Sleep Disorder Drug Is a
Nightmare," TheStreet.com, June 19, 2013, www.thestreet.com/story/11954365/1
/vandas-sleep-disorder-drug-is-a-nightmare.html.

103 **In front of Dr. Sack's committee:** For a full transcript of the committee meeting that led
to Hetlioz's approval, see www.fda.gov/downloads/AdvisoryCommittees/Committees
MeetingMaterials/Drugs/PeripheralandCentralNervousSystemDrugsAdvisoryCommittee
/UCM386061.pdf.

104 **to sell just fifteen hundred:** Rafi Farber, "Vanda's Hetlioz Is Starting to Sell Slowly
After Bumbling Through the Pipeline," TheStreet.com, October 6, 2014, www.thestreet
.com/story/12895655/2/vandas-hetlioz-is-starting-to-sell—slowly—after-bumbling-
through-the-pipeline.html.

105 **$50 million worth of common stock:** "Vanda Pharmaceuticals Prices Public Offering
of Common Stock," *Sleep Review Magazine,* October 31, 2014, www.sleepreviewmag
.com/2014/10/vanda-pharmaceuticals-prices-public-offering-common-stock/.

105 **conducting trials for that indication:** Vanda's "Pipeline," on its Web site, shows that it
is already testing Hetlioz for jet lag too; see www.vandapharmaceuticals.com/pipeline
.html.

105 **"Wild, Wild West":** Elisabeth Rosenthal, "Lawmakers Look for Ways to Provide Relief

for Rising Cost of Generic Drugs," *New York Times,* November 25, 2014, www.nytimes
.com/2014/11/25/us/lawmakers-look-for-ways-to-provide-relief-for-rising-cost-of-generic
-drugs.html.

106 **because each new application:** For a great review of the issues, see Jessica Wapner,
"How Much Money Do Drug Companies Pay the FDA?," *PLOS Blog,* January 25, 2012,
http://blogs.plos.org/workinprogress/2012/01/25/how-much-money-do-drug-companies
-pay-the-fda/.

106 **"If you're persistent you can":** Lisa Larrimore Ouellette, personal interview/
communication, 2015.

107 **"Why is it I can order":** Comment on an article ("The Rising Price of Insulin") on the
RxRights.org campaign site. Chat rooms of diabetics are filled with outrage and despair
about the rising price of insulin; see www.rxrights.org/the-rising-price-of-insulin/.

107 **she was open about the strategy:** Susan Brooks, personal interview/communication,
2014.

107 **Hatch-Waxman "waiting period":** John Carroll, "Sanofi Blocks Eli Lilly's Biosimilar of
Lantus at the Goal Line, Buys Time," FierceBiotech.com, January 31, 2014, www
.fiercebiotech.com/story/sanofi-blocks-eli-lillys-biosimilar-lantus-goal-line-buys
-time/2014-01-31. FierceBiotech is a good site to follow such conflicts.

107 **the patent was set to expire in December 2016:** Tracy Staton, "Sanofi Patent Deal Lets
Lilly Roll Out a Lantus Biosim in U.S. Next December," FiercePharma.com, September
28, 2015, www.fiercepharma.com/legal/sanofi-patent-deal-lets-lilly-roll-out-a-lantus-
biosim-u-s-next-december.

107 **it was no longer available:** Dr. Laura Schiller, personal interview/communication, 2015.

108 **sales of Loestrin 24 Fe:** "Warner Chilcott Tops in 4Q," Nasdaq.com, February 25, 2013,
www.nasdaq.com/article/warner-chilcott-tops-in-4q-analyst-blog-cm220734#ixzz
3cTthqP6l.

108 **every six months of delay:** Markian Hawryluk, "Blocking Generics," *Bend Bulletin,*
July 28, 2013. "The industry has had a history of presenting very weak patents and
then litigating to protect these weak patents for as long they can," said Daniel Berger,
an attorney with the Philadelphia-based law firm Berger & Montague. "Because if
you can delay generic entry for six months, that's worth billions of dollars."
www.bendbulletin.com/csp/mediapool/sites/BendBulletin/News/story.csp?cid=1372219
&sid=497&fid=151.

109 **between $130 and $150:** Pricing from GoodRx.com.

109 **succeeded in delaying competition:** "Product Hopping—the FTC Weighs In," *Orange
Book Blog,* December 6, 2012, www.orangebookblog.com/2012/12/product-hopping-the
-ftc-weighs-in.html.

110 **All generics were banned:** Only one thing was different: the Colcrys prescribing label
now cautioned about an obscure interaction between colchicine and an antibiotic.

110 **URL was acquired by a big pharmaceutical firm:** Two articles discuss the rebranding
of colchicine and how little it did to help patients: "Takeda Again Sues Par over Generic
Gout Drug," Law360.com, September 3, 2015, www.law360.com/articles/469534/takeda
-again-sues-par-over-generic-gout-drug; "Study Says No Good Has Come from FDA's
Action on Gout Drug Colchicine," FiercePharma.com, April 10, 2015, http://www
.fiercepharma.com/regulatory/study-says-no-good-has-come-from-fda-s-action-on-gout
-drug-colchicine.

110 **even pressure to do so:** Steven Francesco, a longtime pharmaceutical consultant, whose

specialty is over-the-counter switches, personal interview/communication, 2015. In 1996 an FDA advisory committee was slated to review taking the sprays over the counter, but the meeting was canceled when drug companies declined to participate.

111 **gave it a six-month patent extension:** G. Harris, "Court Rules Against Schering on Claritin Patent Protection," *Wall Street Journal,* August 9, 2002, www.wsj.com/articles /SB1028832783118577960.

111 **lost valuable time:** M. Herper, "Schering-Plough Stands to Lose Claritin Patent," *Forbes,* June 30, 2000, www.forbes.com/2000/06/30/mu3.html.

111 **for longer periods of time:** Under those conditions, steroids are well known to leave patients vulnerable to infection, to induce bone loss, and to disrupt functioning of crucial hormonal feedback loops that handle vital functions like children's growth. In the mid-1990s, right around the first time the FDA considered taking nasal sprays off prescription, a few studies had shown that asthmatic children who used high doses of steroid inhalers that penetrate deep into the lungs might have a slightly reduced short-term growth rate—although further research concluded this was not significant in the long run. There was no data on nasal sprays that used lower doses and presumably presented even less chance of absorption into the blood. But it was in no company's interest to do the studies, because showing the sprays were safe for wider sale would also necessitate a lower price. With potential liability added on, in the United States there was no pressure from the increasingly lawyerly FDA to switch: if one patient is harmed by OTC availability, the FDA is in trouble.

112 **delay less expensive generics:** "GSK Faces Flonase Lawsuit," BigClassAction.com, February 10, 2015, www.bigclassaction.com/lawsuit/gsk-faces-flonase-lawsuit.php.

112 **to protest the entry of generics:** In 2013 Glaxo paid $35 million to settle a class action lawsuit with a law firm representing purchasers of Flonase who averred the company "had lodged sham citizen petitions with the Food & Drug Administration in order to delay entry of generic versions of Flonase." According to the terms of the settlement Glaxo admitted no fault. For a good review of the legal action, see http://pennrecord.com /stories/510553178-judge-approves-35-million-in-flonase-indirect-purchasers-antitrust -class-action-11-7-million-will-go-to-plaintiffs-lawyers.

112 **the same product cannot be on the market:** Francesco, personal interview/ communication.

113 **"There really is no benefit":** P. Crutcher, "HZNP—Horizon Pharma's Unsustainable Business Model," August 9, 2012, www.chimeraresearchgroup.com/2012/08/horizon -pharmas-unsustainable-business-model. He also noted that the trials Horizon ran to gain FDA approval of the drug overstated its usefulness because they compared Duexis with ibuprofen alone.

113 **rose to $85.5 million:** "Horizon Pharma Reports 2013 Financial Results and Provides Business Update (NASDAQ: HZNP)," March 13, 2014, http://ir.horizon-pharma.com /releasedetail.cfm?releaseid=832380.

113 **Horizon "vigorously" defends:** Statement from Horizon CEO Timothy Walbert; see http://ipfrontline.com/2015/05/horizon-pharma-settles-with-perrigo/.

116 **A 2016 survey:** Bari Talente, "Perceptions of and Experiences with the High Cost of MS Disease-Modifying Therapies," abstract presented at the 2016 Consortium of Multiple Sclerosis Care Centers annual conference, https://cmsc.confex.com/cmsc/2016 /webprogram/Paper4090.html.

117 **its IRS Form 990:** The form can be accessed at https://panfoundation.org/files /PAN_990_2015.pdf.

117 **one over $100 million:** Ibid.

117 **According to a report:** For the letter and report of the Office of the Inspector General of the U.S. Department of Health and Human Services, see https://www.panfoundation .org/index.php/en/donors/office-of-inspector-general-advisory-opinion.

117 **presumably the ones their drugs treat:** Ibid.

117 **Pharmaceutical firms are skirting:** For more on the controversy over patient-assistance programs, see Lisa Schencker, "Lifesavers or Kickbacks? Critics Say Patient-Assistance Programs Help Keep Drug Prices High," *Modern Healthcare,* March 7, 2015, www.modernhealthcare.com/article/20150307/MAGAZINE/303079980.

117 **"would not constitute grounds":** Office of the Inspector General of the U.S. Department of Health and Human Services, letter. It can be accessed at www .panfoundation.org/index.php/en/donors/office-of-inspector-general-advisory-opinion.

119 **suggesting it made more:** C. Noles, "Express Scripts' Q4, Full-Year Profit Rises," *St. Louis Business Journal,* February 23, 2015, www.bizjournals.com/stlouis/blog/2015 /02/express-scripts-q4-full-year-profit-rises.html.

119 **"As Express Scripts Attacks Costs":** J. Bennett, "As Express Scripts Attacks Costs, Investors Profit," *Barron's,* May 21, 2015, http://online.barrons.com/articles/as-express -scripts-attacks-costs-investors-will-profit-1432251332.

120 **struggling to treat patients:** Dr. James Larson, personal interview/communication, 2015.

120 **which studies showed worked:** T. J. Gan, P. F. White, P. E. Scuderi, M. F. Watcha, and A. Kovac, "FDA 'Black Box' Warning Regarding Use of Droperidol for Postoperative Nausea and Vomiting: Is It Justified?," *Journal of the American Society of Anesthesiologists* 97, no. 1 (2002): 287, http://anesthesiology.pubs.asahq.org/Article.aspx?articleid =1944490.

121 **handed over a very lucrative market:** C. W. Jackson, A. H. Sheehan, and J. G. Reddan, "Evidence-Based Review of the Black-Box Warning for Droperidol," *American Journal of Health-System Pharmacy* 64, no. 11 (2007): 1174–86, doi:10.2146/ajhp060505.

121 **$1.3 billion in global sales:** *Wikipedia,* s.v. "Ondansetron," accessed August 3, 2016, https://en.wikipedia.org/wiki/Ondansetron.

121 **actually charging doctors $22.61:** C. Rizo, "Kansas AG Sues 13 Drug Companies Over Pricing," Legal NewsLine, October 24, 2008, http://legalnewsline.com/stories/510520064 -kansas-ag-sues-13-drug-companies-over-pricing.

121 **U.S. Department of Justice:** "GlaxoSmithKline to Plead Guilty and Pay $3 Billion to Resolve Fraud Allegations and Failure to Report Safety Data," Justice News, U.S. Department of Justice, July 2, 2012, www.justice.gov/opa/pr/glaxosmithkline-plead -guilty-and-pay-3-billion-resolve-fraud-allegations-and-failure-report.

121 **South Korea sued Glaxo:** Jacqueline Bell, "South Korea Fines GSK $2.6M Over Pay-For-Delay Deal," Law360, October 24, 2011, http://www.law360.com/articles/279947 /south-korea-fines-gsk-2-6m-over-pay-for-delay-deal.

122 **twofold risk of having a baby:** For information on the problem as well as the lawsuits that followed, see M. Llamas, "Popular Nausea Drug Zofran May Increase Risk of Birth Defects," Drugwatch, February 18, 2015, www.drugwatch.com/2015/02/18/zofran-may -increase-risk-of-birth-defects/; J. Mundy, "Plaintiff Claims Zofran Maker Uses Expectant Mothers and Unborn Children as Human Guinea Pigs," LawyersandSettlements.com,

May 24, 2015, www.lawyersandsettlements.com/articles/zofran-birth-defects
/glaxosmithkline-gsk-united-states-district-court-of-20662.html.

122 **have become the new normal:** The FDA compiles a list of drug shortages, which it
updates frequently; see www.accessdata.fda.gov/scripts/drugshortages/default.cfm#P.

122 **Well over 80 percent:** All statistics in this paragraph are from the Generic
Pharmaceutical Association's *Generic Drug Savings in the U.S., Seventh Annual Edition,*
2015, www.gphaonline.org/media/wysiwyg/PDF/GPhA_Savings_Report_2015.pdf.

123 **He was shocked to discover:** Dr. John Siebel, personal interview/communication, 2015.

123 **Medicaid data show:** Aaron Carroll, "Generic Drug Competition and Pricing
Nightmares," *The Incidental Economist* (a health services research blog), November 13,
2014, http://theincidentaleconomist.com/wordpress/generic-drug-competition-and
-pricing-nightmares/.

123 **to corner a niche market:** J. D. Alpern, W. M. Stauffer, and A. S. Kesselheim, "High-
Cost Generic Drugs—Implications for Patients and Policymakers," *New England Journal
of Medicine* 371, no. 20 (2014): 1859–62, doi:10.1056/nejmp1408376.

123 **rose from 6.3 cents to $3.36:** "U.S. Prices Soaring for Some Generic Drugs, Experts
Say," *U.S. News & World Report,* November 12, 2014, http://health.usnews.com/health
-news/articles/2014/11/12/us-prices-soaring-for-some-generic-drugs-experts-say.

124 **the single biggest drug outlay:** Dr. Gene Bishop, who is on the Pennsylvania
Department of Public Welfare Pharmacy and Therapeutics Committee, personal
interview/communication, 2015.

124 **to really bring down prices:** Dr. Aaron Kesselheim, personal interview/communication,
2014.

124 **the fastest-growing company:** L. Lorenzetti, "This Is the Fastest Growing Company in
the U.S.," *Fortune,* August 19, 2015, http://fortune.com/2015/08/19/lannett-fastest
-growing-company/.

125 **"The United States leads the world":** www.fda.gov/AboutFDA/ReportsManualsForms
/Reports/ucm454955.htm.

125 **Opdivo, which costs $150,000:** On the hype versus reality of this drug, see Michael
Wilkes, "Opdivo Ads vs. the Reality of Stage IV Cancer Treatment," HealthNewsReview,
December 16, 2015, www.healthnewsreview.org/2015/12/opdivo-ads-vs-the-reality-of
-stage-iv-cancer-treatment/.

125 **British health regulators ultimately decided:** For more about the British decision,
see "NICE Rejects BMS Cancer Drug in Draft Guidance," Pharmafile, June 12, 2015,
www.pharmafile.com/news/501839/nice-rejects-bms-cancer-drug-draft-guidance;
Andrew McConaghie, "NICE Rejects Opdivo in Lung Cancer as Too Expensive,"
Pharmaphorum, December 16, 2015, http://pharmaphorum.com/news/nice-rejects
-opdivo-in-lung-cancer-as-too-expensive/.

126 **there were no further cases:** The charges are $168 in the United States for each of two
shots, compared with a list price of half that in Great Britain, where authorities negotiated
a national price. Today, both GSK and Pfizer have licensed meningitis B vaccines in
America, partly because the FDA said it would accept the data from elsewhere, thereby
reducing the outlays for new trials. But widespread press coverage surrounding the
outbreaks also contributed toward creating a market. Although the CDC's Advisory
Committee on Immunization Practices says that whether to take the shot is a personal
decision, many parents will likely want their children vaccinated before attending college
and many colleges now encourage it. The vaccine is even advertised on TV.

127 **patients with allergies:** Peter S. Creticos, "Sublingual Immunotherapy for Allergic Rhinoconjunctivitis and Asthma," UpToDate, May 26, 2016, www.uptodate.com /contents/sublingual-immunotherapy-for-allergic-rhinoconjunctivitis-and-asthma.

CHAPTER 5: THE AGE OF MEDICAL DEVICES

128 **Robin Miller's forty-eight-year-old:** Robin Miller, personal interview/communication, 2013.

129 **a doctor who owned a small:** Dr. Larry Teuber, a South Dakota surgeon.

129 **Dr. Blair Rhode:** Dr. Blair Rhode, personal interview/communication, 2013.

129 **Peter Cram, a doctor and an MBA:** Dr. Peter Cram, personal interview/communication, 2013, when he was at the University of Iowa.

130 **Congressional Research Service:** Paul N. Van DeWater, "Excise Tax on Medical Devices Should Not Be Repealed," Report from the Center on Budget and Policy Priorities, February 23, 2015, www.cbpp.org/research/health/excise-tax-on-medical-devices-should -not-be-repealed.

130 **individual donations going to:** Information on donations to politicians is from the OpenSecrets database of the Center for Responsive Politics.

130 **estimated to be in the range:** David J. Dykeman and Michael A. Cohen, "Stake Your Claim in the Medical Device Patent Gold Rush," *Medical Device and Diagnostic Industry,* May 16, 2014, www.mddionline.com/article/stake-your-claim-medical-device-patent -gold-rush.

130 **Advanced Medical Technology Association:** To learn more, see www.medicaldevices.org/.

131 **"hamper the growth of the growth":** For the January 2015 report from the market research firm MarketsandMarkets, see www.marketsandmarkets.com/Market-Reports /automated-external-defibrillator-market-549.html.

131 **Zimmer Biomet:** For the history of Zimmer, see www.zimmer.com/corporate/about -zimmer/our-history.html.

131 **Albert Starr coinvented the first:** www.sts.org/news/dr-albert-starr-historical -commentary.

132 **defined three different classes of devices:** www.fda.gov/MedicalDevices/Device RegulationandGuidance/GuidanceDocuments/ucm094526.htm.

132 **"life-threatening or life sustaining":** FDA Medical Device Classifications Procedures, Code of Federal Regulations, Title 21, Volume 8, www.accessdata.fda.gov/scripts/cdrh /cfdocs/cfcfr/CFRSearch.cfm?fr=860.3.

132 **which devices should fall:** A huge number of opinions have been rendered on how to define "substantial equivalence"; for example, see www.lexology.com/library/detail .aspx?g=ffc86914-a44c-4729-9bcd-0c936e65d7a6.

133 **1,200 hours for class 3 devices:** Depending on the complexity of the new or modified medical device, the FDA review of a 510(k) submission takes between twenty and ninety or more days. The more complex the changes or comparison required to support the safety and effectiveness of the new or modified medical device, the longer the FDA review process. See www.qrasupport.com/FDA_MED_DEVICE.html and http://ita .doc.gov/td/health/medical%20device%20industry%20assessment%20final%20ii%203 -24-10.pdf.

133 **According to another report:** "Institute of Medicine Report. Medical Devices and the Public's Health: The FDA 510(k) Clearance Process at 35 Years," July 29, 2011, www

.policymed.com/2011/07/institute-of-medicine-report-medical-devices-and-the-publics
-health-the-fda-510k-clearance-process-a.html.

134 **its descendants continued to sell:** For example, see A. Nussbaum and D. Voreacos, "J&J
Mesh Approved by FDA Based on Recalled Device," Bloomberg, October 27, 2011, www
.bloomberg.com/news/articles/2011-10-20/j-j-vaginal-mesh-approved-by-fda-based-on
-older-recalled-device.

134 **A report by the Institute of Medicine:** "Institute of Medicine Report."

134 **FDA held a public meeting:** For a summary, see "Washington Wrap-Up: 510(k)'s
Critics and Supporters Discuss IOM Report at Public Meeting," *Mechanical Device and
Diagnostic Industry,* November 3, 2011, www.mddionline.com/article/510k%E2%
80%99s-critics-and-supporters-discuss-iom-report-public-meeting.

135 **"required, but never received":** Minutes of the FDA hearing are available at www.fda
.gov/downloads/MedicalDevices/NewsEvents/WorkshopsConferences/UCM275006.pdf.

135 **Dr. Diana Zuckerman:** Dr. Zuckerman's presentation on the 510(k) issue for the FDA
is filled with alarming statistics, such as "We found 113 high-risk recalls between 2005
and 2009. Those translated to almost exactly 113 million devices"; see www.fda.gov
/downloads/MedicalDevices/NewsEvents/WorkshopsConferences/UCM358915.pdf.

135 **surpassing the previous record of 13,699:** Figures are taken from the most recent U.S.
Patent and Trademark Office (USPTO) Patent Technology Monitoring Team report;
see www.uspto.gov/learning-and-resources/electronic-data-products/patent-technology
-monitoring-team-ptmt-patent.

135 **a gold rush:** Dykeman and Cohen, "Stake Your Claim in the Medical Device Patent
Gold Rush."

137 **had their own unique patents:** www.510kdecisions.com/product_codes/index.cfm?fusea
ction=companies&product_code=MEH.

137 **"The Rejuvenate wasn't even put in a dog":** C. Calvin Warriner, malpractice attorney,
West Palm Beach, Florida, personal interview/communication, 2015.

138 **a drug-resistant superbug:** "Deadly Superbug-Related Scopes Sold Without FDA
Approval," *Outpatient Surgery,* March 5, 2015, www.outpatientsurgery.net/outpatient
-surgery-news-and-trends/general-surgical-news-and-reports/deadly-superbug-related
-scopes-sold-without-fda-approval—03-05-15.

138 **"Can you imagine":** www.cnn.com/2015/03/04/us/superbug-endoscope-no-permission.

139 **there wasn't a great need:** Dr. Paul Manner, who presented grand rounds at the
University of Washington, said, "They last a very very long time. So the question is
where's the problem? Why are we still talking about this?" You can watch it at www
.youtube.com/embed/jNCnPQZyjp8. "Three decades later, 80 percent of people who had
first-generation implants were still walking on the originals." Dr. Scott Kelley of Duke
University, personal interview/communication.

139 **"They are largely interchangeable":** Dr. Rory Wright, personal interview/
communication.

140 **became comfortable installing:** Dr. Alexandra Page, orthopedic surgeon, personal
interview/communication, 2015. Before 2000 the royalties went directly to the doctor, but
as federal restrictions on such payments tightened, the money often was passed through
to the hospital, in the form of funding for research or pet projects.

140 **"it's nearly impossible":** Dr. Blair Rhode, orthopedic surgeon and president of RōG
Sports Medicine, personal interview/communication, 2013. Also see www.omtecexpo

.com/agenda/34-ot-art-forattendees/ot-cat-attcontent/302-blair-rhode-md-orthopaedic-surgeon-and-founder-of-rhode-orthopedic-group-2013.

141 **get permission each time:** "I used to be seen as added value—now it's all about dollars and cents and who keeps the money," said John Nieradka, who spent much of his career selling devices for orthopedic trauma surgery. Personal interview/communication, 2015.

142 **"We're already making":** Dr. Larry Teuber, physician, entrepreneur, and former surgical hospital owner, personal interview/communication, 2015.

142 **Edwards Lifesciences' McCarthy Annuloplasty Ring:** The *Chicago Tribune* did an in-depth investigation on her case: "Medical Devices: A Cautionary Tale of Two Heart Rings," May 22, 2011, http://articles.chicagotribune.com/2011-05-22/health/ct-met -medical-devices-patients-20110522_1_antonitsa-vlahoulis-medical-device-inventions.

143 **the original holder of its patent:** See www.google.com/patents/US20050192666 for the original patent.

143 **and he had relied on its judgment:** For an investigation of the incident and Dr. McCarthy's response, see Shelley Wood, "Questions Raised About Northwestern Use of Valve Device; Prominent Surgeon Denies Wrongdoing," Medscape, October 7, 2008, www.medscape.com/viewarticle/790268.

144 **than any other class 2 device:** For an analysis of the FDA data, see "Medical Devices: Rules on Annuloplasty Rings Raise Questions," *Chicago Tribune,* May 22, 2011, http:// articles.chicagotribune.com/2011-05-22/health/ct-met-medical-devices-20110521_1 _annuloplasty-rings-faulty-heart-valve-diana-zuckerman.

144 **make it available to more patients:** For McCarthy's explanation of the concept behind the ring in a lawsuit, see www.topsecretwriters.com/wp-content/uploads/2011/11 /mccarthy.pdf.

144 **Federal regulators did not hear:** Nalini Rajamannan, *The Myxo File: The Tale of Three Rings,* www.amazon.com/Myxo-File-Part-XXIV-Three-ebook/dp/B0178XRF22.

144 **and wrote to the agency himself:** Patients and doctors can report adverse events through this FDA database: www.accessdata.fda.gov/scripts/cdrh/cfdocs/cfmaude/detail .cfm?mdrfoi__id=1344261.

145 **who published a fascinating monograph:** Rajamannan, *The Myxo File.*

145 **"at least as safe and effective":** In the course of a 2014 congressional investigation, Stephen R. Mason, the FDA's acting assistant commissioner for legislation, told the committee that the agency did not "have the opportunity to evaluate that decision in advance to determine if it was appropriate. However, the Agency educates sponsors about how to make the correct decision in this regard"; see www.grassley.senate.gov/sites /default/files/news/upload/CEG%20to%20Northwestern%20%28Myxo-Ring %29%2C%204-28-14.pdf.

145 **the wholesale price was about $4,000:** I was surprised to find an Edwards wholesale price list online; see the Edwards Price List for 2010, http://market360online.com /sqlimages/1246/125029.pdf.

145 **pay royalties on a percentage:** Michael Gibney, "Baxter," FierceBiotech.com, www.fiercemedicaldevices.com/special-reports/medtronic-med-tech-patent-battles.

145 **"On a weekly basis":** Dr. Elliott's August 19, 2011, letter to the FDA can be found at www.citizen.org/documents/1963-Elliott_statement_in_support_of_HRG_petition.pdf.

146 **thousands of injuries:** A law firm describes the state of play at www.rxinjuryhelp.com /transvaginal-mesh/recall/.

146 **propose moving the mesh:** Nussbaum and Voreacos, "J&J Mesh Approved by FDA Based on Recalled Device."

146 **The switch was enacted in 2016:** www.meshmedicaldevicenewsdesk.com/just-in-fda -moves-to-reclassify-pop-vaginal-mesh-as-high-risk/.

146 **avoid many billions:** For a report on the settlements, see www.drugwatch.com/2014 /12/17/judge-tells-bard-to-settle-mesh-lawsuits/.

147 **"There was a promise":** Dr. Daniel Elliott, personal interview/communication, 2015.

147 **they were identical:** M. R. de Cógáin and D. Elliott, "The Impact of an Antibiotic Coating on the Artificial Urinary Sphincter Infection Rate," *Journal of Urology* 190, no. 1 (2013): 113–17, www.ncbi.nlm.nih.gov/pubmed/23313209.

CHAPTER 6: THE AGE OF TESTING AND ANCILLARY SERVICES

148 **between $17 and $618:** From UnitedHealthcare's cost estimator, accessed by Jerri Solomon, February 2013.

150 **"the new income from them":** Leigh Page, "Six Ancillary Services Worth Considering," Medscape, October 15, 2012, www.medscape.com/viewarticle/772417.

150 **suddenly spiked impressively:** The Harvey L. Neiman Health Policy Institute's interactive graphics are fabulous; check out this one showing the trends: www.neimanhpi.org/data _series/medicare-part-b-magnetic-resonance-imaging-procedures-per-1000-beneficiaries /#/graph/2004/2014/true/Arizona%7CGeorgia%7CIndiana%7CMassachusetts.

151 **well under $1,000:** Jeanne Pinder of ClearHealthCosts did an interesting post on *The Healthcare Blog* about the varying price of an MRI. Medicare in San Francisco paid $255, which is about what it pays all over the country; see http://thehealthcareblog.com /blog/2014/08/06/how-much-does-an-mri-cost-in-california-255-973-25-2925/.

152 **Dr. Awaad became the top-paid doctor:** The link to the original *Detroit Free Press* story is no longer functional, but much of the story can be read in excerpt on this legal blog: http://medicalmalpracticeblog.nashandassociates.com/tag/dr-yasser-awaad/.

153 **more likely than primary care doctors:** M. Bassett, "Nurse Practitioners, PAs Order More Imaging Exams Than Primary-Care Docs," FierceHealthcare.com, www.fierce healthit.com/story/nurse-practitioners-pas-order-more-imaging-exams-primary-care -docs/2014-11-27.

153 **Björn Kemper:** Björn Kemper, personal interview/communication, 2015.

153 **Jacqui Bush:** Jacqui Bush, personal interview/communication, 2015.

154 **"The offices refused to allow":** Melanie Dukas, personal interview/communication, 2015.

155 **intense competition for these specimens:** Dr. William Watkin, pathologist, personal interview/communication, 2015.

155 **"These are tiny specimens":** Dr. Jeffrey Crespin, personal interview/communication, 2015.

155 **"new business models":** In interviews in 2015–2016, Dr. Henneberry graciously took me through the changes in her field, pathology.

156 **"exception" for certain types of care:** "Overview of the Stark Law Exceptions," Atlantic Information Systems, 2015, https://aishealth.com/sites/all/files/comp_lsta_ch400.pdf.

156 **she sold it for $80 million *cash* to Caris Diagnostics:** From a blog for pathologists: http://pathologyblawg.com/pathology-news/dermatopathologists-sued-miraca-life- sciences-breach-contract/.

157 **she received a bill for $835:** Kathleen Williams, personal interview/communication, 2015.

158 **"We found ourselves struggling":** History of the Bensonhurst Volunteer Ambulance

Service, prepared for a New York City Web site, www.nycservice.org/organizations/index
.php?org_id=1592.

159 **bought by private equity firms:** See Bob Sullivan's great post on credit.com, October 10,
2013, http://blog.credit.com/2013/10/consumer-rage-ambulance-ride-69734/. While I was
finishing this book, the *New York Times* did a nice deep dive on Rural Metro: Danielle
Ivory, Ben Protess, and Kitty Bennett, "When You Call 911 and Wall Street Answers,"
June 26, 2016, www.nytimes.com/2016/06/26/business/dealbook/when-you-dial-911
-and-wall-street-answers.html.

159 **Los Angeles's receipts:** Here are three budget reports to illustrate how revenues from
ambulance services have changed: http://cao.lacity.org/budget2004-05/Proposed_04-05
_Revenue_Outlook.pdf, p. 102; http://cao.lacity.org/budget-09-10/2009-10RevenueBook
.pdf; and http://cao.lacity.org/budget15-16/2015-16Revenue_Outlook.pdf, p. 91.

159 **"The Fire Department's attitude":** Richard Dickinson, personal interview/
communication, 2015.

159 **budget analyst for the city:** For a Dickinson bio, see page 6 of this newsletter: www
.waterandpower.org/sitebuildercontent/sitebuilderfiles/april-06.cwk.pdf.

160 **the City of New York:** A. Hotz, "City Readies Sharp Increase in Ambulance Fees," *New
York World,* January 12, 2012, www.thenewyorkworld.com/2012/01/12/city-readies
-sharp-increase-in-ambulance-fees/.

161 **series of moratoriums and exceptions:** These are outlined in great detail on the Web site
of the American Physical Therapy Association: www.apta.org/FederalIssues/TherapyCap
/History/.

161 **moratorium on a cap:** Ibid. "From December 8, 2003, through December 31, 2005,
there is no dollar limit on claims received for physical therapy, occupational therapy, and
speech-language pathology services," the Centers for Medicare and Medicaid Services
announced.

162 **supervise no more than three:** Ibid.

162 **expected to grow 7 percent:** Market report from Harris Williams & Co., an investment
bank; see www.harriswilliams.com/sites/default/files/industry_reports/physical_therapy
_market_overview.pdf.

162 **rose 5 percent in 2012:** A study by the Congressional Budget Office found that the
volume of services delivered by physical therapy centers that were not owned by
physicians rose by 41 percent; see www.gao.gov/products/GAO-14-270.

162 **"At this point the procedure":** Dr. Rebecca Bechhold, a Cincinnati oncologist, personal
interview/communication, 2015.

163 **encouraged to have a screening colonoscopy:** Pam Farris, personal interview/
communication, 2015.

163 **"This procedure kills people":** Dr. James Goodwin, personal interview/communication,
2015.

164 **can count on getting $2,000 to $4,000:** Fred Schulte, "Medicare Advantage Money
Grab: Home Is Where the Money Is for Medicare Advantage Plans," Center for Public
Integrity, June 10, 2014, www.publicintegrity.org/2014/06/10/14880/home-where-money
-medicare-advantage-plans.

165 **according to a venture capital firm:** Stacy Coggeshall, MSN/MBA, director of risk
adjustment operations at Tufts Health Plan Medicare Preferred, said that "by using the
concise and accurate information from the Predilytics model, we're optimizing our

prospective targeting, and improving our in-home assessment resource utilization"; see www.hcp.com/predilytics-launches-two-healthcare-analytics-solutions.

165 **8 percent *higher* per patient:** From a study by the Commonwealth Fund: www .commonwealthfund.org/publications/press-releases/2008/sep/extra-payments-to -medicare-advantage-plans-to-total-$8-5-billion.

165 **extracting billions in dubious billing:** Schulte, "Medicare Advantage Money Grab."

165 **Poor Americans are less likely:** Office of Disease Prevention and Health Promotion, data from the Healthy People 2020 campaign, www.healthypeople.gov/2020/leading -health-indicators/2020-lhi-topics/Clinical-Preventive-Services/data.

CHAPTER 7: THE AGE OF CONTRACTORS: BILLING, CODING, COLLECTIONS, AND NEW MEDICAL BUSINESSES

171 **charge patients who are uninsured:** Gerard Anderson, "Hospitals Charge Uninsured and 'Self-Pay' Patients More Than Double What Insured Patients Pay," news release, Johns Hopkins, Bloomberg School of Public Health, May 8, 2007, www.jhsph.edu /news/news-releases/2007/anderson-hospital-charges.html.

172 **University of Virginia and its lawyers:** Ms. Wickizer, it turns out, is not the only patient who has faced the University of Virginia Health System and its debt-collecting lawyers in court. In June 2014 the Rector and Visitors of the University of Virginia filed 506 claims against debtors in Albemarle General District Court—more than 55 percent of the total civil claims sought by any plaintiff that month. Sentara Martha Jefferson, the other hospital in town, filed none (and it gives uninsured people a 40 percent discount). In the process of its work, Ms. Wickizer's dream team discovered that "the aggressive UVA medical establishment" was suing 30,392 patients in mid-2015.

172 **"NO CODES=NO PAY":** Letter provided by Nora Johnson, Medical Expense Review and Recovery, Caldwell, West Virginia, who was on Ms. Wickizer's "dream team."

173 **A detailed itemized bill:** Provided to me by Michael Shopenn, an American who paid privately to have his hip replaced at Sint Rembert's Hospital in Belgium.

173 **periodically revised by an international commission:** It was called the Mixed Commission, a group composed of representatives from the International Statistical Institute and the Health Organization of the League of Nations.

174 **ICD-9-CM:** The "9" stands for the ninth version of the ICD. "CM" is added for a U.S. adaptation. The United States belatedly adopted the tenth version after more than a decade of delay in 2015.

174 **"In order to code for the more lucrative code":** Isela Coutin, a professional coder who helped out in the Wickizer case, personal interview/communication, 2015. When she started working in healthcare more than twenty-five years ago, she didn't speak the language—it didn't exist. "I worked for a third-party administrator and the important thing was to understand the disease state. But after a few years everything had to be stated in numbers, in codes, so you had to translate everything in the chart."

175 **found massive evidence of modifier 59 abuse:** Daniel R. Levinson, "Use of Modifier 59 to Bypass Medicare's National Correct Coding Initiative Edits," Department of Health and Human Services, Office of the Inspector General, November 2005, https://oig.hhs .gov/oei/reports/oei-03-02-00771.pdf.

176 **codes to modify modifier 59:** Here are two explanations of modifier 59's modifying codes from coding companies: Moda Health, www.modahealth.com/pdfs/reimburse

/RPM027.pdf; The Business of Spine, http://files.ctctcdn.com/42356a47201/ea6c8a14
-ee15-4766-942e-af756b4ce77c.pdf.

176 **Thomas Goetz of San Francisco:** Thomas Goetz, personal interview/communication,
2015.

177 **Dr. Richard Hayes:** Dr. Richard Hayes, personal interviews/communication, 2014–2016.
Dr. Hayes worked in a hospital urgent care clinic for over a year but didn't like the style of
practice. He is now in a large group practice affiliated with Dartmouth-Hitchcock
Medical Center in New Hampshire.

179 **"ARE YOU KIDDING ME?":** Elisabeth Rosenthal, "Rapid Price Increases for Some
Generic Drugs Catch Users by Surprise," *New York Times,* July 8, 2014, www.nytimes
.com/2014/07/09/health/some-generic-drug-prices-are-soaring.html.

180 **Steven Davidson:** Much of the information in this section is based on my personal
interviews/communication with Mr. Davidson in 2015.

CHAPTER 8: THE AGE OF RESEARCH AND GOOD WORKS FOR PROFIT: THE PERVERSION OF A NOBLE ENTERPRISE

182 **The Web site:** The Web site for the lab of Dr. Denise Faustman is www.faustmanlab.org.

182 **Dr. Denise Faustman:** Dr. Denise Faustman, personal interviews/communication,
2014–2016.

183 **largest private foundation funder:** http://healthaffairs.org/blog/2015/06/29/ahrq-and
-the-essential-bothand-of-federal-investments-in-medical-discoveries/.

184 **"a gift to humanity":** They "licensed their patent for the process of isolating insulin for
one dollar each as a gift to humanity rather than an opportunity for commercial profit."
See J. Luo, J. Avorn, and A. S. Kesselheim, "Trends in Medicaid Reimbursements for
Insulin," *JAMA Internal Medicine* 175, no. 10 (2015), doi:10.1001/jamainternmed
.2015.4338.

185 **funded the Columbia University scientist:** www.nationalmssociety.org/NationalMS
Society/media/MSNationalFiles/Brochures/Brochure-History-of-Multiple-Sclerosis.pdf.

185 **bemoaning the slow pace:** http://juvenilediabetesresearchfoundationintl.orghub.net
/pages/history.html.

186 **allow people with type 1 diabetes:** Researchers and even patients, though grateful for
the progress, resent what they regard as sometimes deceptive branding. "Medtronic went
ahead and used an unqualified 'Artificial Pancreas' label for its new system knowing
this was somewhat deceiving language in the interest of creating marketing hype. Grrr,"
wrote one patient in an article titled "Keeping It Real on Medtronic's 530G." See
Healthline, October 8, 2013, www.healthline.com/diabetesmine/keeping-it-real-on
-medtronics-530g.

186 **insulin rose between 127 and 325 percent:** The Alliance of Community Health Plans,
www.achp.org/wp-content/uploads/Diabetes_FINAL_Revised-12.7.15.pdf.

186 **has risen to nearly $1,100:** "Sticker Shock at the Pharmacy," *Friday Focus* newsletter,
Baylor Scott & White Health, September 11, 2015, https://legacy.swhp.org/sites/default
/files/Sticker%20Shock%20at%20the%20Pharmacy.pdf.

186 **"It looks like a beeper":** Elisabeth Rosenthal, "Even Small Medical Advances Can Mean
Big Jumps in Bills," *New York Times,* April 6, 2014, www.nytimes.com/2014/04/06
/health/even-small-medical-advances-can-mean-big-jumps-in-bills.html.

187 **"How could the board of Vertex":** Robert F. Higgins and Brent Kazan, "Vertex

Pharmaceuticals and the Cystic Fibrosis Foundation: Venture Philanthropy Funding for Biotech," *Harvard Business Review,* October 15, 2007, https://hbr.org/product/vertex -pharmaceuticals-and-the-cystic-fibrosis-foundation-venture-philanthropy-funding-for -biotech/808005-PDF-ENG.

187 **Kalydeco attacked a biochemical defect:** For information on ivacaftor, the chemical name for Kalydeco, see the DrugBank information service, www.drugbank.ca/drugs /DB08820.

187 **immediately branded "unconscionable":** Criticism of the price came from all quarters. The doctors' letter is available at http://media.jsonline.com/documents/CFletteruse.pdf. Also see on the Healthcare Renewal blog: "Is the Cystic Fibrosis Foundation a Charity or a Venture Capital Firm?," *Health Care Renewal* (blog), http://hcrenewal.blogspot .com/2013/06/is-cystic-fibrosis-foundation-charity.html; L. Hinkes-Jones, "Stop Subsidizing Big Pharma," *New York Times,* January 6, 2015, www.nytimes .com/2015/01/06/opinion/stop-subsidizing-big-pharma.html.

187 **no "price restrictions for these new medicines":** www.forbes.com/sites/johnlamattina /2013/05/20/pharmas-rd-deals-with-foundations-may-negatively-impact-image/.

187 **he had "expressed concern":** www.nytimes.com/2015/01/06/opinion/stop-subsidizing -big-pharma.html.

188 **In 2015 Vertex sought approval:** B. Fidler, "FDA Panel Backs Vertex's Two-Drug Combo for Cystic Fibrosis," Xconomy, May 12, 2015, www.xconomy.com/boston /2015/05/12/fda-panel-backs-vertexs-two-drug-combo-for-cystic-fibrosis/.

188 **not really that impressive:** www.fda.gov/downloads/AdvisoryCommittees/Committees MeetingMaterials/Drugs/Pulmonary-AllergyDrugsAdvisoryCommittee/UCM446193 .pdf. Here's what they said: "Overall, the assessment of efficacy in the phase 3 clinical trials demonstrated that LUM/IVA regardless of dose provided consistent statistically significant benefit over placebo in terms of ppFEV1. However, the clinical meaningfulness of the magnitude of the improvement remains to be determined by the clinical review team. Specifically for the proposed dose of LUM 400mg/IVA 250mg q12h, the average benefit was 2.6% over placebo in study 809-103 and 3.0% in study 809-104. These effect sizes are similar to that of ivacaftor alone."

188 **"While on paper, Orkambi:** A. Pollack, "Cystic Fibrosis Drug Wins Approval of F.D.A. Advisory Panel," *New York Times,* May 14, 2015, www.nytimes.com/2015/05/13/business /cystic-fibrosis-drug-wins-approval-of-fda-advisory-panel.html.

188 **The *Boston Globe* noted:** D. Rudick and R. Weisman, "FDA Clears Vertex's New Treatment for Cystic Fibrosis," *Boston Globe,* July 2, 2015, www.bostonglobe.com /business/2015/07/02/fda-approves-vertex-cystic-fibrosis-medicine/jzn9eCDenCq4rEI671 mDOM/story.html.

188 **Jeffrey Brewer:** He was replaced in 2014 by Derek Rapp, a former executive at Monsanto; see www.healthline.com/diabetesmine/newsflash-ada-and-jdrf-change-leaders#6.

189 **"rebranding" campaign "to more accurately":** http://jdrf.org/press-releases/jdrf -adopts-new-brand-to-better-reflect-its-mission-for-type-1-diabetes/.

189 **It had given Medtronic:** "Medtronic Partners with JDRF and Helmsley Trust to Accelerate Diabetes Research," *San Fernando Valley Business Journal,* June 1, 2012, http:// sfvbj.com/news/2012/jun/01/medtronic-partners-jdrf-and-helmsley-trust-acceler/. See also http://jdrf.org/wp-content/uploads/2013/11/MTI1310_Artificial-Pancreas_2013700119.pdf.

189 **partnered with Tandem Diabetes Care:** http://jdrf.org/wp-content/uploads/2013/11 /MTI1310_Artificial-Pancreas_2013700119.pdf.

189 **invested $4.3 million in BD:** Ibid.
189 **with PureTech Ventures:** B. Fidler, "PureTech Ventures, JDRF Team Up to Form Type 1 Diabetes Startup Creator," Xconomy, October 15, 2013, www.xconomy.com /boston/2013/10/15/puretech-ventures-jdrf-team-form-type-1-diabetes-startup-creator/. To ensure that the profit motive wouldn't tarnish its activities, the joint venture included a "mission committee" to guarantee that investments were ethical and "consistent with the foundation's goals."
189 **doesn't need a few million:** Dr. Aaron Kowalski, who was then JDRF's vice president of artificial pancreas, defended the choice, noting that when products are successful, JDRF recoups its investment with a bit of interest, and plows the money "right back into the next generation of products that we think will be meaningful to you," he told a diabetes Web site, Glu; see https://myglu.org/articles/a-pathway-to-an-artificial-pancreas-an-interview -with-jdrf-s-aaron-kowalski.
189 **By 2013 JDRF research grants:** www.healthline.com/diabetesmine/newsflash-ada-and -jdrf-change-leaders#6.
189 **"If the March of Dimes":** Dr. Michael Brownlee, personal interview/communication, 2014.
190 **Stephen G. Buck:** Stephen G. Buck, personal interview/communication, 2015–2016.
191 **was totally free:** "EHR Software Comparison: Brief Overview of the Top Ten EHRs," *Capterra Medical Software Blog,* October 5, 2015, http://blog.capterra.com/ehr-software -comparison-brief-overview-of-the-top-10-ehrs/. See the section on Practice Fusion in this overview of office electronic medical records offerings.
192 **put the latter's executives in charge:** www.pm360online.com/elite-entrepreneur-mark -heinold-of-pdr-llc/.
192 **"providing the right messages":** "PDR Network Merges with LDM Group," Medical Media and Marketing, November 3, 2014, www.mmm-online.com/digital/pdr-network -merges-with-ldm-group/article/380994/.
192 **distributes co-pay cards:** Announcement from the Illinois Venture Capital Association, December 7, 2015, www.ropesgray.com/newsroom/news/2015/December/Genstar -Capitals-PSKW-Adds-On-PDR-Network.aspx.
192 **"synonymous with credible, comprehensive":** For a press release about the merger, see www.marketwired.com/press-release/pdr-moves-online-and-interactive-with-hcnn -merger-1206803.htm.
193 **Charles Kroll, a forensic accountant:** Much of the material in this section is from my interviews and exchanges with Mr. Kroll, a forensic accountant now based in Wisconsin, who made figuring out the finances of the ABIM his after-hours mission, 2014–2016.
193 **Dr. Westby Fisher:** http://drwes.blogspot.com/2014/12/the-abim-foundation-choosing -wisely-and.html.
193 **"Lifelong learning and education":** Dr. Christopher Dibble, personal interview/ communication, 2015.
194 **ten thousand physicians:** http://medicaleconomics.modernmedicine.com/medical -economics/content/tags/abim/moc-online-petition-swells-more-10000 -signatures?page=full.
194 **left the organization tens of millions:** For one of Mr. Kroll's presentations, see www.pamedsoc.org/PAMED_Downloads/MOCpanelKroll.pdf.
194 **raising fees to break even:** A good summary of Mr. Kroll's findings can be found in his June 13, 2016, presentation at a forum of the Pennsylvania Medical Society; see www .pamedsoc.org/PAMED_Downloads/MOCpanelKroll.pdf.

194 **the $2.3 million condominium was sold:** For a July 10, 2016, blog post from Dr. Westby Fisher on the ABA condominium sale, see http://drwes.blogspot.com/2016/07/too-little-too-late-abim-foundation.html.

195 **The American Medical Association was founded:** For a brief history of the AMA, see www.ama-assn.org/ama/pub/about-ama/our-history/the-founding-of-ama.page?.

195 **"the strongest trade union":** Milton Friedman, *Capitalism and Freedom,* 40th anniversary ed. (Chicago: University of Chicago Press, 2002), 150.

195 **increasing taxes on tobacco:** George E. Curry, "AMA's Proposed Tobacco-Ad Ban Lights Fire," *Chicago Tribune,* December 15, 1985, http://articles.chicagotribune.com/1985-12-15/news/8503260866_1_tobacco-advertising-scott-stapf-tobacco-products.

196 **"As a professional association":** "AMA Urged to Limit Corporate Entanglements; Physicians Group Should Restrain Its Pursuit of Profit, Report Says," *Baltimore Sun,* November 23, 1998, http://articles.baltimoresun.com/1998-11-23/news/1998327118_1_ama-leaders-ama-announced-corporate-relationships.

196 **Dr. James Madara:** I interviewed Dr. Madara at the AMA headquarters in 2015. A former head of the University of Chicago hospitals, he was thoughtful and gracious in answering my questions and filled with ideas about how the AMA could contribute to public health.

196 **AMA owns the copyright:** For AMA policy on CPT code licensing, see www.ama-assn.org/ama/pub/physician-resources/solutions-managing-your-practice/coding-billing-insurance/cpt/cpt-products-services/licensing.page. For a taste of how angry this monopoly makes some providers, see "The Evils of CPT," an essay on the Web site of EP Studios, a billing company: www.epstudiossoftware.com/the-evils-of-cpt/.

197 **"offers today's medical practices":** A description of the deal can be found at www.transworldsystems.com/ama.html.

197 **"commitment to public health":** For a description of the Corporate Roundtable, see www.ama-assn.org/ama/pub/about-ama/ama-foundation/corporate-roundtable.page?.

197 **contributes millions to campaigns:** www.ampaconline.org/ampac-2012-election-wrap-up/.

197 **calculate "usual, customary and reasonable":** For an AMA video about how it is fighting for doctors' reimbursement, see www.youtube.com/watch?v=8VXig5TvxK0&feature=youtu.be.

197 **Walgreens, which has refused:** "As the U.S. retail pharmacy leader and health care partner in offering smoking cessation programs, products and initiatives . . . our goal is to help get the U.S. smoking rate, which has leveled off at around 18% of the adult population for a decade, moving lower again," its spokesman told *Forbes* magazine. From Barbara Thau, "Walgreens and Walmart Won't Stop Selling Smokes but Will the Decision Backfire?," *Forbes,* September 9, 2014, http://www.forbes.com/sites/barbarathau/2014/09/09/walmart-and-walgreens-wont-stop-selling-smokes-but-will-the-decision-backfire/#4f90573a72f5.

198 **speaking out against pharmaceutical advertising:** "AMA Calls for Ban on Direct to Consumer Advertising of Prescription Drugs and Medical Devices," press release, November 17, 2015, www.ama-assn.org/ama/pub/news/news/2015/2015-11-17-ban-consumer-prescription-drug-advertising.page.

198 **spending nearly half a billion:** For more information, see the OpenSecrets database on lobbying by sector for 2015 at www.opensecrets.org/lobby/top.php?indexType=c&showYear=2015.

198 **raised more than $3 million** : www.aaos.org/news/aaosnow/oct10/advocacy6.asp.

198 **changed its tax status:** "RADPAC Uses Radiology's Money to Build Political Clout," DiagnosticImaging, November 2002, www.diagnosticimaging.com/dimag/legacy/db _area/archives/2002/0211.politicalact.di.shtml.

198 **"is toward the betterment":** "What Is a 501(c)(6)?," http://askville.amazon.com/difference -501c/AnswerViewer.do?requestId=2400614.

199 **"The societies recognized that the hospitals":** Alexandra Page, personal interview/ communication, 2015.

199 **"persons trained in the administration":** Current label warning from RxList, www .rxlist.com/diprivan-drug/warnings-precautions.htm.

199 **gastroenterologists have argued:** "Position Statement: Nonanesthesiologist Administration of Propofol for GI Endoscopy," *Gastrointestinal Endoscopy* 70, no. 6 (2009): 1053–59, www.asge.org/uploadedFiles/Publications_and_Products/Practice _Guidelines/NAAP%20Propofol%20Position%20Statement%20Dec%20GIE%20 FINAL.pdf.

199 **cease and desist order:** Here are two articles about the case, which went all the way to the U.S. Supreme Court; other medical groups watched closely to see if it qualified as a restraint of trade: *Raleigh News Observer,* www.newsobserver.com/news/local /article10071881.html; "Justices: Dentists Can Decide Who Whitens Your Teeth," *USA Today,* February 25, 2015, http://www.usatoday.com/story/news/nation/2015/02/25 /supreme-court-teeth-whitening-dentists/20108545/.

Dr. William Sage, a doctor and a lawyer at the University of Texas, offered this analysis: "Dentistry in North Carolina follows a regulatory pattern typical of established, politically powerful professions. A board composed primarily of members of the profession sets standards for admission to practice, monitors and disciplines the individuals it licenses, and resists efforts by others to deliver services. However, allowing private economic actors to wield the coercive power of the state can create mischief: insularity, poor process, turf protectiveness, and harm to both competition and innovation." William Sage and David Hyman, *Health Affairs Blog,* October 30, 2014, http://healthaffairs.org/ blog/2014/10/30/north-carolina-dental-board-v-ftc-a-bright-line-on-whiter-teeth/.

199 **What was good for patients:** Here's a pretty shocking example: in 2013, in order to make sure that their Medicare payments were not reduced, doctors groups convinced Congress to make up the deficit by cutting reimbursement for diabetics' lifesaving test strips by 72 percent. See D. Scott, "This Is the End for Washington's Most Frenzied Lobbying Extravaganza," *National Journal,* April 6, 2015, www.nationaljournal.com/health-care /this-is-the-end-for-washington-s-most-frenzied-lobbying-extravaganza-20150406.

199 **Daniel Burke proposed a bill:** Daniel Burke's bill, which was defeated, was House Bill 3812. Read this report of the legislative session to see what kinds of causes medical societies care about: www.isms.org/uploadedFiles/Main_Site/Content/Advocacy /Legislative_Action_Hub/2012sessionreport.pdf.

200 **Dr. Scott Norton:** Dr. Scott Norton, personal interview/communication, 2014.

201 **grew 700 percent:** Robert S. Stern, "Cost Effectiveness of Mohs Micrographic Surgery," *Journal of Investigative Dermatology* 133, no. 5 (May 2013): 1129–31, www.jidonline.org /article/S0022-202X(15)36247-3/fulltext.

201 **"the decision to utilize MMS":** Robert S. Stern, "Cost Effectiveness of Mohs Micrographic Surgery," *Journal of Investigative Dermatology,* May 2013, www .jidonline.org/article/S0022-202X(15)36247-3/fulltext.

201 **2 percent of all Medicare recipients:** www.nature.com/jid/journal/v133/n5/full/jid2012473a.html.

201 **"The questions and the methodology":** Dr. Scott Norton, personal interview/communication, 2015.

202 **Doctors who identify themselves:** Pay of Mohs surgeons: http://www.hospitaljobsonline.com/career-center/healthcare-careers/the-highest-paid-md-specialties.html. Hours worked by dermatologists: http://www.medscape.com/features/slideshow/compensation/2012/dermatology.

202 **both John Boehner and Nancy Pelosi:** The SkinPAC Web site lists donations for 2014 to Nancy Pelosi for Congress and Friends of John Boehner. See http://us-campaign-committees.insidegov.com/l/29623/American-Academy-of-Dermatology-Association-Political-Action-Committee-Skinpac.

203 **arthroscopy to shave cartilage:** The jury is still out on exactly who benefits in this patient group, but the procedure was overused; see P. Belluck, "Common Knee Surgery Does Very Little for Some, Study Suggests," *New York Times,* December 25, 2013, www.nytimes.com/2013/12/26/health/common-knee-surgery-does-very-little-for-some-study-suggests.html.

203 **has been critical of profiteering:** Gerald Chodak, "'Samadi Challenge' Misaligns Women's Role in Prostate Cancer," Medscape, November 4, 2014, www.medscape.com/viewarticle/834115.

203 **"normal" or "abnormal" level of testosterone:** Sanjai Sinha, "Testosterone Decline with Age: What Is Normal?," MedPageToday, www.medpagetoday.com/resource-center/hypogonadism/testosterone-decline-with-aging/a/35000.

204 **FDA review of the risk:** For a good summary of the state of understanding and research, see Charlie Schmidt, "Are Testosterone Supplements Linked to Cardiovascular Problems?," *Prostate Knowledge,* Harvard Medical School and Harvard Health Publications, www.harvardprostateknowledge.org/testosterone-supplements-linked-cardiovascular-problems.

CHAPTER 9: THE AGE OF CONGLOMERATES

206 **NewYork-Presbyterian healthcare network:** www.nyp.org/about-us.

207 **An analysis of 306 geographic health markets:** David M. Cutler and Fiona Scott Morton, "Hospitals, Market Share and Consolidation," *JAMA* 310, no. 18 (November 13, 2013): 1966, http://scholar.harvard.edu/files/cutler/files/jsc130008_hospitals_market_share_and_consolidation.pdf.

207 **One dominant healthcare system:** Professor Jaime King, Hastings College of the Law, congressional testimony, September 2015, http://docs.house.gov/meetings/JU/JU05/20150929/103998/HHRG-114-JU05-Wstate-KingJ-20150929.pdf: "A wide body of literature indicates that increased hospital concentration leads to increased hospital prices and insurance premiums. In 2012, health economists Martin Gaynor and Robert Town conducted a systemic review of the literature that found mergers in concentrated markets resulted in price increases over 20 percent. Furthermore, recent analyses suggest that hospital and physician payment rate increases are major contributors to rising premiums in large employer-sponsored plans."

207 **hospital mergers were associated:** Tim Xu, Albert Wu, and Martin Makary, "The Potential Hazards of Hospital Consolidation," *JAMA* 314, no.13 (2015): 1337–38, doi:10.1001/jama.2015.7492.

208 **Wild West foundational myth:** All information about the historical development of
      Sutter pre-2000 is from www.sutterhealth.org/about/history.
209 **more than seventy California hospitals:** Lisa Girion and Mark Medina, "Hospitals Feel
      Ill Effects of Recession," *Los Angeles Times,* January 14, 2009, http://articles.latimes
      .com/2009/jan/14/business/fi-hospitals14.
209 **Sutter Health has assembled:** "Sutter Health Facts at a Glance," www.sutterhealth.org
      /about/news/news_facts.html.
209 **there is now no other choice:** Its longtime CEO, Patrick Fry, earned total compensation
      of $6.4 million in 2012; see www.crainsdetroit.com/article/20140811/NEWS/140819983
      /another-year-of-pay-hikes-for-nonprofit-hospital-ceos.
209 **"Sutter is the tallest Sequoia":** E. Rosenthal, "As Hospital Prices Soar, a Stitch Tops
      $500," *New York Times,* December 17, 2013, www.nytimes.com/2013/12/03/health
      /as-hospital-costs-soar-single-stitch-tops-500.html.
210 **offering to buy his practice:** Dr. Alexander Lakowsky, personal interview/
      communication, 2015–2016.
211 **"one of the largest publicly funded":** From Commonwealth Fund Web site:
      http://www.commonwealthfund.org/about-us/staff-contact-information/executive
      -managers/staff-contact-folder/blumenthal-david. Dr. David Blumenthal, a Harvard
      hospital executive, moved to Washington, DC, to serve as President Obama's national
      coordinator for health information technology and to lead creation of a nationwide health
      information system.
211 **spent $50 million to develop and install:** Dr. Warren Browner, CEO, California Pacific
      Medical Center, personal interview/communication, 2013.
212 **drive Sutter's few competitors:** Dr. Beth Kleiner, partner, Peninsula Diagnostic
      Imaging, personal interview/communication, 2015.
213 **an MRI scan has to be downloaded to a CD and walked over:** Bob Wachter, "Why
      Health-Care IT Systems Must Be Made to Talk to One Another," *Wall Street Journal,*
      March 27, 2105, http://blogs.wsj.com/experts/2015/03/27/why-health-care-it-systems
      -must-be-made-to-talk-to-one-another/. Here's a quote from the article: "There's a rueful
      joke told that circulates around Boston's Longwood Medical area, where several
      prestigious Harvard hospitals share a space of about 10 blocks. What is the fastest way to
      get a patient's record from Brigham & Women's Hospital to Beth Israel Deaconess, a few
      hundred yards away? The answer: a paper airplane."
        "We didn't share records across Brookline Avenue," said Paul Levy, former president
      of Beth Israel Deaconess, referring to the street that divides Deaconess (in the BIDMC
      Community Network) from Brigham and Women's (in Partners HealthCare). "They'd
      get an MRI and you'd have to fight to get results faxed."
213 **building a new $1 billion IT system:** www.businesswire.com/news/home
      /20140219005019/en/Denmark-World-Leader-Health-Tests-Systems-Companies
      #.VehPXrxViko.
214 **began the class with an apology:** Dr. Joanne Roberts, personal interview/
      communication, 2015.
214 **"They made sure we had good equipment":** Dr. Greg Duncan, personal interview/
      communication, 2014–2016.
215 **according to California's Valued Trust:** Letter of documentation provided by Dr. Greg
      Duncan.
217 **increased 300 percent:** From the California Office of Statewide Health Planning and

Development; documents provided by Dr. Greg Duncan: In 2008, Sutter Lakeside Hospital downsized from 69 beds to 25 beds in order to qualify for Critical Access designation. In 2007 (the last full year before converting to CAH designation) Sutter Lakeside reported 257 patient transfers. In 2009 (the first full year after converting to CAH designation) Sutter Lakeside reported 1,064 patient transfers.

217 **costing Medicare an extra $4.1 billion:** For a report on excess billing by critical access hospitals, see www.usnews.com/news/us/articles/2015/03/09/report-rural-hospitals-get-billions-in-extra-medicare-funds.

217 **Sutter Lakeside's charges to Medicare:** Dr. Greg Duncan, personal interview/communication, 2014–2015.

217 **James Skoufis represents:** Much of this section is based on interviews with and documents provided by Assemblyman Skoufis, 2015–2016.

217 **Cornwall Hospital . . . was founded:** For a history of Cornwall Hospital, see www.stlukescornwallhospital.org/about/Pages/History.aspx.

218 **opening of freestanding ERs:** Jessica Chang, "Ten Factors to Consider When Building a Freestanding ER," *Becker's Hospital Review,* March 19, 2014, www.beckershospitalreview.com/capacity-management/top-10-factors-to-consider-when-building-a-freestanding-emergency-department.html. Freestanding emergency rooms are inevitably opened in zip codes where people tend to have insurance; near highways (people with cars tend to be insured) rather than in inner cities (people who are victims of violent street crime are not). Also see http://kaiserhealthnews.org/news/stand-alone-emergency-rooms/.

220 **ninety-two hospitals, coast to coast:** www.munsonhealthcare.org/?id=4016&sid=36.

220 **sell Cadillac Hospital to Munson Healthcare:** That was not a big deal because many patients in the area got healthcare from Munson anyway; see www.mlive.com/business/west-michigan/index.ssf/2014/05/trinity_health_to_sell_cadilla.html.

220 **Katy Huckle, a local banker:** Details in this section based on interviews with and documents provided by Katy Huckle and Helen James Lehman, one of Mr. Pell's grandchildren, 2015–2016

220 **"in the best interest of the hospital":** Trinity said a local group that the Pell family had asked to administer the foundation was charging too much. The family was unconvinced. "Whatever fees drawn from [the hospital foundation] would benefit the area, they would stay in the area, so it was a win, win, win," one granddaughter, Helen James Lehman, wrote in the *Cadillac News.* "At least this way, if they charged $68,000, then the community is enriched by $68,000 a year—yahoo!" Cadillacnews.com, March 25, 2015. You can access the article at http://www.savethepelllegacy.org/2015/03/cadillac-philanthropists-funds-kept-by-trinity/.

221 **received a bill for $500:** She filed a complaint with the New Jersey Department of Banking and Insurance, and shortly thereafter, the hospital and insurer "adjusted" the charge she was expected to pay to $173. "It was like they thought they were doing me a favor but it wasn't a favor to me—if they'd been up front, I could have gotten the X-ray done at a radiologist's office for fifty dollars."

222 **can no longer give infusions:** Dr. Mark Gudesblatt, personal interview/communication, 2015.

CHAPTER 10: THE AGE OF HEALTHCARE AS PURE BUSINESS

223 **"As a consumer":** Uwe Reinhardt, personal interview/communication, 2016.

223 **Helen, a real estate professional:** Personal interview/communication. She would not let her full name be used for fear that she would be abandoned by her surgeons.

225 **Mark Skinner, fifty-six:** Much of material in this section was provided by Mark Skinner and Dr. Glenn Pierce, two thought leaders in the world of hemophilia treatment, in personal interview/communication, 2015.

226 **A community linked by one serious disease:** According to Dr. Pierce, "Although cryo did transmit HIV/HCV (and HBV), by pooling the plasma of 60–120,000   donors (American Red Cross), a single infectious donor would contaminate the entire pool, which would be given to [hundreds] of individuals with hemophilia. At the height of the AIDS epidemic, all plasma pools used by industry to make clotting factor were contaminated. If you were treated with cryo in the Midwest, or out of hotspots like NY, LA, SF, you were relatively safer since HIV had not penetrated these communities much during the early 80s. Remember too, plasma was collected in prisons, skid row, etc, which predisposed to individuals with these infections" (e-mail to author, July 1, 2016).

226 **by various middlemen:** According to Dr. Glenn Pierce, "During this time, most product was delivered by home care delivery companies, most of which have been purchased by Express Scripts–like pharmacy benefit managers. They are the biggest offenders of mark ups, often 50% or more on what the pharmas charge. They also contract with the HTCs [hemophilia treatment centers] to administer their 340B programs, so the HTC gets some money, and the PBM gets some money. It's complicated but there is big money involved in US" (e-mail to author, July 1, 2016). The 340B program provides discounts to hospitals that treat a high number of low-income patients, who are less likely to be insured.

228 **half or less of the $1 per unit price:** In those counties factor VIII is now selling for 25 cents a unit. "But here in the US they're still happy to sell it for $1," said Dr. Marion Koerper, a hemophilia expert at the University of California at San Francisco.

228 **hired dozens of full-time reps:** This information comes from interviews with my "deep throat" marketing consultant. And that doesn't count the mothers, siblings, and patients themselves who are paid to promote a particular brand—called variously community relations managers, peer-to-peer educators, or brand ambassadors.

My marketing consultant told me the marching orders for 2015 were simply: "How do I get this guy to switch? What do I have to give?" One company's flow chart, titled "Patient Experience Mapping: Consideration Phase," advises representatives how to approach each "high value" patient and how to address potential concerns, complete with visual aids and an invitation to participate in an Ambassador program for reluctant targets.

229 **rate increases of 40 percent:** R. Pear, "Why Do Health Costs Keep Rising? These People Know," *New York Times,* June 10, 2016, www.nytimes.com/2016/06/10/us/health -insurance-affordable-care-act.html?.

CHAPTER 11: THE AGE OF THE AFFORDABLE CARE ACT (ACA)

231 **the ACA promoted some programs:** For some great analysis and insight into the political maneuvering that castrated the final Affordable Care Act, see Steven Brill, *America's Bitter Pill: Money, Politics, Backroom Deals, and the Fight to Fix Our Broken Healthcare System* (New York: Random House, 2015), and Brendan W. Williams, *Compromised: The Affordable Care Act and Politics of Defeat* (CreateSpace Independent Publishing Platform, 2015).

232 **novel medical arrangement:** For an interim report card on the accountable care organization program, see Kerry Young, "Closely Watched Accountable-Care Program Saved $385 Million, Study Says," *Washington Health Policy Week in Review, CQ HealthBeat,* May, 11, 2015, www.commonwealthfund.org/publications/newsletters

/washington-health-policy-in-review/2015/may/may-11-2015/accountable-care-program-saved-385-million.

232 **"So much has happened"**: Brendan Williams, personal interview/communication, 2015.

233 **Steve Carlson's NovoLog insulin:** Steve Carlson, personal interview/communication, 2015.

233 **have difficulty affording them:** Dr. Huseyin Naci, personal interview/communication, 2016. Also see H. Naci et al., "Medication Affordability Gains Following Medicare Part D Are Eroding Among Elderly with Multiple Chronic Conditions," *Health Affairs* 33, no. 8 (2014): 1435–43, doi:10.1377/hlthaff.2013.1067.

233 **plans to close the donut hole:** For a helpful consumer article from *NJ Spotlight*, February 14, 2014, that nicely describes the effect of the Medicare donut hole over time on seniors, see www.njspotlight.com/stories/14/02/13/obamacare-slowly-but-surely-closes-donut-hole-gap/.

234 **many thousands of dollars:** Dr. Chien-Wen Tseng, Hawaii Medical Service Association chair of Healthcare Research and Quality at the University of Hawaii's medical school, looked at how Medicare beneficiaries are holding up under the cost of new medicines for rheumatoid arthritis, a not uncommon condition in patients over sixty-five. Dr. Tseng found that most patients would fall into the Medicare Part D donut hole by February or March when their cost-sharing would increase to 45 percent of drug costs—an amount that would force many to drop treatment or to make major sacrifices in retirement to continue. From a personal interview/communication, 2015; also see www.ncbi.nlm.nih.gov/pmc/articles/PMC4464809/.

234 **Health insurance cooperatives:** For a review of the cooperative concept, see Louise Norris, "Co-op Health Plans: Patients' Interests First," Healthinsurance.org, August 3, 2016, www.healthinsurance.org/obamacare/co-op-health-plans-put-patients-interests-first/.

235 **only seven of the original twenty-three:** Press release, House Committee on Energy and Commerce, July 16, 2016, https://energycommerce.house.gov/news-center/press-releases/another-one-bites-dust-co-ops-dwindle-7-illinois-collapse-losses-eclipse.

236 **mostly just avoided any interactions:** An informative piece from Vox details how high-deductible health plans influence patient behavior; see www.vox.com/2015/10/14/9528441/high-deductible-insurance-kolstad.

237 **"Now, they have my fifteen thousand dollars":** Paul Schwartz, personal interview/communication, 2016.

237 **"Seizing Opportunities Provided by the ACA":** www.physiciansweekly.com/emergency-services-affordable-care-act/, January 4, 2014. For example: "The minimum payment required from health insurers is intended to be a floor to protect patients from excessive balance billing that results from low ball, out-of-network reimbursement. Once minimum payment amounts are made, out-of-network emergency providers can balance bill patients with the difference between its billed charges and the amount paid by the insurance."

237 **"Providers should not leave money on the table":** Ibid.

237 **good behavior and coordinated medical care:** Leigh Page, "8 Ways the ACA Is Affecting Doctors' Incomes," Medscape, August 15, 2013, www.medscape.com/viewarticle/809357.

237 **more consumer complaints:** See the report from the Kaiser Family Foundation at

http://kff.org/report-section/coverage-of-colonoscopies-under-the-affordable-care-acts
-prevention-benefit-report/. While my insurer's list contains hundreds of gastroenterologists
in its plan, when I called to schedule an appointment I found that many will no longer
perform screening colonoscopies under my insurance in-network coverage, but only more
elaborate (and lucrative)—procedures.

238 **18 percent in 2013:** www.gallup.com/poll/182348/uninsured-rate-dips-first-quarter.aspx.

238 *New York Times/*CBS **News poll:** Elisabeth Rosenthal, "How the High Cost of Medical
Care Is Affecting Americans," *New York Times,* December 18, 2014, www.nytimes.com
/interactive/2014/12/18/health/cost-of-health-care-poll.html.

238 **Payments to doctors only 20 percent!:** This graphic from the CDC breaks down
many facets of health spending in the United States: www.cdc.gov/nchs/fastats/health
-expenditures.htm.

238 **Dermatology accounts for only 4 percent:** Dermatology Market Overview from Harris
Williams & Co., an investment bank: www.harriswilliams.com/system/files/industry
_update/dermatology_market_overview.pdf.

CHAPTER 12: THE HIGH PRICE OF PATIENT COMPLACENCY

243 **delivers healthcare for a fraction:** For a fantastic comparison of costs and services
among developed countries, see David Squires and Chloe Anderson, "U.S. Healthcare
from a Global Perspective," Commonwealth Fund, October 8, 2015, www
.commonwealthfund.org/publications/issue-briefs/2015/oct/us-health-care-from
-a-global-perspective.

244 **unique hybrids of government intervention:** For a primer on the underpinnings
of healthcare systems in different countries, see the Commonwealth Fund's *2015
International Profiles of Health Care Systems,* January 2016, www.commonwealthfund
.org/~/media/files/publications/fund-report/2016/jan/1857_mossialos_intl_profiles
_2015_v7.pdf.

244 **set national fee schedules:** Many countries allow for slight variations in fees related to
overhead in different locations. But some, like Japan, do not. The Japanese government
reasons that the greater profit from laboring in the boondocks, where overhead and living
costs are lower, will lure doctors into underserved areas.

244 **Japan and Germany have hundreds:** Japan, which sets fees, has over one thousand
insurers. To make sure patients use healthcare wisely, the system requires patient co-
payments of 10 to 30 percent, depending on family income. (While that 30 percent may
sound high in a country where echocardiograms can cost $8,000, it is reasonable when
they are priced at under $150.)

245 **creating true *nationalized or socialized healthcare*:** In these systems, GPs perform a
gatekeeper function and a referral is generally needed to access specialists and specialty
hospitals. But even here, there is variation. In Canada, the majority of general practice
physicians are self-employed, but payments for office visits come from the government in
accordance with the preset fee schedule.

245 **Hillary Clinton, proposed allowing people:** "Hillary Clinton Offers Healthcare
Proposal Sought by Bernie Sanders," *USA Today,* July 9, 2016, www.usatoday.com/story
/news/2016/07/09/hillary-clinton-offers-health-care-proposal-sought-bernie-sanders
/86894032/.

246 **According to the World Bank:** http://data.worldbank.org/indicator/SH.XPD.TOTL.ZS.

CHAPTER 13: DOCTORS' BILLS

248 **20 to 30 Percent of Our $3 Trillion Bill:** The upper end of the estimate includes ancillary health professionals, such as physical therapists.

249 **banned by a gastroenterology practice:** John Gardner, personal interview/communication, 2015.

252 **nearly $15 billion on advertising annually:** Elisabeth Rosenthal, "Ask Your Doctor If This Ad Is Right for You," *New York Times Sunday Review,* March 4, 2016, www.nytimes.com/2016/02/28/sunday-review/ask-your-doctor-if-this-ad-is-right-for-you.html.

253 **rate of spine surgery:** Jaimy Lee, "Rethinking Spine Care: Some Health Systems Are Moving Beyond Surgery in Serving Back Pain Patients," *Modern Healthcare,* March 22, 2014, www.modernhealthcare.com/article/20140322/MAGAZINE/303229985.

253 **In 2014 Dr. Eric Scaife:** K. Russell et al., "Charge Awareness Affects Treatment Choice: Prospective Randomized Trial in Pediatric Appendectomy," *Annals of Surgery* 262, no. 1 (2014): 189–93, www.ncbi.nlm.nih.gov/pubmed/25185471%20.

255 **The bill for the three stitches:** Dr. Ann Winters, personal interview/communication, 2015.

255 **"They all said it was confidential":** Dr. David Gifford, personal interview/communication, 2015.

256 **quotes a price to privately insured patients:** Dr. Fabrice Gaudot, personal interview/communication, 2013.

256 **"Every medical practitioner is responsible":** "AMA Position Statement on Informed Financial Consent 2015," Australian Medical Association, June 1, 2015, https://ama.com.au/position-statement/informed-financial-consent-2015.

256 **getting fees in advance:** Mark Hall, a professor of health law at Wake Forest University who has studied the Australian system, suggests that contracts—or at least the concept of an implicit contract—should be applied in U.S. medicine as well. He told me, "Generally if you agree to a service and a price isn't stated the provider can only charge what's reasonable. Generally you look at the market to gauge that. But the U.S. healthcare market is so dysfunctional we don't have a good reference point. Medicare? What insurers pay? Providers will say that's too low. But I do think there's a legal principle that indicates that there's a limit."

256 **worries about malpractice suits:** Carol Peckham, "Medscape Malpractice Report 2015: Why Most Doctors Get Sued," December 9, 2015, www.medscape.com/features/slideshow/public/malpractice-report-2015#page=7.

256 **Reforming the malpractice system:** David Hyman and Charles Silver, "Medical Malpractice Litigation and Tort Reform: It's the Incentives, Stupid," *Vanderbilt Law Review,* September 2011, at http://iactprogram.com/wp-content/uploads/2011/09/Hyman_Silver1.pdf.

257 **reasonable compensation to cover their costs:** Ibid.

257 **judge-directed arbitration or dispute resolution:** M. M. Mello, D. M. Studdert, and A. Kachalia, "The Medical Liability Climate and Prospects for Reform," *JAMA* 312, no. 20 (2014): 2146–55, doi:10.1001/jama.2014.10705.

258 **"I had always felt good":** Dr. Hans Rechsteiner, personal interview/communication.

259 **The doctors of the society:** D. Wahlberg, "Health Sense: Rural Wisconsin Doctors Call for Health Care Reform," *Wisconsin State Journal,* February 2, 2014, http://host.madison.com/news/local/health_med_fit/health-sense/health-sense-rural-wisconsin-doctors-call

-for-health-care-reform/article_753b3ef2-f605-5633-8055-0ffa431df94c.html#
ixzz3ipTckkQg.

259 **support the expansion of Medicare:** Their proposal, which they presented at medical
meetings, garnered support from groups like the medical student section of the American
Medical Association and the Madison County Medical Society.

260 **radiologists in Florida perform five times as many tests:** Dr. Richard Duszak, personal
interviews/communication, 2015.

260 **an epidemic of unneeded tests:** The research of Dr. Seth Stein challenges the notion
that doctors order too many scans as a result of legitimate malpractice fears. Examining
national data, he found that states that cap malpractice awards, like California, had some
of the highest rates of testing. In fact, what correlated best with lots of test ordering was
having a high number of test centers in an area. The more machines doctors purchased,
the more they used them. Study published in the *Journal of the American College of
Radiology:* S. Stein, J. R. Barry, and S. Jha, "Are Chargemaster Rates for Imaging Studies
Lower in States That Cap Noneconomic Damages?," August 2014, http://www.ncbi.nlm
.nih.gov/pubmed/25087989.

260 **devoted an entire issue:** Saurabh Jha, "Radiologists and Overdiagnosis," *Academic
Radiology* 22, no. 8 (August 2015): 943–44.

CHAPTER 14: HOSPITAL BILLS

261 **40 to 50 Percent of Our $3 Trillion Bill:** That includes rehab.

262 **a published set of statistical metrics:** http://health.usnews.com/health-news/best
-hospitals/articles/2015/05/20/faq-how-and-why-we-rate-and-rank-hospitals.

262 **grades all general hospitals:** Leapfrog Group Hospital Safety Score Program,
www.hospitalsafetyscore.org.

262 **Hospital Compare program:** www.medicare.gov/hospitalcompare/About/Medicare
-Payment.html.

263 **sent out the press release:** www.cms.gov/newsroom/mediareleasedatabase/press
-releases/2015-press-releases-items/2015-04-16.html.

263 **they had been notified in advance:** Sabriya Rice, "CMS Delays New Hospital Quality
Ratings Amid Pressure from Congress, Industry," *Modern Healthcare,* April 20, 2016,
www.modernhealthcare.com/article/20160420/NEWS/160429991.

263 **information about hospital pricing:** See Medicare Provider Utilization and Payment
Data for inpatient stays, www.cms.gov/Research-Statistics-Data-and-Systems/Statistics
-Trends-and-Reports/Medicare-Provider-Charge-Data/Inpatient.html.

263 **more consumer-friendly formats:** Here is one from the *New York Times:* M. Bloch,
"How Much Hospitals Charge Medicare," *New York Times,* May 8, 2013, www.nytimes
.com/interactive/2013/05/08/business/how-much-hospitals-charge.html.

266 **comedian John Oliver:** Katie Rogers, "For His Latest Trick, John Oliver Forgives $15
Million in Medical Debt," *New York Times,* June 6, 2016, www.nytimes.com/2016/06/07
/arts/television/for-his-latest-trick-john-oliver-forgives-15-million-in-medical-debt.html.

267 **over 90 percent of hospital bills:** "GMA: Hidden Costs in Hospital Bills," April 12,
2007, http://abcnews.go.com/GMA/story?id=127077&page=1.

271 **twenty-five most common inpatient stays:** California patients' rights to see/know
hospital charges are outlined at www.oshpd.ca.gov/HID/Products/Hospitals/Chrgmstr
/PayersBillofRights.pdf.

271 **Chargemasters do not have to be presented:** www.oshpd.ca.gov/HID/Products
/Hospitals/Chrgmstr/.

271 **chargemasters are tailored to obfuscate:** If you're curious, you can look up some
chargemasters of California hospitals at www.oshpd.ca.gov/chargemaster/.

273 **a new surprise billing form:** You can find it at www.dfs.ny.gov/insurance/health/OON
_assignment_benefits_form.pdf.

273 **appeared not to know of the law's existence:** Note that over time this type of solution
protects hospitals' and doctors' balance sheets far better than your wallet. As we've seen,
insurers are more likely than you or I to fork over $50,000 for a few stitches, rather than
take the time to investigate and fight an individual bill. If our insurers are paying
outrageous out-of-network charges on our behalf, we'll pay with higher premiums soon
enough.

273 **Ralph Weber's MediBid:** Ralph Weber, personal interview/communication, 2013.

273 **a total knee or hip replacement:** Sample online price listing for the Surgery Center of
Oklahoma is available at www.surgerycenterok.com/?procedure_category=knee#jump.

274 **$200 extra for twins:** For Maricopa Medical Center's maternity package offerings, see
http://mihs.org/uploads/sites/19/2014/Martha-Maternity_Package_Plan_-_Residents
2014.9.pdf.

274 **cuts into the profit margins:** There are in fact many ways that hospitals and health
insurers could facilitate consumer price comparison. "Private health insurers could
simplify dramatically the structure of their hospital pricing, and thereby facilitate
consumer price comparisons, if they adopted the DRG index," suggests James Robinson,
the Berkeley economist. For example, an insurer might negotiate a price level of 150
percent of Medicare's rate with a freestanding hospital and 200 percent with a large
hospital chain.

274 **"modern nonprofit hospitals":** Lisa Schencker, "New Jersey Hospital's Loss of Tax
Exemption Sends Warning," *Modern Healthcare,* July 11, 2015, www.modernhealthcare
.com/article/20150711/MAGAZINE/307119969.

274 **looming threat of losing tax-exempt status:** This editorial from the *Star Tribune*
outlines the argument against tax breaks for Minnesota's hospitals: Steve Calvin and
Theodore J. Patton, "Minnesota's Healthcare: Can You Heal Me Now?," January 2, 2015,
www.startribune.com/minnesota-s-nonprofit-health-care-can-you-heal-me
-now/287380091/.

275 **"may be substantially to lessen competition":** "Acquisitions and Mergers Under
Section 7 of the Clayton Act," section 35.7 in *The Legal Environment and Business Law:
Master of Accountancy Edition* (v. 1.0), http://2012books.lardbucket.org/books/the-legal
-environment-and-business-law-master-of-accountancy-edition/s38-07-acquisitions-and
-mergers-under.html.

275 **"I do think there's a legal means":** Professor Jaime King, personal interview/
communication.

276 **a spate of enforcement activity:** See the Litigation/Enforcement Timeline compiled by
the Source on Healthcare Price & Competition, a project of UC Hastings College of the
Law: http://sourceonhealthcare.org/news-topic/litigationenforcement/. This is a fantastic
up-to-the-minute resource for following antitrust actions related to healthcare.

278 **Health First has used its monopoly power:** "Florida Hospital Hits Health First with
Antitrust Lawsuit for Trying to Monopolize Cancer Care Market," *Becker's Hospital
Review,* September 1, 2015, www.beckershospitalreview.com/legal-regulatory-issues

/florida-hospital-hits-health-first-with-antitrust-lawsuit-for-trying-to-monopolize-cancer
-care-market.html.

278 **state AGs armed with FTC backing:** A. Ellison, "5 Healthcare Antitrust Cases to Watch
in 2015," *Becker's Hospital Review,* January 30, 2015, www.beckershospitalreview.com
/legal-regulatory-issues/5-healthcare-antitrust-cases-to-watch-in-2015.html.

278 **"market muscle, to exact higher prices":** P. D. McCluskey and R. Weisman, "Partners'
Deal to Acquire Three Hospitals Rejected," *Boston Globe,* January 29, 2015, www
.bostonglobe.com/business/2015/01/29/partners/s9TxpYCBakjPN6pDbBFHGL/story.
html.

278 **the threat of hospitals and doctors:** L. Schencker, "Courts Prove Tough Crowd for
Consolidating Providers," *Modern Healthcare,* February 10, 2015, www.modernhealthcare
.com/article/20150210/news/302109937?template=print. "It did not demonstrate that
efficiencies resulting from the merger would have a positive effect on competition,"
according to the Ninth Circuit opinion written by Judge Andrew D. Hurwitz. The suit
had been brought by the FTC, the Idaho attorney general, and several competing
medical groups.

278 **a "wake up call to hospitals":** Schencker, "Courts Prove Tough Crowd."

279 **because of opposition from credit agencies:** Personal interview/communication, 2014,
with Larry LaRocco, a former congressman who lobbies on behalf of mortgage brokers
upset at how delinquent medical bills are depleting the ranks of creditworthy clients:
"The Consumer Data Industry Association—which mostly represents the three big credit
agencies—opposed the bill. They don't want anyone messing with their algorithms."

CHAPTER 15: INSURANCE COSTS

280 **$67 million to pay "navigators":** See the CMS bulletin "In Person Assistance in the
Health Insurance Marketplaces," www.cms.gov/cciio/programs-and-initiatives/health
-insurance-marketplaces/assistance.html.

281 **employees of community organizations:** C. Fish-Parcham, "Navigators Need Not Be
Licensed as Insurance Brokers or Agents," Families USA, March 2011, http://familiesusa
.org/product/navigators-need-not-be-licensed-insurance-brokers-or-agents.

283 **a more "cost-effective" drug:** Blue Cross Blue Shield cost comparisons can be found at
www.bcbsok.com/pdf/sbc/2016-compare-marketplace-gold-plans-ok.pdf.

286 **"My students say":** Jane Moyer, personal interview/communication, 2015.

286 **great fans of closed medical systems:** Arthur L. Kellermann, "'Socialized' or Not, We
Can Learn from the VA," Rand Corporation, August 8, 2012, www.rand.org
/blog/2012/08/socialized-or-not-we-can-learn-from-the-va.html.

287 **VA's ten-year-old MOVE!:** It is the largest and most comprehensive weight-management
program associated with a medical care system in the United States; see www.move.va.gov/.

287 **Every veteran is screened annually:** M. Romanova et al., "Effectiveness of the MOVE!
Multidisciplinary Weight Loss Program for Veterans in Los Angeles," *Preventing Chronic
Disease* 10:120325 (2013), doi:10.5888/pcd10.120325. Careful follow-up studies have
shown that participants who lose weight maintain weight loss at three years.

287 **"Overall, the available literature":** "Comparison of Quality of Care in VA and Non-VA
Settings: A Systematic Review," September 2010, p. vi, www.hsrd.research.va.gov
/publications/esp/quality.pdf.

288 **Kaiser enjoys a devoted patient clientele:** "Kaiser Permanente No. 1 in Customer
Satisfaction in 2014 Insure.Com Study," Kaiser Permanente Share, April 9, 2014,

http://share.kaiserpermanente.org/article/kaiser-permanente-no-1-in-customer-satisfaction
-in-2014-insure-com-study/.

288 **performs well in J.D. Power's annual health plan:** www.jdpower.com/press
-releases/2016-member-health-plan-study.

289 **"Kaiser focuses on what matters":** Professor James Robinson, personal interview/
communication, 2014.

290 **its behavior didn't qualify:** Chad Terhune, "With Billions in the Bank, Blue Shield of
California Loses Its State Tax-Exempt Status," *Los Angeles Times,* March 18, 2015, www
.latimes.com/business/la-fi-blue-shield-california-20150318-story.html.

290 **ceding to the business of medicine:** "Given that the administration had capitulated on
drug importation and the public option in the ACA, I expected it to be more resolute in
administering the policies," said Brendan Williams, a former elected official from
Washington State. "It is not."

291 **"consumers have been forced to pay":** Press release, California Department of
Insurance, January 5, 2015, www.insurance.ca.gov/0400-news/0100-press-releases/2015
/release001-15.cfm.

291 **the insurance commissioner is a veteran executive:** A brochure detailing the names and
histories of other insurance commissioners can be found at www.naic.org/documents
/members_membershiplist.pdf.

293 **gives state or federal regulators the power:** C. Cox, R. Ma, G. Claxton, and L. Levitt,
"Analysis of 2016 Premium Changes and Insurer Participation in the Affordable Care
Act's Health Insurance Marketplaces," Henry J. Kaiser Family Foundation, June 24,
2015, kff.org/health-reform/issue-brief/analysis-of-2016-premium-changes-and-insurer
-participation-in-the-affordable-care-acts-health-insurance-marketplaces/.

293 **"evaluate whether the proposed":** D. Mangan, "Will These Big Obamacare Rates Get
Approved?," CNBC.com, July 12, 2016, www.cnbc.com/2015/06/01/will-these
-big-obamacare-rates-get-approved.html.

293 **"Generally, the rate review":** Larry Levitt, senior vice president of the Henry J. Kaiser
Family Foundation, personal interview/communication.

293 **Alaska proposed moving its threshold:** A range of insurance co-payments and
deductibles can be found at http://news.ehealthinsurance.com/_ir/68/20152/Price-Index
-report-2015_final.pdf.

294 **pay attention to this down-ballot issue:** A list of insurance commissioners and
their affiliated political parties, and when their office term expires, can be found at
http://ballotpedia.org/Insurance_Commissioner.

294 **1. Reference pricing. CalPERS:** Ann Boynton and James C. Robinson, "Appropriate
Use of Reference Pricing Can Increase Value," *Health Affairs Blog,* July 7, 2015, http://
healthaffairs.org/blog/2015/07/07/appropriate-use-of-reference-pricing-can-increase
-value/.

296 **Epogen was not particularly useful:** S. Swaminathan, V. Mor, R. Mehrotra, and A.
Trivedi, "Medicare's Payment Strategy for End-Stage Renal Disease Now Embraces
Bundled Payment and Pay-for-Performance to Cut Costs," *Health Affairs* 31, no. 9 (2012):
2051–58, www.ncbi.nlm.nih.gov/pmc/articles/PMC3766315/.

296 **the cost of all injectable medications:** Ibid.

296 **It is penalized if they come in:** It is a somewhat awkward construct, still requiring a host
of bills because Medicare has different methods and pots of money for paying out to

different parts of the healthcare system. Hospitals are paid those DRG rates. Doctors are paid through fee schedules. Nursing homes receive a day rate. Home health care is paid for sixty days. The next step is to ask all of these groups to work together proactively to package their services.

297 **At NYU Langone Medical Center:** "Bundled Payments Improve Care for Medicare Patients Undergoing Joint Replacement: Reductions in Patient Length-of-Stay and Readmission Rates," March 2, 2016, www.sciencedaily.com/releases/2016/03 /160302082309.htm.

297 **yearly per capita fee:** Melanie Evans, "Washington Health Systems Contract Directly with Boeing," *Modern Healthcare,* June 13, 2014, www.modernhealthcare.com /article/20140613/NEWS/306139947. According to the agreements, the total costs have to go down 1 percent a year, and the contract measures quality, access, and savings.

298 **need only to get a waiver:** A. Walker, "Federal Government Approves New Medicare Waiver for Maryland," *Baltimore Sun,* January 10, 2014, http://articles.baltimoresun .com/2014-01-10/health/bs-hs-medicare-waiver-approved-20140109_1_john-colmers -waiver-hospital-reimbursement-rates.

298 **less calculated revenue:** Martin Makary and Seth Goldstein, "Maryland's Maverick Health Care Overhaul: A Physician Perspective," *Health Affairs Blog,* July 20, 2015, http://healthaffairs.org/blog/2015/07/20/marylands-maverick-health-care-overhaul-a-physician-perspective/#comments. Also see Brett LoGiurato, "An Amazing Healthcare Revolution Is Happening in Maryland—and Almost No One's Talking About It," Business Insider, August 11, 2014, www.businessinsider.com/maryland-health-care -revolution-2014-8.

300 **enrollees who participate:** www.compassphs.com/consumer-driven-health-plan/case -study-enlink-midstream-transitioned-consumer-directed-health-plan-cdhp/.

301 **Site-neutral payments could save Medicare:** A. Ellison, "25 Things to Know About Site-Neutral Payments," *Becker's Hospital Review,* June 29, 2015, www .beckershospitalreview.com/finance/25-things-to-know-about-site-neutral-payments.html.

301 **prompting a firestorm of protest:** V. Dickson, "CMS Angers Hospitals with Plans for Site-Neutral Rates in Outpatient Payment Rule," *Modern Healthcare,* July 6, 2016, www.modernhealthcare.com/article/20160706/NEWS/160709964?.

301 **a pale compromise:** E. J. Cook, "Congress Takes Step Toward Site-Neutral Medicare Payments in Bipartisan Budget Act of 2015," McDermott Will & Emery, October 29, 2015, www.mwe.com/Congress-Takes-Step-Toward-Site-Neutral-Medicare-Payments-in -Bipartisan-Budget-Act-of-2015-10-29-2015/.

CHAPTER 16: DRUG AND MEDICAL DEVICE COSTS

302 **a proportion that rises dramatically:** B. DiJulio, J. Firth, and M. Brodie, "Kaiser Health Tracking Poll: August 2015," Kaiser Family Foundation, August 20, 2015, http://kff.org/health-costs/poll-finding/kaiser-health-tracking-poll-august-2015.

304 **GoodRx.com began offering:** www.goodrx.com/medicare and www.dropbox.com /s/84tr3wj6bh39opn/GoodRx-for-Medicare-Press-Release.pdf.

305 **technically against the law:** R. A. Cohen, W. K. Kirzinger, and R. M. Gindi, "Strategies Used by Adults to Reduce Their Prescription Drug Costs," NCHS Data Brief, no 119, April 2013, www.cdc.gov/nchs/data/databriefs/db119.pdf.

305 **$250 in the United States:** See the infographic in Elisabeth Rosenthal, "The Soaring

Cost of a Simple Breath," *New York Times,* October 10, 2013, www.nytimes
.com/2013/10/13/us/the-soaring-cost-of-a-simple-breath.html#g-graphic-falling.

306 **The healthcare industry spends:** E. Rosenthal, "Ask Your Doctor If This Ad Is Right for
You," *New York Times Sunday Review,* March 4, 2016, www.nytimes.com/2016/02/28
/sunday-review/ask-your-doctor-if-this-ad-is-right-for-you.html. For auto advertising stats,
see www.statista.com/topics/1601/automotive-advertising/.

306 **Invokana, for example:** "FDA Drug Safety Communication: FDA Revises Label of
Diabetes Drug Canagliflozin (Invokana, Invokamet) to Include Updates on Bone
Fracture Risk and New Information on Decreased Bone Mineral Density," September 10,
2015, www.fda.gov/Drugs/DrugSafety/ucm461449.htm.

307 **Jublia's cure rates are under 20 percent:** Ed Pullen, "What Is a Fungal Nail Cure
Worth? Ask Jublia," Dr. Pullen.com, December 2, 2014, http://drpullen.com
/jubliafungalnail. This post, by Dr. Ed Pullen, a family physician, on his "Medical Blog
for the Informed Patient," expresses reservations common among many doctors about the
cost and cost-effectiveness of Jublia.

307 **calling for a ban on pharmaceutical advertising:** Dr. Patrice Harris, chairwoman of the
AMA, said that advertising "inflates demand for new and more expensive drugs, even
when these drugs may not be appropriate." http://ama-assn.org/ama/pub/news
/news/2015/2015-11-17-ban-consumer-prescription-drug-advertising.page.

308 **The late senator Edward Kennedy championed:** A history of what is called
"reimportation" (the right to buy drugs from overseas) can be found in the following
excerpt from Ken Godwin, Scott H. Ainsworth, and Erik Godwin, *Lobbying and
Policymaking* (Thousand Oaks, CA: Sage Publications, 2013): https://books.google.com/
books?id=QQ2CbU_oGkAC&pg=PT156&lpg=PT156&dq=obama+drug+reimportation
&source=bl&ots=bW88QQsmSE&sig=amOiEzLmwVXNY7ph27qAhQfiiNA&hl=en&s
a=X&ved=0CB0Q6AEwADgKahUKEwj0iaXD_s_HAhWLGx4KHW-HC8E#v=one
page&q=obama%20drug%20reimportation&f=false.

308 **"allow Americans to buy":** http://thehill.com/policy/healthcare/229397-republicans
-senators-slam-obama-on-drug-reimportation.

309 **"its authority to destroy":** www.federalregister.gov/articles/2014/05/06/2014-10304
/administrative-destruction-of-certain-drugs-refused-admission-to-the-united-states.

309 **this rule clearly targets:** Before that, the mechanism for destruction of product was
ambiguous, and the packages were in practice often turned over to the U.S. Postal Service
for return to the sender, an insufficient "deterrent," the FDA said; see http://blogs.fda.
gov/fdavoice/index.php/2015/0.

310 **"cause Maine pharmacists to lose market":** See the legal filing at www.med.uscourts
.gov/Opinions/Torresen/2014/NT_05152014_1_13cv347_Ouellette_v_Mills.pdf.

310 **it overstepped states' purview:** For more on the decision, see www.fdalawblog.net
/Maine%202-23-15%20Decision.pdf; E. Russell, "Judge Strikes Down Maine Law
Allowing Residents to Buy Drugs from Foreign Pharmacies," *Portland Press Herald,*
February 24, 2015, www.pressherald.com/2015/02/24/maine-residents-cant-order-drugs
-from-foreign-pharmacies-judge-rules/.

310 **the FDA has allowed U.S. drugmakers:** S. Tavernise, "Robert Califf, F.D.A. Nominee,
Queried on Industry Ties," *New York Times,* November 18, 2015, www.nytimes
.com/2015/11/18/health/robert-califf-fda-nomination.html.

313 **"All the data was":** Dr. Andrin Oswald, then head of Novartis Vaccines, which made
Bexsero, personal interview/communication, 2014.

313 **assign certain patent licenses:** Here is an informative online guide to the use of march-in rights: http://digitalcommons.wcl.american.edu/cgi/viewcontent.cgi?article=109 4&context=ipbrief.

313 **fifty-one lawmakers wrote a letter:** M. Mezher, "Lawmakers Urge HHS to Exercise 'March-in' Rights to Fight Higher Drug Costs," *Regulatory Focus,* January 11, 2016, www.raps.org/Regulatory-Focus/News/2016/01/11/23878/Lawmakers-Urge-HHS-to -Exercise-March-in-Rights-to-Fight-Higher-Drug-Costs/.

314 **Countries use various strategies:** For more information on these negotiations, see www.rand.org/content/dam/rand/pubs/research_reports/RR200/RR240/RAND _RR240.pdf.

314 **achieving prices one-third of those:** "Let Medicare Negotiate Drug Prices: Our View," *USA Today,* April 20, 2014, www.usatoday.com/story/opinion/2014/04/20/medicare-part -d-prescription-drug-prices-negotiate-editorials-debates/7943745/.

315 **over $95,000 from the health and pharmaceutical industry:** www.opensecrets.org /politicians/summary.php?type=C&cid=N00028958&newMem=N&cycle=2016.

315 **"Our founding legislation prohibits us":** For more on PCORI's policy, see https://help .pcori.org/hc/en-us/articles/213716607-Why-does-PCORI-have-a-specific-policy-on-cost -effectivenesnalysis-.

316 *like the United Kingdom's National Institute for Health:* For more information about NICE, see www.nice.org.uk/.

316 **a third of the U.S. price:** That means, for example, that Advair—called Seretide in the United Kingdom—was in 2015 reimbursed at about £60 for a 120-dose inhaler, or about $92, as opposed to a price of now consistently over $300 in the United States. Tecfidera is £343 for fourteen tabs, or about $528, compared with $1,300 to $1,400 (with a free coupon) in the United States. Sovaldi is £34,980 for a twelve-week supply, or about $54,000, compared with $86,000 in the United States. (Prices for the United States are from GoodRx.com; British prices were provided to me by Thomas Wilkinson, an adviser to NICE.)

316 **whatever they want to beneath that ceiling:** E. J. Emanuel, "The Solution to Drug Prices," *New York Times,* September 14, 2015, www.nytimes.com/2015/09/09/opinion/the -solution-to-drug-prices.html.

316 **set a value-based benchmark:** Laura T. Pizzi, "The Institute for Clinical and Economic Review and Its Growing Influence on the US Healthcare," *American Health & Drug Benefits* 9, no. 1 (February 2016): 9–10, www.ncbi.nlm.nih.gov/pmc/articles /PMC4822973/.

316 **"$5,404–$7,735 linked to long-term value":** "ICER Releases Final Report on Use of PCSK9 Inhibitors for Treatment of High Cholesterol," press release, Institute for Clinical and Economic Review, November 24, 2015, https://icer-review.org/announcements/icer -releases-final-report-on-use-of-pcsk9-inhibitors-for-treatment-of-high-cholesterol-2/.

317 **"Ignoring the cost of ":** P. B. Bach, L. B. Saltz, and R. E. Wittes, "A Hospital Says 'No' to an $11,000-a-Month Cancer Drug," *New York Times,* August 25, 2014, www.nytimes .com/2012/10/15/opinion/a-hospital-says-no-to-an-11000-a-month-cancer-drug.html.

317 **"have been standoffish because":** Dr. Daniel Hartung, personal interview/ communication, 2015.

317 **income of about $100 million:** www.nationalmssociety.org/Get-Involved/Corporate -Support/Corporate-Partners.

318 **about $16 million in direct mail solicitations:** For a list of how much money the

National MS Society raised from different types of activities, see www.nationalmssociety
.org/NationalMSSociety/media/MSNationalFiles/Financials/NMSS-990-Final-FY2013
.pdf?ext=.pdf.

CHAPTER 18: BETTER HEALTHCARE IN A DIGITAL AGE

321 **investment for the quarter reaching nearly $1 billion:** According to Rock Health, a
leading health technology incubator, in early 2016 "our data shows digital health funding
experienced an uptick with 13% TTM [trailing twelve months] growth and almost 50%
YoY [year over year] growth. . . . Total funding for Q1 2016 reached $981.3M"; http://
rockhealth.com/reports/q1-update-2016-digital-health-funding-on-pace-to-surpass-2015/.

322 **Consider the five largest healthcare start-up deals:** Ibid.

323 **the company will be seeking to bill:** S. Hodsden, "Fitbit Expanding into Medical-Grade
Technology," Med Device Online, April 18, 2016, www.meddeviceonline.com/doc/fitbit
-expanding-into-medical-grade-technology-0001.

323 **getting an ultrasound of your neck:** Harriet Hall, "Ultrasound Screening: Misleading
the Public," Science-Based Medicine, March 4, 2008, www.sciencebasedmedicine.org
/ultrasound-screening-misleading-the-public/.

325 **Start-ups like PicnicHealth:** https://picnichealth.com/.

326 **the government describes as "meaningful use":** Here is a guide to the HITECH
program, from HealthITAnswers.net, December 7, 2015: www.hitechanswers.net/can
-your-hospital-benefit-from-e-prescribing/.

327 **That would be "meaningful use":** The data collected by such a system would also make
it easy for state regulators to see if provider networks were adequate or if there were not
enough timely appointments for patients. Researchers could use it to understand the
prevalence of illness in their communities and patterns of medical use.

EPILOGUE

328 *The Fate of Empires:* www.newworldeconomics.com/archives/2014/092814_files
/TheFateofEmpiresbySirJohnGlubb.pdf.

Index